THE COMPLETE
LORD'S TESTS
1884–2013

Jonathan Rice

ORIGINAL FOREWORD BY
Sir Donald Bradman

FOREWORD TO THIS EDITION BY
David Gower OBE

METHUEN

1 3 5 7 9 10 8 6 4 2

First published in 2001 as *One Hundred Lord's Tests* by
Methuen & Co Ltd
35 Hospital Fields Road, York YO10 4DZ
This revised edition published in 2014

Methuen & Co Ltd Reg. No. 5278590

A CIP catalogue record for this book is available
from the British Library

ISBN 978 0 41377741 6

Designed by Roger Walker

Printed and bound in China by
New Era Printing Company Ltd, Hong Kong

Contents

The Author — vii

Foreword by Sir Donald Bradman — ix

Foreword by David Gower OBE — xi

Preface and acknowledgements — xiii

List of Illustrations — xv

THE COMPLETE LORD'S TESTS

1884: England v Australia — 2
1886: England v Australia — 4
1888: England v Australia — 6
1890: England v Australia — 8
1893: England v Australia — 10
1896: England v Australia — 12
1899: England v Australia — 14
1902: England v Australia — 16
1905: England v Australia — 17
1907: England v South Africa — 20
1909: England v Australia — 22
1912: England v South Africa — 24
1912: England v Australia — 26
1912: Australia v South Africa — 28
1921: England v Australia — 30
1924: England v South Africa — 32
1926: England v Australia — 34
1928: England v West Indies — 36
1929: England v South Africa — 38
1930: England v Australia — 40
1931: England v New Zealand — 43
1932: England v India — 46
1933: England v West Indics — 48
1934: England v Australia — 50
1935: England v South Africa — 52

1936: England v India — 54
1937: England v New Zealand — 56
1938: England v Australia — 58
1939: England v West Indies — 60
1946: England v India — 62
1947: England v South Africa — 64
1948: England v Australia — 66
1949: England v New Zealand — 68
1950: England v West Indies — 70
1951: England v South Africa — 72
1952: England v India — 74
1953: England v Australia — 76
1954: England v Pakistan — 78
1955: England v South Africa — 80
1956: England v Australia — 82
1957: England v West Indies — 84
1958: England v New Zealand — 86
1959: England v India — 88
1960: England v South Africa — 90
1961: England v Australia — 92
1962: England v Pakistan — 94
1963: England v West Indies — 96
1964: England v Australia — 98
1965: England v New Zealand — 100
1965: England v South Africa — 102
1966: England v West Indies — 104
1967: England v India — 106
1967: England v Pakistan — 108
1968: England v Australia — 110
1969: England v West Indies — 112
1969: England v New Zealand — 114
1971: England v Pakistan — 116

1971: England v India 118
1972: England v Australia 120
1973: England v New Zealand 122
1973: England v West Indies 124
1974: England v India 126
1974: England v Pakistan 128
1975: England v Australia 130
1976: England v West Indies 132
1977: England v Australia 134
1978: England v Pakistan 136
1978: England v New Zealand 138
1979: England v India 140
1980: England v West Indies 142
1980: England v Australia 144
1981: England v Australia 148
1982: England v India 150
1982: England v Pakistan 152
1983: England v New Zealand 154
1984: England v West Indies 156
1984: England v Sri Lanka 158
1985: England v Australia 160
1986: England v India 162
1986: England v New Zealand 165
1987: England v Pakistan 167
1988: England v West Indies 169
1988: England v Sri Lanka 172
1989: England v Australia 174
1990: England v New Zealand: 177
1990: England v India 179
1991: England v West Indies 182
1991: England v Sri Lanka 184
1992: England v Pakistan 186
1993: England v Australia 188
1994: England v New Zealand 190
1994: England v South Africa 192
1995: England v West Indies 194
1996: England v India 196
1996: England v Pakistan 198

1997: England v Australia 200
1998: England v South Africa 202
1999: England v New Zealand 204
2000: England v Zimbabwe 206
2000: England v West Indies 208
2001: England v Pakistan 210
2001: England v Australia 213
2002: England v Sri Lanka 216
2002: England v India 218
2003: England v Zimbabwe 220
2003: England v South Africa 222
2004: England v New Zealand 224
2004: England v West Indies 226
2005: England v Bangladesh 228
2005: England v Australia 230
2006: England v Sri Lanka 232
2006: England v Pakistan 235
2007: England v West Indies 237
2007: England v India 239
2008: England v New Zealand 241
2008: England v South Africa 243
2009: England v West Indies 245
2009: England v Australia 248
2010: England v Bangladesh 250
2010: Pakistan v Australia 252
2010: England v Pakistan 254
2011: England v Sri Lanka 256
2011: England v India 258
2012: England v West Indies 260
2012: England v South Africa 262
2013: England v New Zealand 264
2013: England v Australia 266

1970: England v Rest of the World 268

Appendix: The Records 271

Index 280

THE AUTHOR

Jonathan Rice is a writer and anthologist on sport and popular culture, who has written and compiled over fifty books, including *The Pavilion Book of Pavilions* (Pavilion), *Presidents of M.C.C.* (Methuen) and *Wisden on India* (Bloomsbury).

He is a member of M.C.C., Kent C.C.C., Heartaches C.C. and the Cricket Writers' Club, and was Chairman of The Lord's Taverners from 2006 to 2008. He is also President of Saltwood C.C. in Kent, where his left arm slows fail to worry many batsmen.

Sir Donald Bradman meets King George VI and Queen Elizabeth at Lord's in 1948.

Foreword to original edition

It is now over seventy years since I first played a Test match at Lord's. That was in a team captained by Bill Woodfull, and featuring great names such as Ponsford, McCabe, Oldfield, Grimmett and Richardson. In the England team that year were some of the greats of English cricket history – Jack Hobbs, Frank Woolley, Walter Hammond, Maurice Tate and Gubby Allen among others. Allen's uncle Reginald played one Test for Australia in the 1880s, and Maurice Tate's father played for England at the turn of the century. Duleepsinhji, who scored a beautiful hundred against us that year, was the nephew of the great Ranjitsinhji. Victor Richardson was the grandfather of the Chappell brothers, so the links with cricket through the entire period of Test match history were in place that day.

Since then I have played and watched cricket countless times at Lord's, and it has always been a happy ground for me. My final century in England was scored there, in 1948 against the Gentlemen of England, fitting opposition for any touring side at Lord's. One of my proudest honours since my retirement from playing is that of Life Vice-Presidency of M.C.C.

Test matches at the headquarters of cricket are special occasions for all tourists, today as much as 120 years ago, and this book highlights some of the achievements and the atmosphere which have made each of the first one hundred Tests at Lord's a special occasion for all those who have played or watched them.

I'm sure the next one hundred will be special as well.

Don Bradman

Sir Donald Bradman AC

Foreword

It is as simple as this; there is no more famous cricket ground in the world than Lord's. Legends abound and cricketers from all over the world want to play there. Just to walk from the dressing room, down the stairs, through the Long Room, down the steps and onto the field, if only once in one's life, is the fulfilment of a childhood dream.

There is an aura to Lord's even when it is empty. Even on those non match days you still feel you are somewhere special. Without cricket on the beautifully kept field there is time to linger in the museum, time to admire the fabulous works of art in that Long Room. You'll even find me in there somewhere in one of the group portraits.

But there is nothing to compare with the buzz around the ground on a Test match day. As a player the butterflies start as you approach the Grace Gates and as you make your way to your chosen spot in the dressing room. When you first take your place in that room for a Test match you just take whatever seat is left after the senior players have claimed spots that might have been theirs for years. Later on your own seniority allows you to claim a particular sofa or armchair as yours.

When you take the field as an England player that buzz becomes a roar and if you don't feel your chest swell with pride there has to be something medically wrong with you! As a batsman there was nothing more special than to hear the applause as you strode to the crease, except of course for the even better feeling of being able to walk off to a standing ovation. Sadly that was never guaranteed.

I had my moments at Lord's, more than a few, I am happy to say, including a hundred in my first match there for Leicestershire and the odd Test hundred to boot. I loved playing there, still treasure the memories of the better days and smile ruefully when I look back at the not so good times.

Great though it is to be able to depart via WG's ironmongery knowing you have made the headlines in tomorrow's Sunday Times for all the right reasons, there were days too when one had to slink away as anonymously as possible. In the '89 Ashes, after one of those days, an eve of rest day (remember them?) Saturday, I abruptly left the press conference, which I was as England captain supposed in theory to see through, and grabbed the first cab still in somewhat low dudgeon. The reasons for that abrupt departure? Firstly I had had more than enough of the line of questioning that evening and secondly I had an appointment at the theatre as a guest of the author's brother, Sir Tim. The show? Anything Goes. I went!

My memories are but a fraction of the history of this great ground. Collected here are the stories of the first 125 Tests at Lord's and what stories they are. There will be something for everyone here, whichever of the world's cricketing nations they hail from.

Nowadays back at Lord's I am just another avid spectator with the best view in the house from the heights of the extraordinary media centre. I have never lost that sense of anticipation that marks a journey to Lord's and still get that tingling sensation in the spine as I walk round the ground of a morning. For me familiarity has bred nothing but affection.

David Gower
September 2013

David Gower played 17 Tests for England at Lord's, captaining the side on six occasions. He scored 1,241 runs at an average of 44.32.

Preface

The first edition of this book, "One Hundred Lord's Tests" was published in 2001, and quickly became the best selling title in the M.C.C. Cricket Library, a minor commercial distinction which it holds to this day. So it seemed logical to update the book to reflect the story of Lord's Test matches a little more than one decade on, after England had played 125 Tests at headquarters.

The format of the book has not changed, although much of the commentary and photographs are new. We have also added a new section of Lord's Test Records, and a look at the 1970 'Test' versus the Rest of the World, which was considered a Test at the time by the T.C.C.B. and the sponsors, Guinness, but which was never fully ratified by the I.C.C. as an official Test match. The series was of course arranged hurriedly to fill the gap in that year's calendar caused by the cancellation of the tour by the South Africans, but the then governing body of cricket eventually ruled that the matches could not be classified as full Test matches because they were not between two full member countries. It is not only Alan Jones of Glamorgan – the one person who thus missed a full Test cap – who wonders why the ridiculous Australia v I.C.C. World XI match in 2005 is accorded full Test status, while the 1970 series is not.

In writing this book, I have been aware of the many statistical works that already exist, so we took the decision from the outset not to create yet another book of cricket records. The statistics of 127 Tests are recorded in the scorecards of every Test, which are reproduced within the text of the book, and the brief statistical section at the back of the book allows you time to gasp in astonishment at some of the overall achievements of the cricketers who have played Tests at Lord's. Who would have guessed, for example, that Warren Bardsley of Australia has scored more Test runs at headquarters than any other overseas player? Or that the result of the 125th Test, which South Africa won by 51 runs, was the closest of all in terms of runs margin?

I have tried to keep personal observations out of the text. My first Lord's Test was the 1966 match against the West Indies. I remember watching Sobers and Holford bat England out of the game, and realizing that I was watching a genius at work. I distinctly recall where I was when the bomb scare happened in 1973 (in the Mound Stand), when the 1975 streaker appeared (in the Grand Stand) and when India were all out for 42 in 1974 (arriving late at the ground, and seeing just the final three balls of the game). I saw Graham Gooch's 333, the guard of honour for Dickie Bird in 1996 and the rain in 1987, 1997 and 2007. I saw Greenidge's 214 not out, and felt the frisson of excitement in the Long Room as Australia went out to bat at the start of the 2005 Test. I have watched the redevelopments, the sponsors and the advertisements come and go, and I still find myself looking in the wrong place for Father Time. But this is not a personal record of my watching Test cricket at Lord's, and I hope it does not read like one.

Thanks and acknowledgements must go to many people. Within M.C.C., I have had tremendous support from Hubert Doggart, who was the main driving force behind the first edition of the book; M.C.C. curators past and present Stephen Green and Adam Chadwick and many of their colleagues, most notably Glenys Williams, Neil Robinson and the late and much missed Michael Wolton. Alastair Lack, Guy Curry, David Rayvern Allen, Michael Down and other members of the Arts and Library Committee at M.C.C. have given me much useful guidance, and Clare Skinner has been a huge help with the photographs. At Methuen, Peter Tummons has once again shouldered the burden of turning my manuscript into a book, without us ever once coming to blows.

The foreword that Sir Donald Bradman wrote for the first edition is reprinted here, and we are also very grateful to David Gower for his foreword to this updated edition.

Finally I'd like to thank my wife Jan, for putting up with my long absences in my office at the top of the house, while I search for literary inspiration and the 1935 scorecard.

All these people have helped to create this book, but any mistakes arc, as always, mine.

Jonathan Rice
Kent
September 2013

List of Illustrations

Year

1884	The England team. © M.C.C.
1886	English and Australian cricketers. © M.C.C.
1888	W. G. Grace. © Roger Mann Collection
1890	The new pavilion. © M.C.C.
1893	Arthur Shrewsbury. © Roger Mann Collection
1896	Harry Trott. © Roger Mann Collection
1899	The Australian team. © M.C.C.
1905	The twelfth Australian touring party. © M.C.C.
1907	The South African team. © M.C.C.
1909	Warwick Armstrong. © Roger Mann Collection
1912	England vs South Africa: Sydney Barnes. © M.C.C.
1912	England's Team vs Australia. © Roger Mann Collection
1912	The Australian team. © M.C.C.
1921	Warren Bardsley of Australia. © Roger Mann Collection
1924	JB Hobbs. © M.C.C.
1926	The England team. © M.C.C.
1928	The first official West Indian touring side. © M.C.C.
1929	Cameron felled by Larwood. © David Frith Collection
1930	JB Hobbs and FE Woolley. © M.C.C.
1931	The New Zealand team. © M.C.C.
1932	The Indian touring team. © M.C.C.
1933	Walter Robins. © Sport & General
1934	Bradman batting. © Sport & General
1935	Victory at Lord's for South Africa. © Sport & General
1936	Wazir Ali, caught in the gully by Verity. © Sport & General
1937	The New Zealand team. © Sport & General
1938	Lord's, painted by Charles Cundall. © M.C.C./Bridgeman Art Library
1939	The West Indies team. © Sport & General
1946	England and India. © Sport & General
1947	Denis Compton and Bill Edrich. © Sport & General
1948	Don Bradman's 'Invincibles'. © Press Association Images
1949	Hutton and Robertson. © Sport & General
1950	Calypso cricket. © Sport & General
1951	Roy Tattersall. © Sport & General
1952	Len Hutton. © Sport & General

Year

1953	Willie Watson and Trevor Bailey. © Sport & General
1954	The first Pakistan team to play official Test Matches in England. © Sport & General
1955	The England team. © Sport & General
1956	A famous catch by Benaud. © Sport & General
1957	The crowd on the pitch at the end of the third day's play. © Sport & General
1958	Lock collides with Richardson. © Sport & General
1959	The England team. © Sport & General
1960	Peter Walker. © Sport & General
1961	Bill Lawry. © Sport & General
1962	Tom Graveney. © Sport & General
1963	Colin Cowdrey. © Sport & General
1964	A pair of mallard enjoy a match much affected by rain. © Sport & General
1964	England vs New Zealand: Fred Trueman. © Sport & General
1965	England vs South Africa: Colin Bland. © Sport & General
1966	Gary Sobers and David Holford. © Sport & General
1967	England vs India: The England team. © Sport & General
1967	England vs Pakistan: Hanif Mohammad. © Sport & General
1968	David Brown and Colin Cowdrey. © Sport & General
1969	England vs West Indies: Illingworth leads England out. © Sport & General
1969	England vs New Zealand: Alan Knott. © David Frith Collection
1971	England vs Pakistan: Boycott at work. © Sport & General
1971	England vs India: The Snow–Gavaskar incident. © Sport & General
1972	Bob Massie. © Patrick Eagar
1973	England vs New Zealand: Mark Burgess. © Patrick Eagar
1973	England vs West Indies: West Indies fielding. © Patrick Eagar
1974	England vs India: Geoff Arnold and Chris Old. © Patrick Eagar

Year

1974 England vs Pakistan: Zaheer Abbas. © Patrick Eagar

1975 Michael Angelow. © Patrick Eagar

1976 Brian Close. © Patrick Eagar

1977 Thomson bowls Amiss. © Patrick Eagar

1978 England vs Pakistan: Ian Botham. © Patrick Eagar

1978 England vs New Zealand: Ian Botham. © Patrick Eagar

1979 'Start delayed!' © Patrick Eagar

1980 England vs West Indies: Graham Gooch. © Patrick Eagar

1980 Centenary Test: Kim Hughes; A great gathering of the clans. © Patrick Eagar

1981 A pair for Botham. © Patrick Eagar

1982 England vs India: Derek Randall. © Patrick Eagar

1982 England vs Pakistan: Mohsin Khan. © Patrick Eagar

1983 The tools of a groundsman's trade. © Patrick Eagar

1984 England vs West Indies: Gordon Greenidge. © Patrick Eagar

1984 England vs Sri Lanka: The teams. © Patrick Eagar

1985 Three cheers for Her Majesty. © Patrick Eagar

1986 England vs India: Dilip Vengsarkar. © Patrick Eagar

1986 England vs India: The Grand Stand scoreboard. © Patrick Eagar

1986 England vs New Zealand: Martyn Moxon. © Patrick Eagar

1987 Groundsmen at work. © Patrick Eagar

1988 England vs West Indies: Viv Richards. © Patrick Eagar

1988 England vs Sri Lanka: Jack Russell on Test debut. © Patrick Eagar

1989 Australia get their first view of the new Mound Stand. © Ken Kelly

1990 England vs New Zealand: Honouring Sir Richard Hadlee. © Patrick Eagar

1990 England vs India: Kapil Dev; Graham Gooch. © Patrick Eagar

1991 England vs West Indies: Robin Smith. © Patrick Eagar

1991 England vs Sri Lanka: Alec Stewart. © Patrick Eagar

1992 Wasim Akram. © Patrick Eagar

1993 Michael Slater and Mark Taylor. © Patrick Eagar

1994 England vs New Zealand: Martin Crowe. © Patrick Eagar

1994 England vs South Africa: South Africa, welcomed back. © Patrick Eagar

1995 Sherwin Campbell and Dominic Cork. © Patrick Eagar

Year

1996 England vs India: Dickie Bird. © Patrick Eagar

1996 England vs Pakistan: Inzamam-ul-Haq. © Patrick Eagar

1997 Glenn McGrath. © Patrick Eagar

1998 The view from the pavilion. © Patrick Eagar

1999 Chris Read and Chris Cairns. © Patrick Eagar

2000 England vs Zimbabwe: Alec Stewart and Graeme Hick. © Patrick Eagar

2000 England vs West Indies: A sight to warm English hearts. © Patrick Eagar

2001 England's match winners, Darren Gough and Andrew Caddick © Press Association Images

2001 Mark Waugh on his way to a another hundred © Press Association Images

2001 Gilchrist in typically aggressive form © Press Association Images

2002 Marvan Atapattu guides a ball from Caddick for four © Press Association Images

2002 John Crawley, one of his best Test innings © Press Association Images

2003 Mark Butcher hits out on his way to a big score © Press Association Images

2003 Makhaya Ntini, 10 wickets in the match. © M.C.C.

2004 Nasser Hussain. © M.C.C.

2004 Robert Key, a double centurion. © M.C.C.

2005 Trescothick and Vaughan. © M.C.C.

2005 Ricky Ponting on his way to 7,000 Test runs © Press Association Images

2006 Marcus Trescothick, a century for England and taking a good catch in the slips © Press Association Images

2006 Ian Bell, a maiden Test century. © M.C.C.

2007 Matthew Prior, a century in his first Test. © M.C.C.

2007 Sachin Tendulkar. © M.C.C.

2008 Michael Vaughan. © M.C.C.

2008 Bell and Pietersen in a record partnership. © M.C.C.

2009 Ravi Bopara. © M.C.C.

2009 Graham Onions. © M.C.C.

2009 Andrew Flintoff, match winner. © M.C.C.

2010 Spectators view the Lord's square. © M.C.C.

2010 The 'Baggy Greens' celebrate. © M.C.C.

2010 Marred by the betting scandal. © M.C.C.

2011 Dishan, a record score. © M.C.C.

2011 Kevin Pietersen, a double century. © M.C.C.

2012 Stuart Broad. © M.C.C.

2012 Andrew Stauss, his final Test match. © M.C.C.

2013 Jonny Bairstow top scored in England's first innings © Press Association Images

2013 Bairstow and Root both batted well against Australia © Press Association Images

THE COMPLETE
LORD'S TESTS
1884–2013

1884: England v Australia

(2nd Test) July 21, 22, 23
England won by an innings and 5 runs

The first Test Match to be played at Lord's was the fifteenth Test ever contested, and the fourth to take place in England. The great sports administrator and innovator Charles Alcock, secretary of Surrey County Cricket Club, had staged Test matches against Australia at the Kennington Oval in 1880 and 1882, but the powers that be at Lord's took some convincing that international matches would have the same appeal as county, school and university matches, which were the staple diet of the Lord's calendar. It was perhaps appropriate that the England captaincy, held by 'Monkey'

The England team. *L–r, top*: umpire Fullin, Peate, Lucas, Lyttelton, Shrewsbury, umpire Farrands. *Middle*: Steel, Lord Harris (captain), Grace, Read, Ulyett. *Front*: Christopherson, Barlow.

Hornby for the First Test at Old Trafford, should be handed on to that pillar of the cricketing establishment Lord Harris for the first Test at Lord's.

England won this encounter by a wide margin, thanks mainly to a brilliant innings of 148 by the Lancashire amateur Allan Steel, and to some conclusive bowling by Ted Peate of Yorkshire in the first innings and his county team-mate 'Happy Jack' Ulyett in the second innings. For the Australians, only 'Tup' Scott was able to cope with the two Yorkshire bowlers, top-scoring in both innings. He could argue that the English never got him out, because in the first innings, after a tenth-wicket partnership of 69 with Harry Boyle, he was last man out – caught at point by his own captain, Billy Murdoch, fielding as substitute for WG Grace who had injured his finger.

Ted Peate was the first in a line of great Yorkshire slow left arm bowlers, which stretched through Bobby Peel, Wilfred Rhodes and Hedley Verity to Johnny Wardle and Don Wilson almost a hundred years later. Peate was perhaps as gifted as any of them, but his personal life was chaotic. He began his cricketing career as part of a troupe of cricketing clowns – apparently a paying proposition in the 1870s before sport and entertainment divorced each other – but soon established a reputation for length and accuracy that would become the benchmark for all Yorkshire slow left armers. However, he lasted with Yorkshire only a comparatively short time, and died in 1900, aged 44.

Stanley Christopherson scored 17 runs and took only one wicket in this his only Test appearance, but went on to achieve a far greater fame at Lord's. He became President of M.C.C. in 1939 and because of the outbreak of war remained in office until 1946, the longest tenure of that office in the history of the club.

1886: England v Australia

(2nd Test) July 19, 20, 21
England won by an innings and 106 runs

The 1886 Australian team was not a happy one. The captain, 'Tup' Scott, was unable to build any semblance of team spirit and it was said that bloodstains in the railway carriages were frequent signs of the disagreements that raged within the side as they travelled around England. It was their misfortune, too, that at a time when their bowling was weaker than it had been for some years they came up against a very strong England batting side.

England chose to bat on what looked like a good batting wicket, but within fifteen minutes of the start there was a heavy shower and play was suspended for an hour and a half. When the players came back onto the field the nature of the wicket had changed completely, and the batsmen now had to cope with a very sticky dog. Grace had gone before lunch, and afterwards Scotton, Read and the captain Steel soon joined him, but Arthur Shrewsbury, accompanied by his Nottinghamshire team-mate Billy Barnes, played one of the great Test innings of the century in making 164. Pelham Warner (who did not see it first hand, but whose authority we should not doubt) described it as 'one of the masterpieces of the art of batting under conditions favourable to the bowlers'. Shrewsbury batted for six hours and 51 minutes until he was last out at 3 o'clock on the second afternoon. His 164 was the highest Test score made by an

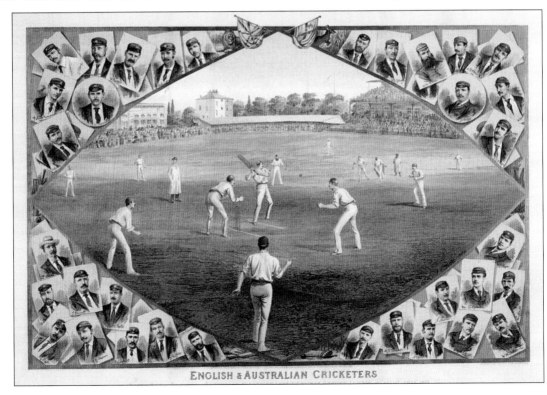

ENGLISH & AUSTRALIAN CRICKETERS

ENGLAND

WG Grace	c Jarvis b Palmer	18
WH Scotton	b Garrett	19
A Shrewsbury	c Bonnor b Trumble	164
WW Read	c Spofforth b Giffen	22
† AG Steel	lbw b Spofforth	5
W Barnes	c Palmer b Garrett	58
RG Barlow	c Palmer b Spofforth	12
G Ulyett	b Spofforth	19
* EFS Tylecote	b Spofforth	0
J Briggs	c Jones b Trumble	0
GA Lohmann	not out	7
	(B 24, LB 4, NB 1)	29
Total		353

AUSTRALIA

SP Jones	c Grace b Briggs	25	b Briggs	17
† HJH Scott	lbw b Briggs	30	b Briggs	2
G Giffen	b Steel	3	b Barlow	1
* AH Jarvis	b Briggs	3	not out	13
GJ Bonnor	c Grace b Steel	0	b Briggs	3
JW Trumble	c Tylecote b Briggs	0	c Tylecote b Barnes	20
GE Palmer	c Shrewsbury b Barnes	20	c Lohmann b Barlow	48
JMcC Blackham	b Briggs	23	b Briggs	5
TW Garrett	not out	7	b Briggs	4
FR Spofforth	b Barnes	5	c & b Briggs	0
E Evans	c Ulyett b Barnes	0	run out	0
	(B 4, LB 1)	5	(B 13)	13
Total		121		126

AUSTRALIA	O	M	R	W
Garrett	72	40	77	2
Evans	36	20	37	0
Palmer	38	15	45	1
Spofforth	56	26	73	4
Trumble	14	4	27	2
Giffen	40	18	63	1
Jones	3	1	2	0

ENGLAND	O	M	R	W	O	M	R	W
Barnes	14.3	7	25	3	10	5	18	1
Lohmann	7	3	21	0	14	9	11	0
Briggs	34	22	29	5	38.1	17	45	6
Steel	21	8	34	2	16	9	14	0
Barlow	6	3	7	0	25	20	12	2
Ulyett					8	3	13	0

FALL OF WICKETS

Wkt.	Eng. 1st	Aus. 1st	Aus. 2nd
1st	27	45	6
2nd	77	52	56
3rd	112	59	91
4th	119	60	95
5th	280	62	98
6th	303	67	105
7th	333	99	120
8th	333	109	126
9th	340	121	126
10th	353	121	126

† Captain   * Wicketkeeper

England batsman to that day, but that record lasted only three weeks before Grace took it back with 170 (in much easier batting conditions) at the Oval.

Australia batted feebly against Barnes, Briggs and Steel, and were all out for 121 in their first innings. Briggs had taken six wickets, five in the first innings as well as the wicket of second innings nightwatchman-cum-opener Garrett before the day was finished. The crowd of 15,663, rather fewer than on many great occasions at Lord's in the 1880s, went home satisfied. Their satisfaction might have seemed misplaced when Palmer and Trumble, batting at numbers one and three in the reshuffled batting order, put on 50 for the second wicket, followed by a further 35 for the third wicket by Palmer and the first innings opening bat Sammy Jones. But once Jones was out, bowled by Briggs, who had come back on at the Pavilion end, the result was not in doubt. Only Arthur Jarvis, who was keeping wicket for Australia despite the presence of the great Jack Blackham in the team, also reached double figures as Briggs took six for 45 to win England the match.

1888: England v Australia

(1st Test) July 16, 17
Australia won by 61 runs

The summer of 1888 was a particularly wet one. Australia had arrived with two of the most formidable bowlers in the long history of the Ashes Tests, JJ Ferris and CTB Turner. Ferris, later to play for England on tour in South Africa, was a left arm medium-paced bowler with a remarkable change of pace, while Charlie Turner, the 'Terror' in succession to the 'Demon' Spofforth, bowled right arm fast medium. Between them, in all matches on the muddy pitches of 1888, they took 534 wickets 314 for Turner and 220 for Ferris. England had no answer, especially with Arthur Shrewsbury still in Australia after touring there the previous winter and showing no inclination to hurry home. His wet wicket skills, as shown in making 164 at Lord's two years before, might have swung the match.

Play did not start until 3 pm on the first day and winning the toss was critical. England's bowling was less suited to the conditions than Australia's, but still Lohmann, Peel and Briggs ran quickly through the Australian side, who reached the dizzy heights of 116 thanks to a last-wicket stand of 34 – the highest of the match – between Jack Edwards, playing in his first Test match, and JJ Ferris. Edwards averaged only 12 for the whole summer but this was undoubtedly his finest hour. John James Ferris was known to all as 'JJ', as was his Test-playing contemporary, John James Lyons. Fortunately for the Australian captain, Ferris and Lyons only played together at the Oval that year. By the time yet another 'JJ', James Joseph Kelly, played the first of his 36 Tests for Australia in 1896, Ferris had retired from Test cricket.

Ferris and Turner tore through the England batting, reducing them to 18 for 3 overnight, and then to 26 for 7 before some lusty blows from

Briggs brought the score to 53, the lowest total by England against Australia in England until the 1948 Test at the Oval when Lindwall, Miller and Johnston dismissed England for just 52. Australia fared scarcely any better in the second innings, and were 18 for 7 before Turner and Ferris showed how to bat against their own type of bowling – hit

WG Grace – still one of England's most recognised cricketers.

out and trust to luck. England were left 124 to win, but once Grace was out for 24, the highest individual score of the match, the game was lost. They made exactly half the runs needed and lost by 61 runs at 4.25 on the second afternoon, in front of a vast crowd. The match aggregate, 291, remains the lowest in all completed Tests in England, and the number of wickets to fall on the second day, 27, is the highest in any one day of Test match cricket anywhere in the world. What's more, the 61 run margin of victory remained the closest in terms of runs of any Test at Lord's, until South Africa's 51 run victory in 2012.

AUSTRALIA

AC Bannerman	c Grace b Lohmann	0	b Peel	0
† PS McDonnell	c O'Brien b Peel	22	b Lohmann	1
GHS Trott	c Lohmann b Peel	0	b Lohmann	3
GJ Bonnor	b Lohmann	6	c Lohmann b Peel	8
* JMcC Blackham	b Briggs	22	run out	1
SMJ Woods	c Gunn b Briggs	18	c Grace b Peel	3
CTB Turner	c Lohmann b Peel	3	c Grace b Briggs	12
JD Edwards	not out	21	c Sherwin b Lohmann	0
AH Jarvis	c Lohmann b Peel	3	(11) c Barnes b Peel	4
J Worrall	c Abel b Briggs	2	b Lohmann	4
JJ Ferris	c Sherwin b Steel	14	(9) not out	20
	(B 5)	5	(B 3, LB 1)	4
Total		116		60

ENGLAND

† WG Grace	c Woods b Ferris	10	c Bannerman b Ferris	24
R Abel	b Ferris	3	c Bonnor b Ferris	8
W Barnes	c Jarvis b Turner	3	st Blackham b Ferris	1
GA Lohmann	lbw b Turner	2	st Blackham b Ferris	0
WW Read	st Blackham b Turner	4	b Turner	3
TC O'Brien	b Turner	0	b Turner	4
R Peel	run out	8	b Turner	4
AG Steel	st Blackham b Turner	3	not out	10
W Gunn	c Blackham b Ferris	2	b Ferris	8
J Briggs	b Woods	17	b Turner	0
* M Sherwin	not out	0	c Ferris b Turner	0
	(LB 1)	1		
Total		53		62

ENGLAND	O	M	R	W	O	M	R	W
Lohmann	20	9	28	2	14	4	33	4
Peel	21	7	36	4	10.2	3	14	4
Briggs	21	8	26	3	4	1	9	1
Barnes	6	0	17	0				
Steel	3.2	2	4	1	1	1	0	0

AUSTRALIA	O	M	R	W	O	M	R	W
Turner	25	9	27	5	24	8	36	5
Ferris	21	13	19	3	23	11	26	5
Woods	4	2	6	1				

FALL OF WICKETS

	Aus.	Eng.	Aus.	Eng.
Wkt.	1st	1st	2nd	2nd
1st	0	5	1	29
2nd	3	14	1	34
3rd	28	18	13	38
4th	32	22	15	39
5th	65	22	18	44
6th	76	22	18	55
7th	76	26	18	56
8th	79	35	42	57
9th	82	49	49	57
10th	116	53	60	62

† Captain   * Wicketkeeper

1890: England v Australia

(1st Test) July 21, 22, 23
England won by 7 wickets

The 1890 Test Match at Lord's was notable for two major changes. The first was the disappearance of the four ball over, which had been the norm in English cricket until the previous season. It had been replaced in 1889 by the brief experiment of a five ball over, the English authorities being unable to see the benefits of the six ball over which had been introduced in Australia in 1887. It was not until 1900 that six ball overs came to England.

The second change was obvious to all who came to Lord's that July. There was a new pavilion in place. Designed by Thomas Verity, its foundation stone had been laid on 17 September 1889 by Sir Spencer Ponsonby-Fane, and was ready for the Annual General Meeting of the Marylebone Cricket Club on 17 May 1890. Just eight months from foundation stone to completion was an astonishing achievement, one which the M.C.C. committee and membership might have wished

had been replicated a century later when the Compton and Edrich stands were being built. The Pavilion, with its Long Room from which members can have a fine and almost uninterrupted view of the play, is now a symbol of the traditions of cricket and a template for many other pavilions around the world. It is a daunting thought for cricketers who walk through the Long Room onto the field of play that the first England captain to lead his team through that room was WG Grace himself.

England were almost at full strength for the match, although according to *Wisden*, 'Mr Stoddart preferred playing for Middlesex against Kent at Tonbridge' and was thus not available. Not even the current policy of central contracts would have made a difference to Mr Stoddart's attitude, because Mr Stoddart was an amateur, and thus had no contract with anybody.

The new pavilion, designed by Thomas Verity and opened in 1890. From the *Architect*, November 1889.

Even without Stoddart, England won at a canter. Turner and Ferris were not the threat they had been two years before, and Grace, a few days after his forty-second birthday, made both his highest and lowest Test scores at Lord's, and also achieved his best Test bowling there – two wickets for 12 in fourteen of those odd five ball overs. The only men to delay England's triumph were Barrett and JJ Lyons. Lyons hit 55 out of 66 in 45 minutes on the first morning, and also took 5 for 30 when England batted, being five sixths of his entire tally of Test wickets over a twelve-year career. He then hit 33 out of 48 in 25 minutes in Australia's second innings. Barrett, who opened in place of Lyons in the second innings, became the first man to carry his bat through a Lord's Test innings.

AUSTRALIA

JJ Lyons	b Barnes	55	(4) c Attewell b Peel	33
CTB Turner	b Attewell	24	lbw b Peel	2
† WL Murdoch	c & b Attewell	9	(5) b Lohmann	19
JE Barrett	c Grace b Ulyett	9	(1) not out	67
GHS Trott	run out	12	(3) b Peel	0
SE Gregory	b Attewell	0	c Lohmann b Barnes	9
PC Charlton	st MacGregor b Peel	6	lbw b Grace	2
* JMcC Blackham	b Peel	5	c Barnes b Grace	10
JJ Ferris	b Attewell	8	lbw b Lohmann	8
KE Burn	st MacGregor b Peel	0	(11) c MacGregor b Attewell	19
H Trumble	not out	1	(10) c Barnes b Lohmann	5
	(LB 3)	3	(LB 2)	2
Total		132		176

ENGLAND

† WG Grace	c & b Turner	0	not out	75
A Shrewsbury	st Blackham b Ferris	4	lbw b Ferris	13
W Gunn	run out	14	c & b Ferris	34
WW Read	c & b Ferris	1	b Trumble	13
JM Read	b Lyons	34	not out	2
G Ulyett	b Lyons	74		
R Peel	c & b Trumble	16		
W Barnes	b Lyons	9		
GA Lohmann	c & b Lyons	19		
* G MacGregor	b Lyons	0		
W. Attewell	not out	0		
	(LB 2)	2		
Total		173	(3 wkts)	137

ENGLAND	O	M	R	W		O	M	R	W
Lohmann	21	10	43	0	....	29	19	28	3
Peel	24	11	28	3	....	43	23	59	3
Attewell	32	15	42	4	....	42.2	22	54	1
Barnes	6	2	16	1	....	6	3	10	1
Ulyett	3	3	0	1	....	6	2	11	0
Grace					....	14	10	12	2

AUSTRALIA	O	M	R	W		O	M	R	W
Turner	35	17	53	1	....	22	12	31	0
Ferris	40	17	55	2	....	25	11	42	2
Trott	3	0	16	0	....				
Lyons	20.1	7	30	5	....	20	6	43	0
Trumble	12	7	17	1	....	8	1	21	1

FALL OF WICKETS

	Aus.	Eng.	Aus	Eng.
Wkt	1st	1st	2nd	2nd
1st	66	0	6	27
2nd	82	14	8	101
3rd	93	20	48	135
4th	109	20	84	
5th	111	92	106	
6th	113	133	109	
7th	120	147	119	
8th	131	162	136	
9th	131	166	142	
10th	132	173	176	

† Captain   * Wicketkeeper

1893: England v Australia

(1st Test) July 17, 18, 19
Match drawn

WG Grace, aged 45 but still an essential part of any England team, had injured his finger and was unable to play the First Test of the summer, the first home Test match he had missed. In his place, AE Stoddart, who had refused to play in the 1890 Test, captained the side and FS Jackson came in for his first Test match. Although Australia still had Charlie Turner in their side, the weather in 1893 was far drier than it had been on Turner's previous tours and he was not as deadly as before. Even so, the Lord's Test match weather proved true to form, and once again the match was curtailed by rain.

Stoddart won the toss and knew enough to bat first. He made 24 out of the first-wicket partner-ship of 29, but from there on, the innings belonged to his partner Arthur Shrewsbury and the new boy Stanley Jackson. Shrewsbury became the first man to score three Test hundreds for England, a mark already achieved by Percy McDonnell for Australia, and also became the first man to reach 1000 Test runs. He and Jackson put on 137 for the fourth wicket, and when Jackson was finally out, he was only nine short of a cen-tury on debut – a feat that Harry Graham did then accomplish when Australia batted. Jackson's dis-missal came from a brilliant catch by Australia's wicket-keeper captain Jack Blackham off the bowling of Charlie Turner. As the disconsolate Jackson headed back to the pavilion, Blackham called after him, 'Bad luck, young fellow! It was an awful fluke.' Sledging has moved on quite some distance since Blackham's day.

England eventually reached 334, and when Australia batted Nottinghamshire's Bill Lockwood (also on debut) skittled the top order. At 75 for 5 he had all five to his credit, but a superb sixth-wicket stand of 162 between Graham, who flayed

the bowling to all parts, and Syd Gregory restored the balance somewhat. All the same, Australia were all out 65 runs behind England, and when Shrewsbury and Gunn put on 152 for England's second wicket the game seemed to be heading

Arthur Shrewsbury, the first Englishman to score three Test centuries.

ENGLAND

		1st innings		2nd innings
† AE Stoddart	b Turner	24	b Turner	13
A Shrewsbury	c Blackham b Turner	106	b Giffen	81
W Gunn	c Lyons b Turner	2	c Graham b Giffen	77
FS Jackson	c Blackham b Turner	91	c Bruce b Giffen	5
JM Read	b Bruce	6	c McLeod b Bruce	1
R Peel	c Bruce b Trumble	12	not out	0
W Flowers	b McLeod	35	b Turner	4
E Wainwright	c Giffen b Turner	1	b Giffen	26
WH Lockwood	b Bruce	22	b Giffen	0
* G MacGregor	not out	5		
A Mold	b Turner	0		
	(B 19, LB 9, NB 2)	30	(B 16, LB 9, W 1, NB 1)	27
Total		334	(8 wkts dec)	234

AUSTRALIA

AC Bannerman	c Shrewsbury b Lockwood	17
JJ Lyons	b Lockwood	7
G Giffen	b Lockwood	0
GHS Trott	c MacGregor b Lockwood	33
RW McLeod	b Lockwood	5
SE Gregory	c MacGregor b Lockwood	57
H Graham	c MacGregor b Mold	107
W Bruce	c Peel b Mold	23
CTB Turner	b Flowers	0
H Trumble	not out	2
†* JMcC Blackham	lbw b Mold	2
	(B 15, LB 1)	16
Total		269

AUSTRALIA	O	M	R	W	O	M	R	W
Turner	36	16	67	6	32	15	64	2
Bruce	22	4	58	2	20	10	34	1
Trumble	19	7	42	1	11	2	33	0
Trott	9	2	38	0	2	0	5	0
McLeod	21	6	51	1	25	11	28	0
Giffen	18	3	48	0	26.4	6	43	5

ENGLAND	O	M	R	W
Peel	22	12	36	0
Lockwood	45	11	101	6
Mold	20.1	7	44	3
Jackson	5	1	10	0
Wainwright	11	3	41	0
Flowers	11	3	21	1

FALL OF WICKETS

	Eng.	Aus.	Eng.
Wkt	1st	1st	2nd
1st	29	7	27
2nd	31	7	179
3rd	168	50	195
4th	189	60	198
5th	213	75	198
6th	293	217	198
7th	298	264	234
8th	313	265	234
9th	333	265	
10th	334	269	

† Captain   * Wicketkeeper

England's way. Stoddart, taking advantage of the new regulations, became the first captain to declare a Test innings closed, at lunch on the third day. This left Australia exactly 300 to win, but then the heavens opened and no further play was possible.

LORD'S GROUND

1896: England v Australia

(1st Test) June 22, 23, 24
England won by 6 wickets

Hooliganism came to Lord's in a major way in 1896. On the first day, a Saturday, around 30,000 people were packed into the ground to see England begin the defence of the Ashes won in 1893 and retained in a hard fought series in Australia in 1894/95. At Lord's barely ten days earlier M.C.C. had dismissed the Australians for 18 on their way to an innings victory, and nine of that Australian team and five of the Englishmen renewed the battle on a bright day perfect for batting. However, the crowd was too large for the ground. Many spectators spilled over onto the playing area, getting in the way of the fielders and throwing bottles and other objects at each other when their view was obstructed, which it frequently was. *The Times*, always keen to take the pompous approach, declared that 'Lord's has scarcely ever before been the scene of so much noisiness and rowdyism as was displayed yester-day when the crowds encroached on the ground.'

Australia, perhaps demoralised by their appalling showing ten days before, fared scarcely better this time. They finished up at 53 all out, setting a record low total by Australia in England which exactly equalled England's lowest score in England, set eight years earlier, but which the Australians would ignominiously improve upon by being all out for 44 just two Tests later. JT Hearne, who had taken 4 for 4 for M.C.C., did not even get a bowl this time: it was left to the Surrey pairing of Tom Richardson and George Lohmann to tear them apart, Richardson bowling from the Pavilion end to take 6 for 39, all clean bowled. When England replied, Grace and Bobby Abel put on 105 for the second wicket, and put the match beyond Australia's reach.

This was the game in which a legend was made: Ernie Jones, the very quick Australian opening bowler, bowled a bouncer to WG first ball of the first innings, which reputedly went through the good doctor's beard, past the wicketkeeper and to the boundary for four byes. Jones was heard to

Harry Trott, captain of Australia.

apologise: 'Sorry, Doctor, she slipped.' Luckily for Jones, the vast crowd did not riot.

It was also the match in which captain Harry Trott and Syd Gregory put on 221 for the fourth wicket in Australia's second innings in barely more than 150 minutes. It was the highest stand in Test cricket to that time, and meant that Australia at least gave themselves a chance, setting England 109 to win. But despite overnight rain, England got home by six wickets.

AUSTRALIA

Batsman	Dismissal (1st)	Score	Dismissal (2nd)	Score
H Donnan	run out	1	b Hearne	8
J Darling	b Richardson	22	b Richardson	0
G Giffen	c Lilley b Lohmann	0	b Richardson	32
† GHS Trott	b Richardson	0	c Hayward b Richardson	143
SE Gregory	b Richardson	14	c Lohmann b Hearne	103
H Graham	b Richardson	0	b Richardson	10
C Hill	b Lohmann	1	b Hearne	5
CJ Eady	not out	10	c Lilley b Richardson	2
H Trumble	b Richardson	0	c Lilley b Hearne	4
* JJ Kelly	c Lilley b Lohmann	0	not out	24
E Jones	b Richardson	4	c Jackson b Hearne	4
	(B 1)	1	(B 7, LB 4, W 1)	12
Total		53		347

ENGLAND

Batsman	Dismissal (1st)	Score	Dismissal (2nd)	Score
† WG Grace	c Trumble b Giffen	66	c Hill b Trumble	7
AE Stoddart	b Eady	17	not out	30
R Abel	b Eady	94	c sub (Iredale) b Jones	4
JT Brown	b Jones	9	c Kelly b Eady	36
W Gunn	c Kelly b Trumble	25	not out	13
FS Jackson	c Darling b Giffen	44		
T Hayward	not out	12		
* AA Lilley	b Eady	0		
GA Lohmann	c sub (Iredale) b Giffen	1		
JT Hearne	c Giffen b Trott	11		
T Richardson	c Hill b Trott	6	b Jones	13
	(B 5, LB 2)	7	(B 3, LB 4, W 1)	8
Total		292	(4 wkts)	111

ENGLAND	O	M	R	W	O	M	R	W
Richardson	11.3	3	39	6	47	15	134	5
Lohmann	11	6	13	3	22	6	39	0
Hayward					11	3	44	0
Hearne					36	14	76	5
Jackson					11	5	28	0
Grace					6	1	14	0

AUSTRALIA	O	M	R	W	O	M	R	W
Jones	26	6	64	1	23	10	42	2
Giffen	26	5	95	3	1	0	9	0
Eady	29	12	58	3	3	0	11	1
Trott	7.4	2	13	2	0.1	0	4	0
Trumble	19	3	55	1	20	10	37	1

FALL OF WICKETS

	Aus.	Eng.	Aus.	Eng.
Wkt	1st	1st	2nd	2nd
1st	3	38	0	16
2nd	3	143	3	20
3rd	4	152	62	42
4th	26	197	283	82
5th	26	256	289	
6th	31	266	300	
7th	41	266	304	
8th	45	267	308	
9th	46	286	318	
10th	53	292	347	

† Captain   * Wicketkeeper

1899: England v Australia

(2nd Test) June 15, 16, 17
Australia won by 10 wickets

The 1899 season was a very high scoring one. Bobby Abel made 357 not out as Surrey compiled 811 against Somerset at the Oval; Major R.M. Poore and E.G. Wynyard put on 411 together for Hampshire, also against Somerset; and A.E.J. Collins, a thirteen year old schoolboy at Clifton College made what is still the highest score in any organised cricket match, 628 not out.

The 1899 Lord's Test did not really reflect these high scores, but it was significant for one reason more than any other: it was the first time that England had voluntarily gone into a home Test match without WG Grace. WG had been captain in the First Test, but was dropped and replaced by Archie MacLaren for the Second Test. He never played for England again, although even at almost 51 years of age, few would have thought his England career was over. Dropping Grace was not the only change the selectors made, and by the end of the match it was probably one of the least controversial. The batting order, on paper at least, was very strong, with the big-hitting Jessop at number eight. The only trouble was the bowling: Jessop had actually been picked to open the bowling, which he did

The Australian team. *L–r, top*: V Trumper, H Trumble, AE Johns, WP Howell, Maj. Wardill, MA Noble, F Laver, CE McLeod.
Middle: JJ Kelly, C Hill, J Worrall, J Darling, FA Iredale, E Jones. *Front*: SE Gregory.

with Walter Mead of Essex. It was Jessop's first Test appearance, and Mead's only one.

Jessop did his best to postpone the moment when he took the new ball for England by scoring a fine 51, but of the rest of the team only Stanley Jackson made any meaningful runs, and before tea Jessop was bowling, trying to help defend a total of 206. At 59 for 3 things seemed to be going fairly well, but then Clem Hill and Monty Noble climbed into the weak England attack, and by stumps had reached 156 for 3. The next morning,

Victor Trumper, in only his second Test, took over where Hill had left off. At the age of just 21, Trumper made an undefeated 135 out of 232, to announce the arrival of a genius.

In England's second innings Hayward opened in place of MacLaren, and the change worked for both of them. Hayward made 77 and MacLaren 88 not out, an innings described by Pelham Warner as 'masterly'. But it was not masterly enough to leave the Australians more than 26 to win, which they did with ease. Who were the masters now?

ENGLAND

Batsman	Dismissal	Score	2nd innings	Score
CB Fry	c Trumble b Jones	13	b Jones	4
† AC MacLaren	b Jones	4	not out	88
KS Ranjitsinhji	c & b Jones	8	c Noble b Howell	0
CL Townsend	st Kelly b Howell	5	b Jones	8
FS Jackson	b Jones	73	c & b Trumble	37
T Hayward	b Noble	1	c Trumble b Laver	77
JT Tyldesley	c Darling b Jones	14	c Gregory b Laver	4
GL Jessop	c Trumper b Trumble	51	c Trumble b Laver	4
* AA Lilley	not out	19	b Jones	12
W Mead	b Jones	7	lbw b Noble	0
W Rhodes	b Jones	2	c & b Noble	2
	(B 2, LB 6, W 1)	9	(B 2, LB 2)	4
Total		206		240

AUSTRALIA

Batsman	Dismissal	Score	2nd innings	Score
J Worrall	c Hayward b Rhodes	18	not out	11
† J Darling	c Ranjitsinhji b Rhodes	9	not out	17
C Hill	c Fry b Townsend	135		
SE Gregory	c Lilley b Jessop	15		
MA Noble	c Lilley b Rhodes	54		
VT Trumper	not out	135		
* JJ Kelly	c Lilley b Mead	9		
H Trumble	c Lilley b Jessop	24		
F Laver	b Townsend	0		
E Jones	c Mead b Townsend	17		
WP Howell	b Jessop	0		
	(LB 4, NB 1)	5		
Total		421	(0 wkt)	28

AUSTRALIA	O	M	R	W	O	M	R	W
Jones	36.1	11	88	7	36	15	76	3
Howell	14	4	43	1	31	12	67	1
Noble	15	7	39	1	19.4	8	37	2
Trumble	15	9	27	1	15	6	20	1
Laver					16	4	36	3

ENGLAND	O	M	R	W	O	M	R	W
Jessop	37.1	10	105	3	6	0	19	0
Mead	53	24	91	1				
Rhodes	39	14	108	3	5	1	9	0
Jackson	18	6	31	0				
Townsend	15	1	50	3				
Ranjitsinhji	2	0	6	0				
Hayward	6	0	25	0				

FALL OF WICKETS

	Eng.	Aus.	Eng.
Wkt	1st	1st	2nd
1st	4	27	5
2nd	14	27	6
3rd	20	59	23
4th	44	189	94
5th	45	271	160
6th	66	306	166
7th	161	386	177
8th	184	387	212
9th	190	421	240
10th	206	421	240

† Captain   * Wicketkeeper

1902: England v Australia

(2nd Test) June 12, 13, 14
Match drawn

This was the Lord's Test most completely ruined by rain. Only an hour and three-quarters of play was possible on the first day, and none at all on the second and third days. So much rain fell on the second day, the Friday, that the pitch was almost completely under water, and the match was abandoned even before play was due to start on the Saturday.

The Australians cannot have been too upset about it all, except insofar as it impacted on the profits of the tour. England were unchanged from the team which had skittled Australia at Birmingham for just 36 (Rhodes 7 for 17), and apart from a devastating bowling combination in Hirst and Rhodes, had eleven batsmen all of whom scored first class centuries. The Australians, on the other hand, were in the midst of a sea of troubles which meant that Hugh Trumble (injured), who would take 26 wickets in the next three Tests, and Bill Howell (flu) were unfit for selection. Howell's replacement was Jack Saunders, but he was suffering from tonsillitis and was far from fit. They had only brought fourteen players to England, so their captain, Joe Darling, and Monty Noble, both recovering from the flu, also had to play although they were probably too ill to have withstood a complete game.

England won the toss and decided to bat. It was less than three months since the teams had met in the Fifth Test of the winter series at the MCG, so the players should have known a great deal about each other. However, the amateurs Fry, Ranji and Jackson had all missed the Australian tour, and certainly had never played against off-spinner Bert Hopkins who was about the only fully fit bowler on the pitch. Despite the fact that he had never opened the bowling for his country before, and would never do so again, Darling gave him the second over and he immediately dismissed Fry and Ranji. But that was the limit of his success – in fact he took no more wickets in the series. MacLaren and Jackson then put on 102 in even time before the rains came again and the match disappeared under water.

ENGLAND

† AC MacLaren	not out	47
CB Fry	c Hill b Hopkins	0
KS Ranjitsinhji	b Hopkins	0
FS Jackson	not out	55
Total	(2 wkts)	102

Did not bat: JT Tyldesley, *AA Lilley, GH Hirst, GL Jessop, LC Braund, WH Lockwood, W Rhodes.

AUSTRALIA	O	M	R	W
Jones	11	4	31	0
Hopkins	9	3	18	2
Saunders	3	0	15	0
Trumper	8	1	33	0
Armstrong	5	0	5	0
Noble	2	2	0	0

FALL OF WICKETS

	Eng.
Wkt	1st
1st	0
2nd	0

Australia: VT Trumper, RA Duff, AJ Hopkins, C Hill, SE Gregory, †J Darling, MA Noble, WW Armstrong, *JJ Kelly, E Jones, JV Saunders.

† Captain   * Wicketkeeper

1905: England v Australia

(2nd Test) June 15, 16, 17 (no play on 3rd day)
Match drawn

The England captain, Stanley Jackson, won the toss at Lord's as he was to do in every Test that summer. By the end of the series, Joe Darling, Australia's captain, was reported as saying, 'What's the good of tossing with you, Jacker? I might just as well give you first innings.' At the Scarborough Festival at the end of the season, when Jackson was captaining CI Thornton's XI against the Australians, Darling challenged him to wrestle for the right to choose innings. Jackson

The twelfth Australian touring party. *L – r, top*: Gehrs, Howell, Armstrong, Hopkins, Cotter, Kelly. *Middle*: Trumper, Hill, Darling (captain), Noble, McLeod, Laver. *Seated*: Duff, Newlands, Gregory.

ENGLAND

AC MacLaren	b Hopkins	56	b Armstrong	79
T Hayward	lbw b Duff	16	c Laver b McLeod	8
JT Tyldesley	c Laver b Armstrong	43	b Noble	12
CB Fry	c Kelly b Hopkins	73	not out	36
† FS Jackson	c Armstrong b Laver	29	b Armstrong	0
AO Jones	b Laver	1	c Trumper b Armstrong	5
BJT Bosanquet	c & b Armstrong	6	not out	4
W Rhodes	b Hopkins	15		
* AA Lilley	lbw b McLeod	0		
S Haigh	b Laver	14		
EG Arnold	not out	7		
	(B 20, LB 2)	22	(B 2, LB 4, NB 1)	7
Total		282	(5 wkts)	151

AUSTRALIA

VT Trumper	b Jackson	31
RA Duff	c Lilley b Rhodes	27
C Hill	c Bosanquet b Jackson	7
MA Noble	c Fry b Jackson	7
WW Armstrong	lbw b Jackson	33
† J Darling	c Haigh b Arnold	41
SE Gregory	c Jones b Rhodes	5
AJ Hopkins	b Haigh	16
CE McLeod	b Haigh	0
F Laver	not out	4
* JJ Kelly	lbw b Rhodes	2
	(B 3, LB 5)	8
Total		181

AUSTRALIA	O	M	R	W	O	M	R	W
McLeod	20	7	40	1	15	5	33	1
Laver	34	8	64	3	10	4	39	0
Armstrong	30	11	41	2	10	2	30	3
Noble	34	13	61	0	13	2	31	1
Duff	7	4	14	1				
Hopkins	15	4	40	3	2	0	11	0

ENGLAND	O	M	R	W
Haigh	12	3	40	2
Rhodes	16.1	1	70	3
Jackson	15	0	50	4
Arnold	7	3	13	1

FALL OF WICKETS

	Eng.	Aus.	Eng.
Wkt	1st	1st	2nd
1st	59	57	18
2nd	97	73	63
3rd	149	73	136
4th	208	95	136
5th	210	131	146
6th	227	138	
7th	257	171	
8th	258	175	
9th	258	175	
10th	282	181	

† Captain   * Wicketkeeper

wisely declined the offer, and won the toss yet again.

The game that followed the toss was once again spoilt by rain, with the last day completely washed out. England were already one up in the series, so were in no mood to take risks. Even so their strong batting line-up barely survived on a poor wicket, the result of many days' rain. Neither side had picked a truly quick bowler (Jackson was probably England's quickest, and he was not expected to be more than a support bowler), but the medium pace of Laver and McLeod, backed by the slower bowling of Bert Hopkins and Warwick Armstrong, kept England's batsmen tied down. Only MacLaren, Tyldesley and Fry made good starts, but none of the three was able to press on to a really big score. Fry was very annoyed to be given out. As he recorded later, 'when I had made 73 and was well set for a century, that obstinate umpire Jim Phillips gave me out caught at the wicket when I hit the toe of my front boot at least a foot away from the ball.' Fry, like all batsmen,

hated being out, and was never one to concede that he might actually have snicked it or had his leg in front of the stumps. But he preserved his particular disgust for Jim Phillips, an Australian who stood in over twenty Tests in three different countries over almost two decades. Fry described him as having been 'a second rate elephantine slow-medium bowler. He was quite honest, but ambitious to achieve the reputation of a "strong umpire".' And he had no-balled Fry for throwing when Sussex played Oxford University. If anything was elephantine, it was Fry's memory for an imagined slight to his reputation.

After England were all out for 282, Duff and Trumper took advantage of a wicket that was briefly easy paced and hit 57 in 33 minutes. The collapse to 181 all out that followed was in no way due to England's bowling hero of the previous Test, BJT Bosanquet, who did not even bowl. How many times has a man taken 8 wickets in a Test innings, as Bosanquet did, and then not been asked to bowl in the next Test?

1907: England v South Africa

(1st Test) July 1, 2, 3 (no play on 3rd day)
Match drawn

Having lost the 1905/06 series in South Africa by four matches to one, England were keen to redeem themselves on home turf. But for 'home turf', read 'home mud'. For the third successive Lord's Test, at least one complete day was lost to the weather, and no result was possible. South Africa, playing their first Test in England after thirteen against England in South Africa, retained almost all the players who had so thoroughly dispensed with England two years earlier – most notably their leg-spin and googly attack of Schwarz, Vogler, White and Faulkner. England's selectors rang the changes, retaining only Crawford and Blythe of the second string eleven who had lost the final Test at Cape Town in March 1906, and yet still

managing not to give a first Test cap to anybody. They paid South Africa the compliment of fielding a full-strength side, and it almost worked. It probably would have worked if they had not left Walter Brearley out of the side on the first morning. England wanted to fight spin with spin, but in the event a fast bowler like Brearley might have sewn the game up even more quickly.

Bert Vogler, a professional cricketer when they were a very rare breed outside England, took 7 for 128 on his first Test appearance at Lord's, but the South Africans were unable to prevent England from compiling a solid 428 on the first day, thanks mainly to a stand of 145 in 75 minutes between Len Braund and the big-hitting Gilbert Jessop,

The South African team. *L – r, top*: Nourse, Smith, Shalders, Hathorn, Faulkner, manager G A Allsop. *Middle*: Sinclair, Schwarz, Robinson, Sherwell, Tancred, Vogler, Kotze. *Seated*: S J Snooke, White, S D Snooke.

whose share was 93. When South Africa batted the next day, they lost three wickets for 18 runs before Nourse and Faulkner added 98 for the fourth wicket. The score was 123 for 4 at lunch, but then the first rain fell, and on resumption after lunch South Africa lost their last six wickets for 17 runs in 24 balls. The Tourists followed on 288 runs behind and despite the efforts of Percy Sherwell, who scored 115 before playing on to Colin Blythe, they were still over 100 runs short of making England bat again when bad light stopped play for the day.

On the third day, it rained, and South Africa floated free. England's victory would have to wait four weeks until the Second Test at Headingley.

Lord's Ground.

ENGLAND v. SOUTH AFRICA.

MONDAY & TUESDAY, (WEDNESDAY no play), JULY 1, 2, 3, 1907.

ENGLAND.

		First Innings.		Second Innings.
1	C. B. Fry	b Vogler	33	
2	Hayward	st Sherwell, b Vogler	21	
3	Tyldesley	b Vogler	52	
4	R. E. Foster	st Sherwell, b Vogler	8	
5	Braund	c Kotze, b Faulkner	104	
6	Hirst	b Vogler	7	
7	G. L. Jessop	c Faulkner, b Vogler	93	
8	J. N. Crawford	c Sherwell, b Schwarz	22	
9	Arnold	b Schwarz	4	
10	Lilley	c Nourse, b Vogler	48	
11	Blythe	not out	4	
		B 24, l-b 6, w 2, n-b ,	32	B , l-b , w n-b ,
		Total	428	Total

FALL OF THE WICKETS.

1-54 2-55 3-79 4-140 5-158 6-303 7-335 8-347 9-401 10-428

1- 2- 3- 4- 5- 6- 7- 8- 9- 10-

ANALYSIS OF BOWLING.

Name.	1st Innings.						2nd Innings.					
	O.	M.	R.	W.	Wd.	N-b.	O.	M.	R.	W.	Wd.	N-b.
Kotze	12	2	43	0								
Schwarz	34	7	90	2	2							
Vogler	47.2	12	128	7								
White	15	2	52	0								
Nourse	1	0	2	0								
Faulkner	12	1	59	1								
Sinclair	6	1	22	0								

SOUTH AFRICA.

		First Innings.		Second Innings.	
1	W. A. Shalders	c Lilley, b Arnold	2	b Hirst	0
2	P. W. Sherwell	run out	6	b Blythe	115
3	M. Hathorn	c Foster, b Hirst	6	c Fry, b Blythe	30
4	A. D. Nourse	b Blythe	62	not out	11
5	G. A. Faulkner	c Jessop, b Braund	44	not out	12
6	S. J. Snooke	l b w, b Blythe	5		
7	G. C. White	b Arnold	0		
8	J. H. Sinclair	b Arnold	0		
9	R. O. Schwarz	not out	0		
10	A. E. Vogler	c Lilley, b Arnold	3		
11	J. J. Kotze	b Arnold	0		
		B 9, l-b 2, w 1, n-b ,	12	B 15, l-b 2, w , n-b ,	17
		Total	140	Total	185

FALL OF THE WICKETS.

1-8 2-8 3-18 4-116 5-134 6-135 7-135 8-137 9-140 10-140

1-1 2-140 3-153 4- 5- 6- 7- 8- 9- 10-

ANALYSIS OF BOWLING.

Name.	1st Inning						2nd Innings.					
	O.	M.	R.	W.	Wd.	N-b.	O.	M.	R.	W.	Wd.	N-b.
Hirst	18	7	35	1			16	8	26	1		
Arnold	22	7	37	5			13	2	41	0		
Jessop	2	0	8	0								
Crawford	8	1	20	0			4	0	19	0		
Blythe	8	3	18	2			21	5	56	2		
Braund	7	4	10	1			4	0	26	0		

Umpires—Millward and White.

Scorers—G. G. Hearne and Martin.

Play commences 1st day at 11.30, 2nd and 3rd day at 11.

1909: England v Australia

(2nd Test) June 14, 15, 16
Australia won by 9 wickets

Having won the low-scoring First Test at Edgbaston by ten wickets, England came to Lord's hoping for their first Test victory at headquarters since 1896. However, the selection policy seemed to defy belief as England made five changes to the winning team, and failed to include more than one opening bowler. There had been other quick bowlers in the selectors' minds, but Thomas Jayes of Leicestershire (who never won a Test cap) was made twelfth man on the morning of the match. Walter Brearley of Lancashire was asked to play at the last minute, but turned the invitation down. The selectors were Lord Hawke, CB Fry and HDG Leveson-Gower, but Lord Hawke was ill in France and Fry was involved as a witness in a lawsuit, which explains why he did not select or play at Lord's. So Leveson-Gower and the captain Archie MacLaren were left with the job of picking the team. Colin Blythe, Kent's great slow left arm bowler, was ill, so his place was taken by John King of Leicestershire, playing his only Test at the age of 38. King may have been old to make his Test debut, but he was not even half way through a county career which stretched from 1895 to 1925. In 1923, aged 52, he hit a double century against Hampshire. Wilfred Rhodes, a youngster of 32 yet already perhaps the greatest of all the slow left armers, was omitted for no obvious reason. Of the eleven selected, Hayward was still lame from a leg injury, a factor in his run out in the second innings for just six.

Monty Noble won the toss for Australia as he did in every Test that summer, but for the only time that summer he put England in to bat. It was in fact the first time ever in a Test match in England that the winner of the toss had not chosen to bat, but Noble's daring move paid off. Only the much maligned King stood firm against Laver,

Cotter and Noble himself, although wicketkeeper Dick Lilley hit 47 of the final 64 runs added. Australia built a first innings lead around Vernon Ransford's 143 not out, his only Test century. If

Warwick Armstrong of Australia.

ENGLAND

Batsman		1st innings		2nd innings	
T Hayward	st Carter b Laver	16	run out	6
JB Hobbs	c Carter b Laver	19	c & b Armstrong	9
JT Tyldesley	lbw b Laver	46	st Carter b Armstrong	3
G Gunn	lbw b Cotter	1	b Armstrong	0
JH King	c Macartney b Cotter	60	b Armstrong	4
† AC MacLaren	c Armstrong b Noble	7	b Noble	24
GH Hirst	b Cotter	31	b Armstrong	1
AO Jones	b Cotter	8	lbw b Laver	26
AE Relf	c Armstrong b Noble	17	b Armstrong	3
* AA Lilley	c Bardsley b Noble	17	not out	25
S Haigh	not out	1	run out	5
	(B 8, LB 3, W 3, NB 2)	16	(B 2, LB 3, NB 10)	15
Total		269		121

AUSTRALIA

Batsman		1st innings		2nd innings	
PA McAlister	lbw b King	22	not out	19
F Laver	b Hirst	14		
W Bardsley	b Relf	46	c Lilley b Relf	0
WW Armstrong	c Lilley b Relf	12		
VS Ransford	not out	143		
VT Trumper	c MacLaren b Relf	28		
† MA Noble	c Lilley b Relf	32		
SE Gregory	c Lilley b Relf	14	not out	18
A Cotter	run out	0		
CG Macartney	b Hirst	5		
* H Carter	b Hirst	7		
	(B 16, LB 8, W 1, NB 2)	27	(B 4)	4
Total		350	(1 wkt)	41

AUSTRALIA	O	M	R	W	O	M	R	W
Laver	32	9	75	3	14	5	24	1
Macartney	8	2	10	0				
Cotter	23	1	80	4	18	3	35	0
Noble	24.2	9	42	3	5	1	12	1
Armstrong	20	6	46	0	24.5	10	35	6

ENGLAND	O	M	R	W	O	M	R	W
Hirst	26.5	2	83	3	8	1	28	0
King	27	5	99	1				
Relf	45	14	85	5	7.4	4	9	1
Haigh	19	5	41	0				
Jones	2	0	15	0				

FALL OF WICKETS

	Eng.	Aus.	Eng.	Aus.
Wkt	1st	1st	2nd	2nd
1st	23	18	16	4
2nd	41	84	22	
3rd	44	90	22	
4th	123	119	23	
5th	149	198	34	
6th	175	269	41	
7th	199	317	82	
8th	205	317	90	
9th	253	342	101	
10th	269	350	121	

† Captain   * Wicketkeeper

MacLaren had caught him at slip when he had only scored 12, Noble's gamble might have proved much less successful.

England's second innings was a pitiful procession back to the pavilion, chased there by Warwick Armstrong's leg breaks. From 41 for 6 there was no way back, and Australia won comfortably by nine wickets. Having started the 1909 tour badly, Australia did not lose again for three months after this Test. The England selectors went on making changes all summer, using 25 players in the series to little effect.

1912: England v South Africa

(Triangular Tournament, 2nd Match) June 10, 11, 12
England won by an innings and 62 runs

Largely thanks to the enthusiasm and backing of the South African millionaire Sir Abe Bailey, a Triangular Tournament of Test Matches was arranged for the summer of 1912, with a total of nine tests being played; England, Australia and South Africa each played each other three times. Three of these Tests, one in each series, were played at Lord's. England were captained by CB Fry.

South Africa won the toss, and their captain Frank Mitchell, a Yorkshireman who had played two Tests for England against South Africa in 1899, decided to bat. Perhaps his team were still shell-shocked from Jimmy Matthews' two hat-tricks in a day against them in their first Test against Australia two weeks earlier, as their first innings lasted barely an hour and a half. On a mud wicket, Foster and Barnes took just 159 balls to dismiss South Africa for 58, with extras the top scorer on 17. Second top scorer was 'Dave' Nourse, another Englishman who went out to South Africa in 1895 as a teenage trumpeter with the West Riding regiment and stayed there after the Boer War ended. For the first quarter of the Twentieth century he was the batting pillar around which the South African side was built, but on this occasion the pillar crumbled.

This was the first time in Test Match history that extras had top-scored in a completed innings. EJ 'Tiger' Smith was the guilty wicketkeeper, although standing up to Sydney Barnes and Frank Foster cannot have been easy. Foster and Barnes, fresh from a triumphant tour of Australia, were one of the very best opening bowling partnerships England has ever had, even though neither of them bowled above fast-medium pace. In South Africa's first innings, they needed no help from anybody else as they tore through the hapless South Africans: six clean bowled, one lbw, two caught by

Sydney Barnes.

Foster and one caught by Barnes! Formerly of Warwickshire and Lancashire, Barnes was at the time playing for Staffordshire. Since his retirement, no English cricketer has played for his country while playing domestic cricket at minor county level.

In the second innings, Jack Hobbs had the longest bowl of his Test career. CB Fry decided Hobbs would make a decent fast bowler, so gave him a long bowl 'when we had the situation in hand'. His idea did not win approval with the press, but Fry was unrepentant. 'But for his innate modesty,' said Fry, 'I would have made a bowler of Hobbs.' Fry was never one to suffer from innate modesty.

SOUTH AFRICA

GPD Hartigan	c Foster b Barnes	0	b Foster	1
HW Taylor	lbw b Barnes	1	b Barnes	5
AW Nourse	b Foster	13	run out	17
GCB Llewellyn	b Foster	9	c Smith b Foster	75
GA Faulkner	b Foster	7	b Barnes	15
SJ Snooke	b Barnes	2	b Foster	16
† F Mitchell	c & b Barnes	1	b Barnes	1
RO Schwarz	c Foster b Barnes	4	b Barnes	28
SJ Pegler	b Foster	4	b Barnes	10
CP Carter	b Foster	0	not out	27
* T Campbell	not out	0	c Jessop b Barnes	3
	(B 12, l R 3, NB 2)	17	(B 17, LB 1, NB 1)	19
Total		58		217

ENGLAND

JB Hobbs	b Nourse	4
W Rhodes	b Nourse	36
RH Spooner	c Llewellyn b Nourse	119
† CB Fry	b Pegler	29
PF Warner	st Campbell b Pegler	39
FE Woolley	b Pegler	73
GL Jessop	b Pegler	3
FR Foster	lbw b Pegler	11
* EJ Smith	b Pegler	2
SF Barnes	not out	0
W Brearley	b Pegler	0
	(B 11, LB 9, W1)	21
Total		337

ENGLAND	O	M	R	W	O	M	R	W
Foster	13.1	7	16	5	27	10	54	3
Barnes	13	3	25	5	34	9	85	0
Brearley					6	2	4	0
Woolley					4	0	19	0
Hobbs					11	2	36	0

SOUTH AFRICA	O	M	R	W	O	M	R	W
Nourse	16	5	46	3				
Pegler	31	8	65	7				
Faulkner	29	6	72	0				
Carter	4	0	15	0				
Llewellyn	9	0	60	0				
Schwarz	20	3	44	0				
Hartigan	10	2	14	0				

FALL OF WICKETS

	SA	Eng.	SA
Wkt	1st	1st	2nd
1st	2	4	5
2nd	3	128	17
3rd	28	183	36
4th	35	207	104
5th	36	320	132
6th	42	323	135
7th	45	324	147
8th	54	330	176
9th	55	337	197
10th	58	337	217

† Captain   * Wicketkeeper

1912: England v Australia

(Triangular Tournament, 2nd Match) June 24, 25, 26
Match drawn

England's team v. Australia at Lord's, 1912.

England won the toss and CB Fry, captain as well as chief selector for the summer, elected to bat. The weather was always going to be a factor, with less than four hours' play being possible on the first two days, and Fry's idiosyncratic captaincy adapted itself to conditions perfectly. Fry claimed later in his 1939 autobiography, *Life Worth Living*, that 'never in any species of representative match from Oxford and Cambridge onwards have I ever been on the losing side as captain.' If so, he was no doubt saved by the weather or innings such as the one Jack Hobbs produced on this occasion, a 'proper

hundred,' as Fry described it. Hobbs was dismissed by a ball that all reports described as unplayable: the medium-paced Sid Emery made one pitch on leg stump and spit from a length to hit off stump low down. The ball that spits, turns and does not bounce is one to which even the Master had no answer.

By the time Fry declared on 310 for 7, it was obvious that a result would not be possible. Charles Kelleway, as solid as ever, and Charles Macartney put on 146 for the second wicket, Macartney eventually falling to a catch behind for a hard hit 99. The snick was so thin that even

ENGLAND

JB Hobbs	b Emery	107
W Rhodes	c Carkeek b Kelleway	59
RH Spooner	c Bardsley b Kelleway	1
† CB Fry	run out	42
PF Warner	b Emery	4
FE Woolley	c Kelleway b Hazlitt	20
FR Foster	c Macartney b Whitty	20
JW Hearne	not out	21
* EJ Smith	not out	14
	(B 16, LB 4, NB 2)	22
Total	(7 wkts dec)	310

Did not bat: SF Barnes, H Dean.

AUSTRALIA

CB Jennings	c Smith b Foster	21
C Kelleway	b Rhodes	61
CG Macartney	c Smith b Foster	99
W Bardsley	lbw b Rhodes	21
† SE Gregory	c Foster b Dean	10
D Smith	not out	24
TJ Matthews	b Dean	0
GR Hazlitt	b Rhodes	19
	(B 17, LB 5, W 1, NB 4)	27
Total	(7 wkts)	282

Did not bat: SH Emery, WJ Whitty, *W Carkeek.

AUSTRALIA	O	M	R	W
Whitty	12	2	69	1
Hazlitt	25	6	68	1
Matthews	13	4	26	0
Kelleway	21	5	66	2
Emery	12	1	46	2
Macartney	7	1	13	0

ENGLAND	O	M	R	W
Foster	36	18	42	2
Barnes	31	10	74	0
Dean	29	10	49	2
Hearne	12	1	31	0
Rhodes	19.2	5	59	3

FALL OF WICKETS

	Eng.	Aus.
Wkt.	1st	1st
1st	112	27
2nd	123	173
3rd	197	226
4th	211	233
5th	246	243
6th	255	243
7th	285	282
8th		
9th		
10th		

† Captain   * Wicketkeeper

today's technology might not have picked it up, but in those gentler days Macartney walked as soon as the appeal went up. Fry let the Australians compile their total without once turning to the Kent all-rounder Frank Woolley, and making comparatively little use of Wilfred Rhodes, perhaps the best slow left arm bowler the game has ever produced. Critics at the time (Fry called them 'scribes, Pharisees and dramatists') could not understand Fry's reluctance to use two of his best wet-wicket bowlers more, but Fry in his defence maintained that he was thinking of the tournament as a whole, being reluctant to let Australia, and in particular the big-hitting Dave Smith, get at his key bowlers when the match was already, in his opinion, dead. Barnes and Foster did the bulk of the work, with Barnes bowling 31 overs for 74 runs and no wickets – by some way his worst analysis in Test cricket.

Fry had the last laugh: in the ninth and final match of the Tournament, at the Oval, Woolley took five Australian wickets in each innings, to give England victory by 244 runs while Foster bowled only two overs in the match.

LORD'S GROUND

1912: Australia v South Africa

(Triangular Tournament, 5th Match) July 15, 16, 17
Australia won by 10 wickets

The first Test Match at Lord's not to feature England resulted in a convincing win for Australia. The dogged Charles Kelleway and the more consistent and attacking Warren Bardsley put on 244 for Australia's third wicket, and by the time they were separated the result was virtually decided, always assuming that the rain held off which it did. Kelleway, in his first Test series for Australia, soon earned the nickname 'The Rock of Gibraltar', for his dour defence rather than for being originally Spanish, and for a further fifteen years was to be the basis upon which Australia built their scores. He and Warren Bardsley both hit

two centuries during the Triangular series, while no other Australian reached three figures even once. Kelleway was also a very useful fast-medium swing bowler, who took ten Test wickets during the tournament.

The Triangular Tournament was certainly a failure, so much so that nothing like it was attempted until the one-day game took its thorough grip, but the failings were not so much on the field of play as in the weather, which was truly awful throughout the summer, and in the Australian camp, where internal disputes meant that barely half of their full-strength Test team came to England. The

The fourteenth Australian squad. *L – r, top*: Minnett, Kelleway, Mayne, Smith, Emery, Crouch (manager). *Middle*: McLaren, Carkeek, Whitty, Gregory (captain), Bardsley, Macartney, Hazlitt. *Seated*: Webster, Jennings, Matthews.

weather was disastrous throughout the summer, but even so, South Africa could only manage to draw one Test, losing the other five by margins that ranged from a mere 174 runs to two ten-wicket defeats and two innings defeats.

On the afternoon of the second day, King George V visited Lord's for the first time since coming to the throne two years before. The visit of the monarch to Lord's during a Test match became something of a tradition from the reign of George V onwards, and could often be relied on to bring a wicket or two in its wake, as batsmen strove to recover concentration after being presented to the King. King George V was not a keen cricketer – nor indeed a sportsman of any particular note – but the enthusiasm he felt for watching the game was real enough. He would not have persisted with the custom otherwise. These days, the sight of the Royal Standard fluttering from the flagpole at the top of the Pavilion, and the presence of the monarch in the Committee Room below, is a sign that Lord's is still the centre of cricket, where the pomp and circumstance still remain, even if the power has moved elsewhere.

SOUTH AFRICA

GA Faulkner	b Whitty	5	c & b Matthews		6
LJ Tancred	lbw b Matthews	31	c Bardsley b Hazlitt		19
GC White	c Carkeek b Minnett	0	b Matthews		18
GCB Llewellyn	c Jennings b Minnett	8	b Macartney		59
AW Nourse	b Hazlitt	11	lbw b Kelleway		10
HW Taylor	c Kelleway b Hazlitt	93	not out		10
LA Stricker	lbw b Kelleway	48	b Hazlitt		13
† F Mitchell	b Whitty	12	b Matthews		3
RO Schwarz	b Whitty	0	c Macartney b Matthews		1
SJ Pegler	c Bardsley b Whitty	25	c Kelleway b Macartney		14
* TA Ward	not out	1	b Macartney		7
	(B 12, LB 14, W 1, NB 2)	29	(B 9, LB 4)		13
Total		263			173

AUSTRALIA

CB Jennings	b Nourse	0	not out		22
C Kelleway	lbw b Faulkner	102			
CG Macartney	b Nourse	9			
W Bardsley	lbw b Llewellyn	164			
† SE Gregory	b Llewellyn	5			
ER Mayne	st Ward b Pegler	23	not out		25
RB Minnett	b Pegler	39			
TJ Matthews	c Faulkner b Pegler	9			
GR Hazlitt	b Nourse	0			
* W Carkeek	not out	6			
WJ Whitty	lbw b Pegler	3			
	(B 24, LB 3, W 2, NB 1)	30	(B 1)		1
Total		390	(0 wkt)		48

AUSTRALIA	O	M	R	W	O	M	R	W
Minnett	15	6	49	2				
Whitty	31	9	68	4	9	0	41	0
Hazlitt	19	9	47	2	13	1	39	2
Matthews	13	5	32	1	13	2	29	4
Kelleway	11	3	38	1	8	1	22	1
Macartney					14.1	5	29	3

SOUTH AFRICA	O	M	R	W	O	M	R	W
Nourse	36	12	60	3	6.1	2	22	0
Pegler	29.5	7	79	4	4	1	15	0
Schwarz	11	1	44	0				
Faulkner	28	3	86	1	2	0	10	0
Llewellyn	19	2	71	2				
Taylor	2	0	12	0				
Stricker	3	1	8	0				

FALL OF WICKETS

	SA	Aus.	SA
Wkt	1st	1st	2nd
1st	24	0	28
2nd	25	14	54
3rd	35	256	62
4th	56	277	102
5th	74	316	134
6th	171	353	136
7th	203	375	142
8th	213	379	146
9th	250	381	163
10th	263	390	173

† Captain   * Wicketkeeper

1921: England v Australia

(2nd Test) June 11, 13, 14
Australia won by 8 wickets

The 1921 Australians are generally regarded as the strongest team to have come from Australia up to that time, and even eighty years on probably only Bradman's 1948 side are spoken of in the same breath. Warwick Armstrong's Australia won three of the five Tests, and drew the other two, and it was not until 30 August that the Australians lost a single game on the tour. That was against a team put together by the 49-year-old former England captain, Archie MacLaren, and including the 40-year-old South African all-rounder Aubrey Faulkner.

The England selectors were not frightened of picking good old 'uns either. CB Fry was asked on his 49th birthday, 25 April, to captain England that summer, but as he himself admitted, 'could not see much fun in taking on Gregory and McDonald so early in the season'. The selectors persisted all summer, and Fry almost played at Lord's, but 'did not fancy taking on the Australian fast bowlers on a fast wicket. Had there been likelihood of a wet wicket, I would have played.' England, having given five men their first caps at Nottingham, promptly dropped four of them after

Warren Bardsley of Australia, who has scored more Test runs at Lord's than any other overseas player.

one game and gave four others their debuts. They also brought back Lionel Tennyson, on the advice of Fry (according to his account, at least), and it was Tennyson, along with the incomparable 34-year-old Kent left-hander Frank Woolley who at least forced Australia to bat again after gaining a first innings lead of 155.

Gregory and McDonald, a fearsome fast bowling combination, took thirteen of the England wickets to fall in the match, following the 16 they had taken in the First Test. All summer they were too good for a rather feeble England, who were without Hobbs all year, and few of the 30 players used that summer enhanced their reputations. The team at Lord's was considered one of the worst fielding sides ever assembled in England colours, and for much of the season the batting and bowling were little better. Whether the 1921 Australians were as good as they seemed at the time, or whether they were just up against very poor opposition after the ravages of the First World War, is something that will be debated as long as there is a Lord's.

ENGLAND

Batsman	Dismissal (1st)	R	Dismissal (2nd)	R
DJ Knight	c Gregory b Armstrong	7	c Carter b Gregory	1
AE Dipper	b McDonald	11	b McDonald	40
FE Woolley	st Carter b Mailey	95	c Hendry b Mailey	93
E Hendren	b McDonald	0	c Gregory b Mailey	10
† JWHT Douglas	b McDonald	34	b Gregory	14
AJ Evans	b McDonald	4	lbw b McDonald	14
Hon. LH Tennyson	st Carter b Mailey	5	not out	74
NE Haig	c Carter b Gregory	3	b McDonald	0
CH Parkin	b Mailey	0	c Pellew b McDonald	11
* H Strudwick	c McDonald b Mailey	8	b Gregory	12
TJ Durston	not out	6	b Gregory	2
Extras	(B 1, LB 11, W 1, NB 1)	14	(B 4, LB 3, NB 5)	12
Total		**187**		**283**

AUSTRALIA

Batsman	Dismissal (1st)	R	Dismissal (2nd)	R
W Bardsley	c Woolley b Douglas	88	not out	63
TJE Andrews	c Strudwick b Durston	9	lbw b Parkin	49
CG Macartney	c Strudwick b Durston	31	b Durston	8
CE Pellew	b Haig	43	not out	5
JM Taylor	lbw b Douglas	36		
† WW Armstrong	b Durston	0		
JM Gregory	c & b Parkin	52		
HL Hendry	b Haig	5		
* H Carter	b Durston	46		
AA Mailey	c & b Parkin	5		
EA McDonald	not out	17		
Extras	(B 2, LB 5, NB 3)	10	(B 3, LB 2, NB 1)	6
Total		**342**	(2 wkts)	**131**

AUSTRALIA	O	M	R	W	O	M	R	W
Gregory	16	1	51	1	26.2	4	76	4
McDonald	20	2	58	4	23	3	89	4
Armstrong	18	12	9	1	12	6	19	0
Mailey	14.2	1	55	4	25	4	72	2
Hendry					4	0	15	0

ENGLAND	O	M	R	W	O	M	R	W
Durston	24.1	2	102	4	9.3	0	34	1
Douglas	9	1	53	2	6	0	23	0
Parkin	20	5	72	2	9	0	31	1
Haig	20	4	61	2	3	0	27	0
Woolley	11	2	44	0	3	0	10	0

FALL OF WICKETS

Wkt	Eng. 1st	Aus. 1st	Eng. 2nd	Aus. 2nd
1st	20	19	3	103
2nd	24	73	97	114
3rd	25	145	124	
4th	108	191	165	
5th	120	192	165	
6th	145	230	198	
7th	156	263	202	
8th	157	277	235	
9th	170	289	263	
10th	187	342	283	

† Captain   * Wicketkeeper

1924: England v South Africa

(2nd Test) June 28, 30, July 1
England won by an innings and 18 runs

The difference between the England of 1921 and the side that played its next Lord's Test three years later was amazing. Only Woolley and Hendren remained from the disaster of 1921, and the England selectors had unearthed several major cricketing talents in the interim. Hobbs, now aged 41, was back at his rightful number one position, but now he was joined by his most famous partner, Herbert Sutcliffe, who had made his debut in the previous Test. There the new England opening pair put on 136 for the first wicket as England strolled to an innings victory, but at Lord's they went several degrees further. Their partnership of 268 for the first wicket was not only England's highest opening partnership at Lord's (it still is), but also a record in all matches against South Africa to that time. The runs came in very quick time: England, who had been 28 for 0 overnight, scored 503 more runs in the day, the most ever compiled by one side in one day in a Test. Sutcliffe went soon after lunch and when Hobbs was dismissed with the score on 410, Hendren and Woolley put on a further 121 in 55 minutes. South Africa, who included the now 43-year-old Aubrey Faulkner, were outclassed, with England scoring at exactly 4.5 an over through their innings.

England's other new discovery was Maurice Tate. On debut at Edgbaston two weeks earlier he had taken four for 12 as he and Gilligan (six for 7) dismissed South Africa for 30, including 11 extras. At Lord's he took only four wickets, but by the end of the series he had taken 27 in all to establish himself as one of England's greatest fast-medium bowlers.

Apart from the massive England innings, there were two odd statistical happenings at Lord's. Firstly, Bob Catterall hit 120 for the second successive Test: the highest score ever made by any batsman in consecutive Test innings. But to add to the coincidence, he was on the losing side both times, and on both occasions by exactly the same margin, an innings and eighteen runs. Never before had consecutive Test matches produced exactly the same result – drawn matches always excluded, of course.

JB Hobbs, 'the Master'

Lord's Ground.

ENGLAND v. SOUTH AFRICA.

SATURDAY, MONDAY & TUESDAY, JUNE 28, 30, JULY 1, 1924.

SOUTH AFRICA.	First Innings.		Second Innings.	
† 1 H. W. Taylor	c Wood, b Gilligan	4	b Gilligan	8
2 J. M. Commaille	b Gilligan	0	l b w, b Tyldesley	37
3 M. J. Susskind	c Tate, b Hearne	64	l b w, b Tyldesley	53
4 A. D. Nourse	c Woolley. b Tate	4	l b w, b Gilligan	11
5 R. H. Catterall	b Gilligan	120	c Gilligan, b Tyldesley	45
6 J. M. Blanckenberg	b Tate	12	c Hobbs, b Fender	15
7 H. G. Deane	b Tyldesley	33	c Sutcliffe, b Hearne	24
8 G. A. Faulkner	b Fender	25	run out	12
* 9 T. A. Ward	b Tyldesley	1	not out	3
10 S. J. Pegler	c Fender, b Tyldesley	0	b Tate	8
11 G. M. Parker	not out	1	b Tate	0
	B 3, l-b 2, w , n-b 4,	9	B 13, l-b 8, w , n-b 3,	24
	Total	273	Total	240

FALL OF THE WICKETS.

1-4	2-5	3-17	4-129	5-182	6-212	7-265	8-271	9-272	10-273
1-50	2-78	3-103	4-117	5-171	6-204	7-224	8-231	9-240	10-240

ANALYSIS OF BOWLING.

Name.	1st Innings.						2nd Innings.					
	O.	M.	R.	W.	Wd.	N-b.	O.	M.	R.	W.	Wd.	N-b.
Gilligan	31	7	70	3	...	3	24	6	54	2	...	1
Tate	34	12	62	2	...	...	26.4	8	43	2	...	...
Tyldesley	24	10	52	3	...	...	36	18	50	3	...	2
Hearne	18	3	35	1	...	...	19	4	35	1	...	...
Fender	9	1	45	1	...	1	14	5	25	1	...	...
Woolley	...	...	...	...	...	...	4	1	9	0	...	...
	...	...	...	...	...	...	...	...	...	...	...	...

ENGLAND.	First Innings.		Second Innings.	
1 Hobbs	c Taylor, b Parker	211		
2 Sutcliffe	b Parker	122		
3 Woolley	not out	134		
4 Hendren, E.	not out	50		
5 Hearne, J. W.	Innings closed.			
6 A. P. F. Chapman				
7 P. G. H. Fender				
8 Tate				
9 Tyldesley, R.				
†10 A. E. R. Gilligan				
*11 G. E. G. Wood				
	B 11, l-b 1, w , n-b 2,	14	B , l-b , w , n-b ,	
	Total	531	Total	

FALL OF THE WICKETS.

1-268	2-410	3-	4-	5-	6-	7-	8-	9-	10-
1-	2-	3-	4-	5-	6-	7-	8-	9-	10-

ANALYSIS OF BOWLING.

Name.	1st Innings.						2nd Innings.					
	O.	M.	R.	W.	Wd.	N-b.	O.	M.	R.	W.	Wd.	N-b.
Parker	24	0	121	2	...	2	...					
Blanckenberg	28	3	113	0	...	...	...					
Pegler	31	4	120	0	...	...	...					
Nourse	15	1	57	0	...	...	...					
Faulkner	17	0	87	0	...	...	...					
Catterall	3	0	19	0	...	...	...					
	...	...	...	...	...	...	...					

Umpires—Chester and Young.

Luncheon at 1.30   †Captain.   * Wicket-keeper.

Scorers—Caldicott and Rippon.

Stumps drawn at 6.30

ENGLAND WON BY AN INNINGS AND 18 RUNS.

1926: England v Australia

(2nd Test) June 26, 28, 29
Match drawn

In 1926 England regained the Ashes in a hard fought series of four drawn games and a Fifth Test triumph at the Oval, an outcome that would be repeated 27 years later in 1953. The years between the two series were dominated by one player, Don Dradman, but in June 1926 he was a seventeen-year-old playing for Bowral Cricket Club.

The 1926 Lord's Test marked the end of an Australian era, and in one way the start of an English one. Harold Larwood made his Test debut, as did the Lord's Grandstand, which was opened that summer to the general criticism that it cost a lot of money and held remarkably few people. All

the same, it lasted another 70 years, as did Harold Larwood.

The Lord's Test was the only one of the summer to be played on a hard batting surface, and the scores emphasised the fact. Bardsley made 193 not out, carrying his bat through the innings at the age of 42. He is still the oldest Australian to score a Test hundred against England. The England attack was not the strongest of all time, with Larwood coming on as second change, but all the same Bardsley's was a remarkable feat. At 338 for 8 at the end of the Saturday's play, Australia were in for a shock when it was discovered on the Monday morning

The England team. *L–r, standing*: Kilner, Larwood, Tate, Woolley, Root, Sutcliffe.
Sitting: Strudwick, Chapman, Carr (captain), Hobbs, Hendren.

AUSTRALIA

HL Collins	b Root	1	c Sutcliffe b Larwood	24
W Bardsley	not out	193	
CG Macartney	c Sutcliffe b Larwood	39	not out	133
† WM Woodfull	c Strudwick b Root	13	c Root b Woolley	0
TJE Andrews	c & b Kilner	10	b Root	9
JM Gregory	b Larwood	7	c Sutcliffe b Root	0
JM Taylor	c Carr b Tate	9	
AJ Richardson	b Kilner	35	
JS Ryder	c Strudwick b Tate	28	not out	0
* WA Oldfield	c Sutcliffe b Kilner	19	c Sutcliffe b Tate	11
AA Mailey	lbw b Kilner	1	
	(B 12, LB 16)	28	(B 5, LB 12)	17
Total		383	(5 wkts)	194

ENGLAND

JB Hobbs	c Richardson b Macartney	119
H Sutcliffe	b Richardson	82
FE Woolley	lbw b Ryder	87
E Hendren	not out	127
APF Chapman	not out	50
	(B 4, LB 4, W 1, NB 1)	10
Total	(3 wkts dec)	475

Did not bat: R Kilner, † AW Carr, MW Tate, H Larwood, F Root, * H Strudwick.

ENGLAND	O	M	R	W	O	M	R	W
Tate	50	12	111	2	25	11	38	1
Root	36	11	70	2	19	9	40	2
Kilner	34.5	11	70	4	22	2	49	0
Larwood	32	2	99	2	15	3	37	1
Woolley	2	0	5	0	7	1	13	1

AUSTRALIA	O	M	R	W
Gregory	30	3	125	0
Macartney	33	8	90	1
Mailey	30	6	96	0
Richardson	48	18	73	1
Ryder	25	3	70	1
Collins	2	0	11	0

FALL OF WICKETS

	Aus.	Eng.	Aus.
Wkt	1st	1st	2nd
1st	11	182	2
2nd	84	219	125
3rd	127	359	164
4th	150		187
5th	187		194
6th	208		
7th	282		
8th	338		
9th	379		
10th	383		

† Captain   * Wicketkeeper

that a hose had been left near the pitch the previous evening and a part of the wicket had been soaked. Australia added 45 to their overnight score, but if the water affected the batting surface England's batsmen did not show it. Hobbs and Sutcliffe put on 182 for the first wicket, which remained the highest first wicket partnership against Australia at Lord's until it was beaten by Strauss and Cook in 2009, and the last century opening stand for England in Ashes Tests at Lord's until 1975. On top of that, Patsy Hendren scored a brilliant 127 not out. Every batsman who came to the wicket made at least 50, and Australia's bowling was made to look mediocre. The opening bowler was Macartney, then aged nearly 40 and best known as a great batsman. He proved this in the second innings when he made 133 not out, the first of three Test hundreds he was to make that summer.

This was the last Test series between England and Australia in England where Tests were scheduled to last just three days, and the fact that England did not have time to finish off Australia from a winning position at Lord's was one factor in the change. Perhaps if they had only allowed Bradman three days to compile his runs, England might have had more chance over the next two decades.

1928: England v West Indies

(1st Test) June 23,25,26
England won by an innings and 58 runs

In 1928 the West Indies became the first team to play their first ever Test Match at headquarters. Even England did not manage that, and since 1928, only India in 1932 have joined this exclusive club. Besides Lord's, only the Melbourne Cricket Ground, where England and Australia began their Test match rivalries in March 1877, can claim to be the birthplace of Test cricket of two countries.

West Indies were well beaten in this First Test, but there were signs of their greatness to come. As the *Cricketer* said at the time, 'Warmth and sun, which mean so much to the West Indians, have at times been conspicuous by their absence.' But they also commented that 'better bowling than the

West Indies on a hard wicket has not been seen in a Test Match in England since Gregory, McDonald, Armstrong and Mailey were here in 1921.' Praise indeed.

The most famous name to us now, Learie Constantine, did little with the bat, but took four England wickets and made three catches. The Trinidad-born Pelham Warner described him at the time as 'one of the most interesting personalities now before the public.' His impact on the tour had already been considerable, but he was to distinguish himself even more when the West Indians moved to Northampton the day after the Test finished. Against the county side (admittedly then one of the weakest in the country), Constantine

The first official West Indian touring side. *L–r, standing*: St Hill, Rae, Hoad, Small, Martin, Constantine, Neblett.
Sitting: Bartlett, Fernandes, Wight, Nunes (captain), Challenor, Brown.

took 13 wickets for 112, including the hat-trick, and scored 107 as the tourists won by an innings and 126 runs. George Challenor and CLR James' childhood friend Wilton St Hill were two more 'most interesting personalities' in the Test side, but neither distinguished himself in what was an uneventful one-sided match. The main significance of the game was the Test debut of Douglas Jardine, playing with Harold Larwood for the first time.

England also gave a rare Test cap to 'Tich' Freeman, the Kent leg-spinner who took a vast number of wickets around this time. He only played for England 12 times in all, despite finishing his career second in the all-time list of wicket-takers. In 1928 he took 304 wickets, an unimaginable total these days, including 22 in the three Tests. But although he was picked for the Australian tour that winter, he did not play in a single Test.

ENGLAND

H Sutcliffe	c Constantine b Francis	48
C Hallows	c Griffith b Constantine	26
E Tyldesley	c Constantine b Francis	122
WR Hammond	b Constantine	45
DR Jardine	lbw b Griffith	22
† APF Chapman	c Constantine b Small	50
VWC Jupp	b Small	14
MW Tate	c Browne b Griffith	22
* H Smith	b Constantine	7
H Larwood	not out	17
AP Freeman	b Constantine	1
	(B 6, LB 19, NB 2)	27
Total		401

WEST INDIES

G Challenor	c Smith b Larwood	29	b Tate	0
FR Martin	lbw b Tate	44	b Hammond	12
MP Fernandes	b Tate	0	c Hammond b Freeman	8
†* RK Nunes	b Jupp	37	lbw b Jupp	10
WHSt. Hill	c Jardine b Jupp	4	lbw b Freeman	9
CA Roach	run out	0	c Chapman b Tate	16
LN Constantine	c Larwood b Freeman	13	b Freeman	0
JA Small	lbw b Jupp	0	c Hammond b Jupp	52
CR Browne	b Jupp	10	b Freeman	44
GN Francis	not out	19	c Jardine b Jupp	0
HC Griffith	c Sutcliffe b Freeman	2	not out	0
	(B 13, LB 6)	19	(B 10, LB 5)	15
Total		177		166

WEST INDIES	O	M	R	W
Francis	25	4	72	2
Constantine	26.4	9	82	4
Griffith	29	9	78	2
Browne	22	5	53	0
Small	15	1	67	2
Martin	8	2	22	0

ENGLAND	O	M	R	W	O	M	R	W
Larwood	15	4	27	1				
Tate	27	8	54	2	22	10	28	2
Freeman	18.3	5	40	2	21.1	10	37	4
Jupp	23	9	37	4	15	4	66	3
Hammond					15	6	20	1

FALL OF WICKETS

	Eng.	WI	WI
Wkt	1st	1st	2nd
1st	51	86	0
2nd	97	86	22
3rd	174	88	35
4th	231	95	43
5th	327	96	44
6th	339	112	44
7th	360	123	100
8th	380	151	147
9th	389	156	147
10th	401	177	166

† Captain   * Wicketkeeper

1929: England v South Africa

(2nd Test) June 29, July 1, 2
Match drawn

For the first time ever, Test matches were played at Lord's in consecutive years. England very nearly managed a second successive victory, but bad light stopped play at 5.45 pm on the third evening and South Africa were able to escape with a draw. That was probably a fair result, because before lunch that day, with Christy and Mitchell going well, it looked as though South Africa might sneak a win despite the brilliant batting of Leyland and Tate in England's second innings. It was Walter Robins, in his first Test, who brought England close with his leg spin, but it was Larwood whose pace brought the match to a premature end. At around 5.30, a very fast short delivery from the Nottinghamshire man struck the South African wicketkeeper Jock Cameron on the side of the head, knocking him out. Nobody in the ground was either surprised or particularly upset when the umpires decided fifteen minutes later that the light was too bad for play to continue.

The whole match was a chapter of injuries. Apart from Cameron's dreadful blow, Hammond and O'Connor were both unable to field at times, and Larwood and Robins were both carrying niggling injuries which got worse during the match. The *Cricketer* decided that 'Larwood is not the bowler he was.' Neither Cameron nor the Australians three years later would agree with that verdict.

The Yorkshiremen Sutcliffe and Leyland made 285 of the 587 runs scored from the bat by England, but the star of the game was probably Denys Morkel

H B Cameron, the South African wicketkeeper, being carried off the field
after being hit on the head by a ball from Larwood in the second Test at Lord's.

of South Africa. He opened the bowling and had England reeling at 18 for 3, and then top-scored with 88 in South Africa's first innings. He was left not out at the end of the match, having stood at the other end when Cameron was hit.

While Frank Woolley was elsewhere, hitting his one hundredth first-class hundred, which was also his third successive century for Kent, England introduced Essex's Jack O'Connor to Test cricket, and he duly joined that most distinguished club of players who have scored a duck on Test debut. Woolley came back into the Test side for the next match, and finished the summer with a Test average of 126.

ENGLAND

H Sutcliffe	c Mitchell b Bell	100	c Catterall b Morkel ... 10
ET Killick	b Morkel	3	c Morkel b Christy ... 24
WR Hammond	c Christy b Morkel	8	b Morkel ... 5
J O'Connor	b Morkel	0	c Cameron b Ochse ... 11
E Hendren	b Morkel	43	b Morkel ... 11
M Leyland	b Bell	73	c Cameron b Ochse ... 102
MW Tate	c Cameron b Bell	15	not out ... 100
RWV Robins	c Mitchell b Bell	4	c Mitchell b Ochse ... 0
H Larwood	b Bell	35	b Ochse ... 9
† JC White	b Bell	8	not out ... 18
* G Duckworth	not out	8	
	(LB 4, W 1)	5	(B 11, LB 6, W 2, NB 3) ... 22
Total		302	(8 wkts dec) ... 312

SOUTH AFRICA

RH Catterall	b Larwood	0	b Tate ... 3
B Mitchell	st Duckworth b Hammond	29	c Hendren b Robins ... 22
JAJ Christy	run out	70	c Hendren b Robins ... 41
DPB Morkel	lbw b Tate	88	not out ... 17
† HG Deane	b Tate	1	st Duckworth b Robins ... 2
* HB Cameron	c Leyland b Robins	32	retired hurt ... 0
HG Owen-Smith	not out	52	not out ... 1
EL Dalton	b Tate	6	c Killick b Larwood ... 1
Q McMillan	c Killick b White	17	
AL Ochse	c Duckworth b White	1	
AJ Bell	b Robins	13	
	(B 9, LB 4)	13	(B 2, LB 1) ... 3
Total		332	(5 wkts) ... 90

SOUTH AFRICA	O	M	R	W	O	M	R	W
Ochse	24	5	51	0	20	0	99	4
Morkel	31	6	93	4	24	6	63	3
Bell	30.4	7	99	6	18.2	2	60	0
Christy	6	2	20	0	3	0	15	1
McMillan	7	0	31	0	13	0	34	0
Owen-Smith	1	0	3	0				
Mitchell					4	0	19	0

ENGLAND	O	M	R	W	O	M	R	W
Larwood	20	4	65	1	12	3	17	1
Tate	39	9	108	3	11	3	27	1
Hammond	8	3	19	1				
White	35	12	61	2	9	3	11	0
Robins	24	5	47	2	19	4	32	3
Leyland	5	2	9	0				

FALL OF WICKETS

	Eng.	SA	Eng.	SA
Wkt	1st	1st	2nd	2nd
1st	8	0	28	9
2nd	18	82	46	60
3rd	18	125	83	77
4th	111	126	93	82
5th	199	189	117	85
6th	243	237	246	
7th	249	253	250	
8th	252	272	260	
9th	287	279		
10th	302	322		

† Captain   * Wicketkeeper

1930: England v Australia

(2nd Test) June 27, 28, 30, July 1
Australia won by 7 wickets

The *Cricketer* magazine noted, in its Spring Annual of 1930 that 'the man whose appearance is most eagerly awaited is D.J. BRADMAN [sic].' They noted that he 'sometimes makes a tentative tap at a ball just outside his off stump', but this was a man averaging 127 in domestic cricket, with a newly-established world record score of 452 not out to his name. This was the man who scored 124

and 225 in Australia's Test Trial match, and made 236 and 185 not out in his first two innings of the tour of England. No wonder his appearance was eagerly awaited, although the England bowlers did not necessarily share that eagerness.

By the time of the Second Test, Bradman's initials had been learnt and his greatness was no longer doubted. But he had to wait for the proof

of his greatness. England won the toss and batted against what was, Grimmett apart, an ordinary Australian attack. Duleepsinhji emulated his uncle Ranjitsinhji by scoring a hundred in his first Test against Australia. Duleep's performance was the only one of real substance but England still reached 425, a good total under normal circumstances. Unfortunately, circumstances, were not normal. King George V confirmed his reputation as a wicket taker when Ponsford was out to the first ball after the teams had been presented to His Majesty, but by then the score was 162 for 1 and now Bradman was striding to the wicket. The Friday crowd of 31,000 (during the four days, over 110,000 people watched the game) sat back

to enjoy one of the great displays of batsmanship in history. Even Bradman described this as one of his greatest innings. His 254 was then the highest Test innings played in England, and it was achieved in five hours and twenty minutes. When he was out, to a great catch at cover by the captain, Percy Chapman, it was said to be the first time that Bradman had lifted the ball off the ground in his entire innings. 'It would be impossible to overpraise Bradman's wonderful cricket,' wrote the *Cricketer*, a sentiment echoed by every correspondent at the time.

With a lead of 304 (a Bradman Test score on the next tour of England), England had to try to avoid an innings defeat. They did, largely thanks

A panoramic view of JB Hobbs and FE Woolley batting.

to a magnificent innings of 121 by Chapman, but they could not avoid defeat altogether. Bradman was out for 1 in the second innings – caught by Chapman again, this time cutting Tate with one of the best shots of the match, in a manner that made Neville Cardus declare that 'I have never seen a finer catch or a more beautiful one.' Even so, Australia cantered home by seven wickets. A new era of Test cricket had begun.

This card does not necessarily include the fall of the last wicket.

2d. Lord's MCC Ground

ENGLAND v. AUSTRALIA.

FRI. SAT. MON. JUNE 27, 28, 30, & TUES. JULY 1, 1930.

ENGLAND.

			First Innings		Second Innings	
1 Hobbs	Surrey	c Oldfield b Fairfax	1		b Grimmett	19
2 Woolley	Kent	c Wall b Fairfax	41		hit wicket, b Grimmett	28
3 Hammond	Gloucestershire	b Grimmett	38		c Fairfax, b Grimmett	32
4 K. S. Duleepsinhji	Sussex	c Bradman, b Grimmett	173		c Oldfield, b Hornibrook	48
5 Hendren	Middlesex	c McCabe, b Fairfax	48		c Richardson, b Grimmett	9
†6 A. P. F. Chapman	Kent	c Oldfield, b Wall	11		c Oldfield, b Fairfax	121
7 G. O Allen	Middlesex	b Fairfax	3		l b w, b Grimmett	57
8 Tate	Sussex	c McCabe, b Wall	54		c Ponsford, b Grimmett	10
9 R. W. V. Robins	Middlesex	c Oldfield, b Hornibrook	5		not out	11
10 J. C. White	Somerset	not out	23		run out	10
*11 Duckworth	Lancashire	c Oldfield, b Wall	18		l b w, b Fairfax	0
		B 2, l b 7, w , n-b 1,	10		B 16, - 13 w 1, n-b ,	30
		Total	425		Total	375

FALL OF THE WICKETS.

1-13	2 53	3 105	4 209	5 236	6 239	7 337	8 363	9 387	10 425
1 45	2 58	3-129	4 141	5 147	6-272	7-329	8 354	9 372	10-375

ANALYSIS OF BOWLING.

Name.	1st Innings.						2nd Innings.					
	O.	M.	R.	W.	Wd.	N-b.	O	M	R	W	Wd	N-b.
Wall	29.4	2	118	3	...	...	25	2	80	0	...	1
Fairfax	31	6	101	4	...	1	12 4	2	37	2	...	...
Grimmett	33	4	105	2	...	...	53	13	167	6	...	...
Hornibrook	26	6	62	1	...	...	22	6	49	1	...	...
McCabe	9	1	29	0	...	...	3	1	11	0	...	...
Bradman					...	...	1	0	1	0		

AUSTRALIA.

			First Innings.		Second Innings.	
†1 W. M. Woodfull	Victoria	st Duckworth b Robins	155		not out	26
2 W. H. Ponsford	Victoria	c Hammond, b White	81		b Robins	14
3 D. G. Bradman	New South Wales	c Chapman, b White	254		c Chapman, b Tate	1
4 A. F. Kippax	New South Wales	b White	83		c Duckworth, b Robins	3
5 S J. McCabe	New South Wales	c Woolley, b Hammond	44		not out	25
6 V. Y. Richardson	South Australia	c Hobbs, b Tate	30			
7 A. G Fairfax	New South Wales	not out	20			
*8 W. A. Oldfield	New South Wales	not out	43			
9 C. V. Grimmett	South Australia					
10 T. M. Wall	South Australia	Innings closed.				
11 P. M. Hornibrook	Queensland					
		B 6, l-b 8, w 5, n-b	19		B 1, l-b 2, w , n-b ,	3
		Total	729		Total	72

FALL OF THE WICKETS

1-162	2 393	3-585	4 588	5-643	6 672	7	8.	9-	10-
1 16	2 17	3-22	4-	5-	6-	7-	8.	9	10-

ANALYSIS OF BOWLING.

Name.	1st Innings.						2nd Innings.					
	O.	M.	R.	W.	Wd.	N-b.	O	M	R	W	Wd	N-b.
Allen	34	7	115	0	4	...						
Tate	64	16	148	1	...	...	13	6	21	1	...	...
White	51	7	158	3	...	...	2	0	8	0	...	...
Robins	42	1	172	1	1	...	9	1	34	2	...	...
Hammond	35	8	82	1	...	...	4.2	1	6	0	...	...
Woolley	6	0	35	0	...	...						

Umpires—Chester and Oates.

Scorers—Caldicott and Ferguson.

The figures on the Scoring Board show the Batsmen in.

Play commences 1st day at 11.30, 2nd 3rd and 4th days at 11.

Luncheon at 1.30.

†Captain   *Wicket-keeper.

Stumps drawn 6.30 each day.

TEA INTERVAL—There will probably be a Tea Interval at 4.30-4.45 but it will depend on the state of the game.

ENGLAND WON THE TOSS

1931: England v New Zealand

(1st Test) June 27, 29, 30
Match drawn

The first Test Match between England and New Zealand in England was meant to be the only Test of the summer. The England authorities, i.e. M.C.C., still considered New Zealand to be second-class fare and after the condescension of playing Tests simultaneously in both West Indies and New Zealand in 1929/30 England still made little effort to treat their opponents seriously. There is little doubt that England were a better side than New Zealand at the time, but the gulf was not as large as the home side liked to believe.

At the end of the first day, a Saturday, England were on 190 for 7 chasing New Zealand's 224. New Zealand had also lost their seventh wicket at 190, so honours were as even as they could possibly have been. England were perhaps surprised to

The New Zealand touring team. *L-r, standing:* HG Vivian, AM Matheson, RO Talbot, IB Cromb, JE Mills, GL Weir, JL Kerr. *Middle:* RC Blunt, ML Page, TC Lowry (captain), CFW Allcott, CS Dempster. *Front:* KC James, WE Merritt.

Lord's ✠ Ground

ENGLAND v. NEW ZEALAND.

SATURDAY, MONDAY & TUESDAY, JUNE 27, 29, 30, 1931.

NEW ZEALAND.		First Innings.		Second Innings.	
1 C. S. Dempster	Wellington	l b w, b Peebles	53	b Hammond	120
2 J. E. Mills	Auckland	b Peebles	34	b Allen	0
3 G. L. Weir	Auckland	l b w, b Peebles	37	b Allen	40
4 J. L. Kerr	Canterbury	st Ames, b Robins	2	l b w, b Peebles	0
5 R. C. Blunt	Otago	c Hammond, b Robins	7	b Robins	96
6 M. L. Page	Canterbury	b Allen	23	c and b Peebles	104
†7 T. C. Lowry	Wellington	c Hammond, b Robins	1	b Peebles	34
8 I. B. Cromb	Canterbury	c Ames, b Peebles	20	c Voce, b Robins	14
9 C. F. W. Allcott	Auckland	c Hammond, b Peebles	13	not out	20
10 W. E. Merritt	Canterbury	c Jardine, b Hammond	17	b Peebles	5
*11 K. C. James	Wellington	not out	1	Innings closed.	
		B 2, l-b 12, w 1, n-b 1,	16	B 23, l-b 10, w 1, n-b 2,	36
		Total	224	Total	469

FALL OF THE WICKETS.

1-58	2-130	3-136	4-149	5-153	6-161	7-190	8-191	9-209	10-224
1-1	2-160	3-218	4-360	5-360	6-389	7-404	8-405	9-469	10-

ANALYSIS OF BOWLING.

Name.	1st Innings.						2nd Innings.					
	O.	M.	R.	W.	Wd.	N-b.	O.	M.	R.	W.	Wd.	N-b.
Voce	10	1	40	0	...	...	32	11	60	0	...	2
Allen	15	2	45	1	...	...	25	8	47	2	1	...
Hammond	10.3	5	8	1	...	...	21	2	50	1	...	...
Peebles	26	3	77	5	...	1	42.4	6	150	4	...	...
Robins	13	3	38	3	1	1	37	5	126	2	...	...

ENGLAND.		First Innings.		Second Innings.	
1 Arnold	Hampshire	c Page, b Cromb	0	c and b Blunt	34
2 Bakewell	Northamptonshire	l b w, b Cromb	9	c Blunt, b Cromb	27
3 Hammond	Gloucestershire	b Cromb	7	run out	46
4 K. S. Duleepsinhji	Sussex	c Kerr, b Merritt	25	c James, b Allcott	11
†5 D. R. Jardine	Surrey	c Blunt, b Merritt	38	not out	0
6 Woolley	Kent	l b w, b Merritt	80	b Cromb	9
*7 Ames	Kent	c James, b Weir	137	not out	17
8 I. A. R. Peebles	Middlesex	st James, b Merritt	0		
9 G. O. Allen	Middlesex	c Lowry, b Weir	122		
10 R. W. V. Robins	Middlesex	c Lowry, b Weir	12		
11 Voce	Nottinghamshire	not out	1		
		B 15, l-b 8, w , n-b ,	23	B , l-b 2, w , n-b ,	2
		Total	454	Total	146

FALL OF THE WICKETS.

1-5	2-14	3-31	4-62	5-129	6-188	7-198	8-436	9-447	10-454
1-62	2-62	3-94	4-105	5-144	6-	7-	8-	9-	10-

ANALYSIS OF BOWLING.

Name.	1st Innings.						2nd Innings.					
	O.	M.	R.	W.	Wd.	N-b.	O.	M.	R.	W.	Wd.	N-b.
Cromb	37	7	113	3	...	...	25	5	44	2	...	...
Weir	8	1	38	3	...	...	5	1	18	0	...	...
Blunt	46	9	124	0	...	...	14	5	54	1	...	...
Allcott	17	3	34	0	...	...	10	2	26	1	...	...
Merritt	23	2	104	4	...	...	1	0	2	0	...	...
Page	3	1	13	0	...	...	...	...	...	...	...	...

Scorers—Mavins and Ferguson.

Umpires—Chester and Hardstaff.

†Captain.   *Wicket-keeper.

Luncheon at 1.30.

NEW ZEALAND WON THE TOSS.

DRAWN.

have evened up the match from a position of 31 for 3 when Cromb hit Hammond's off-stump. It was what happened on the Monday that tipped the balance. Tom Lowry, the New Zealand captain, took note that Peebles and Robins for England and Bill Merritt for New Zealand had all been very effective with their leg breaks and googlies on the first day, and he stuck to the slow attack on the Monday. Merritt and Roger Blunt wheeled away along with the quicker bowling of Ian Cromb, but Les Ames and Gubby Allen both hit centuries as they compiled an eighth-wicket partnership of 246 which put victory out of New Zealand's reach. This remained a record eighth-wicket Test partnership until Wasim Akram and Saqlain Mushtaq put on 313 together against Zimbabwe in October 1996, a record that was reclaimed for England when Trott and Broad added 332 at Lord's against Pakistan in 2010.

England's first innings lead of 230 should have been enough to force a victory, but without Larwood the attack lacked edge. Dempster, a great batsman by any yardstick, and Page both made hundreds and Blunt made 96. After being so far behind on first innings, New Zealand were able to declare 239 ahead with only two and a quarter hours left for play. In that time, New Zealand bowled 55 overs – about 23 overs an hour – and England made 146 for 5. This was Douglas Jardine's first match as captain of England, and he emerged from it with mixed reviews. Yes, England were probably ahead on points, but was the new man at the helm original and determined enough to become a great captain?

The success of the tourists in this Test Match allowed the authorities to arrange two more at short notice, at the Oval and Old Trafford. England won the Oval match easily, but the Manchester game was spoilt by the weather.

1932: England v India

(1st and only Test) June 25, 27, 28
England won by 158 runs

The first ever Test Match played by India (or All-India as the newspapers of the day described the team) began on Saturday 25 June in wonderful weather in front of a packed house of 25,000 spectators. It was described by one journalist as 'an event of more than mere cricketing importance', for it also helped encapsulate the concept of nationhood within the sub-continent which fifteen years later would culminate in independence for two new nations, India and Pakistan.

The Indian captain, the Maharajah of Porbandar, had decided to stand down from the Test side as he was out of form – as he had been throughout his career – so CK Nayudu led his country into their first Test match. He called wrong when

Jardine tossed, but twenty minutes later England were 19 for 3. Jardine and Hammond steadied the ship, but comment at the time was not about the bowling of Mahomed Nissar or the electric fielding of Lall Singh, who had run out Woolley. People were more concerned that two of the victims were Sutcliffe and Holmes, Yorkshire team-mates who had travelled (with Bill Bowes) down from Leeds the night before and had not arrived at their London hotel until after midnight. As 'Onlooker' in the *Cricketer* said, 'If Test matches are necessary – which they certainly are – some arrangement must in future be come to so as to ensure our representatives having a long night's rest before a Test match begins.' It was only two

The Indian touring team, captained by CK Nayudu.

ENGLAND

H Sutcliffe	b Nissar	3	c Nayudu b Amar Singh	19
P Holmes	b Nissar	6	c J Khan	11
FE Woolley	run out	9	c Colah b J Khan	21
WR Hammond	b Amar Singh	35	b J Khan	12
† DR Jardine	c Navle b Nayudu	79	not out	85
E Paynter	lbw b Nayudu	14	b J Khan	54
* LEG Ames	b Nissar	65	b Amar Singh	6
RWV Robins	c Lall Singh b Nissar	21	c J Khan b Nissar	30
FR Brown	c Amar Singh b Nissar	1	c Colah b Naoomal	29
W Voce	not out	4	not out	0
WE Bowes	c Nissar b Amar Singh	7		
	(B 3, LB 9, NB 3)	15	(B 2, LB 6)	8
Total		259	(8 wkts. dec)	275

INDIA

* JG Navle	b Bowes	12	lbw b Robins	13
Naoomal Jeoomal	lbw b Robins	33	b Brown	25
S Wazir Ali	lbw b Brown	31	c Hammond b Voce	39
† CK Nayudu	c Robins b Voce	40	b Bowes	10
SHM Colah	c Robins b Bowes	22	b Brown	4
S Nazir Ali	b Bowes	13	c Jardine b Bowes	6
PE Palia	b Voce	1	not out	1
Lall Singh	c Jardine b Bowes	15	b Hammond	29
M Jahangir Khan	b Robins	1	b Voce	0
Amar Singh	c Robins b Voce	5	c & b Hammond	51
M Nissar	not out	1	b Hammond	0
	(B 5, LB 7, W 1, NB 2)	15	(B 5, LB 2, NB 2)	9
Total		189		187

INDIA	O	M	R	W	O	M	R	W
Nissar	26	3	93	5	18	5	42	1
Amar Singh	31.1	10	75	2	41	13	84	2
Jahangir Khan	17	7	26	0	30	12	60	4
Nayudu	24	8	40	2	9	0	21	0
Palia	4	3	2	0	3	0	11	0
Naoomal Jeoomal	3	0	8	0	8	0	40	1
Wazir Ali					1	0	9	0

ENGLAND	O	M	R	W	O	M	R	W
Bowes	30	13	49	4	14	5	30	2
Voce	17	6	23	3	12	3	28	2
Brown	25	7	48	1	14	1	54	2
Robins	17	4	39	2	14	5	57	1
Hammond	4	0	15	0	5.3	3	9	3

FALL OF WICKETS

	Eng.	Ind.	Eng.	Ind.
Wkt	1st	1st	2nd	2nd
1st	8	39	30	41
2nd	11	63	38	41
3rd	19	110	54	52
4th	101	139	67	65
5th	149	160	156	83
6th	166	165	169	108
7th	229	181	222	108
8th	231	182	271	182
9th	252	188		182
10th	258	189		187

† Captain   * Wicketkeeper

paragraphs later that 'Onlooker' acknowledged that 'the bowling of Nissar, Amar Singh, Nayudu and Khan was really good.'

On the Monday, another huge crowd came to St John's Wood. So did the King of England and Emperor of India, no doubt impartially to cheer on both his teams. His presence seemed to help England more than India, who slumped from 153 for 4 at lunch to 189 all out at 3.20 pm. Bowes and Voce both bowled with several short legs and no slip, keeping the ball short of a length and forcing Ames into a succession of difficult leg side takes. This was a dress rehearsal for the bodyline tactics to be used in the forthcoming tour to Australia, but of course nobody had thought of the word then. None of the newspapers thought much of the tactic (although Larwood, the fastest and best proponent of bodyline, was not playing: he had injured his leg), and all thought Bowes in particular wasted the new ball by bowling far too short. Little did they realise.

1933: England v West Indies

(1st Test) June 24, 26, 27
England won by an innings and 27 runs

Walter Robins: Middlesex, England and ever loyal to Lord's.

Fresh from the 'Bodyline Tour' of Australia, England introduced four players who had not been on the tour, although only one, Cyril Walters, was completely new to Test cricket. West Indies were without Learie Constantine, who was playing that summer as professional in the Lancashire League but his club, Nelson, refused to release him. He was sorely missed. It was George Headley's debut in a Test at Lord's, but even he could not save his side.

Harold Larwood, who had badly injured his foot at the end of the Australian tour, was not considered, even though he was playing as a non-bowling number eight batsman for Notting-

hamshire against Yorkshire as the Test match unfolded. The wicket would probably not have suited him anyway. Almost the entire first day was washed out by rain, with only 45 minutes play being possible. On the second day, England, thanks mainly to Les Ames, reached 296, and by stumps had West Indies at 55 for 6. Macaulay was bowling with three short legs, and Verity's flight and Robins' sharp turning leg breaks and googlies proved too much for the tourists. Their captain, Grant, was the last man out the next morning, and his team followed on 199 behind. This time they did rather better than the first time round, with

George Headley hitting a half century, earning the description of 'a great and glorious batsman' from the English press. But it was never enough and when the ninth wicket fell at 146, it was all apparently over. By this time Macaulay was bowling with five short legs, but the 40-year-old fast bowler Herman Griffith (no relation of Charlie Griffith's, but like him a Bajan) was not concerned. He scattered the leg trap with a well timed sweep, and seeing the success of the stroke spent ten minutes sweeping everything to leg, until inevitably he missed one and Hedley Verity bowled him. England had won with a couple of hours to spare despite the first day washout, but Griffith had made 18, his highest ever Test score.

Ellis Achong, a Trinidadian of Chinese extraction known to all and sundry as 'Puss', took two wickets with his unorthodox slow left arm in this his only Lord's Test appearance. His greater contribution to cricket history is that he is sometimes regarded as the origin of the word 'Chinaman', as a description of the left-arm bowler's googly.

ENGLAND

CF Walters	c Barrow b Martindale	51
H Sutcliffe	c Grant b Martindale	21
WR Hammond	c Headley b Griffith	29
M Leyland	c Barrow b Griffith	1
† DR Jardine	c Da Costa b Achong	21
MJ Turnbull	c Barrow b Achong	28
* LEG Ames	not out	83
GO Allen	run out	16
RWV Robins	b Martindale	8
H Verity	c Achong b Griffith	21
GG Macaulay	lbw b Martindale	9
	(B 3, LB 5)	8
Total		296

WEST INDIES

CA Roach	b Allen	0	c Sutcliffe b Macaulay		0
* I Barrow	c & b Verity	7	lbw b Robins		12
G Headley	lbw b Allen	13	b Allen		50
ELG Hoad	lbw b Robins	6	c & b Verity		36
† GC Grant	hit wkt. b Robins	26	lbw b Macaulay		28
OC Da Costa	b Robins	6	lbw b Verity		1
CA Merry	lbw b Macaulay	9	b Macaulay		1
E Achong	b Robins	15	c Hammond b Verity		10
GN Francis	b Robins	4	not out		11
EA Martindale	b Robins	4	b Macaulay		4
HC Griffith	not out	1	b Verity		18
	(B 3, LB 1, NB 2)	6	(B 1)		1
Total		97			172

WEST INDIES	O	M	R	W
Martindale	24	3	85	4
Francis	18	3	52	0
Griffith	20	7	48	3
Achong	35	9	88	2
Da Costa	4	0	15	0

ENGLAND	O	M	R	W	O	M	R	W
Macaulay	18	7	25	1	20	6	57	4
Allen	13	6	13	2	11	2	33	1
Verity	16	8	21	1	18.1	4	45	4
Robins	11.5	1	32	6	12	2	36	1

† Captain * Wicketkeeper

FALL OF WICKETS

Wkt	Eng. 1st	WI 1st	WI 2nd
1st	49	1	0
2nd	103	17	56
3rd	105	27	56
4th	106	31	116
5th	154	40	119
6th	155	51	120
7th	194	87	133
8th	217	92	138
9th	265	96	146
10th	296	97	172

1934: England v Australia

(2nd Test) June 22, 23, 25
England won by an innings and 38 runs

The only time in the twentieth century that England beat Australia at Lord's was when the Yorkshire left arm spinner Hedley Verity took fourteen wickets in a day and Australia lost by an innings and 38 runs. Bob Wyatt, the England captain, was extremely proud of this achievement, perhaps above all others, until the day he died. He was often to be found in his old age in Sir Paul Getty's box at Lord's, always fervently looking for an England victory against Australia but secretly half hoping his team's achievement would remain unique.

It has to be admitted, though, that the weather played a crucial role in England's win. Wyatt did the right thing by winning the toss (or rather

Woodfull did the wrong thing by calling incorrectly and losing it), and choosing to bat. Thanks in particular to Leyland who scored his second Test century at Lord's, and to Les Ames who scored the first hundred by a wicketkeeper in England–Australia Tests, England reached 440 by the early afternoon. Wyatt, incidentally, was much castigated in the press for not declaring sooner, but like many others before and after him, he had the last laugh. At the close of the second day, though, with Australia on 192 for 2, it looked as though castigation was the right line for the press to take.

On the Sunday, it rained. As *Wisden* said, the Australians 'suffered the cruellest luck, rain ... rendering their chances almost hopeless.' It was

Bradman batting – England's wicketkeeper Les Ames can only stand and admire.

England's good luck that they had a bowler able to exploit the conditions, which were not really those to give a 'sticky' wicket, but were nevertheless alien to the tourists. A successful appeal against the light as soon as the batsmen reached the wickets at the start of the morning delayed play for twenty minutes, but after that Verity took over. During the day, he took six first innings wickets for 37 runs (having taken 1 for 24 the day before) and when Australia followed on 156 behind, he took another eight wickets for 43.

Nobody before or since has taken fourteen wickets in a day in a Test: at Lord's it is the record for all matches. Verity bowled impeccably, varying his flight and his length, and making the ball lift and turn almost at will. He was backed up by some brilliant fielding 'with Hammond shining as a star of the first magnitude', as Pelham Warner wrote in the *Daily Telegraph*. After the match, Warner reported, Wyatt 'spoke a few modest words' from the pavilion balcony, 'and acknowledged the great part that the rain had played in England's success.'

ENGLAND

CF Walters	c Bromley b O'Reilly	82
H Sutcliffe	lbw b Chipperfield	20
WR Hammond	c & b Chipperfield	2
E Hendren	c McCabe b Wall	13
† RES Wyatt	c Oldfield b Chipperfield	33
M Leyland	b Wall	109
* LEG Ames	c Oldfield b McCabe	120
G Geary	c Chipperfield b Wall	9
H Verity	st Oldfield b Grimmett	29
K Farnes	b Wall	1
WE Bowes	not out	10
	(LB 12)	12
Total		440

AUSTRALIA

† WM Woodfull	b Bowes	22	c Hammond b Verity	43
WA Brown	c Ames b Bowes	105	c Walters b Bowes	2
DG Bradman	c & b Verity	36	c Ames b Verity	13
SJ McCabe	c Hammond b Verity	34	c Hendren b Verity	19
LS Darling	c Sutcliffe b Verity	0	b Hammond	10
AG Chipperfield	not out	37	c Geary b Verity	14
EH Bromley	c Geary b Verity	4	c & b Verity	1
* WA Oldfield	c Sutcliffe b Verity	23	lbw b Verity	0
CV Grimmett	b Bowes	9	c Hammond b Verity	0
WJ O'Reilly	b Verity	4	not out	8
TW Wall	lbw b Verity	0	c Hendren b Verity	1
	(B 1, LB 9)	10	(B 6, NB 1)	7
Total		284		118

AUSTRALIA	O	M	R	W				
Wall	49	7	108	4				
McCabe	18	3	38	1				
Grimmett	53.3	13	102	1				
O'Reilly	38	15	70	1				
Chipperfield	34	10	91	3				
Darling	6	2	19	0				
ENGLAND	O	M	R	W	O	M	R	W
Farnes	12	3	43	0	4	2	6	0
Bowes	31	5	98	3	14	4	24	1
Geary	22	4	56	0				
Verity	36	15	61	7	22.3	8	43	8
Hammond	4	1	6	0	13	0	38	1
Leyland	4	1	10	0				

FALL OF WICKETS

Wkt	Eng. 1st	Aus. 1st	Aus. 2nd
1st	70	68	10
2nd	78	141	43
3rd	99	203	57
4th	130	204	94
5th	182	205	94
6th	311	218	95
7th	359	258	95
8th	409	273	95
9th	410	284	112
10th	440	284	118

† Captain   * Wicketkeeper

1935: England v South Africa

(2nd Test) June 29, July 1, 2
South Africa won by 157 runs

After his triumph against the Australians the year before, England's captain Bob Wyatt had to learn to treat the other impostor – disaster – just the same. He led England to defeat, making this South Africa's first Test victory in England. If in 1934 he had had help from the rain in securing victory, it could be argued that in 1935 he was hindered by the leather-jackets. As *The Times*' leader writer so succinctly put it, 'In the second Test match South Africa won the toss and the game. In the University match Cambridge won the toss and the game. The conclusion is too obvious to be disputed. To

win the toss at Lord's this summer is to win the game . . . It is all the fault of the leather-jackets.'

Leather-jackets are the larvae of the daddy-long-legs, which had apparently been deposited under the surface of the pitch, creating a surface which crumbled quickly. Bat first and you could compile a decent score to keep ahead of your opponents: bat second and you would always be faced by a treacherous pitch. That was the theory. Spin bowlers did indeed prosper at Lord's in 1935, but as England had the best of the lot at the time – Verity – why did they not win? What's more, the highest

Victory at Lord's: a great moment in South Africa's cricket history.

individual score of the match, 164 not out by Bruce Mitchell, came in South Africa's second innings. The newsmen had it right when they put England's defeat down to inept batting. Howard Marshall, the BBC broadcaster who pioneered cricket commentary in England, asked the question, 'What's wrong with our cricket?' For neither the first nor the last time, the answer was, 'I don't know.'

South Africa's spin hero was Xenophon Balaskas, a man of Greek extraction who only played one Test that summer because of recurring injuries. His nine wickets in the match sealed the victory which Mitchell and Jock Cameron had set up. The only man with the initial X to play Test cricket until Xavier Marshall (West Indies) and Xavier Doherty (Australia) in the 21st century, Balaskas never repeated the triumph of his one Lord's Test. If you are going to have one good Test, it might as well be at Lord's.

For wicketkeeper Jock Cameron, it was his finest hour. As *Wisden* said, his 'powerful driving and pulling captured the imagination of everyone'. Later in the tour he hit Verity for 30 runs in an over in the game against Yorkshire at Sheffield. But he caught enteric fever on his return to his homeland, and before the year was out, he was dead, aged just 30. He became *Wisden*'s only posthumous Cricketer of The Year.

SOUTH AFRICA

B Mitchell	lbw b Nichols	30	not out		164
IJ Siedle	b Mitchell	6	c Farrimond b Mitchell		13
EAB Rowan	c Farrimond b Verity	40	lbw b Nichols		44
AD Nourse	b Verity	3	b Verity		2
† HF Wade	c Hammond b Langridge	23	b Verity		0
* HB Cameron	b Nichols	90	c Ames b Mitchell		3
EL Dalton	c & b Langridge	19	c Wyatt b Verity		0
XC Balaskas	b Verity	4			
ABC Langton	c Holmes b Hammond	4	c & b Hammond		44
RJ Crisp	not out	4			
AJ Bell	b Hammond	0			
	(B 1, LB 1, W 1, NB 2)	5	(B 3, LB 5)		8
Total		228	(7 wkts dec)		278

ENGLAND

† RES Wyatt	c Nourse b Dalton	53	b Balaskas		16
H Sutcliffe	lbw b Bell	3	lbw b Langton		38
M Leyland	b Balaskas	18	b Crisp		4
WR Hammond	b Dalton	27	c Cameron b Langton		27
* LEG Ames	b Balaskas	5	lbw b Langton		8
ERT Holmes	c Bell b Balaskas	10	b Langton		8
James Langridge	c Mitchell b Balaskas	27	lbw b Balaskas		17
WF Farrimond	b Balaskas	13	b Crisp		13
MS Nichols	c Cameron b Langton	10	not out		7
H Verity	lbw b Langton	17	c Langton b Balaskas		8
TB Mitchell	not out	5	st Cameron b Balaskas		1
	(B 4, LB 5, W 1)	10	(LB 4)		4
Total		198			151

ENGLAND	O	M	R	W	O	M	R	W
Nichols	21	5	47	2	18	4	64	1
Wyatt	4	2	9	0	4	2	2	0
Hammond	5.3	3	8	2	14.4	4	26	1
Mitchell	20	3	71	1	33	5	93	2
Verity	28	10	61	3	38	16	56	3
Langridge	13	3	27	2	10	4	19	0
Holmes					4	2	10	0

SOUTH AFRICA	O	M	R	W	O	M	R	W
Crisp	8	1	32	0	15	4	30	2
Bell	6	0	16	1	12	3	21	0
Langton	21.3	3	58	2	11	3	31	4
Balaskas	32	8	49	5	27	8	54	4
Dalton	13	1	33	2				
Mitchell					2	0	11	0

FALL OF WICKETS

Wkt	SA 1st	Eng. 1st	SA 2nd	Eng. 2nd
1st	27	5	32	24
2nd	59	46	136	45
3rd	62	100	158	89
4th	98	109	169	90
5th	158	116	169	102
6th	187	121	177	111
7th	196	158	278	129
8th	224	161		141
9th	228	177		149
10th	228	198		151

† Captain   * Wicketkeeper

1936: England v India

(1st Test) June 27, 29, 30
England won by 9 wickets

All-India, as they were still known, were captained by Sir Gajapatairaj Vijaya Ananda, the Maharajkumar of Vizianagram, or 'Vizzy' for short. He had been knighted by King Edward VIII a few days before the match began, and thus became the first knight to play in a Test match at Lord's. That particular list doubled in length 54 years later when Sir Richard Hadlee played for New Zealand.

Nobody would pretend that Vizzy was anywhere near as good a player as Hadlee. In fact, there is a case to be made for the Maharajkumar as the worst cricketer ever to play in a Test match. In this, his Test debut, he made a few useful runs at the end of the All-India first innings, but his main contribution to the outcome may well have been his action in sending home one of his team's best players, Lala Amarnath, allegedly for disciplinary reasons, before the Test began. Having scored more runs than anybody else in his team and taken 32 wickets on tour, Amarnath was not the kind of player a weak touring side could lightly

Wazir Ali, one of Allen's ten victims, is caught in the gully by Verity.

This card does not necessarily include the fall of the last wicket

2d. Lord's (MCC) Ground

ENGLAND v. ALL INDIA

SATURDAY, MONDAY & TUESDAY, JUNE 27, 29, 30, 1936.

ALL INDIA.

	First Innings.		Second Innings.	
1 V. M. Merchant	b Allen	35	c Duckworth, b Allen	0
*2 D. R. Hindlekar	b Robins	26	l b w, b Robins	17
3 Mushtaq Ali	c Langridge, b Allen	0	l b w, (n) b Allen	8
4 Major C. K. Nayudu	l b w, (n) b Allen	1	c Robins, b Allen	3
5 Lieut. Syed Wazir Ali	b Allen	11	c Verity, b Allen	4
6 Amar Singh	c Langridge, b Robins	12	l b w, b Verity	7
7 P. E. Palia	c Mitchell, b Verity	11	c Leyland, b Verity	16
8 Jehangir Khan	b Allen	13	c Duckworth, b Verity	13
†9 Maharaj Kumar of Vizianagram	not out	19	c Mitchell, b Verity	6
10 C. S. Nayudu	c Wyatt, b Robins	6	c Hardstaff, b Allen	9
11 Mohamed Nissar	st Duckworth, b Verity	9	not out	2
	B 4, l-b , w , n-b	4	B 4, l-b 3, w , n-b 1,	8
	Total	147	Total	93

FALL OF THE WICKETS.

1-62 2-62 3-64 4-66 5-85 6-97 7-107 8-119 9-137 10-147
1-0 2-18 3-22 4-28 5-39 6-45 7-64 8-80 9-90 10-93

ANALYSIS OF BOWLING.

Name.	1st Innings. O.	M.	R.	W.	Wd.	N-b.	2nd Innings. O.	M.	R.	W.	Wd.	N-b.
Allen	17	7	35	5	...	...	18	1	43	5	...	1
Wyatt	3	2	7	0	...	...	7	4	8	0	...	...
Verity	18.1	5	42	2	...	...	16	8	17	4	...	...
Langridge	4	1	9	0	...	...	5	1	17	1	...	...
Robins	13	4	50	3	...	...	...	...	...	...	...	...

ENGLAND.

		First Innings.		Second Innings.	
1 Mitchell	Yorkshire	b Amar Singh	14	c Merchant, b Nissar	0
2 Gimblett	Somerset	c Mu'taq Ali, b Amar Singh	11	not out	67
3 M. J. Turnbull	Glamorgan	b Amar Singh	0	not out	37
4 Leyland	Yorkshire	l b w, b Amar Singh	60		
5 R. E. S. Wyatt	Warwickshire	c J'gir K, b Amar Singh	0		
6 Hardstaff	Notts	b Nissar	2		
7 Langridge, James	Sussex	c J'gir K, b C. K. Nayudu	19		
†8 G. O. Allen	Middlesex	c J'gir K, b Amar Singh	13		
*9 Duckworth	Lancashire	c Vizianagram, b Nissar	2		
10 R. W. V. Robins	Middlesex	c C. K. Nayudu, b Nissar	0		
11 Verity	Yorkshire	not out	2		
		B 4, l-b 4, w , n-b 3,	11	B 4, l-b , w , n-b ,	4
		Total	134	Total	108

FALL OF THE WICKETS.

1-16 2-16 3-30 4-34 5-41 6-96 7-129 8-132 9-132 10-134
1-0 2- 3- 4- 5- 6- 7- 8- 9- 10-

ANALYSIS OF BOWLING.

Name.	1st Innings. O.	M.	R.	W.	Wd.	N-b.	2nd Innings. O.	M.	R.	W.	Wd.	N-b.
Nissar	17	5	36	3	...	3	6	3	26	1	...	...
Amar Singh	25.1	11	35	6	...	...	16.3	6	36	0	...	...
Jehangir Khan	9	0	27	0	...	...	10	3	20	0	...	...
C. K. Nayudu	7	2	17	1	...	...	7	2	22	0	...	...
C. S. Nayudu	3	0	8	0	...	...	...	...	...	...	...	...

Scorers—Mavins and Ferguson.

Umpires—Dolphin and Walden.

The figures on the scoring board indicate the batsmen who are in.

Play begins 1st day at 11.30, 2nd and 3rd days at 11.

*Wicket-keeper.

†Captain.

Luncheon at 1.30.

Stumps drawn at 6.30 each day.

TEA INTERVAL—There will probably be a Tea Interval at **4.30-4.45** but it will depend on the state of the game.

(n) Signifies L.B.W. under the new experimental rule.

ENGLAND WON THE TOSS.

discard. He finally got his chance to play in a Lord's Test in 1946.

Vizzy did at least win the toss, and duly batted. But after Merchant and the wicket-keeper Hindlekar had put on 62 for the first wicket, the rot set in. England's new captain, Gubby Allen, was the main destroyer, taking 5 for 35, and after the opening partnership was broken no Indian batsman scored even 20 in the match.

That did not stop the Indians from making a fight of it, at least until the halfway stage. Though they could manage only 147, England did even worse. The weather had stepped in to play its part, so that Monday's play could not start until after lunch. England, 132 for 7 overnight, were all out for 134, of which Maurice Leyland, who usually excelled at Lord's, made 60. Then India, on a wicket which had been artificially dried, had to face Allen and the double threat of Verity and Robins, both bowling spin that turned away from the right-handers. They could not handle it, and were all out for 93. The weather tried hard to save the Indians, and play did not begin until 3.15 pm on the last day. But Somerset's Harold Gimblett, on his debut, made the highest score of the match to bring his side home with some ease.

1937: England v New Zealand

(1st Test) June 26, 28, 29
Match drawn

The year 1937 was the 150th anniversary of the founding of the Marylebone Cricket Club, and two major celebration fixtures were arranged for the last week of May. The North played the South from May 22 to 25 and then the M.C.C. Australian side played the Rest from May 26 to 28. By scoring 102 for the North and then 50 for the Rest, a young Yorkshireman called Len Hutton earned himself a Test call-up a month later at Lord's against New Zealand.

Hutton opened the batting with another debutant, JH Parks of Sussex, both of whom went on to have sons who played for England in their turn. When Hutton was out for a duck, his place at the wicket was taken by 'Young Joe' Hardstaff, whose father had played for England in 1907/08, and who had umpired seventeen Tests until his son's selection had eliminated him from consideration. England's new captain, Walter Robins, had a two-year-old son who would go on to play county cricket but not Test cricket. Making his debut in the New Zealand side was Walter Hadlee, three of whose sons, Dayle, Barry and Richard, would reach international level.

The New Zealand team. *L-r, standing*: TC Lowry (manager), WN Carson, J Cowie, N Gallichan, WA Hadlee, JR Lamason, JA Dunning, DAR Moloney, W Ferguson (scorer). *Middle*: EWT Tindill, AW Roberts, HG Vivian, ML Page (captain), GL Weir, JL Kerr. *Front*: MW Wallace, MP Donnelly.

This card does not necessarily include the fall of the last wicket

2d. Lord's ⊕ Ground

ENGLAND v. NEW ZEALAND

SATURDAY, MONDAY & TUESDAY, JUNE 26, 28, 29, 1937.

ENGLAND.		First Innings.		Second Innings.	
1 Hutton	Yorkshire	b Cowie	0	c Vivian, b Cowie	1
2 Parks, J.	Sussex	b Cowie	22	b Cowie	7
3 Hardstaff	Nottinghamshire	c Moloney, b Roberts	114	c Tindill, b Roberts	64
4 Hammond	Gloucestershire	c Roberts, b Vivian	140		
5 Paynter	Lancashire	c Dunning, b Roberts	74	not out	83
6 Barnett	Gloucestershire	b Cowie	5	c sub, b Roberts	20
*7 Ames	Kent	b Vivian	5	not out	38
†8 R. W. V. Robins	Middlesex	c Tindill, b Roberts	18		
9 Voce	Nottinghamshire	c Tindill, b Cowie	27	Innings closed.	
10 Verity	Yorkshire	c Cowie, b Roberts	3		
11 Gover	Surrey	not out	2		
		B 4, l-b 9, w 1, n-b	14	B 5, l-b 8, w , n-b	13
		Total	424	Total	226

FALL OF THE WICKETS.

1-13	2 31	3 276	4 284	5-302	6 307	7 339	8 402	9-415	10-424
1-8	2-19	3-123	4-163	5-	6-	7-	8-	9	10

ANALYSIS OF BOWLING.

	1st Innings.						2nd Innings.				
Name.	O.	M.	R.	W.	Wd.	N-b.	O.	M.	R.	W.	Wd.	N-b.
Cowie	41	10	118	4	...	...	15	2	49	2	...	...
Roberts	43.3	11	101	4	1		14	3	73	2	...	...
Dunning	20	3	64	0			9	0	60	0	...	...
Vivian	46	10	106	2	...	...	4	0	31	0	...	...
Moloney	2	1	9	0	...	...	...					
Page	3	0	12	0	...	...	...					

NEW ZEALAND.		First Innings.		Second Innings.	
1 H. G. Vivian	Auckland	l b w, b Gover	5	c Verity, b Voce	11
2 J. L. Kerr	Canterbury	c Ames, b Robins	31	not out	38
3 W. A. Hadlee	Canterbury	c Verity, b Voce	34	b Voce	3
†4 M. L. Page	Canterbury	c Paynter, b Robins	9	c and b Robins	13
5 W. M. Wallace	Auckland	l b w, b Parks	52	l b w, b Parks	56
6 M. P. Donnelly	Wellington	l b w, b Parks	0	c Ames, b Voce	21
7 D. A. R. Moloney	Wellington	c and b Verity	64	run out	0
*8 E. W. T. Tindill	Wellington	c Hammond, b Robins	8	l b w, b Verity	3
9 A. W. Roberts	Canterbury	not out	66	c sub, b Gover	17
10 J. A. Dunning	Otago	b Gover	0		
11 J. Cowie	Auckland	l b w, b Voce	2		
		B 4, l-b 18, w , n-b	24	B 4, l-b 8, w 1, n-b	13
		Total	295	Total	175

FALL OF THE WICKETS.

1 9	2-36	3-66	4-131	5-131	6 147	7-176	8 280	9 281	10-295
1-15	2-15	3-15	4-85	5-87	6-143	7-146	8 175	9	10

ANALYSIS OF BOWLING.

	1st Innings.						2nd Innings.				
Name.	O.	M.	R.	W.	Wd.	N-b.	O.	M.	R.	W.	Wd.	N-b.
Gover	22	8	49	2	...	2	18	7	27	1	...	...
Voce	24.2	2	74	2	...	...	18.5	8	41	3	1	...
Hammond	6	2	12	0	...	...	...					
Robins	21	5	58	3	...	...	16	3	51	2	...	...
Verity	25	13	48	1	...	...	14	7	33	1	...	...
Parks	11	3	26	2	...	...	10	6	10	1	...	...
Hutton	2	1	4	0	...	...						

Scorers—Mavins and Ferguson.

Umpires—Chester and Walden.

The figures on the scoring board indicate the batsmen who are in.

Play begins 1st day at 11.30, 2nd and 3rd days at 11.

Luncheon at 1.30. †Captain. *Wicket-keeper.

Stumps drawn at 6.30 each day.

TEA INTERVAL—There will probably be a Tea Interval at **4.30-4.45** but it will depend on the state of the game.

ENGLAND WON THE TOSS.

This was New Zealand's first Test Match against any opposition since they played England in March and April 1933. In that match, Walter Hammond had hit 336 not out, the record Test score, so at Lord's a mere 140 could be seen as a great success for the New Zealand bowlers. England's innings was built around a third wicket partnership of 245 bet-ween Hammond and Hardstaff. Hammond hit a six and fourteen fours (as opposed to ten sixes and 34 fours in his 336), and incidentally passed Jack Hobbs' Test record run aggregate of 5,410. This was Hammond's final season as a professional: during the winter he turned amateur and was immediately awarded the captaincy of England.

England's batting line-up for this Test was very strong and, with six front-line bowlers as well, the home side should have been too strong for New Zealand. But three days was not quite enough to force a victory, especially with a break for bad light at a crucial point in the third day. Another new New Zealand cap, Mervyn Wallace, hit two fifties in the game and, with Martin Donnelly who was out caught behind off the last ball of the match, managed to stave off defeat.

LORD'S GROUND

1938: England v Australia

(2nd Test) June 24, 25, 27, 28
Match drawn

After the amazing high scores of the First Test of the 1938 series (1,496 runs scored for the loss of 24 wickets), which ended in a draw, hopes were high for an enthralling Lord's occasion. The general public wanted to see two very strong Test teams playing at Lord's for the Ashes, and the press did their best to encourage them to come. In the event, a total of 100,933 people paid for entry to the ground over the four days, including 33,800 on the second day, the Saturday. This number was not only the largest crowd ever seen at Lord's, it was also too large for the ground to cope with, and the gates had to be closed well before the start of play (England were 409 for 5 overnight).

After consultation with the ground authorities, the players and the umpires (one of whom, Fanny Walden, had won two caps for England at football during his Spurs playing days), it was decided that the spectators would be allowed to encroach a little on the previous day's playing area, so the boundary ropes were moved in a few yards. It was slightly to Australia's advantage that they batted on a smaller playing area than England had done, but the alternative was the likelihood of a riot if some of those who had already paid were ejected.

Lord's painted by Charles Cundall from the roof of the works department, with the cooling towers behind the first Mound Stand.

ENGLAND

L Hutton	c Brown b McCormick	4	c McCormick b O'Reilly 5
CJ Barnett	c Brown b McCormick	18	c McCabe b McCormick 12
WJ Edrich	b McCormick	0	c McCabe b McCormick 10
† WR Hammond	b McCormick	240	c sub b McCabe 2
E Paynter	lbw b O'Reilly	99	run out 43
D Compton	lbw b O'Reilly	6	not out 76
* LEG Ames	c McCormick b Fleetwood-Smith	83	c McCabe b O'Reilly 6
H Verity	b O'Reilly	5	b McCormick 11
AW Wellard	c McCormick b O'Reilly	4	b McCabe 38
DVP Wright	b Fleetwood-Smith	6	not out 10
K Farnes	not out	5	
	(B 1, LB 12, W 1, NB 10)	24	(B 12, LB 12, W 1, NB 4) 29
Total		494	(8 wkts dec) 242

AUSTRALIA

JH Fingleton	c Hammond b Wright	31	c Hammond b Wellard 4
WA Brown	not out	206	b Verity 10
† DG Bradman	b Verity	18	not out 102
SJ McCabe	c Verity b Farnes	38	c Hutton b Verity 21
AL Hassett	lbw b Wellard	56	b Wright 42
CL Badcock	b Wellard	0	c Wright b Edrich 0
* BA Barnett	c Compton b Verity	8	c Paynter b Edrich 14
AG Chipperfield	lbw b Verity	1	
WJ O'Reilly	b Farnes	42	
EL McCormick	c Barnett b Farnes	0	
LO'B Fleetwood-Smith	c Barnett b Verity	7	
	(B 1, LB 8, NB 6)	15	(B 5, LB 3, W 2, NB 1) 11
Total		422	(6 wkts) 204

AUSTRALIA	O	M	R	W	O	M	R	W
McCormick	27	1	101	4	24	5	72	3
McCabe	31	4	86	0	12	1	58	2
Fleetwood-Smith	33.5	2	139	2	7	1	30	0
O'Reilly	37	6	93	4	29	10	53	2
Chipperfield	9	0	51	0				

ENGLAND	O	M	R	W	O	M	R	W
Farnes	43	6	135	3	13	3	51	0
Wellard	23	2	96	2	9	1	30	1
Wright	16	2	68	1	8	0	56	1
Verity	35.4	9	103	4	13	5	29	2
Edrich	4	2	5	0	5.2	0	27	2

FALL OF WICKETS

Wkt	Eng. 1st	Aus. 1st	Eng. 2nd	Aus. 2nd
1st	12	69	25	8
2nd	20	101	28	71
3rd	31	152	43	111
4th	253	276	64	175
5th	271	276	76	180
6th	457	307	128	204
7th	472	308	142	
8th	476	393	216	
9th	483	393		
10th	494	422		

† Captain   * Wicketkeeper

As at Trent Bridge, batsmen ruled the roost. Wally Hammond, now an amateur and therefore eligible to captain England, made the highest score by an England player against Australia at Lord's, and the highest by an England captain in Ashes Tests. Eddie Paynter was out for 99, only the second player to fall one short of a Test century at Lord's. Since 1938 four others have joined the list to make six in all – Mike Smith in 1960, Ross Edwards in 1975 and Mark Waugh and Michael Atherton, both in 1993. Of the six only two went on to score a Lord's Test century. One was the first '99 man', Charles Macartney, who waited fourteen years until 1926 for his hundred. The other was Mark Waugh who hit three figures in 2001.

Hammond's innings was matched if not bettered by Bill Brown, who became only the third Australian ever to bat right through a Test innings at the ground. What is more, his score of 206 is still the highest ever achieved by anyone carrying his bat at Lord's.

1939: England v West Indies

(1st Test) June 24, 26, 27
England won by 8 wickets

The England team had perhaps an even more trau-
matic journey to this First Test at Lord's than their
opponents, the West Indies. Many of the team had
been playing in South Africa during the winter, but
had had to cut short the final Test against their
hosts when just 43 runs short of victory, in order to
make the two-day train journey from Durban to
Cape Town to catch their ship back to England for
the new season. The West Indians had had a far
simpler journey, sailing across the Atlantic.

England did without Bill Edrich, who had
scored 219 in the Durban Test three months ear-

lier, but were still too good for the West Indies. In
1939, the tourists' team consisted of George
Headley, still considered by many to be the greatest of all West Indian batsmen, an ageing Learie
Constantine and nine others. England had the
makings of a brilliant side, with Hutton, Compton,
Hammond, Wright, Verity and Bowes all in their
prime. In this Test match, the only one at Lord's
ever played with eight ball overs, the limelight
belonged to Headley, Hutton and Compton.
George Headley scored almost half of the West
Indies' runs off the bat, with only Jeffrey

The West Indies team. *L–r, back*: W Ferguson (scorer), Gomez, J Stollmeyer, Hylton, Johnson, Clarke, Bayley, Williams. *Middle*:
Headley, Barrow, Grant (captain), JM Kidney (manager), Cameron, Constantine, Martindale. *Front*: Weekes, Sealey, V Stollmeyer.

Stollmeyer, of all his team mates, getting above 30 in either innings. Headley became only the second man, after Herbert Sutcliffe, to score two hundreds in a Test match for a second time (his first such achievement was against England at Georgetown in 1930), and the first man to achieve the feat at Lord's.

But it was not enough. Hutton batted superbly for 196 and Compton, after a bit of luck at the start of his innings, played the sort of innings that only he could – powerful, unorthodox and apparently carefree. England had a lead of 127, and nobody could cope with Copson on his Test debut and stay with Headley to make a game of it. The weather, which had started very cold indeed, had warmed up considerably by the final afternoon, but even with the sun on their backs, the West Indians could not build an innings. As DR Jardine noted in the *Daily Telegraph* at the time, 'it was a case of "Headley out, West Indies out"'.

Things would change, though. West Indies were to win six of their next eight Lord's Test matches, and it was not until the late 1990s that the tide turned back in England's favour.

WEST INDIES

† RS Grant	c Compton b Copson	22		b Bowes		23
JB Stollmeyer	b Bowes	59		c Verity b Copson		0
G Headley	c Wood b Copson	106		c Hutton b Wright		107
JED Sealey	c Wood b Wright	13		c Wood b Copson		29
KH Weekes	c Gimblett b Copson	20		c Wood b Verity		16
LN Constantine	lbw b Copson	14		c Hammond b Verity		17
JH Cameron	c Hutton b Bowes	12		c & b Wright		0
* I Barrow	lbw b Copson	2		not out		6
EA Martindale	lbw b Wright	22		c Bowes b Wright		3
LG Hylton	not out	2		c Hardstaff b Copson		13
CB Clarke	b Bowes	1		c & b Copson		0
	(B 3, LB 9, NB 3)	15		(B 6, LB 4, W 1)		11
Total		277				225

ENGLAND

L Hutton	c Grant b Hylton	196		b Hylton		16
H Gimblett	b Cameron	22		b Martindale		20
E Paynter	c Barrow b Cameron	34		not out		32
† WR Hammond	c Grant b Cameron	14		not out		30
DCS Compton	c Stollmeyer b Clarke	120				
J Hardstaff	not out	3				
* A Wood	not out	0				
	(B 8, LB 6, W 1)	15		(LB 2)		2
Total	(5 wkts dec)	404		(2 wkts)		100

Did not bat: DVP Wright, H Verity, WH Copson, WE Bowes.

ENGLAND	O	M	R	W	O	M	R	W
Bowes	28.4	5	86	3	19	7	44	1
Copson	24	2	85	5	16.4	2	67	4
Wright	13	1	57	2	17	0	75	3
Verity	16	3	34	0	14	4	20	2
Compton					3	0	8	0

WEST INDIES	O	M	R	W	O	M	R	W
Martindale	20	2	86	0	7.7	0	51	1
Hylton	24	4	98	1	7	1	36	1
Constantine	13	0	67	0	3	0	11	0
Cameron	26	6	66	3				
Clarke	6	0	28	1				
Sealey	3	0	21	0				
Grant	3	0	23	0				

FALL OF WICKETS

	WI	Eng.	WI	Eng.
Wkt	1st	1st	2nd	2nd
1st	29	49	0	35
2nd	147	119	42	39
3rd	180	147	105	
4th	226	395	154	
5th	245	402	190	
6th	250		199	
7th	250		200	
8th	261		204	
9th	276		225	
10th	277		225	

† Captain   * Wicketkeeper

1946: England v India

(1st Test) June 22, 24, 25
England won by 10 wickets

This was the first Test match England had played at Lord's – or anywhere else – for seven years, so it was not surprising that on each of the first two days, despite the overcast weather, the gates were closed by noon with about 30,000 in the ground. Astonishingly, six of the eleven who played against West Indies in the previous Lord's Test in June 1939 were still in the England team in 1946. Only Gimblett, Paynter, Wood, Verity (who died a prisoner of war in Italy in 1943) and Copson had been replaced, by Washbrook, Ikin, Gibb, Smailes and Bedser, and of those five, Washbrook and Gibb had played Tests before the war. India were introducing six men to Test cricket, including Gul Mahomed and Abdul Hafeez, both of whom would later also play for a country that did not exist in 1946: Pakistan. They also brought back the bad boy of 1936, Lala Amarnath, for his first Test appearance since February 1934. What's more, their captain, the Nawab of Pataudi, was making his debut for India having already played three times for England in the early 1930s.

The most significant of the debutants was Alec Bedser. The Surrey fast-medium bowler began his record breaking Test career with a record-breaking performance, taking eleven wickets for 145

The two teams. *L–r, back*: Gul Mahomed, Washbrook, Abdul Hafeez, Ikin, umpire Ferguson. *Standing*: Mankad, Compton, Nayudu, Smailes, Hazare, A V Bedser, Modi, Hardstaff, Shinde, Wright. *Sitting*: P Gupta (manager), Hutton, Amarnath, Colonel RS Rait Kerr (Secretary of M.C.C. 1936-52), the Nawab of Pataudi (India captain), Hammond (England captain), Merchant, Gibb, Hindlekar, Holmes (an England selector). *Front*: Brookes (England reserve), Sohni (India reserve).

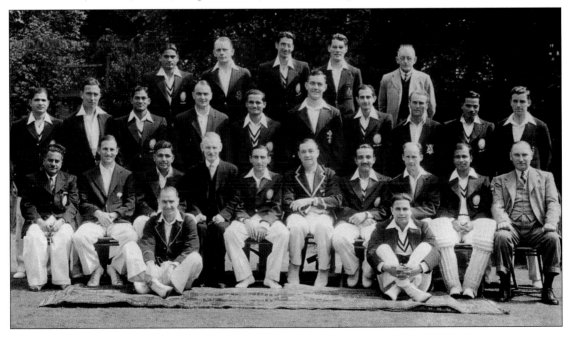

INDIA

Batsman	Dismissal	R		2nd innings	R
VM Merchant	c Gibb b Bedser	12		lbw b Ikin	27
V Mankad	b Wright	14		c Hammond b Smailes	63
L Amarnath	lbw b Bedser	0		b Smailes	50
VS Hazare	b Bedser	31		c Hammond b Bedser	34
RS Modi	not out	57		lbw b Smailes	21
† Nawab of Pataudi	c Ikin b Bedser	9		b Wright	22
Gul Mahomed	b Wright	1		lbw b Wright	9
Abdul Hafeez	b Bowes	43		b Bedser	0
* DD Hindlekar	lbw b Bedser	3		c Ikin b Bedser	17
CS Nayudu	st Gibb b Bedser	4		b Bedser	13
SG Shinde	b Bedser	10		not out	4
	(B 10, LB 6)	16		(B 10, LB 2, NB 3)	15
Total		200			275

ENGLAND

Batsman	Dismissal	R		2nd innings	R
L Hutton	c Nayudu b Amarnath	7		not out	22
C Washbrook	c Mankad b Amarnath	27		not out	24
DCS Compton	b Amarnath	0			
† WR Hammond	b Amarnath	33			
J Hardstaff	not out	205			
* PA Gibb	c Hazare b Mankad	60			
JT Ikin	c Hindlekar b Shinde	16			
IF Smailes	c Mankad b Amarnath	25			
AV Bedser	b Hazare	30			
DVP Wright	b Mankad	3			
WE Bowes	lbw b Hazare	2			
	(B 11, LB 8, NB 1)	20		(LB 1, W 1)	2
Total		428		(0 wkt)	48

ENGLAND	O	M	R	W	O	M	R	W
Bowes	25	7	64	1	4	1	9	0
Bedser	29.1	11	49	7	32.1	3	96	4
Smailes	5	1	18	0	15	2	44	3
Wright	17	4	53	2	20	3	68	2
Ikin					10	1	43	1

INDIA	O	M	R	W	O	M	R	W
Hazare	34.4	4	100	2	4	2	7	0
Amarnath	37	18	118	5	4	0	15	0
Gul Mahomed	2	0	2	0				
Mankad	48	11	107	2	4.5	1	11	0
Shinde	23	2	66	1				
Nayudu	5	1	15	0	4	0	13	0

FALL OF WICKETS

Wkt	Ind. 1st	Eng. 1st	Ind. 2nd
1st	15	16	67
2nd	15	16	117
3rd	44	61	126
4th	74	70	129
5th	86	252	174
6th	87	284	185
7th	144	344	190
8th	147	416	249
9th	157	421	263
10th	200	428	275

† Captain   * Wicketkeeper

runs in the match, an analysis described by *Wisden* as 'probably the finest performance ever recorded by a bowler in his first Test match', and it certainly was the best debut at Lord's until Bob Massie's match of 1972. It is interesting to read, over fifty years on, the scoreline 'CS Nayudu, st Gibb b Bedser, 4' when Bedser was bowling at full fast-medium pace. These days the wicketkeeper would be standing so far back to a bowler of Bedser's pace that a stumping would not be even a distant thought in the back of his mind.

The other key player was Joe Hardstaff, whose 205 not out was the highest of his four Test centuries. He came in at 16 for 2 after Denis Compton had been dismissed first ball, and carried his bat through the rest of the innings. Only the quick and fearless wicketkeeper Paul Gibb gave him much support, scoring 60 in a fifth-wicket stand of 182. For India, Vinoo Mankad top-scored in their second innings after having bowled 48 overs in England's first innings, a sign of the heavy load he was to bear for India over the next decade.

1947: England v South Africa

(2nd Test) June 21, 23, 24, 25
England won by 10 wickets

The glorious summer weather of 1947 threatened to misbehave as Lord's filled with up to 30,000 people coming to watch the hometown heroes, Bill Edrich and Denis Compton, take on the South Africans. However, the weather held, and England's captain Norman Yardley won the toss and duly batted. By lunch, the 30,000 patient souls had watched one and a half hours' cricket and seen Hutton and Washbrook, Yorkshire and Lancashire at their most obdurate, working their way carefully past the 50 mark. It was not exciting cricket, but it was necessary and it set the stage for what followed. In the second over after lunch, Hutton was out, and by the time the score had reach one hundred, not only had the second new ball been taken, but Washbrook had gone too. South Africa looked to be on top.

But 1947 was the summer of Compton and Edrich. In the first Test, Compton had scored 65 and 163, and this time he all but matched that aggregate in one innings. Edrich, who had made 57 and 50 at Trent Bridge, almost doubled that amount in his one knock at Lord's. John Arlott, describing this innings, pointed out that 'Edrich's initial care is familiar' and that 'Compton was again and again checking the attacking shot,' but despite this careful defensive attitude to their batting the Middlesex twins had put on 111 at more than a run a minute by tea, and by close of play had both reached their centuries. In less than three and a half hours' batting on the first day (there had been thirty minutes lost through rain) they put on 216 runs. They added a further 154 runs the next day until, a few minutes after lunch, Edrich was bowled. Their partnership of 370 was at the time the record third-wicket partnership in all Test cricket, and it remains after 125 Lord's Tests the highest partnership for any Test wicket at head-

quarters. After that it was almost certain that England would win the match, and they did.

To win, England had to bowl South Africa out twice, of course, and to help in that task they turned to two of the best bowlers in England that summer, Edrich and Compton. After scoring 189 and having not even a couple of hours' rest before going out to field, Edrich was thrown the new ball and told to make the breakthrough. He didn't, but then nor did Alec Bedser at the other end. It was

Denis Compton and Bill Edrich on the Nursery ground.

left to the two unorthodox spinners – Doug Wright with his quickish leg spin and Compton (DCS) with his left arm finger spin with the occasional chinaman in the mix – to break the back of the South African innings. Wright took five wickets in each innings, and England were left to score just 26 for victory. Edrich, who had bowled three South Africans in the second innings and caught three more, no doubt had his pads on in the pavilion, but was not needed.

Lord's ⓂⒸⒸ Ground

ENGLAND v. SOUTH AFRICA
SAT., MON., TUES. & WED., JUNE 21, 23, 24, 25, 1947. (4-day Match)

ENGLAND

	First Innings		Second Innings	
1 L. Hutton	b Rowan	18	not out	13
2 C. Washbrook	c Tuckett, b Dawson	65	not out	13
3 W. J. Edrich	b Mann	189		
4 D. Compton	c Rowan, b Tuckett	208		
5 C. J. Barnett	b Tuckett	33		
†6 N. W. D. Yardley	c Rowan, b Tuckett	5		
*7 T. G. Evans	b Tuckett	16		
8 G. H. Pope	not out	8		
9 A. V. Bedser	b Tuckett	0		
10 D. V. P. Wright				
11 W. E. Hollies				

Innings closed

B 2, l-b 10, w , n-b , 12 B , l-b , w , n-b ,
Total .... 554 Total 26

FALL OF THE WICKETS
1 75 2 96 3 466 4 515 5 526 6 541 7 554 8 554 9 .... 10 ....
1 .... 2 .... 3 .... 4 .... 5 .... 6 .... 7 .... 8 .... 9 .... 10 ....

ANALYSIS OF BOWLING

Name	1st Innings						2nd Innings					
	O.	M.	R.	W.	Wd.	N-b	O.	M.	R.	W.	Wd.	N-b
Tuckett	47	7	115	5	...	...						
Dawson	33	11	81	1	...	...	3	0	4	0	...	...
Mann	53	16	99	1	...	...	6	2	6	0	...	...
Rowan	65	11	174	1	...	...	3.1	1	16	0	...	...
Smith	17	2	73	0	...	...						

SOUTH AFRICA

	First Innings		Second Innings	
†1 A. Melville	c Bedser, b Hollies	117	b Edrich	8
2 B. Mitchell	st Evans, b Compton	46	c Edrich, b Wright	80
3 K. G. Viljoen	b Wright	1	b Edrich	6
4 D. Nourse	l b w, b Wright	61	b Edrich	58
5 O. C. Dawson	c Barnett, b Hollies	36	c Edrich, b Compton	33
6 T. A. Harris	st Evans, b Compton	30	c Yardley, b Compton	3
7 A. M. B. Rowan	b Wright	8	not out	38
8 L. Tuckett	b Wright	5	l b w, b Wright	9
*9 N. B. F. Mann	b Wright	4	b Wright	5
10 J Lindsay	not out	7	c Yardley, b Wright	5
11 V. I. Smith	c Edrich, b Pope	11	c Edrich, b Wright	0
	B , l-b , l w , n-b ,	1	B 3, l-b 4, w , n-b ,	7
	Total	327	Total	252

FALL OF THE WICKETS
1 95 2 104 3 222 4 230 5 290 6 300 7 302 8 308 9 309 10 327
1 16 2 28 3 120 4 192 5 192 6 201 7 224 8 236 9 252 10 252

ANALYSIS OF BOWLING

Name	1st Innings						2nd Innings					
	O.	M.	R.	W.	Wd.	N-b	O.	M.	R.	W.	Wd.	N-b
Edrich	9	1	22	0	...	...	13	5	31	3	...	...
Bedser	26	1	76	0	...	...	14	6	20	0	...	...
Pope	19.2	5	49	1	...	...	17	7	36	0	...	...
Wright	39	10	95	5	...	...	32.2	6	80	5	...	...
Hollies	28	10	52	2	...	...	20	7	32	0	...	...
Compton	21	11	32	2	...	...	31	10	46	2	...	...

Umpires—Baldwin & Davies   †Captain   * Wicket-keeper   Scorers—Mavins & Ferguson

1948: England v Australia

(2nd Test) June 24, 25, 26, 28, 29
Australia won by 409 runs

Rarely can two consecutive Lord's Tests have had such differing results. After crushing South Africa a year earlier, England were in turn crushed by the mighty Australians of 1948. Eight of England's 1947 team were still there in 1948, but the difference was in the opposition. England had brought in Alec Coxon for his first and, as it turned out, his last Test appearance, so when Bradman won the toss and chose to bat, England opened the bowling with two Alecs, for the first and only time in Test history. Coxon proved the smarter of the Alecs in the first session, capturing the wicket of Barnes for a duck, but thereafter, nothing really went England's way. Coxon, incidentally, is the one regularly forgotten in answering the quiz question, 'Which four players with an 'x' in their names have played cricket for England since the war?' – the others being Dexter, Prideaux and Moxon. Before the First World War, there was also NA Knox, who played twice for England in 1907.

By the start of the fourth day, Australia, 343 for 4 in their second innings, were already 478 ahead of England. Arthur Morris had survived an entire Test without losing his wicket to Alec Bedser, and Donald Bradman had passed 50 for the fourteenth successive Test against England (excluding the 1938 Oval Test, in which he broke his ankle bowling before he could bat in either innings). Sid Barnes made up for his first innings duck by making 141 in the second, but still

Don Bradman's 'Invincibles'. The 1948 Australian Tourists.

SG Barnes	c Hutton b Coxon	0	c Washbrook b Yardley	141
AR Morris	c Hutton b Coxon	105	b Wright	62
† DG Bradman	c Hutton b Bedser	38	c Edrich b Bedser	89
AL Hassett	b Yardley	47	b Yardley	0
KR Miller	lbw b Bedser	4	c Bedser b Laker	74
WA Brown	lbw b Yardley	24	c Evans b Coxon	32
IW Johnson	c Evans b Edrich	4	(8) not out	9
* D Tallon	c Yardley b Bedser	53		
RR Lindwall	b Bedser	15	(7) st Evans b Laker	25
WA Johnston	st Evans b Wright	29		
ERH Toshack	not out	20		
	(B 3, LB 7, NB 1)	11	(B 22, LB 5, NB 1)	28
Total		350	(7 wkts dec)	460

ENGLAND

L Hutton	b Johnson	20	c Johnson b Lindwall	13
C Washbrook	c Tallon b Lindwall	8	c Tallon b Toshack	37
WJ Edrich	b Lindwall	5	c Johnson b Toshack	2
DCS Compton	c Miller b Johnston	53	c Miller b Johnston	29
HE Dollery	b Lindwall	0	b Lindwall	37
† NWD Yardley	b Lindwall	44	b Toshack	11
A Coxon	c and b Johnson	19	lbw b Toshack	0
* TG Evans	c Miller b Johnston	9	not out	24
JC Laker	c Tallon b Johnson	28	b Lindwall	0
AV Bedser	b Lindwall	9	c Hassett b Johnston	9
DVP Wright	not out	13	c Lindwall b Toshack	4
	(LB 3, NB 4)	7	(B 16, LB 4)	20
Total		215		186

ENGLAND	O	M	R	W	O	M	R	W
Bedser	43	14	100	4	34	6	112	1
Coxon	35	10	90	2	28	3	82	1
Edrich	8	0	43	1	2	0	11	0
Wright	21.3	8	54	1	19	4	69	1
Laker	7	3	17	0	31.2	6	111	2
Yardley	15	4	35	2	13	4	36	2
Compton					3	0	11	0

AUSTRALIA	O	M	R	W	O	M	R	W
Lindwall	27.4	7	70	5	23	9	61	3
Johnston	22	4	43	2	33	16	62	2
Johnson	35	13	72	3	2	1	3	0
Toshack	18	11	23	0	20.1	6	40	5

FALL OF WICKETS

Wkt	Aus. 1st	Eng. 1st	Aus. 2nd	Eng. 2nd
1st	3	17	122	42
2nd	87	32	296	52
3rd	166	46	296	65
4th	173	46	329	106
5th	216	133	416	133
6th	225	134	445	133
7th	246	145	460	141
8th	275	186		141
9th	320	197		158
10th	350	215		186

† Captain   * Wicketkeeper

Bradman batted on. Rain was in the air and showers interrupted play more than once. Lindsay Hassett made a duck, but Keith Miller hit a jaunty 74, and finally in mid-afternoon Bradman declared. England needed a mere 596 to win.

Against South Africa in the glorious sunshine of a year earlier, an adventurous punter might have put a tenner on England, but against Australia in the cold and gloom there were no takers. Overnight after four days Denis Compton was not out, batting carefully with Dollery, but to the second ball of the fifth morning he snicked a leg cutter from Bill Johnston low to Keith Miller at second slip, who dived wide to his right and took the catch at the second attempt. And that was that. 106 for 4 became 186 all out, with five wickets to Ernie Toshack, one of the lesser known heroes of Bradman's all-conquering 1948 team and the only person who could confidently hold down a place lower in the batting order than Bill Johnston.

1949: England v New Zealand

(2nd Test) June 25, 27, 28
Match drawn

EW Swanton, writing in the *Daily Telegraph*, decided that 'the second Test at Lord's expired painlessly this evening.' The match, like all the Tests that summer, was only scheduled to last three days and the batting of both sides was too good, or the bowling was too poor, for a result to be possible. All four Tests of 1949 were drawn, and as a result it was decided never again to play Tests over just three days in England.

Hutton and Robertson opening for England, Hutton in an M.C.C. touring cap, Robertson in his Middlesex cap.

England's innings was distinguished only by the partnership of 189 for the sixth wicket between Denis Compton and Trevor Bailey. in only his second Test, Bailey fell just short of what would have been his maiden Test century. His dismissal was very unlucky: he cut the ball onto wicketkeeper Mooney's foot and from there it bounced up into the hands of Bert Sutcliffe at second slip.

Once Compton was out the England innings fell rapidly apart so George Mann, the captain, decided to give his bowlers fifteen minutes at the New Zealand openers at the end of the first day. This was the first time ever that a Test innings had been declared closed on the first day, for the not surprising reason that until that season it had been illegal to declare on the first day of a three-day game. What neither Mann nor the umpires seemed to know, however, was that the experimental law that season allowing such declarations did not apply to the Test matches, so Mann's daring new tactic was illegal. No New Zealand wickets fell that evening, so no advantage was gained.

The hero of the New Zealand innings was Martin Donnelly. An Oxford graduate who was already an established star in England (and an England rugby international in 1946/47), he hit 206 without giving a glimmer of a chance in just short of six hours. One ludicrous statistic was that when Hollies bowled Smith he became the first England bowler to hit the stumps that summer, after 733 runs had been scored for the loss of 17 wickets. No England bowler that summer hit the stumps in more than one Test. Hollies in the Second Test; Bailey (five times) and Jackson in the Third Test; and Compton in the Fourth Test were the only bowlers to hit the New Zealanders' stumps all year. No wonder the matches were all drawn.

ENGLAND

JD Robertson	c Mooney b Cowie	26	c Cave b Rabone ... 121
L Hutton	b Burtt	23	c Cave b Rabone ... 66
WJ Edrich	c Donnelly b Cowie	9	c Hadlee b Burtt ... 31
DCS Compton	c Sutcliffe b Burtt	116	b Burtt ... 6
A Watkins	c Wallace b Burtt	6	not out ... 49
† FG Mann	b Cave	18	c Donnelly b Rabone ... 17
TE Bailey	c Sutcliffe b Rabone	93	not out ... 6
* TG Evans	b Burtt	5	
C Gladwin	run out	5	
JA Young	not out	1	
	(B 9, LB 2)	11	(B 9, LB 1) ... 10
Total	(9 wkts dec)	313	(5 wkts) ... 306

Did not bat: WE Hollies.

NEW ZEALAND

B Sutcliffe	c Compton b Gladwin	57
VJ Scott	c Edrich b Compton	42
† WA Hadlee	c Robertson b Hollies	43
WM Wallace	c Evans b Hollies	2
MP Donnelly	c Hutton b Young	206
FB Smith	b Hollies	23
GO Rabone	b Hollies	25
* FLH Mooney	c Watkins b Young	33
TB Burtt	c Edrich b Hollies	23
HB Cave	c & b Young	6
J Cowie	not out	1
	(B 16, LB 3, W 3, NB 1)	23
Total		484

NEW ZEALAND	O	M	R	W	O	M	R	W
Cowie	26.1	5	64	2	14	3	39	0
Cave	27	2	79	1	7	1	23	0
Rabone	14	5	56	1	28	6	116	3
Burtt	35	7	102	4	37	12	58	2
Sutcliffe	1	0	1	0	16	1	55	0
Wallace					1	0	5	0

ENGLAND	O	M	R	W
Bailey	33	3	136	0
Gladwin	28	5	67	1
Edrich	4	0	16	0
Hollies	58	18	133	5
Compton	7	0	33	1
Young	26.4	4	65	3
Watkins	3	1	11	0

FALL OF WICKETS

Wkt	Eng. 1st	NZ 1st	Eng. 2nd
1st	48	89	143
2nd	59	124	216
3rd	72	137	226
4th	83	160	226
5th	112	197	252
6th	301	273	
7th	307	351	
8th	307	436	
9th	313	464	
10th		484	

† Captain   * Wicketkeeper

1950: England v West Indies

(2nd Test) June 24, 26, 27, 28, 29
West Indies won by 326 runs

One of the most famous of all the Lord's Tests was not a close contest at all: it was a one-sided slaughter made all the more surprising because England had just come from an easy victory, by 202 runs, in the First Test at Old Trafford. That victory was won on a wicket that 'turned most of the time', according to Hubert Doggart, who made his debut at Manchester and continued in the side at Lord's.

England were without Compton, Simpson and Bailey, but even with them, the result would probably have been no different. The selectors decided to pick three spinners – Jenkins, Wardle and Berry – covering all the options of leg break and googly, left arm orthodox or unorthodox and off break, but it was the West Indian spinners who proved unplayable.

Sonny Ramadhin and Alf Valentine were both twenty years old when they came to England, and had played barely a handful of first-class games between them before they landed at Southampton. At Old Trafford, Valentine had taken the first eight English wickets to fall and ended up with 11 for 204 in 106 overs, probably more bowling in one

'Those two little pals of mine, Ramadhin and Valentine.' West Indies supporters invaded the ground and sang calypsos to celebrate their country's first ever Test victory over England.

WEST INDIES

Batsman	Dismissal	Runs		2nd Innings	Runs
AF Rae	c and b Jenkins	106		b Jenkins	24
JB Stollmeyer	lbw b Wardle	20		b Jenkins	30
FM Worrell	b Bedser	52		c Doggart b Jenkins	45
E Weekes	b Bedser	63		run out	63
*CL Walcott	st Evans b Jenkins	14		not out	168
GE Gomez	st Evans b Jenkins	1		c Edrich b Bedser	70
RJ Christiani	b Bedser	33		not out	5
†JD Goddard	b Wardle	14		c Evans b Jenkins	11
PE Jones	c Evans b Jenkins	0			
S Ramadhin	not out	1			
AL Valentine	c Hutton b Jenkins	5			
	(B10, LB 4, W 1, NB 1)	17		(LB 8, NB 1)	9
Total		326		(6 wkts)	425

ENGLAND

Batsman	Dismissal	Runs		2nd Innings	Runs
L Hutton	st Walcott b Valentine	35		b Valentine	10
C Washbrook	st Walcott b Ramadhin	36		b Ramadhin	114
WJ Edrich	c Walcott b Ramadhin	8		c Jones b Ramadhin	8
GHG Doggart	lbw b Ramadhin	0		b Ramadhin	25
WGA Parkhouse	b Valentine	0		c Goddard b Valentine	48
†NWD Yardley	b Valentine	16		c Weekes b Valentine	19
*TG Evans	b Ramadhin	8		c Rae b Ramadhin	2
RO Jenkins	c Walcott b Valentine	4		b Ramadhin	4
JH Wardle	not out	33		lbw b Worrell	21
AV Bedser	b Ramadhin	5		b Ramadhin	0
R Berry	c Goddard b Jones	2		not out	0
	(B 2, LB 1, W1)	4		(B 16, LB 7)	23
Total		151			274

ENGLAND	O	M	R	W	O	M	R	W
Bedser	40	14	60	3	44	16	80	1
Edrich	16	4	30	0	13	2	37	0
Jenkins	35.2	6	116	5	59	13	174	4
Wardle	17	6	46	2	30	10	58	0
Berry	19	7	45	0	32	15	67	0
Yardley	4	1	12	0				

WEST INDIES	O	M	R	W	O	M	R	W
Jones	8.4	2	13	1	7	1	22	0
Worrell	10	4	20	0	22.3	9	39	1
Valentine	45	28	48	4	71	47	79	3
Ramadhin	43	27	66	5	72	43	86	6
Gomez					13	1	25	0
Goddard					6	6	0	0

FALL OF WICKETS

	WI 1st	Eng. 1st	WI 2nd	Eng. 2nd
1st	37	62	48	28
2nd	128	74	75	57
3rd	233	74	108	140
4th	262	75	146	218
5th	273	86	199	228
6th	274	102	410	238
7th	320	110		245
8th	320	113		258
9th	320	122		258
10th	326	151		274

† Captain * Wicketkeeper

match than he had done in all his career in the West Indies. At Lord's the mastery continued, although it was Ramadhin who took centre stage.

After Allan Rae, Frank Worrell and Everton Weekes had set West Indies up well, 'those two little pals of mine' bowled 88 of the 106.4 overs it took England to crawl to 151 all out. 'Ramadhin, with his short arms and shirtsleeves buttoned down, and no sightscreen in the pavilion, was very difficult to pick,' says Doggart. True, but no excuse, of course. In the fourth innings, having set England 601 to win with two days to play

(Walcott 168 not out – dropped when on nine at first slip off Edrich, bowling very quickly), the West Indians relied on Ramadhin and Valentine to do it again. This time they bowled 143 of the 191.3 overs and took 9 for 165. Washbrook made a brave century, but only Gilbert Parkhouse, on debut, stayed with him for long, and West Indies won by 326 runs fairly early on the final day.

Almost 112,000 people, many of them West Indians recently arrived to live in England, watched the match, and a lot of them stayed behind afterwards to sing and dance in victory.

1951: England v South Africa

(2nd Test) June 21, 22, 23
England won by 10 wickets

The last Test match that South Africa had won against any opposition anywhere before they came to England in 1951 was the Second Test against England at Lord's in 1935. They relieved themselves of that unwanted record at Trent Bridge, beating England by 71 runs, and came to Lord's full of confidence. They retained the same eleven, while England brought in Statham for Bailey. This meant that the England side contained three Yorkshiremen and three Lancastrians. The difference between the two teams this time, on yet another rain-affected pitch, was Roy Tattersall, the Lancashire off-spinner.

England's total, completed by the end of the first day, was adequate if not brilliant, and they owed this adequacy to 79 apiece from Compton and Watson and 51 from Ikin. The South African opening attack of the fast but erratic 22-year-old Cuan McCarthy and the steady medium pace of the 40-year-old Geoff Chubb was certainly a contrast in styles, but they kept England in check in their different ways. Chubb had made his Test

Tattersall, a willowy cajoler.

debut at Trent Bridge, the oldest South African on Test debut until overtaken by Omar Henry after the end of their apartheid isolation in 1992/93 and still one of only thirteen men to have played his first Test after the age of 40.

On the second day, South Africa fell apart. Roy Tattersall, at this time England's number one off-spinner ahead of Jim Laker, took nine of the fourteen wickets to fall that day for just 88 runs. The other bowlers took 5 for 160 between them. *Wisden* remarked on 'the failure of Wardle on a surface more or less made for him', but it did not really matter. Going into the third day, South Africa were 137 for four, needing 196 to make England bat again. Thanks to Jack Cheetham, batting with a stiff neck, and George Fullerton, they narrowly succeeded.

Against tradition, but in view of the King's poor health, there was no royal presence on the Saturday. Instead, the teams were presented to Princess Elizabeth and her husband, the Duke of Edinburgh, during the tea interval on the Friday. This brief interruption did not slow the regular fall of South African wickets.

ENGLAND

L Hutton	lbw b McCarthy	12	not out	12
JT Ikin	b Mann	51	not out	4
RT Simpson	lbw b McCarthy	26		
DCS Compton	lbw b McCarthy	79		
W Watson	c McCarthy b Chubb	79		
† FR Brown	b Chubb	1		
* TG Evans	c Fullerton b McCarthy	0		
JH Wardle	lbw b Chubb	18		
AV Bedser	not out	26		
JB Statham	b Chubb	1		
R Tattersall	b Chubb	1		
	(B 8, LB 9)	17		
Total		311	(0 wkt)	16

SOUTH AFRICA

EAB Rowan	c Ikin b Tattersall	24	c Ikin b Statham	10
JHB Waite	c Hutton b Wardle	15	c Compton b Tattersall	17
DJ McGlew	c Evans b Tattersall	3	b Tattersall	2
AD Nourse	c Watson b Tattersall	20	lbw b Wardle	3
JE Cheetham	c Hutton b Tattersall	12	b Statham	54
GM Fullerton	b Tattersall	12	lbw b Bedser	60
CB van Ryneveld	lbw b Wardle	0	c Ikin b Tattersall	18
AMB Rowan	c Ikin b Tattersall	3	c Brown b Bedser	10
NBF Mann	c Brown b Tattersall	14	c Brown b Tattersall	13
GWA Chubb	c Tattersall b Wardle	5	b Tattersall	3
CN McCarthy	not out	1	not out	2
	(LB 3)	3	(B 11, B 8)	19
Total		115		211

SOUTH AFRICA	O	M	R	W	O	M	R	W
McCarthy	23	2	76	4				
Chubb	34.4	9	77	5				
A Rowan	13	1	63	0				
Mann	32	12	51	1				
van Ryneveld	5	0	27	0				
Nourse					2	0	9	0
E Rowan					1.5	0	7	0

ENGLAND	O	M	R	W	O	M	R	W
Bedser	8	5	7	0	24	8	53	2
Statham	6	3	7	0	18	6	33	2
Tattersall	28	10	52	7	32.2	14	49	5
Wardle	22.5	10	46	3	20	5	44	1
Compton					2	0	13	0

FALL OF WICKETS

Wkt	Eng. 1st	SA 1st	SA 2nd
1st	20	25	21
2nd	89	38	29
3rd	103	47	32
4th	225	72	58
5th	226	88	152
6th	231	91	160
7th	265	91	178
8th	299	103	196
9th	301	112	200
10th	311	115	211

† Captain   * Wicketkeeper

1952: England v India

(2nd Test) June 19, 20, 21, 23, 24
England won by 8 wickets

Len Hutton, who made 150 and 39 not out.

England, captained by a professional for the first time at Lord's, swept India aside by a margin slightly bigger (eight rather than seven wickets) than they had done in the First Test at Headingley. The problem with this Indian team was their weakness against fast bowling. Fred Trueman had made his debut in the previous game, and at one point in their second innings had four wickets down without a run on the board. Things were slightly better for them at Lord's, but Trueman was still there, and still too much for most of their

batsmen. He hit the stumps six times, including the number three batsman's wicket twice. As Godfrey Evans remembered, 'Polly Umrigar had his leg stump knocked over by Fred as he was trying to cover drive him, but he was so far away from the wicket that he couldn't reach the ball.'

The match was a particular triumph for two people: Vinoo Mankad and Godfrey Evans. Mankad scored 72 in India's first innings, took 5 for 196 in 73 overs and then hit a brilliant 184 in a losing cause. He scored more runs in the match

LORD'S **GROUND**

ENGLAND v. INDIA

THURSDAY, FRIDAY, SATURDAY, MONDAY & TUESDAY,
JUNE 19, 20, 21, 23, 24, 1952   (5-day Match)

INDIA	First Innings		Second Innings	
1 P. Roy	c and b Bedser	35	b Bedser	0
2 V. Mankad	c Watkins b Trueman	72	b Laker	184
3 P. R. Umrigar	b Trueman	5	b Trueman	14
†4 V. S. Hazare	not out	69	c Laker b Bedser	49
5 V. L. Manjrekar	l b w b Bedser	5	b Laker	1
6 D. G. Phadkar	b Watkins	8	b Laker	16
7 H. R. Adhikari	l b w b Watkins	0	b Trueman	16
8 G. S. Ramchand	b Trueman	18	b Trueman	42
*9 M. K. Mantri	st Evans b Watkins	5	c Compton b Laker	5
10 S. G. Shinde	b Jenkins	0	c Hutton b Trueman	14
11 Ghulam Ahmed		0	not out	1
	B 7, 1 b , w , n b 10,	17	B 29, 1-b 3, w , n-b 4	36
	Total	235	Total	378

FALL OF THE WICKETS

1 — 106   2 — 116   3 — 118   4 — 126   5 — 135   6 — 139   7 — 167   8 — 180   9 — 221   10 — 235

1 — 7   2 — 59   3 — 270   4 — 272   5 — 289   6 — 312   7 — 314   8 — 323   9 — 377   10 — 378

ANALYSIS OF BOWLING

Name	1st Innings						2nd Innings					
	O.	M.	R.	W.	Wd.	N-b.	O.	M.	R.	W.	Wd.	N-b
Bedser	33	8	62	2	...	4	36	13	60	2	...	3
Trueman	25	3	72	4	...	6	27	4	110	4	...	1
Jenkins	7.3	1	26	1	...	...	10	1	40	0	...	...
Laker	12	5	21	0	...	...	39	15	102	4	...	...
Watkins	17	7	37	3	...	...	8	0	20	0	...	...
Compton	...	...	...	...	...	...	2	0	10	0	...	...

ENGLAND	First Innings		Second Innings	
†1 Hutton, L.	c Mantri b Hazare	150	not out	39
2 R. T. Simpson	b Mankad	53	run out	2
3 P. B. H. May	c Mantri b Mankad	74	c Roy b G. Ahmed	26
4 Compton, D. C. S.	l b w b Hazare	6	not out	4
5 Graveney, T. W.	c Mantri b G. Ahmed	73		
6 Watkins, A. J.	b Mankad	0		
*7 Evans, T. G.	c and b Ghulam Ahmed	104		
8 Jenkins, R. O.	st Mantri b Mankad	21		
9 Laker, J. C.	not out	23		
10 Bedser, A. V.	c Ramchand b Mankad	3		
11 Trueman, F. S.	b Ghulam Ahmed	17		
	B 8, 1-b 5, w , n-b ,	13	B 4, 1 b 4, w , n-b	8
	Total	537	Total	79

FALL OF THE WICKETS

1 — 106   2 — 264   3 — 272   4 — 292   5 — 292   6 — 451   7 — 468   8 — 506   9 — 514   10 — 537

1 — 8   2 — 71   3 —   4 —   5 —   6 —   7 —   8 —   9 —   10 —

ANALYSIS OF BOWLING

Name	1st Innings						2nd Innings					
	O.	M.	R.	W.	Wd.	N-b	O.	M.	R.	W.	Wd.	N-b
Phadkar	27	8	44	0	...	...	1	0	5	0	...	...
Ramchand	29	8	67	0	...	...	1	1	0	0	...	...
Hazare	24	4	53	2	...	...	24	12	35	0	...	...
Mankad	73	24	196	5	...	...	23.2	9	31	1	...	...
Ghulam Ahmed	43.4	12	106	3	...	...	...	...	...	...	...	...
Shinde	6	0	43	0	...	...	...	...	...	...	...	...
Umrigar	4	0	15	0	...	...	...	...	...	...	...	...

Scorers—W. Mavins & W. Ferguson

Umpires—F. Chester & F. S. Lee

† Captain   * Wicket-keeper

Play begins at 11.30 each day   Stumps drawn at 6.30 each day

Spectators are requested not to enter or leave their seats during the progress of an over

This card does not necessarily include the fall of the last wicket

INDIA WON THE TOSS

than any other five of his team-mates added together; in England's first innings he bowled more overs than any two of his team-mates added together, and took half the wickets. It was truly a monumental all-round performance. Godfrey Evans claimed his one hundredth Test victim when he stumped Sadu Shinde in the first innings, and he then went on to hit 104, completing his hundred after lunch on the second day. He always claimed that he could have reached his century before lunch, and thus become the third man to achieve this feat in a Test at Lord's (after Warren Bardsley and Jack Hobbs), if Indian captain Vijay Hazare had not taken so long to move his fielders about between overs and umpire Frank Chester had not so delighted in dramatic gestures. At the time, Evans was 98 not out, thanks to Tom Graveney at the other end giving Evans as much of the strike as possible to give him his hundred before lunch. 'I don't know for certain whether Hazare was deliberate in his slowness,' wrote Evans in his autobiography eight years later. 'The clock moved on. And then Frank Chester swung up his metal arm, pointed it at no one in particular . . . and stated dramatically, "And that concludes the morning's play."'

Evans completed his hundred in the over after lunch, and then was out. After the traumas of his hundred, it was perhaps not unexpected that he should let through 29 byes in India's second innings, the most byes ever conceded in a Test innings at Lord's.

1953: England v Australia

(2nd Test) June 25, 26, 27, 29, 30
Match drawn

Rarely can the simple words 'match drawn' have masked such an exciting game as the 1953 Test, although ten years later the same phrase was to seem equally inadequate. After rain had probably cost England victory in the First Test at Trent Bridge two weeks earlier, England were hoping for great things at Lord's. After all, they were trying in Coronation Year to win back the Ashes which had been held by the Australians for nineteen years.

Lindsay Hassett won the toss for Australia, and by tea they had made 180 for 1. Hassett went on to score the first of four hundreds in the match, but after he went only Alan Davidson made many runs and Alec Bedser finished with yet another five-wicket haul. Len Hutton scored 41 more than his opposite number, and was well supported in century partnerships with Tom Graveney and

Denis Compton – what England would give for a batting line-up like that at almost any time in our Test history – but the rest of the batsmen failed. All the same, a first innings lead of 26 was scraped together.

Keith Miller, one of cricket history's great all-rounders, had bowled 25 overs in England's innings, but when Hassett was first out with only three on the board Miller came in and by the close of play on the third day had made 58 out of the total 96 for 1. The next day he completed his century and his bowling partner Ray Lindwall attacked Freddie Brown's leg spin for a quick fifty. England were eventually left with 343 to win in a day and a bit.

The bit of a day was a bit of a disaster. By close of play, England were 20 for 3, with Hutton,

Watson and Bailey during their legendary partnership.
L–r: Langley, Watson, Lindwall, Miller, Bailey, umpire Baldwin, Benaud and Hole.

AUSTRALIA

† AL Hassett	c Bailey b Bedser	104		c Evans b Statham	3
AR Morris	st Evans b Bedser	30		c Statham b Compton	89
RN Harvey	lbw b Bedser	30		(4) b Bedser	21
KR Miller	b Wardle	25		(3) b Wardle	109
GB Hole	c Compton b Wardle	13		lbw b Brown	47
R Benaud	lbw b Wardle	0		c Graveney b Bedser	5
AK Davidson	c Statham b Bedser	76		c & b Brown	15
DT Ring	lbw b Wardle	18		lbw b Brown	7
RR Lindwall	b Statham	9		b Bedser	50
* GRA Langley	c Watson b Bedser	1		b Brown	9
WA Johnston	not out	3		not out	0
	(B 4, LB 4)	8		(B 8, LB 5)	13
Total		**346**			**368**

ENGLAND

† L Hutton	c Hole b Johnston	145		c Hole b Lindwall	5
D Kenyon	c Davidson b Lindwall	3		c Hassett b Lindwall	2
TW Graveney	b Lindwall	78		c Langley b Johnston	2
DCS Compton	c Hole b Benaud	57		lbw b Johnston	33
W Watson	st Langley b Johnston	4		c Hole b Ring	109
TE Bailey	c & b Miller	2		c Benaud b Ring	71
FR Brown	c Langley b Lindwall	22		c Hole b Benaud	28
* TG Evans	b Lindwall	0		not out	11
JH Wardle	b Davidson	23		not out	0
AV Bedser	b Lindwall	1			
JB Statham	not out	17			
	(B 11, LB 1, W 1, NB 7)	20		(B 7, LB 6, W 2, NB 6)	21
Total		**372**		**(7 wkts)**	**282**

ENGLAND	O	M	R	W	O	M	R	W
Bedser	42.4	8	105	5	31.5	8	77	3
Statham	28	7	48	1	15	3	40	1
Brown	25	7	53	0	27	4	82	4
Bailey	16	2	55	0	10	4	24	0
Wardle	29	8	77	4	46	18	111	1
Compton					3	0	21	1

AUSTRALIA	O	M	R	W	O	M	R	W
Lindwall	23	4	66	5	19	3	26	2
Miller	25	6	57	1	17	8	17	0
Johnston	35	11	91	2	29	10	70	2
Ring	14	2	43	0	29	5	84	2
Benaud	19	4	70	1	17	6	51	1
Davidson	10.5	2	25	1	14	5	13	0
Hole					1	1	0	0

FALL OF WICKETS

	Aus.	Eng.	Aus.	Eng.
Wkt	1st	1st	2nd	2nd
1st	65	9	3	6
2nd	190	177	168	10
3rd	225	279	227	12
4th	229	291	235	73
5th	240	301	248	236
6th	280	328	296	246
7th	291	328	305	282
8th	330	332	308	
9th	331	341	362	
10th	346	372	368	

† Captain   * Wicketkeeper

Kenyon and Graveney all back in the pavilion. With all hope of a victory apparently gone, England had to try to survive to the end of the fifth day, with no prospect of rain to let them off the hook. Denis Compton and Willie Watson began well, putting on 61 for the fourth wicket, but then Bill Johnston (the number eleven who averaged 102 with the bat that summer) trapped Compton lbw, and Trevor Bailey came in to join Watson. What followed was one of the epic rearguard actions in Test history – a stand of 163 in 345 minutes, with Watson scoring 109 in his first Test against Australia, and Bailey enhancing his reputation for defensive doggedness with 71. Both men were out before the end of the match, but by then the game was saved: England ended 60 runs short with three wickets in hand. Miller had conceded just 17 runs in 17 overs, and Davidson only 13 in 14 overs: it was hard going out there, but Watson and Bailey wrote their names indelibly into Lord's Test history.

1954: England v Pakistan

(1st Test) June 10, 11, 12, 14, 15 (no play on first three days)
Match drawn

In direct contrast to the thrilling drawn Test a year earlier, the 1954 match was a rain-soaked disappointment. It was Pakistan's first official Test match in England, so it had a significance for the visitors that the circumstances could not reflect. The only reflections were in the puddles on the outfield.

England did at least pay their new opponents the compliment of fielding a full-strength team, with only Alec Bedser unfit. This was, in fact, the first time ever that England fielded a side all of whom had already played a Test at Lord's. However, we were not to discover how strong the full-strength team might be until the fourth day, as rain washed out any chance of play on any of the first three days. By the time the match began, at 3.45 pm on the Monday, it was obvious that no result would be possible. Pakistan were led by Abdul Hafeez Kardar, the Oxford Blue who had played for India in the 1946 Test at Lord's, who

The first Pakistan team to play official Test Matches in England.
L–r, back: Wazir Mohammad, Khalid Hassan, Shuja-ud-din, Shakoor Ahmed, Zulfiqar Ahmed. *Standing*: Khan Mohammad, Mohammad Aslam, Ikram Elahi, Mahmood Hussain, Waqar Hassan, Alim-ud-din, Hanif Mohammad.
Sitting: MEZ Ghazali, Fazal Mahmood, AH Kardar (captain), Imtiaz Ahmed, Maqsood Ahmed.

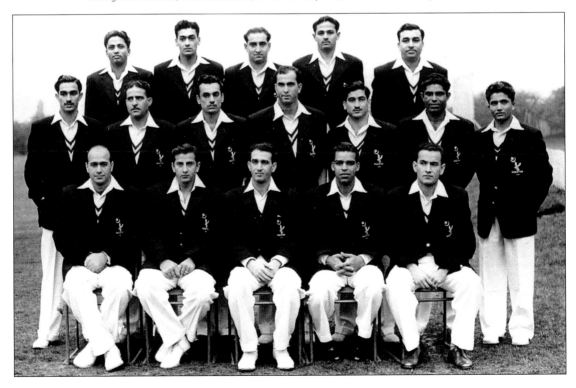

lost the toss and was asked by Len Hutton to bat. The achingly slow pace at which they did so made absolutely sure that there would be no result, even though they made very few runs. Their total of 87 occupied 83.5 overs: Brian Statham's 4 for 18 in thirteen overs looked positively profligate in the circumstances. Hanif Mohammad top-scored, as he would many times in the future for Pakistan, but they were never at home in conditions that were alien to them and favoured the English attack absolutely.

England tried to force the pace when they batted, but the pitch which had helped the English bowlers helped Fazal Mahmood and Khan Mohammad just as much. Hutton was out to Khan Mohammad's first ball in a Test in England, and only Simpson, May and Evans made much headway. Fazal and Khan became the first pair of bowlers to bowl unchanged through a Test innings of more than 25 overs at Lord's since Foster and Barnes routed the South Africans in 1912. Khan, like Foster 40 years before, clean bowled all five of his victims. England's 117 for 9 took 31 overs, almost four times as quick a scoring rate as Pakistan's, but neither side could create a platform for victory. Hanif, who batted 340 minutes for 59 runs in the match, and Waqar Hassan made sure that the only result possible was a draw.

PAKISTAN

Hanif Mohammad	b Tattersall	20	lbw b Laker	39
Alim-ud-din	c Edrich b Wardle	19	b Bailey	0
Waqar Hassan	c Compton b Wardle	9	c Statham b Compton	53
Maqsood Ahmed	st Evans b Wardle	0	not out	29
*Imtiaz Ahmed	b Laker	12		
†AH Kardar	b Statham	2		
Fazal Mahmood	b Wardle	5		
Khalid Wazir	b Statham	3		
Khan Mohammad	b Statham	0		
Zulfiqar Ahmed	b Statham	11		
Shuja-ud-din	not out	0		
	(b 4, lb 1, nb 1)	6		
Total		87	(3 wkts)	121

ENGLAND

†L Hutton	b Khan Mohammad	0
RT Simpson	lbw b Fazal Mahmood	40
PBH May	b Khan Mohammad	27
DCS Compton	b Fazal Mahmood	0
WJ Edrich	b Khan Mohammad	4
JH Wardle	c Maqsood Ahmed b Fazal Mahmood	3
*TG Evans	b Khan Mohammad	25
TE Bailey	b Khan Mohammad	3
JC Laker	not out	13
JB Statham	b Fazal Mahmood	0
	(b 2)	2
Total	(9 wkts dec)	117

Did not bat: R Tattersall.

PAKISTAN	O	M	R	W				
Fazal Mahmood	16	2	54	4				
Khan Mohammad	15	3	61	5				

ENGLAND	O	M	R	W	O	M	R	W
Statham	13	6	18	4	5	2	17	0
Bailey	3	2	1	0	6	2	13	1
Wardle	30.5	22	33	4	8	6	6	0
Tattersall	15	8	12	1	10	1	27	0
Laker	22	12	17	1	10.2	5	22	1
Compton					13	2	36	1

FALL OF WICKETS:

	Pak.	Eng.	Pak.
Wkt	1st	1st	2nd
1st	24	9	0
2nd	42	55	71
3rd	43	59	121
4th	57	72	
5th	67	75	
6th	67	79	
7th	71	85	
8th	71	110	
9th	87	117	
10th	87		

† Captain   * Wicketkeeper

1955: England v South Africa

(2nd Test) June 23, 24, 25, 27
England won by 71 runs

England, fresh from the famous 'Typhoon Tyson' Ashes triumph in Australia the previous winter, were expected to brush South Africa aside, but a sequence of injuries and a touring side that included a number of younger players destined for great things meant that in the end, England took the rubber 3-2 by winning at the Oval. At Lord's, however, everything looked good for a successful summer.

England had won the first Test thanks to Frank Tyson's 6 for 28 in the South African second innings, but he was injured before the Lord's match and his place was taken by Fred Trueman. Tyson never played a Test at Lord's, and injuries meant that England had a different opening bowling partnership every Test that summer – Statham and Tyson, Statham and Trueman, Bedser and Tyson, Statham and Loader, and finally Statham and Bailey.

England were all out for a very disappointing 133, with Peter Heine, the six foot four fast bowler, taking 5 for 60 on his debut. This was to

The England team. *L–r, back*: Barrington, Trueman, Statham, Graveney, Morgan (twelfth man), Kenyon, Titmus *Front*: Wardle, Bailey, May (captain), Compton, Evans.

prove to be the only Test in Lord's history in which none of the four opening partnerships reached double figures, as Brian Statham took a wicket with the first ball of South Africa's innings. Even though Trueman also struck very early, Roy McLean hit 142 (and was dropped half a dozen times on the way), while Russell Endean and Headley Keith made useful scores to give South Africa a lead of 173 on first innings – safe enough, you might think. England's new captain and two old reliables had other ideas. Peter May hit a hundred on his first appearance as England captain at Lord's, and Tom Graveney, a makeshift opener in the absence of Len Hutton, and Denis Compton hit

good half centuries. Compton clocked up 5,000 Test runs during his innings, joining a list that then only contained Bradman, Hammond, Hobbs and Hutton. 'Toey' Tayfield became South Africa's leading wicket taker in Tests in taking 5 for 80, but England were able to make 353, and leave South Africa 183 to win.

Brian Statham then took over. He bowled unchanged throughout the innings (which admittedly did include a two-hour break for bad light), to take 7 for 39 as England won by 71 runs. 'I couldn't have gone off for a rest and come back again,' said Statham afterwards. 'I just had to keep it up or I was finished.'

ENGLAND

Batsman	Dismissal	Runs	Dismissal	Runs
D Kenyon	b Adcock	1	lbw b Goddard	2
TW Graveney	c Waite b Heine	14	c Heine b Goddard	60
† PBH May	c Tayfield b Heine	0	hit wkt b Heine	112
DCS Compton	c Keith b Heine	20	c Mansell b Goddard	69
K Barrington	b Heine	34	c McLean b Tayfield	18
TE Bailey	lbw b Goddard	13	c Adcock b Tayfield	22
* TG Evans	c Waite b Heine	20	c & b Tayfield	14
FJ Titmus	lbw b Goddard	4	c Waite b Adcock	16
JH Wardle	c Tayfield b Goddard	20	c Heine b Tayfield	4
JB Statham	c McLean b Goddard	0	b Tayfield	11
FS Trueman	not out	2	not out	6
	(B 2, LB 2)	4	(B 15, L B 2, N B 2)	19
Total		133		353

SOUTH AFRICA

Batsman	Dismissal	Runs	Dismissal	Runs
DJ McGlew	c Evans b Statham	0	lbw b Statham	0
TL Goddard	c Evans b Trueman	0	c Evans b Statham	10
† JE Cheetham	lbw b Bailey	13	retired hurt	3
WR Endean	lbw b Wardle	48	c Evans b Statham	28
RA McLean	b Statham	142	b Statham	8
* JHB Waite	c Evans b Trueman	8	lbw b Statham	9
HJ Keith	c Titmus b Wardle	57	c Graveney b Statham	5
PNF Mansell	c Graveney b Wardle	2	c Kenvon b Wardle	16
HJ Tayfield	b Titmus	21	c Evans b Statham	3
P Heine	st Evans b Wardle	2	c Kenyon b Wardle	14
NAT Adcock	not out	0	not out	0
	(B 6, LB 1, NB 4)	11	(B 9, LB 5, NB 1)	15
Total		304		111

ENGLAND	O	M	R	W	O	M	R	W
Statham	27	9	49	2	29	12	39	7
Trueman	16	2	73	2	19	2	39	0
Bailey	16	2	56	1				
Wardle	29	10	65	4	9.4	4	18	2
Titmus	14	3	50	1				

SOUTH AFRICA	O	M	R	W	O	M	R	W
Heine	25	7	60	5	29	5	87	1
Adcock	8	3	10	1	25	5	64	1
Goddard	21.2	8	59	4	55	23	96	3
Tayfield					38.5	12	80	5
Mansell					2	0	7	0

FALL OF WICKETS

Wkt	Eng. 1st	SA 1st	Eng. 2nd	SA 2nd
1st	7	0	9	0
2nd	8	7	141	17
3rd	30	51	237	40
4th	45	101	277	54
5th	82	138	285	63
6th	98	247	302	75
7th	111	259	306	78
8th	111	302	336	111
9th	111	304	336	111
10th	133	304	353	111

† Captain   * Wicketkeeper

1956: England v Australia

(2nd Test) June 21, 22, 23, 25, 26
Australia won by 185 runs

In a summer which everybody remembers for Jim Laker's 19 for 90 in the Fourth Test at Manchester, the Lord's Test still stands out. It was the only one of the series that Australia won, but after a drawn First Test, it meant that Australia went one up with three to play. The Ashes, which England held, were in jeopardy.

Australia owed their victory largely to one man. Thirty-six year old Keith Miller, still one of the best and most glamorous all-rounders Australia has ever produced, was always a man for the big occasion. The little occasion often bored him, as was famously proved when he gave up his wicket for a duck while his team-mates were compiling 721 runs in a day against Essex in 1948. That day he was more interested in the horse racing, and his gambling streak was always a feature of his play. The England team's most avid gambler at the time, Godfrey Evans, thought it would be easy money to take Miller's bet, even at 2-1, that Australia would win. 'In the end,' noted Evans, 'he had some £40 or £50 laid out on the result of the game.'

Australia, who had avoided defeat at Nottingham only through meteorological intervention, were missing Ray Lindwall and Alan Davidson (both injured), so Miller had to open the bowling with a Test debutant, Pat Crawford. Crawford then broke down in his fifth over and did not bowl again in the match. But Miller then put in what

A famous catch – Benaud's to dismiss Cowdrey.

 **LORD'S GROUND**

3D. 3D.

ENGLAND v. AUSTRALIA

Thur., Fri., Sat., Mon. & Tues., 21, 22, 23, 25 & 26 June, 1956 (5-day Match)

AUSTRALIA

			First Innings		Second Innings	
1	C. C. McDonald	Victoria	c Trueman b Bailey	78	c Cowdrey b Bailey	26
2	J. Burke	New South Wales	st Evans b Laker	65	c Graveney b Trueman	16
3	R. N. Harvey	Victoria	c Evans b Bailey	0	c Bailey b Trueman	10
4	P. Burge	Queensland	b Statham	21	b Trueman	14
5	K. R. Miller	New South Wales	b Trueman	28	c Evans b Trueman	30
6	K. Mackay	Queensland	c Bailey b Laker	38	c Evans b Statham	31
7	R. G. Archer	Queensland	b Wardle	5	c Evans b Bailey	1
8	R. Benaud	New South Wales	b Statham	6	c Evans b Trueman	97
†9	I. W. Johnson	Victoria	c Evans b Trueman	14	l b w b Bailey	17
*10	G. R. Langley	S. Australia	c Bailey b Laker	0	not out	7
11	P. Crawford	New South Wales	not out	2	l b w b Bailey	0
			B , l b 2, w n-b		B 2, l-b 2, w , n b 4,	8
			Total	285	Total	257

FALL OF THE WICKETS

1—137   2—137   3— 151   4—185   5—196   6—249   7—255   8—265   9—285   10—285

1—36   2—47   3—69   4—70   5—79   6—112   7—229   8—243   9—257   10—257

ANALYSIS OF BOWLING

Name	1st Innings						2nd Innings					
	O.	M.	R.	W.	Wd.	N-b	O.	M.	R.	W.	Wd.	N-b
Statham	35	9	70	2	...	...	26	5	59	1	...	2
Trueman	27	6	54	2	...	...	28	2	90	5	...	2
Bailey	34	11	72	2	...	...	24.5	8	64	4	...	...
Laker	29.1	10	47	3	...	...	7	3	17	0	...	...
Wardle	20	7	40	1	...	...	7	2	19	0	...	...
	...	...	...	...	...	...	...	...	...	...	...	...

ENGLAND

			First Innings		Second Innings	
1	M. C. Cowdrey	Kent	c Benaud b Mackay	23	l b w b Benaud	27
2	P. E. Richardson	Worcester	c Langley b Miller	9	c Langley b Archer	21
3	Graveney, T. W.	Gloucester	b Miller	5	c Langley b Miller	18
†4	P. B. H. May	Surrey	b Benaud	63	c Langley b Miller	53
5	Watson, W.	Yorkshire	b Benaud b Miller	6	b Miller	18
6	T. E. Bailey	Essex	b Miller	32	c Harvey b Archer	18
*7	Evans, T. G.	Kent	st Langley b Benaud	12	c Langley b Miller	20
8	Laker, J. C.	Surrey	b Archer	0	c Langley b Archer	4
9	Wardle, J. H.	Yorkshire	c Langley b Archer	0	b Miller	0
10	Trueman, F. S.	Yorkshire	c Langley b Miller	7	b Archer	2
11	Statham, J. B.	Lancashire	not out	0	not out	0
			B , l-b 14, w , n-b	14	B , l-b 5, w , n b	5
			Total	171	Total	186

FALL OF THE WICKETS

1—22   2—32   3—60   4—87   5—128   6—128   7—161   8—161   9—170   10—171

1—35   2—59   3—87   4—91   5—142   6—175   7—180   8—184   9—184   10—186

ANALYSIS OF BOWLING

Name	1st Innings						2nd Innings					
	O.	M.	R.	W.	Wd.	N-b	O.	M.	R.	W.	Wd.	N-b
Miller	34.1	9	72	5	...	...	36	12	80	5	...	...
Crawford	5	2	4	0	...	...	31.2	8	71	4	...	...
Archer	23	9	47	2	...	...					...	...
Mackay	11	3	15	1	...	...	28	14	27	1	...	...
Benaud	9	2	19	2	...	...	4	2	3	0	...	...
Johnson	...	...	...	...	...	...	...	...	...	...	...	...

Scorers—A. Fowler & N. Gorman

Umpires—E. Davies & F. S. Lee   * Wicket-keeper

† Captain   Stumps drawn at 6.30 each day

Play begins at 11.30 each day

Spectators are requested not to enter or leave their seats during the progress of an over

AUSTRALIA WON THE TOSS

---

umpire Frank Lee described as 'probably the greatest piece of sustained fast bowling I have ever seen'. Ten for 152 in 70.1 overs at an age when most fast bowlers have long since hung up their boots was an astonishing match and bet-winning performance.

The role of Richie Benaud in the match should not be forgotten, though. Not only did he take one of the truly amazing Test catches to dismiss Cowdrey off a full blooded square drive to give 'Slasher' Mackay his first Test wicket, but he also hit 97 in Australia's second innings. Godfrey Evans reckoned he should have gone first ball, caught behind off Trueman, but the umpire turned down the appeal. Such is Test luck. When Tom Graveney was out, caught behind in the second innings (one of Gil Langley's record nine victims in the match), he knew he had failed. 'To fail at Lord's,' he later wrote, 'seems to be a personal matter, and the sight of those silent, illustrious members looking the other way as you pass through their ranks leaves no doubt as to their feelings.' Ian Botham would learn all about members looking the other way 25 years later.

1957: England v West Indies

(2nd Test) June 20, 21, 22
England won by an innings and 36 runs

Lord's drew the short straw in 1957. After the epic First Test at Edgbaston, in which May and Cowdrey put on 411 for the fourth wicket and blunted the threat of Sonny Ramadhin for the summer, and before Graveney's huge double century in the Third Test, before Loader's hat-trick in the Fourth and Tony Lock's eleven for 48 in the Fifth, the Lord's crowd endured a bland, one-sided contest which England won by an innings and 36 runs.

The West Indies tourists of 1957 were just past their peak and just short of greatness. It was the first England tour for both Garfield Sobers and Wes Hall (who did not play in any Tests), not to mention Rohan Kanhai and Collie Smith, but it was also the beginning of the end for the three Ws: Worrell, Weekes and Walcott. England on the other hand had a very strong side, with only the position of Peter Richardson's opening partner in any doubt. For this Test, the place went to the Sussex left-hander Don Smith.

Jim Laker and Tony Lock, England's best spin partnership since the Second World War, were both injured, so Johnny Wardle was left in charge of spin duties, but in the event was hardly needed.

The crowd on the pitch at the end of the third day's play.

WEST INDIES

Batsman	1st innings		2nd innings	
N Asgarali	lbw b Trueman	0	(4) c Trueman b Wardle	26
*Rohan Kanhai	c Cowdrey b Bailey	34	(1) c Bailey b Statham	0
CL Walcott	lbw b Bailey	14	c Trueman b Bailey	21
G Sobers	c May b Statham	17	(5) c May b Bailey	66
ED Weekes	c Evans b Bailey	13	(6) c Evans b Bailey	90
†FM Worrell	c Close b Bailey	12	c Evans b Trueman	10
OG Smith	c Graveney b Bailey	25	(2) lbw b Statham	5
JD Goddard	c Cowdrey b Bailey	1	c Evans b Trueman	21
S Ramadhin	b Trueman	0	c Statham b Bailey	0
R Gilchrist	c & b Bailey	0	not out	11
AL Valentine	not out	0	b Statham	1
	(B 2, LB 1, W 4)	7	(B 4, LB 6)	10
Total		127		261

ENGLAND

PE Richardson	b Gilchrist	76
DV Smith	lbw b Worrell	8
TW Graveney	lbw b Gilchrist	0
†PBH May	c Kanhai b Gilchrist	0
MC Cowdrey	c Walcott b Sobers	152
TE Bailey	b Worrell	1
DB Close	c Kanhai b Goddard	32
*TG Evans	b Sobers	82
JH Wardle	c Sobers b Ramadhin	11
FS Trueman	not out	36
JB Statham	b Gilchrist	7
	(B 7, LB 11, W 1)	19
Total		424

ENGLAND	O	M	R	W	O	M	R	W
Statham	18	3	46	1	29.1	9	71	3
Trueman	12.3	2	30	2	23	5	73	2
Bailey	21	8	44	7	22	6	54	4
Wardle					22	5	53	1

WEST INDIES	O	M	R	W
Worrell	42	7	114	2
Gilchrist	36.3	7	115	4
Ramadhin	22	5	83	1
Valentine	3	0	20	0
Goddard	13	1	45	1
Sobers	7	0	28	2

FALL OF WICKETS

	WI	Eng.	WI
Wkt	1st	1st	2nd
1st	7	25	0
2nd	34	34	17
3rd	55	34	32
4th	79	129	80
5th	85	134	180
6th	118	192	203
7th	120	366	233
8th	123	379	241
9th	127	387	256
10th	127	424	261

† Captain * Wicketkeeper

The West Indies misjudged the nature of the wicket when they brought in Alf Valentine, who in the end only bowled three expensive overs. England, especially Trevor Bailey, got it right. With 7 for 44, the best Test analysis against West Indies in England at the time, he ripped through the opposition, and only the makeshift opener and wicketkeeper Rohan Kanhai made over 30. England's innings produced 297 more runs than the West Indies', largely due to Cowdrey's second successive Test innings of over 150, an aggressive 76 from Richardson, an equally pugnacious 82 from Evans and a belligerent cameo of 36 not out from Fred Trueman, including three sixes in one over from Ramadhin. Oh, and at least a dozen dropped catches.

The West Indian second innings was a catalogue of disasters from the outset. Asgarali, in his first Test, could not open because he had pulled muscles in both legs, so he batted at number four with a runner. Weekes made a superb 90, but cracked a bone in one finger on his right hand. Sobers stayed four hours for his 66, but when his wicket fell, it was all over bar the celebrations, which they began ten minutes after tea on the third day, and lasted for the rest of the summer.

1958: England v New Zealand

(2nd Test) June 19, 20, 21
England won by an innings and 148 runs

The last Test to be played at Lord's before the Press Box was positioned in the back of the Warner Stand (where it would stay for forty years) was a very one-sided affair indeed. It was an odd irony that the New Zealanders, who had been granted four-day Tests after all four matches on their previous tour in 1949 had ended in stalemate, should have come with such a weak side in 1958 that three of the matches were over well within three days. The Lord's Test was one of them. Apart from John Reid and Bert Sutcliffe, both survivors from the 1949 tour, New Zealand were remarkably short of players even of county standard, let alone Test class.

Even so, New Zealand performed very poorly indeed and made the lowest Test score ever recorded at Lord's, surpassed in awfulness only once, by the 1974 Indian team, who batted one man short. In their second innings, the visitors scarcely did any better – 74 all out – and the total number of runs scored in the match, 390, was the second lowest total ever in a completed Test at Lord's. New Zealand's aggregate of 121 runs in two innings was also the second lowest. In 1888 England made 115 in two innings against Australia.

As has so often been the case, the weather played its part. England definitely had the best of

In catching Hayes, to finish off the match, Lock collides with Richardson.

LORD'S GROUND

ENGLAND v. NEW ZEALAND

Thur., Fri., Sat., Mon. & Tues., 19, 20, 21, 23, 24 June 1958. (5-day Match)

ENGLAND		First Innings		Second Innings
1 M. J. K. Smith	Warwickshire	c Petrie b Hayes	47	
2 P. E. Richardson	Worcestershire	c Petrie b Hayes	36	
3 Graveney, T. W.	Gloucestershire	c Petrie b Alabaster	37	
†4 P. B. H. May	Surrey	c Alabaster b MacGibbon	19	
5 M. C. Cowdrey	Kent	b Hayes	65	
6 T. E. Bailey	Essex	c Petrie b Reid	17	
*7 Evans, T. G.	Kent	c Hayes b MacGibbon	11	
8 Lock, G. A. R.	Surrey	not out	23	
9 Trueman, F. S.	Yorkshire	b Hayes	8	
10 Laker, J. C.	Surrey	c Blair b MacGibbon	1	
11 Loader, P. J.	Surrey	c Playle b MacGibbon	4	
		B , lb 1, w , n-b	1	B , l-b , w , n-b ,
		Total	269	Total

FALL OF THE WICKETS

1—54 2—113 3—139 4—141 5—201 6—222 7—237 8—259 9—260 10—269

1— 2— 3— 4— 5— 6— 7— 8— 9— 10—

ANALYSIS OF BOWLING	1st Innings						2nd Innings					
Name	O.	M.	R.	W.	Wd.	N-b	O.	M.	R.	W.	Wd.	N-b
Hayes	22	5	36	4	...	...	...	...	...	...	...	...
MacGibbon	36.4	11	86	4	...	...	...	...	...	...	...	...
Blair	25	6	57	0	...	...	...	...	...	...	...	...
Reid	24	12	41	1	...	...	...	...	...	...	...	...
Alabaster	16	6	48	1	...	...	...	...	...	...	...	...

NEW ZEALAND		First Innings		Second Innings	
1 J. W. D'Arcy	Canterbury	c Trueman b Laker	14	c Bailey b Trueman	33
2 L. S. M. Miller	Wellington	l b w b Trueman	4	c Trueman b Loader	0
3 W. R. Playle	Auckland	c Graveney b Laker	1	b Loader	3
4 N. S. Harford	Central Districts	c and b Laker	0	c May b Lock	3
†5 J. R. Reid	Otago	c Loader b Lock	6	c Cowdrey b Trueman	5
6 B. Sutcliffe	Otago	b Lock	18	b Bailey	0
7 A. R. MacGibbon	Canterbury	c May b Lock	2	c May b Lock	7
8 J. C. Alabaster	Otago	c and b Lock	0	b Laker	5
*9 E. C. Petrie	Northern Districts	c Trueman b Laker	0	not out	4
10 R. W. Blair	Wellington	not out	0	b Lock	0
11 J. A. Hayes	Auckland	c Cowdrey b Lock	1	c and b Lock	14
		B , l-b 1, w , n-b	1	B , l-b , w , n b ,	74
		Total	47	Total	74

FALL OF THE WICKETS

1—4 2—12 3—12 4—19 5—25 6—31 7—34 8—46 9—46 10—47

1—11 2—21 3—34 4—41 5—44 6—44 7—56 8—56 9—56 10—74

ANALYSIS OF BOWLING	1st Innings						2nd Innings					
Name	O.	M.	R.	W.	Wd.	N-b	O.	M.	R.	W.	Wd.	N-b
Trueman	4	1	6	1	...	...	11	6	24	2	...	...
Loader	4	2	6	0	...	...	9	6	7	2	...	...
Laker	12	6	13	4	...	...	13	8	24	1	...	...
Lock	11.3	7	17	5	...	...	12.3	8	12	4	...	...
Bailey	1	0	4	0	...	...	5	1	7	1	...	...

Umpires—D. Davies & C. S. Elliott

Scorers—A. Fowler & G. Duckworth

† Captain   * Wicket-keeper

Play begins at 11.30 each day   Stumps drawn at 6.30 each day

Spectators are requested not to enter or leave their seats during the progress of an over

England won the toss

the conditions when they batted, and Cowdrey made the most of the true pitch, hitting 65 in 140 minutes. 'It was sheer joy,' reported Norman Preston in *Wisden*, 'to see Cowdrey pierce the field with dazzling cover drives and powerful on-side strokes.' England reached 237 for 7 at the end of the day, but overnight, it rained so heavily that play was not possible until 3.20 pm. In half an hour of slogging England added another 32 runs to their total, and then set about New Zealand on a spiteful wicket. Trueman and Loader bowled eight token overs (during which Trueman trapped Miller lbw), and then Laker and Lock took over. Tony Lock, on his Lord's Test debut in his twenty-third appearance for England over six years, finished with nine wickets for 29 runs and was pretty well unplayable throughout. Laker, five for 37, backed him up brilliantly while the close catching of Trueman, May, and Cowdrey turned the screw on the hapless Kiwis. Only Bert Sutcliffe in the first innings, and John D'Arcy (who never hit a first-class century) in both innings showed any sort of defiance, although Johnny Hayes, another veteran from 1949, hit Laker for two big sixes at the very end to make the final New Zealand partnership their biggest of the match.

1959: England v India

(2nd Test) June 18, 19, 20
England won by 8 wickets

The England team. *L–r, back*: Taylor, Barrington, Milton, Moss, Horton, Greenhough, Mortimore (twelfth man).
Front: Statham, Cowdrey, May (captain), Evans, Trueman.

'In June 1959, the Indians came to Lord's and were defeated by eight wickets in a pleasant but unmemorable game.' So wrote Benny Green in his *Lord's Companion*, going on to comment that 'no centuries were scored: no bowler took more than seven wickets. The weather was fine and the crowds fairly large.' An apt description of the majority of Test matches all over the world, because without the ordinary games, there would be no extraordinary ones.

In fact, it was a little less ordinary than Green would have us believe. It was the only Test of the series in which no centuries were scored, and it was part of a series in which no bowler on either side took more than seven wickets in any match. It was the ninety-first and final Test played by Godfrey Evans, whose last Test victim (Gupte st Evans b Greenhough 7) was his 219th, then easily a Test record. It was also the Test in which Brian Statham took his 150th wicket (Roy, acting as captain in place of the bronchitic Gaekwad, c Evans b Statham 15); in which the Indians' injury list, already topped by Borde, injured at Trent Bridge, was added to by Statham breaking one of Nari Contractor's ribs during his innings of 81; and in which the unorthodox batting of Statham and Moss put on 62 for the ninth English wicket.

It was also notable for the cat. Peter, the Lord's cat, became so famous that he even earned an obituary in *Wisden* when his 'ninth life ended on November 5, 1964,' as the obituarist noted. 'He preferred a close-up view of the proceedings and his sleek, black form could often be seen prowling on the field of play when the crowds were biggest. He frequently appeared on the television screen.' He also appeared, nameless, in a leading article in *The Times* of 20 June 1959. 'A fair minded man might well assert' (and here 'The Thunderer' was merely asserting, not thundering) 'that the most composed of all those who have taken the field at

Lord's during the past few days was the resident cat – the cat which, in the middle stages of India's first innings and in fine full view of the spectators and the television camera, fielded for a short period at square leg, changed comfortably to mid-off at the end of an over, and then stalked majestically off the field.' The whimsical leader writer indulged his fantasies and literary allusions on the nature of walking with confidence for a couple more paragraphs before having to admit that 'the Lord's cat directed his stately walk from the wicket not to the pavilion, but to the bar.'

INDIA

† P Roy	c Evans c Statham	15	c May b Trueman	0
NJ Contractor	b Greenhough	81	not out	11
PR Umrigar	b Statham	1	c Horton b Trueman	0
VL Manjrekar	lbw b Trueman	12	lbw b Statham	61
JM Ghorpade	lbw b Greenhough	41	c Evans b Statham	22
AG Kripal Singh	b Greenhough	0	b Statham	41
ML Jaisimha	lbw b Greenhough	1	lbw b Moss	8
* PG Joshi	b Horton	4	b Moss	6
R Surendranath	b Greenhough	0	run out	0
SP Gupte	c May b Horton	0	st Evans b Greenhough	7
RB Desai	not out	2	b Greenhough	5
	(LB 11)	11	(LB 4)	4
Total		168		165

ENGLAND

CA Milton	c Surendranath b Desai	14	c Joshi b Desai	3
K Taylor	c Gupte b Desai	6	lbw b Surendranath	3
MC Cowdrey	c Joshi b Desai	34	not out	63
† PBH May	b Surendranath	9	not out	33
KF Barrington	c sub b Desai	80		
MJ Horton	b Desai	2		
* TG Evans	b Surendranath	0		
FS Trueman	lbw b Gupte	7		
JB Statham	c Surendranath b Gupte	38		
AE Moss	b Surendranath	26		
T Greenhough	not out	0		
	(B 5, LB 4, W 1)	10	(B 5, LB 1)	6
Total		226	(2 wkts)	108

ENGLAND	O	M	R	W	O	M	R	W
Trueman	16	4	40	1	21	3	55	2
Statham	16	6	27	2	17	7	45	3
Moss	14	5	31	0	23	10	30	2
Greenhough	16	4	35	5	18	8	31	2
Horton	15.4	7	24	2				

INDIA	O	M	R	W	O	M	R	W
Desai	31.4	8	89	5	7	1	29	1
Surendranath	30	17	46	3	11	2	32	1
Umrigar	1	1	0	0	1	0	8	0
Gupte	19	2	62	2	6	2	21	0
Kripal Singh	3	0	19	0	1	1	0	0
Jaisimha					1	0	8	0
Roy					0.2	0	4	0

FALL OF WICKETS

	Ind.	Eng.	Ind.	Eng.
Wkt	1st	1st	2nd	2nd
1st	32	9	0	8
2nd	40	26	0	12
3rd	61	35	22	
4th	144	69	42	
5th	152	79	131	
6th	158	80	140	
7th	163	100	147	
8th	163	184	147	
9th	164	226	159	
10th	168	226	165	

† Captain   * Wicketkeeper

1960: England v South Africa

(2nd Test) June 23, 24, 25, 27
England won by an innings and 73 runs

This was a bizarre and one-sided match, one that has gone down in Test history for both the right and the wrong reasons. The central figure in all this was a young Rhodesian who had celebrated his twenty-first birthday on the rest day of his debut Test match two weeks earlier at Birmingham, their very quick opening bowler Geoff Griffin. The problem was that the main

reason why Griffin was very quick was that he threw, rather than bowled, the ball.

Before the Lord's Test, Griffin had been called for throwing seventeen times by six umpires in three games against the counties (and twice in South Africa before coming to England on tour), but had bowled 42 overs in the First Test without any incident. Griffin certainly looked like a chucker, with his elbow clearly bent at delivery, but his defenders pointed out that he had a permanent bend in his arm after an accident during his school-days. And nobody ever described him as anything other than a charming and pleasant young man, entirely without malice on the cricket field.

On the first day, Griffin became the first man to be no-balled for throwing in a Test at Lord's, and by the last session of the day had been called six times, each time by umpire Frank Lee at square leg. All the same, his captain Jackie McGlew brought him back for one more session at the end of the day, and he responded by having Mike Smith caught behind for 99 off the final ball of the over. With the first ball of his next over, he clean bowled Peter Walker and with his next ball he also bowled the man with one of the most classically correct bowling actions of all time, Fred Trueman. So Griffin achieved something that nobody else has ever achieved – a Test hat-trick at Lord's.

Maybe the throwing controversy demoralized the South Africans, for they lost within three days. With a Saturday crowd of 25,000, both sides agreed to an exhibition game. This time Griffin was no-balled for throwing four times out of five balls by umpire Syd Buller at square leg, so the unfortunate young man switched to underarm. Umpire Lee immediately no-balled him again for not telling the batsman he was changing his action. Griffin never played Test cricket again.

Peter Walker becomes the second victim of Geoff Griffin's hat-trick, bowled for 52.

England won by an innings and 73 runs

 LORD'S GROUND

ENGLAND v. SOUTH AFRICA

Thurs., Fri., Sat., Mon. & Tues., June 23, 24, 25, 27 & 28, 1960 (5-day Match)

ENGLAND

			First Innings		Second Innings
†1	M. C. Cowdrey	Kent	c McLean b Griffin	4	
2	R. Subba Row	Northamptonshire	l b w b Adcock	90	
3	E. R. Dexter	Sussex	c McLean b Adcock	56	
4	Barrington, K. F.	Surrey	l b w b Goddard	24	
5	M. J. K. Smith	Warwickshire	c Waite b Griffin	99	
*6	Parks, J. M.	Sussex	c F. Smith b Adcock	3	
7	Walker, P. M.	Glamorgan	b Griffin	52	
8	Illingworth, R.	Yorkshire	not out	0	
9	Trueman, F. S.	Yorkshire	b Griffin	0	
10	Statham, J. B.	Lancashire	not out	2	
11	Moss, A. E.	Middlesex			

Innings closed

B 6, l-b 14, w 1, n-b 11, 32   B , l b , w , n b ,

Total 362   Total ....

FALL OF THE WICKETS
1—7 2—103 3—165 4—220 5—227 6—347 7—360 8—360 9— 10—

1— 2— 3— 4— 5— 6— 7— 8— 9— 10—

ANALYSIS OF BOWLING

Name	1st Innings						2nd Innings					
	O.	M.	R.	W.	Wd.	N-b	O.	M.	R.	W.	Wd.	N-b
Adcock	36	11	70	3								
Griffin	30	7	87	4	1	11						
Goddard	31	6	96	1								
Tayfield	27	9	64	1								
Fellows-Smith	5	0	13	0								

SOUTH AFRICA

			First Innings		Second Innings	
†1	D. J. McGlew	Natal	l b w b Statham	15	b Statham	17
2	T. L. Goddard	Natal	b Statham	19	c Parks b Statham	24
3	S. O'Linn	Transvaal	c Walker b Moss	18	l b w b Trueman	8
4	R. A. McLean	Natal	c Cowdrey b Statham	15	c Parks b Trueman	13
*5	J. H. B. Waite	Transvaal	c Parks b Statham	3	l b w b Statham	0
6	P. R. Carlstein	Transvaal	c Cowdrey b Moss	12	c Parks b Moss	6
7	C. Wesley	Natal	c Parks b Statham	11	b Dexter	35
8	J. P. Fellows-Smith	Transvaal	c Parks b Moss	29	not out	27
9	H. J. Tayfield	Transvaal	c Smith b Moss	12	b Dexter	4
10	G. Griffin	Natal	b Statham	5	b Statham	0
11	N. A. T. Adcock	Transvaal	not out	8	b Statham	2

B 4, l-b , w , n-b 1, 5   B , l b , w , n b 1, 1

Total 152   Total 137

FALL OF THE WICKETS
1—33 2—48 3—56 4—69 5—78 6—88 7—112 8—132 9—138 10—152

1—26 2—49 3—49 4—50 5—63 6—72 7—126 8—132 9—133 10—137

ANALYSIS OF BOWLING

Name	1st Innings						2nd Innings					
	O.	M.	R.	W.	Wd.	N-b	O.	M.	R.	W.	Wd.	N-b
Statham	20	5	63	6		1	21	6	34	5		
Trueman	13	2	49	0			17	5	44	2		
Moss	10.3	0	35	4			14	1	41	1		1
Illingworth							1	1	0	0		
Dexter							4	0	17	2		

Umpires—J. S. Buller & F. S. Lee   Scorers—A. Fowler & M. McLennan

† Captain   * Wicket-keeper

Play begins 1st, 2nd & 3rd days at 11.30, 4th & 5th days at 11

Stumps drawn 1st, 2nd, 3rd & 4th days at 6.30, 5th day at 5 or 5.30

Spectators are requested not to enter or leave their seats during the progress of an over

England won the toss

1961: England v Australia

(2nd Test) June 22, 23, 24, 26
Australia won by 5 wickets

England won the toss for the twelfth consecutive time, a record stretching back to the Fifth Test of 1959, and Colin Cowdrey, captain of England even though Peter May was back after injury, was celebrating his ninth consecutive winning of the toss, a Test record for any captain. It was also eighteen Tests since England had last lost a match (the Fifth Test of the 1958/59 series against Australia). May, Cowdrey, Dexter and Trueman were the only four survivors from that previous loss, although Lock and Statham had also known what it was like to lose in England colours. What is more, Richie Benaud, England's nemesis on so many occasions, was unable to play, so Neil Harvey took

Bill Lawry, a regular thorn in England's side.

over the captaincy. The omens may have been good for England, but the realities were not.

England batted indifferently against Alan Davidson, one of the very best of the many left arm quick bowlers who have played for Australia over the years, and twenty-year-old newcomer Graham McKenzie. The contrast between the previous season's young fast bowler Geoff Griffin and 'Garth' McKenzie could not have been greater. Where poor Griffin's career ended in ignominy at Lord's, McKenzie's began in a blaze of glory and continued over 60 Tests, until when he retired he was second only to Benaud in the list of all-time Australian Test wicket takers. Raman Subba Row, who had scored a hundred in the First Test – his debut against Australia – and would score another in the Fifth Test, his final Test against Australia, was the only man to look even slightly at ease, and nobody else got into the thirties. England were all out for 206, and by stumps on the first day Australia were 42 for 2. It was reported with some astonishment at the time that 'no spin was used all day,' a sign of the changing times, maybe. In the new millennium the papers might remark with equal astonishment if spin were used on the first day of a Test.

At 88 for 4 the next morning, Australia might have been in a dangerous position, had not Lawry, in only his second Test, and Peter Burge, both played very well. Thanks also to a typically determined innings by Ken Mackay, and some sensible hitting by McKenzie and Misson, Australia built up a winning lead of 134. England, with the honourable exception of Ken Barrington, failed again and Australia needed only 69 to win. Trueman and Statham had them at 19 for 4, but could not press the slim chance home.

After the match, a survey of the pitch revealed what players had suspected for some time – there was a 'ridge' at Lord's.

ENGLAND

G Pullar	b Davidson	11	c Grout b Misson	42
R Subba Row	lbw b Mackay	48	c Grout b Davidson	8
ER Dexter	c McKenzie b Misson	27	b McKenzie	17
† MC Cowdrey	c Grout b McKenzie	16	c Mackay b Misson	7
PBH May	c Grout b Davidson	17	c Grout b McKenzie	22
KF Barrington	c Mackay b Davidson	4	lbw b Davidson	66
R Illingworth	b Misson	13	c Harvey b Simpson	0
* JT Murray	lbw b Mackay	18	c Grout b McKenzie	25
GAR Lock	c Grout b Davidson	5	b McKenzie	1
FS Trueman	b Davidson	25	c Grout b McKenzie	0
JB Statham	not out	11	not out	2
	(LB 9, W 2)	11	(B 1, I B 10, W 1)	12
Total		206		202

AUSTRALIA

WM Lawry	c Murray b Dexter	130	c Murray b Statham	1
CC McDonald	b Statham	4	c Illingworth b Trueman	14
RB Simpson	c Illingworth b Trueman	0	(6) c Illingworth b Statham	15
† RN Harvey	c Barrington b Trueman	27	(3) Murray b Trueman	4
NC O'Neill	b Dexter	1	(4) b Statham	0
PJ Burge	c Murray b Statham	46	(5) not out	37
AK Davidson	lbw b Trueman	6	not out	0
KD Mackay	c Barrington b Illingworth	54		
* ATW Grout	lbw b Dexter	0		
GD McKenzie	b Trueman	34		
FM Misson	not out	25		
	(B 1, LB 12)	13		
Total		340	(5 wkts)	71

AUSTRALIA	O	M	R	W	O	M	R	W
Davidson	24.3	6	42	5	24	8	50	2
McKenzie	26	7	81	1	29	13	37	5
Misson	16	4	48	2	17	2	66	2
Mackay	12	3	24	2	8	6	5	0
Simpson					19	10	32	1

ENGLAND	O	M	R	W	O	M	R	W
Statham	44	10	89	2	10.5	3	31	3
Trueman	34	3	118	4	10	0	40	2
Dexter	24	7	56	3				
Lock	26	13	48	0				
Illingworth	11.3	5	16	1				

FALL OF WICKETS

Wkt	Eng. 1st	Aus. 1st	Eng. 2nd	Aus. 2nd
1st	26	5	33	15
2nd	87	6	63	15
3rd	87	81	67	19
4th	111	88	80	19
5th	115	183	127	58
6th	127	194	144	
7th	156	238	191	
8th	164	238	199	
9th	167	291	199	
10th	206	340	202	

† Captain   * Wicketkeeper

1962: England v Pakistan

(2nd Test) June 21, 22, 23
England won by 9 wickets

Pakistan's return to England for their second tour, eight years after the first, proved to be a disappointment. England won four of the five Tests, with the remaining one a rain-affected draw, which was not what the Pakistanis had hoped for after the high promise of the 1954 series. But the Lord's Test still had its high points. Two England stalwarts, Fred Trueman and Tom Graveney, will remember the game with particular affection. Trueman, in his forty-seventh Test appearance,

enjoyed his best bowling analysis at Lord's, six for 31 including his 200th Test victim, the Pakistan captain Javed Burki. With Tom Graveney, he added a then record ninth-wicket partnership against Pakistan of 76. Graveney hit a typically stylish 153, his first Test century at Lord's, which more than made up for the disappointment of being dismissed for 97 in the previous Test, at Edgbaston.

Despite England's comfortable victory, all was not bleakness for the tourists. Their first innings

Tom Graveney, last man out for 153.

was a disaster, with the top score being only 17, by Nasim-ul-Ghani batting at number eight. In the second innings, he was made nightwatchman and came in at number

six, but when he came to the wicket at the end of the second day to join his captain Pakistan were 77 for 4, still 193 runs away from saving the innings defeat. When they were finally separated, Nasim had scored the first hundred by a Pakistan Test batsman in England, and it was Nasim's maiden first class hundred. His captain emulated his feat shortly afterwards, but neither could build on their centuries, and when Len Coldwell, on his Test debut, finished off the Pakistan innings, England needed only 86 to win. Micky Stewart, also on debut, was still there with his captain when the target was reached.

Stewart was unlucky in his Test career. After a prolific few seasons with Surrey, and a reputation as the best slip fielder of his generation, he came into the Test side in 1962, replacing Lancashire's left-handed opener 'Noddy' Pullar. But later that summer the Reverend David Sheppard, undoubtedly in his prime a better batsman than Stewart, took time off from his pastoral duties and scored a century for the Gentlemen against the Players. The England selectors asked him whether he would be available for the winter tour to Australia. When he hinted that he would, he was brought in to the England team for the fourth Test, and scored 83. Stewart was left out in the cold and did not tour Australia. When Sheppard's church duties meant he could not play Test cricket in 1963, Stewart came back, but only until the arrival of Geoff Boycott as a Test cricketer a year later.

England won by 9 wickets

LORD'S GROUND

ENGLAND v. PAKISTAN

Thurs., Fri., Sat., Mon. & Tues., 21, 22, 23, 25 & 26 June, 1962 (5-day match)

PAKISTAN

		First Innings		Second Innings	
1 Hanif Mohammad		c Cowdrey b Trueman	13	l b w b Coldwell	24
‡2 Imtiaz Ahmed		b Coldwell	1	c Trueman b Coldwell	33
3 Saeed Ahmed		b Dexter	10	b Coldwell	20
†4 Javed Burki		c Dexter b Trueman	5	l b w b Coldwell	101
5 Mushtaq Mohammad		c Cowdrey b Trueman	7	c Millman b Trueman	18
6 Alim-Ud-Din		b Coldwell	9	c Graveney b Allen	10
7 Wallis Mathias		b Trueman	15	c Graveney b Trueman	1
8 Nasim-Ul Ghani		c Millman b Trueman	17	c Graveney b Coldwell	101
9 Mahmood Hussain		c Cowdrey b Coldwell	1	b Coldwell	20
10 Antoa D'Souza		not out	6	not out	12
11 Mohammad Farooq		c Stewart b Trueman	13	b Trueman	1
		B 1, l b 2, w , n-b ,	3	B 6, l b 4, w 4, n-b ,	14
		Total	100	Total	365

FALL OF THE WICKETS

1—2 2—23 3—25 4—31 5—36 6—51 7—77 8—78 9—78 10—100
1—36 2—36 3—57 4—77 5—274 6—299 7—300 8—347 9—354 10—355

ANALYSIS OF BOWLING

Name	1st Innings						2nd Innings					
	O.	M.	R.	W.	Wd.	N-b	O.	M.	R.	W.	Wd.	N-b
Coldwell	14	2	25	3	...	...	41	13	85	6	...	...
Trueman	17.4	6	31	6	...	...	33.3	6	85	3	...	4
Dexter	12	3	41	1	...	...	15	4	44	0	...	...
Allen			...	...	...	...	15	6	41	1	...	...
Lock			...	...	...	...	14	1	78	0	...	...
Barrington			...	...	...	...	1	0	8	0	...	...

ENGLAND

			First Innings		Second Innings	
*1 M. C. Cowdrey		Kent	c D'Souza b Farooq	41	c Imtiaz b D'Souza	20
2 M. J. Stewart		Surrey	c Imtiaz b D'Souza	39	not out	34
†*3 E. R. Dexter		Sussex	c Imtiaz b Farooq	65	not out	32
4 T. W. Graveney		Worcestershire	b D'Souza	153		
5 K. F. Barrington		Surrey	c Imtiaz b Farooq	0		
6 D. A. Allen		Gloucestershire	l b w b Farooq	2		
7 P. H. Parfitt		Middlesex	b Mahmood	16		
‡8 G. Millman		Nottinghamshire	c Hanif b Mahmood	7		
9 G. A. R. Lock		Surrey	c Mathais b Saeed	7		
10 F. S. Trueman		Yorkshire	l b w b Saeed	29		
11 L. J. Coldwell		Worcestershire	not out	0		
			B , l-b 5, w , n-b 5,	11	B , l b , w , n-b ,	
			Total	370	Total	86

FALL OF THE WICKETS

1—59 2—137 3—168 4—168 5—184 6—221 7—247 8—290 9—366 10—370
1—36 2— 3— 4— 5— 6— 7— 8— 9— 10—

ANALYSIS OF BOWLING

Name	1st Innings						2nd Innings					
	O.	M.	R.	W.	Wd.	N-b	O.	M.	R.	W.	Wd.	N-b
Mahmood Hussain	40	8	106	2	...	3	7	1	37	0	...	...
Mohammad Farooq	19	4	70	4	...	...	7	0	29	1	...	...
Antao D'Sousa	35.4	3	147	2	...	...						
Nazim-Ul-Ghani	2	0	15	0	...	...	2	0	12	0	...	...
Saeed Ahmed	5	1	21	0	...	...	1	0	8	0	...	...
Mushtaq Mohammad	...	...	...	...	...	...						

Umpires—J. S. Buller & N. Oldfield *Amateur †Captain ‡Wicket-keeper

Scorers—A. Fowler & Intikhab Alam

Play begins 1st, 2nd, 3rd & 4th days at 11.30. 5th day at 11
Stumps drawn 1st, 2nd, 3rd & 4th days at 6.30. 5th day at 5.30 or 6
Luncheon Interval 1.30 p.m.—2.10 p.m.
Tea Interval 4.15 p.m.—4.35 p.m. (may be varied according to state of game)

Pakistan won the toss

1963: England v West Indies

(2nd Test) June 20, 21, 22, 24, 25
Match drawn

For many people, this was the greatest Lord's Test ever. As Wes Hall ran in to bowl the final ball, any one of four results was still possible. England needed six runs to win, and the last pair were together. That pair were David Allen and Colin Cowdrey, batting with his left arm in plaster. Allen blocked the final delivery (hitting a six was not really an option) and the match was drawn.

Throughout the match, the sides had been very evenly matched. There were no players new to Test cricket, although 38-year-old Derek Shackleton was recalled after an eleven-year gap.

He did not let England down. West Indies, batting first on a rain-affected wicket, scored 301 and England replied with 297, including a brilliant, aggressive 70 from Dexter. England looked to have nosed in front when West Indies slipped to 15 for 2 in their second innings, but a truly superb innings of 133 by the much underrated Basil Butcher, aided by his captain Frank Worrell, allowed them to clamber back to 229 all out, leaving England 234 to win in five sessions. Fred Trueman had bowled 70 overs and taken eleven wickets for 152 runs in the match; at the other end

Colin Cowdrey is struck on the arm by a ball from Wes Hall on the fourth day.
Inset: Cowdrey, his left arm in plaster, at the non-striker's end for the last ball of the match.

Match Drawn

LORD'S  GROUND

ENGLAND v. WEST INDIES

Thurs., Fri., Sat., Mon. & Tues., 20, 21, 22, 24 & 25 June, 1963   (5-day Match)

WEST INDIES

		First Innings		Second Innings	
1	C. C. Hunte	c Close b Trueman	44	c Cowdrey b Shackleton	7
2	E. McMorris	l b w b Trueman	16	c Cowdrey b Trueman	8
3	R. Kanhai	c Edrich b Trueman	73	c Cowdrey b Shackleton	21
4	G. Sobers	c Cowdrey b Allen	42	c Parks b Trueman	8
5	B. Butcher	c Barrington b Trueman	14	l b w b Shackleton	133
6	J. Solomon	l b w b Shackleton	56	c Stewart b Allen	5
†7	F. M. Worrell	b Trueman	0	c Stewart b Trueman	33
*8	D. Murray	c Cowdrey b Trueman	20	c Parks b Trueman	2
9	W. Hall	not out	25	c Parks b Trueman	2
10	C. Griffith	c Cowdrey b Shackleton	0	b Shackleton	1
11	L. R. Gibbs	c Stewart b Shackleton	0	not out	1
		B 10, l-b 1, w , n-b	11	B 5, l-b 2, w , n-b 1,	8
		Total	301	Total	229

FALL OF THE WICKETS

1—51 2—64 3—127 4—145 5—219 6—219 7—263 8—297 9—297 10—301
1—15 2—15 3—64 4—84 5—104 6—214 7—224 8—226 9—228 10—229

ANALYSIS OF BOWLING

Name	1st Innings						2nd Innings					
	O.	M.	R.	W.	Wd.	N-b	O.	M.	R.	W.	Wd.	N-b
Trueman	44	16	100	6			26	9	52	5		1
Shackleton	50.2	22	93	3			34	14	72	4		
Dexter	20	6	41	0			...	...	...	...		
Close	9	3	21	0			21	7	50	1		
Allen	10	3	35	1			17	3	47	0		
Titmus							...	...	...	...		

ENGLAND

			First Innings		Second Innings	
1	M. J. Stewart	Surrey	c Kanhai b Griffith	2	c Solomon b Hall	17
2	J. H. Edrich	Surrey	c Murray b Griffith	0	c Murray b Hall	8
†3	E. R. Dexter	Sussex	l b w b Sobers	70	b Gibbs	2
4	K. F. Barrington	Surrey	c Sobers b Worrell	80	c Murray b Griffith	60
5	M. C. Cowdrey	Kent	b Gibbs	4	not out	19
6	D. B. Close	Yorkshire	c Murray b Griffith	9	c Murray b Griffith	70
*7	J. M. Parks	Sussex	b Worrell	35	l b w b Griffith	17
8	F. J. Titmus	Middlesex	not out	52	c McMorris b Hall	11
9	F. S. Trueman	Yorkshire	b Hall	10	c Murray b Hall	0
10	D. A. Allen	Gloucestershire	l b w b Griffith	2	not out	4
11	D. Shackleton	Hampshire	b Griffith	8	run out	4
			B 8, l-b 8, w , n-b 9,	25	B 5, l-b 8, w , n-b 3,	16
			Total	297	Total	228

FALL OF THE WICKETS

1—2 2 20 3—102 4—115 5—151 6—206 7—235 8—271 9—274 10—297
1—15 2—27 3—31 4—130 5—158 6—203 7—203 8—219 9—228 10—

ANALYSIS OF BOWLING

Name	1st Innings						2nd Innings					
	O.	M.	R.	W.	Wd.	N-b	O.	M.	R.	W.	Wd.	N-b
Hall	18	2	65	1		4	40	9	93	4		2
Griffith	26	6	91	5		5	30	7	59	3		1
Sobers	18	4	45	1			4	1	4	0		
Gibbs	27	9	59	1			17	7	56	1		
Worrell	13	6	12	2			...	...	...	...		

Umpires—J. S. Buller & W. E. Phillipson

Scorers—A. Fowler & G. Duckworth

† Captain   * Wicket-keeper

Play begins 1st, 2nd, 3rd & 4th days at 11.30.   5th day at 11
Stumps drawn 1st, 2nd, 3rd & 4th days at 6.30   5th day at 5.30 or 6
Luncheon Interval 1.30 p.m.—2.10 p.m.
Tea Interval 4.15 p.m.—4.35 p.m. (may be varied according to state of the game)

West Indies won the toss

Shackleton bowled 84.2 overs, ending with 7 for 165.

Before play came to an early halt for bad light at 4.45 on the fourth day, England had reached 116 for three, but Cowdrey was also out of action, his wrist broken by a very fast rising ball from Wes Hall. His place was taken by Brian Close, who played an astonishing innings of 70, repeatedly taking short deliveries on his chest and arms. He was out late on the final day (no play had been possible before lunch), having changed his tactics and come down the wicket to try to put Hall and Griffith off their length. For a while he succeeded.

The final over began with England needing eight to win and two wickets in hand, and with Cowdrey plastered and padded up in the pavilion, ready to bat if needed. He was needed, because on the fourth ball Shackleton was run out by Worrell, who ran with the ball in his hand to beat Shackleton to the bowler's end, thus proving a 39-year-old can sometimes beat a 38-year-old over 22 yards. Cowdrey came in to the non-striker's end, and David Allen took the discretionary route and played out the final two balls for a draw.

Wes Hall bowled unchanged throughout the final day. EW Swanton described it as 'surely an unparalleled feat for a man of his pace.' It was just one of many in the Lord's Test of 1963.

LORD'S GROUND

1964: England v Australia

(2nd Test) June 18, 19, 20, 22, 23 (no play on first two days)
Match drawn

The summer of 1964 was not a particularly rainy one but when the Test matches were played, the dark clouds gathered. The Lord's Test was affected most of all. No play was possible on the first two days, and although the Cricket Board of Control suggested adding an extra half hour to each of the remaining three days to make up some lost time, the Australians, holding the Ashes and not wanting to take any unnecessary risks, refused. So the match was almost inevitably a draw before it got started.

There were a few highlights and statistics to keep some of the crowd happy. Fred Trueman took five wickets in the innings for the seventeenth and final time in Test matches, and Graham McKenzie, one of Trueman's five victims, made only 10 when he batted, but six of them came in possibly the biggest hit ever seen in a Lord's Test. Batting at the Nursery End, he hit a ball from Len Coldwell over square leg and on to the roof of the Mound Stand, from where it bounced into St John's Wood Road, hitting Richard Horton (aged 55 of Camden Town,

A pair of mallard enjoy a match much affected by rain.

for those who need to know) in the face and breaking his glasses. John Edrich played far better than anybody else in the match in scoring 120, thus guiding England to a first innings lead of 70, but in the end the rain finished the match off. With Australia just short of 100 ahead and with six second innings wickets still in hand, the heavens opened again shortly after lunch on the Tuesday and that was that.

Or almost that. On that final day a letter appeared in *The Times* from a Mr Keith Falkner, complaining about the drainage at Lord's. 'It was ludicrous,' he wrote, 'to all of us watching despondently yesterday to see the falling rain run off the playing area, by hosepipe, to the very parts of the ground which need redraining. It is an elementary thought that the water could have been drained into mobile tanks or containers. In future, may this be considered for the benefit of thousands of cricketers for whom the Lord's Test is the one event which takes precedence over all else?'

That autumn a new drainage system was installed at Lord's, to help ensure that the Lord's Test remains the one event which takes precedence over all else.

Match Drawn

LORD'S GROUND

ENGLAND v. AUSTRALIA

Thurs., Fri., Sat., Mon. & Tues., June 18, 19, 20, 22 & 23, 1964 (5-day Match)

AUSTRALIA

#	Batsman		First Innings		Second Innings	
1	W. M. Lawry	Victoria	b Trueman	4	c Dexter b Gifford	20
2	I. R. Redpath	Victoria	c Parfitt b Coldwell	30	l b w b Titmus	36
3	N. C. O'Neill	New South Wales	c Titmus b Dexter	26	c Parfitt b Trueman	22
4	P. J. Burge	Queensland	l b w b Dexter	1	c Parfitt b Titmus	59
5	B. C. Booth	New South Wales	l b w b Trueman	14	not out	2
†6	R. B. Simpson	New South Wales	c Parfitt b Trueman	0	not out	15
7	T. R. Veivers	Queensland	b Gifford	54		
8	G. D. McKenzie	Western Australia	b Trueman	10		
*9	A. T. W. Grout	Queensland	c Dexter b Gifford	14		
10	N. J. N. Hawke	South Australia	not out	5		
11	G. E. Corling	New South Wales	b Trueman	0		
			B 8, l b 5, w , n-b 5,	18	B 8, l-b 4, w , n-b 2,	14
			Total	176	Total	168

FALL OF THE WICKETS

1—8 2—46 3—58 4—84 5—84 6—88 7—132 8—163 9—167 10—176

1—35 2—76 3—143 4—148 5— 6— 7— 8— 9— 10—

ANALYSIS OF BOWLING

Name	1st Innings						2nd Innings					
	O.	M.	R.	W.	Wd.	N-b	O.	M.	R.	W	Wd.	N-b
Trueman	25	8	48	5		4	18	6	52	1		1
Coldwell	23	7	51	4			19	4	59	0		1
Gifford	12	6	14	2			17	9	17	1		
Dexter	7	1	16	2		1	3	0	5	0		
Titmus	17	6	29	0			17	7	21	2		

ENGLAND

#	Batsman		First Innings		Second Innings	
†1	E. R. Dexter	Sussex	b McKenzie	2		
2	J. H. Edrich	Surrey	c Redpath b McKenzie	120		
3	M. C. Cowdrey	Kent	c Burge b Hawke	10		
4	K. F. Barrington	Surrey	l b w b McKenzie	5		
5	P. H. Parfitt	Middlesex	l b w b Corling	20		
6	P. J. Sharpe	Yorkshire	l b w b Hawke	35		
*7	J. M. Parks	Sussex	c Simpson b Hawke	12		
8	F. J. Titmus	Middlesex	b Corling	15		
9	F. S. Trueman	Yorkshire	b Corling	8		
10	N. Gifford	Worcestershire	c Hawke b Corling	5		
11	L. J. Coldwell	Worcestershire	not out	6		
			B , l-b 7, w , n-b l,	8	B , l b , w , n-b ,	
			Total	246	Total	

FALL OF THE WICKETS

1—2 2—33 3—42 4—83 5—138 6—170 7—227 8—229 9—235 10—246

1— 2— 3— 4— 5— 6— 7— 8— 9— 10—

ANALYSIS OF BOWLING

Name	1st Innings						2nd Innings					
	O.	M.	R.	W.	Wd.	N-b	O.	M.	R.	W.	Wd.	N-b
McKenzie	26	8	69	3								
Corling	27.3	9	60	4								
Hawke	16	4	41	3								
Veivers	9	4	17	0								
Simpson	21	8	51	0		1						

Umpires—J. S. Buller & J. F. Crapp Scorers—A. Fowler & D. Sherwood

† Captain * Wicket-keeper

Play begins 1st, 2nd, 3rd & 4th days at 11.30 5th day at 11
Stumps drawn 1st, 2nd, 3rd & 4th days at 6.30 5th day at 5.30 or 6
Luncheon Interval 1.30 p.m.—2.10 p.m.
Tea Interval 4.15 p.m.—4.35 p.m. (may be varied according to state of game)
New Ball—may be taken after 200 runs have been scored off, or 85 overs bowled with, the old one

England won the toss and elected to field

1965: England v New Zealand

(2nd Test) June 17, 18, 19, 21, 22
England won by 7 wickets

The summer of 1965 was the first since 1912 that there had been two touring teams playing Tests in England, and the first since that year there had been more than one Test at Lord's. The first series of the summer was of three matches against New Zealand, who had improved out of all recognition since their last appearance at Lord's in 1958. Their captain was still John Reid, easily the best all rounder from New Zealand in their first fifty years playing Test matches, but nobody else remained from seven years before. England still had three survivors of that bygone age – Colin Cowdrey, Mike Smith and Fred Trueman.

This, however, was to be Trueman's final Test. When it finished, his wickets total of 307 was a world record which stood until Lance Gibbs of West Indies overtook him eleven years later. It was also John Snow's first Test, so England's fast bowling mantle was passed on at Lord's in 1965. Actually, it was Somerset's jovial left arm fast medium Fred Rumsey who took more wickets than either of his quicker colleagues: his four for 25 in New Zealand's first innings ensured they never got near to creating a winning total. Vic Pollard made 55 and Bruce Taylor, stepping into Reid's all-rounder shoes, scored 51, but otherwise nobody got going. England were able to pass their total with only four wickets down, thanks to old hands Cowdrey (119), Dexter (62) and Smith (44), and finished 132 ahead.

In 1958 that would have been the signal for an innings victory, but New Zealand in 1965 were a much better side. All of the top six got a start, and Dowling, Sinclair and Pollard went on to make half-centuries. It was the spinners who did the damage, though. First choice off-spinner Fred Titmus, part-time leggie Bob Barber and part-time off-spinner Peter Parfitt took six for 153

between them from 72 overs as New Zealand worked their way to 347 in 148 overs, leaving England 215 to win.

Rain took out five hours of the final twelve on the Monday and Tuesday, but thanks to aggressive batting from Geoff Boycott and Ted Dexter England got home with a quarter of an hour to spare.

Fred Trueman, in his last Test, is bowled by RO Collinge.

England won by 7 wickets

6ᴰ LORD'S ⓂⒸⒸ GROUND 6ᴰ

ENGLAND v. NEW ZEALAND

Thurs., Fri., Sat., Mon. & Tues., June 17, 18, 19, 21 & 22, 1965   (5-day Match)

NEW ZEALAND		First Innings		Second Innings	
1 G. T. Dowling	Canterbury	l b w b Rumsey	12	b Parfitt	66
2 B. E. Congdon	Central Districts	l b w b Rumsey	0	l b w b Titmus	26
3 B. W. Sinclair	Wellington	b Rumsey	1	c Parks b Barber	72
†4 J. R. Reid	Auckland	c Parks b Snow	21	b Titmus	22
5 R. W. Morgan	Wellington	c Parfitt b Rumsey	0	l b w b Rumsey	35
*6 A. E. Dick	Wellington	b Snow	7	c Parks b Snow	3
7 V. Pollard	Central Districts	c and b Titmus	55	run out	55
8 B. R. Taylor	Canterbury	c Parks b Titmus	61	c Smith b Snow	0
9 R. C. Motz	Canterbury	b Trueman	11	c Snow b Barber	8
10 R. O. Collinge	Central Districts	c Parks b Titmus	7	c Parks b Barber	21
11 F. J. Cameron	Otago	b Trueman	3	not out	9
		not out	7		
		B 3, l-b 2, w , n-b 2,	7	B 8, l-b 12, w , n-b 10,	30
		Total	175	Total	347

FALL OF THE WICKETS

1—0   2—4   3—24   4—28   5—49   6—62   7—154   8—160   9—171   10—175

1—59   2—149   3—196   4—206   5—253   6—258   7—259   8—293   9—303   10—347

ANALYSIS OF BOWLING	1st Innings						2nd Innings					
Name	O.	M.	R.	W.	Wd.	N-b	O.	M.	R.	W.	Wd.	N-b
Rumsey	13	4	25	4		1	26	10	42	1		3
Trueman	19.5	8	40	2		1	26	4	69	0		3
Dexter	8	2	27	0			...	...	...	...		4
Snow	11	2	27	2			24	5	53	2		
Titmus	15	7	25	2			39	12	71	2		
Barber	8	2	24	0			28	10	57	3		
Parfitt							6	2	25	1		

ENGLAND		First Innings		Second Innings	
1 G. Boycott	Yorkshire	c Dick b Motz	14	l b w b Motz	76
2 R. W. Barber	Warwickshire	c Dick b Motz	13	b Motz	34
3 E. R. Dexter	Sussex	c Dick b Taylor	62	not out	80
4 M. C. Cowdrey	Kent	c sub b Collinge	119	not out	4
5 P. H. Parfitt	Middlesex	c Dick b Cameron	11		
†6 M. J. K. Smith	Warwickshire	c sub b Taylor	44		
*7 J. M. Parks	Sussex	b Collinge	2	c Dick b Motz	1
8 F. J. Titmus	Middlesex	run out	13		
9 F. S. Trueman	Yorkshire	b Collinge	3		
10 F. E. Rumsey	Somerset	b Collinge	3		
11 J. A. Snow	Sussex	not out	2		
		B 1, l-b 7, w 1, n-b 12,	21	B 9, l-b 5, w , n-b 9,	23
		Total	307	Total	218

FALL OF THE WICKETS

1—18   2—38   3—131   4—166   5—271   6—285   7—292   8—300   9—302   10—307

1—64   2—70   3—196   4—   5—   6—   7—   8—   9—   10—

ANALYSIS OF BOWLING	1st Innings						2nd Innings					
Name	O.	M.	R.	W.	Wd.	N-b	O.	M.	R.	W.	Wd.	N-b
Collinge	28.2	4	85	4		7	15	1	43	0		3
Motz	20	1	62	2	1		19	5	45	3		6
Taylor	25	4	66	2		5	10	0	53	0		
Cameron	19	6	40	1			13	0	39	0		
Morgan	8	1	33	0			3	0	11	0		
Reid	...	...	...	...			0.5	0	4	0		

Scorers—A. Fowler & H. Wilkinson

Umpires—J. S. Buller & W. E. Phillipson

† Captain   * Wicket-keeper

Play begins 1st, 2nd, 3rd & 4th days at 11.30   5th day at 11
Stumps drawn 1st, 2nd, 3rd & 4th days at 6.30   5th day at 5.30 or 6
Luncheon Interval 1.30 p.m.—2.10 p.m.
Tea Interval 4.15 p.m.—4.35 p.m. (may be varied according to state of game)
New Ball—may be taken after 85 overs have been bowled with the old one

New Zealand won the toss

1965: England v South Africa

(1st Test) July 22, 23, 24, 26, 27
Match drawn

Three weeks after the death in Durban of Walter Hammond, one of England's greatest ever players, South Africa were the visitors to Lord's for the first of three Tests, which was also the one hundredth between the two countries since rivalry began in 1888/89. England had won 46 of them, to South Africa's 17, and this would become the 37th draw.

The South African team was improving with each match, it seemed. When apartheid forced the country out of international competition five years later they were generally regarded as the strongest side of all, but even in 1965 most of the elements were in place. The Pollock brothers, all-rounder Eddie Barlow and wicketkeeper-batsman

Denis Lindsay would have been in most people's World XI, while Ali Bacher, making his debut in this game, would soon establish himself as a middle order batsman of the highest quality. And then there was Colin Bland.

People who watch cricket in the present era tend to think of Jonty Rhodes when they think of great South African fielders, but it was Colin Bland who set the standard that Rhodes and others have tried to live up to. The tall Rhodesian would practise for hours throwing a cricket ball at one stump, so that by the time he was in the Test side (and the leading run-scorer at Lord's in 1965), he could expect to hit the stump twice in three attempts. Unfortunately neither Ken Barrington

Colin Bland, fielder supreme, here cutting Fred Titmus for 3 runs.

Match Drawn

 LORD'S GROUND

ENGLAND v. SOUTH AFRICA

Thurs., Fri., Sat., Mon. & Tues., July 22, 23, 24, 26 & 27, 1965   (5-day Match)

		First Innings		Second Innings	
SOUTH AFRICA					
1 E. J. Barlow	E. Province	c Barber b Rumsey	1	c Parks b Brown	52
2 H. R. Lance	Transvaal	c and b Brown	28	c Titmus b Brown	9
*3 D. Lindsay	N. E. Transvaal	c Titmus b Rumsey	40	c Parks b Larter	22
4 R. G. Pollock	E. Province	c Barrington b Titmus	56	b Brown	5
5 K. C. Bland	Rhodesia	b Brown	39	c Edrich b Barber	70
6 A. Bacher	Transvaal	l b w b Titmus	4	b Titmus	37
†7 P. L. Van der Merwe	W. Province	c Barrington b Rumsey	17	c Barrington b Rumsey	31
8 R. Dumbrill	Natal	b Barber	3	c Cowdrey b Rumsey	2
9 J. T. Botten	N. E. Transvaal	b Brown	33	b Rumsey	0
10 P. M. Pollock	E. Province	st Parks b Barber	34	run out	14
11 H. D. Bromfield	W. Province	not out	9	run out	0
		B , l-b **14**, w , n-b **2**,	16	B **4**, l-b **2**, w , n-b ,	6
		Total	**280**	Total	**248**

FALL OF THE WICKETS

1—1 2—60 3—75 4—155 5—170 6—170 7—178 8—212 9—241 10—280

1—55 2—62 3—68 4—120 5—170 6—216 7—230 8—230 9—247 10—248

ANALYSIS OF BOWLING

Name	1st Innings						2nd Innings					
	O.	M.	R.	W.	Wd.	N-b	O.	M.	R.	W.	Wd.	N-b
Larter	26	10	47	0	...	1	17	2	67	1	...	...
Rumsey	30	9	84	3	...	1	21	8	49	3	...	...
Brown	24	9	44	3	...	...	21	11	30	3	...	...
Titmus	29	10	59	2	...	...	26	13	36	1	...	...
Barber	10.3	3	30	2	...	...	25	5	60	1	...	...
	...	...	...	...	...	...	...	...	...	...	...	...

		First Innings		Second Innings	
ENGLAND					
1 G. Boycott	Yorkshire	c Barlow b Botten	31	c and b Dumbrill	28
2 R. W. Barber	Warwickshire	b Bromfield	56	c Lindsay b P. Pollock	12
3 J. H. Edrich	Surrey	l b w b P. Pollock	0	retired hurt	7
4 K. F. Barrington	Surrey	run out	91	l b w b Dumbrill	18
5 M. C. Cowdrey	Kent	b Dumbrill	29	l b w b P. Pollock	37
†6 M. J. K. Smith	Warwickshire	c Lindsay b Botten	26	c Lindsay b Dumbrill	13
*7 J. M. Parks	Sussex	run out	32	c VanderMerwe b D'brill	7
8 F. J. Titmus	Middlesex	c P. Pollock b Bromfield	59	not out	9
9 D. J. Brown	Warwickshire	c Bromfield b Dumbrill	1	c Barlow b R. Pollock	5
10 F. E. Rumsey	Somerset	b Dumbrill	3	not out	0
11 J. D. F. Larter	Northants	not out	0		
		B **1**, l-b **4**, w **1**, n-b **4**,	10	B , l-b **7**, w **1**, n-b **1**,	9
		Total	**338**	Total	**145**

FALL OF THE WICKETS

1—82 2—88 3—88 4—144 5—240 6—240 7—294 8—314 9—338 10—338

1—23 2—70 3—79 4—113 5—121 6—135 7—140 8— 9— 10—

ANALYSIS OF BOWLING

Name	1st Innings						2nd Innings					
	O.	M.	R.	W.	Wd.	N-b	O.	M.	R.	W.	Wd.	N-b
P. Pollock	39	12	91	1	...	1	20	6	52	2	...	...
Botten	33	11	65	2	...	2	12	6	25	0	...	1
Barlow	19	6	31	0	...	...	9	1	25	0	...	...
Bromfield	25.2	5	71	2	...	...	5	4	4	0	...	...
Dumbrill	24	11	31	3	...	1	18	8	30	4	...	...
Lance	5	0	18	0	...	...	...	...	...	...	...	...
R. Pollock	5	1	21	0	...	...	4	4	0	1	1	...

Scorers—A. Fowler & M. McLennan

Umpires—J. S. Buller & A. E. Rhodes

† Captain   * Wicket-keeper

Play begins 1st, 2nd, 3rd & 4th days at 11.30 5th day at 11

Stumps drawn 1st, 2nd, 3rd & 4th days at 6.30 5th day at 5.30 or 6

Luncheon Interval 1.30 p.m.—2.10 p.m.

Tea Interval 4.15 p.m.—4.35 p.m. (may be varied according to state of game)

New Ball—may be taken after 85 overs have been bowled with the old one

South Africa won the toss

---

nor Jim Parks believed the hype. Both England batsmen, when well set in the first innings, made the mistake of believing there was a run to Bland at mid-wicket or cover. Both were run out by direct hits. Parks, in particular, could not believe the evidence of his own eyes when he saw the stumps uprooted before he had made his ground.

In England's second innings, when they needed only 191 runs to win in a few minutes under four hours, they never really recovered from the injury to John Edrich, who was hit on the side of the head by a ball from Peter Pollock. Edrich had been in a very rich vein of form that summer, hitting nine consecutive fifties (including 310 not out against New Zealand at Headingley) before being lbw for a duck in the first innings here. After being hit by Pollock, he never really recovered his dominant form of that summer.

1966: England v West Indies

(2nd Test) June 16, 17, 18, 20, 21
Match drawn

There was really no chance that the 1966 Lord's Test against the West Indies could live up to the drama of the previous encounter between the two teams three years earlier. Only four Englishmen, Barrington, Cowdrey, Parks and Titmus, remained from that famous game, but seven West Indians returned for another go at England. The West Indians were getting stronger and England were rebuilding. Part of the rebuilding process was a Test debut for the most politically significant cricketer of the age, South African-born Basil D'Oliveira. A game as close as that of 1963 was just not possible.

All the same, it nearly happened. Thanks to the cavalier captaincy of Gary Sobers, who always preferred a sporting declaration to the cautious option, England were left having to score 284 in 240 minutes after Sobers and his cousin David Holford put on an unbroken 274 for the sixth wicket. Coming together when their side was leading by just nine runs with only five wickets in hand, Sobers and Holford crafted one of the great

Sobers and Holford, cousins and partners.

Match Drawn

6D LORD'S GROUND 6D

ENGLAND v. WEST INDIES

Thurs., Fri., Sat., Mon. & Tues., June 16, 17, 18, 20 & 21, 1966   (5-day Match)

WEST INDIES

			First Innings		Second Innings	
1	C. C. Hunte	Barbados	c Parks b Higgs	18	c Milburn b Knight	13
2	M. C. Carew	Trinidad	c Parks b Higgs	2	c Knight b Higgs	0
3	R. B. Kanhai	Guyana	c Titmus b Higgs	25	c Parks b Knight	40
4	B. F. Butcher	Guyana	c Milburn b Knight	49	l b w b Higgs	3
5	S. M. Nurse	Barbados	b D'Oliveira	64	c Parks b D'Oliveira	35
†6	G. S. Sobers	Barbados	l b w b Knight	46	not out	163
7	D. Holford	Barbados	l b w b Knight	26	not out	105
*8	D. W. Allan	Barbados	c Titmus b Higgs	13		
9	C. C. Griffith	Barbados	l b w b Higgs	5	Innings closed	
10	L. R. Gibbs	Guyana	c Parks b Higgs	4		
11	W. W. Hall	Barbados	not out	8		
			B 2, l-b 7, w , n-b	9	B , l-b 8, w , n-b 2,	10
			Total	269	Total	369

FALL OF THE WICKETS

1—8   2—42   3—53   4—119   5—205   6—213   7—252   8—252   9—261   10—269
1—2   2—22   3—25   4—91   5—95   6—   7—   8—   9—   10—

ANALYSIS OF BOWLING

Name	1st Innings						2nd Innings					
	O.	M.	R.	W.	Wd.	N-b	O.	M.	R.	W.	Wd.	N-b
Jones	22	3	64	1	...	...	25	2	95	0	...	2
Higgs	33	9	91	6	...	...	34	5	82	2	...	...
Knight	21	0	63	2	...	...	30	3	106	2	...	...
Titmus	5	0	18	0	...	...	19	3	30	0	...	...
D'Oliveira	14	5	24	1	...	...	25	7	46	1	...	...

ENGLAND

			First Innings		Second Innings	
1	G. Boycott	Yorkshire	c Griffith b Gibbs	60	c Allan b Griffith	25
2	C. Milburn	Northamptonshire	l b w b Hall	6	not out	126
3	T. W. Graveney	Worcestershire	c Allan b Hall	96	not out	30
4	K. F. Barrington	Surrey	b Sobers	19	b Griffith	5
†5	M. C. Cowdrey	Kent	c Gibbs b Hall	9	c Allan b Hall	5
*6	J. M. Parks	Sussex	l b w b Carew	91	b Hall	0
7	B. D'Oliveira	Worcestershire	run out	27		
8	B. R. Knight	Essex	b Griffith	6		
9	F. J. Titmus	Middlesex	c Allan b Hall	6		
10	K. Higgs	Lancashire	c Holford b Gibbs	13		
11	I. J. Jones	Glamorgan	not out	0		
			B 7, l-b 10, w , n-b 5,	22	B 4, l-b 2, w , n-b ,	6
			Total	355	Total	197

FALL OF THE WICKETS

1—8   2—123   3—164   4—198   5—203   6—251   7—266   8—296   9—355   10—355
1—37   2—43   3—67   4—67   5—   6—   7—   8—   9—   10—

ANALYSIS OF BOWLING

Name	1st Innings						2nd Innings					
	O.	M.	R.	W.	Wd.	N-b	O.	M.	R.	W.	Wd.	N-b
Sobers	39	12	89	1	...	...	8	4	8	0	...	...
Hall	36	2	106	4	...	2	14	1	65	2	...	...
Griffith	28	4	79	1	...	3	11	2	43	2	...	...
Gibbs	37.3	18	48	2	...	...	13	4	40	0	...	...
Carew	3	0	11	1	...	...	...	...	...	...	...	...
Holford	...	...	...	...	...	...	9	1	35	0	...	...

Umpires—J. S. Buller & W. F. Price

Scorers—A. Fowler & J. A. Griffiths

† Captain   * Wicket-keeper

Play begins 1st, 2nd, 3rd, & 4th days at 11.30   5th day at 11
Stumps drawn 1st, 2nd, 3rd & 4th days at 6.30   5th day at 5.30 or 6
Luncheon Interval 1.30 p.m.—2.10 p.m.
Tea Interval 4.15 p.m.—4.35 p.m. (may be varied according to state of game)
New Ball—may be taken after 85 overs have been bowled with the old one

West Indies won the toss

---

partnerships of post-war Test cricket. In their first innings, the West Indians had disappointed, allowing Lancashire's Ken Higgs to take a personal best 6 for 91 in 33 overs. In reply, two England players made nineties – Tom Graveney, now in his fortieth year, and Jim Parks – and built a useful first innings lead of 86. By the time Higgs and Barry Knight had reduced West Indies to 25 for 3, thoughts of an England victory to square the series were in everybody's minds.

The partnership between Sobers and Holford lasted five hours and twenty minutes. The pair came together with more than a day and a half of the match remaining and the weather forecast was good. There could have been little realistic hope of saving the game, but the cousins did it. Sobers made 163 not out, two more than he had scored at Old Trafford in the First Test, and Holford, in only his second Test, made 105 not out.

England went after the victory that Sobers dangled in front of them by his declaration, but stumbled to 67 for 4. They were saved by the other man playing in his second Test, Colin Milburn, who hit 126 not out.

1967: England v India

(2nd Test) June 22, 23, 24, 26
England won by an innings and 124 runs

It is hard to remember how strong the England team was almost half a century ago, but this Test Match, the second of the three-match series, was their seventh consecutive victory against India. At Lord's this match gave England their sixth win in six attempts, in the series which stretched back to 1932.

England were doing without their best opener, Geoffrey Boycott, by choice. The Yorkshireman had scored 246 not out in the First Test at his home ground, Headingley, but had taken 573 minutes to get there, so the selectors dropped him for slow batting. Ken Barrington, who had missed the Lord's Test two years earlier for exactly the same reason, was promoted to open in his place, and Dennis Amiss came in at number three.

India's woes started early. With the score at 22 for 1, Sardesai was hit on the hand by a ball from John Snow and had to retire hurt. He came back later, but not before the England bowlers had got

The England team. *L–r, back*: Edrich, Hobbs, Snow, Brown, d'Oliveira, Amiss.
Front: Barrington, Graveney, Close (captain), Murray, Illingworth.

England won by an innings and 124 runs

 LORD'S **GROUND**

ENGLAND v. INDIA

THURS., FRI., SAT., MON. & TUES., June 22, 23, 24, 26 & 27, 1967   (5-day Match)

INDIA

		First Innings		Second Innings	
1 D. N. Sardesai	Bombay	c Murray b Illingworth	28	absent hurt	
*2 F. M. Engineer	Bombay	c Murray b Brown	8	c Amiss b Snow	8
3 A. L. Wadekar	Bombay	c Illingw'h b D'Oliveira	57	b Illingworth	19
4 C. G. Borde	Maharashtra	b Snow	0	c Snow b Close	1
†5 Nawab of Pataudi	Hyderabad	c Murray b Brown	5	c Graveney b Close	5
6 R. F. Surti	Gujerat	c Murray b D'Oliveira	6	c D'Oliveira b Illingw'h	0
7 V. Subramanya	Mysore	c Murray b Brown	0	c Edrich b Illingworth	1
8 B. K. Kunderan	Mysore	c Murray b Snow	20	l b w b Illingworth	47
9 E. A. S. Prasanna	Mysore	run out	17	c D'Oliveira b Illingw'h	0
10 B. S. Chandrasekhar	Punjab	not out	2	not out	3
11 B. S. Bedi	Punjab	c Amiss b Snow	5	b Illingworth	11
		B 2, l-b 2, w , n-b	4	B 11, l-b 4, w , n-b	15
		Total	152	Total	110

FALL OF THE WICKETS

1—12 2—24 3—29 4—45 5—58 6—102 7—112 8—144 9—145 10—152
1—8 2—60 3—67 4—79 5—80 6—86 7—90 8—101 9—110 10—

ANALYSIS OF BOWLING

Name	1st Innings						2nd Innings					
	O.	M.	R.	W.	Wd.	N-b	O.	M.	R.	W.	Wd.	N-b
Snow	20.4	5	49	3	...	...	8	4	12	1	...	...
Brown	18	3	61	3	...	...	5	2	10	0	...	...
D'Oliveira	15	6	38	2	...	...	22.3	12	29	6	...	...
Illingworth	2	2	0	1	...	...	6	1	16	0	...	...
Hobbs	...	...	...	...	...	...	15	5	28	2	...	...
Close	...	...	...	...	...	...	...	...	...	...	...	...

ENGLAND

		First Innings		Second Innings
1 J. H. Edrich	Surrey	c and b Surti	12	
2 K. F. Barrington	Surrey	b Chandrasekhar	97	
3 D. L. Amiss	Warwickshire	b Chandrasekhar	29	
4 T. W. Graveney	Worcestershire	st Engineer b Bedi	151	
5 B. D'Oliveira	Worcestershire	c and b Chandrasekhar	33	
†6 D. B. Close	Yorkshire	c Borde b Prasanna	7	
*7 J. T. Murray	Middlesex	b Chandrasekhar	7	
8 R. Illingworth	Yorkshire	l b w b Chandrasekhar	4	
9 R. N. S. Hobbs	Essex	b Bedi	7	
10 D. J. Brown	Warwickshire	c Pataudi b Bedi	5	
11 J. A. Snow	Sussex	not out	8	
		B 5, l-b 18, w 1, n-b 2,	26	B , l-b , w , n-b ,
		Total	386	Total

FALL OF THE WICKETS

1—46 2—107 3—185 4—307 5—334 6—359 7—365 8—372 9—372 10—386
1— 2— 3— 4— 5— 6— 7— 8— 9— 10—

ANALYSIS OF BOWLING

Name	1st Innings						2nd Innings					
	O.	M.	R.	W.	Wd.	N-b	O.	M.	R.	W.	Wd.	N-b
Surti	31	10	67	1	...	2	...	...	...	...	...	...
Subramanya	7	1	20	0	1	...	...	...	...	...	...	...
Chandrasekhar	53	9	127	5	...	...	...	...	...	...	...	...
Bedi	31.2	13	68	3	...	...	...	...	...	...	...	...
Prasanna	32	5	78	1	...	...	...	...	...	...	...	...

Scorer—A. Fowler

Umpires—J. S. Buller & A. Jepson

† Captain   * Wicket-keeper

Play begins 1st, 2nd, 3rd & 4th days at 11.30   5th day at 11
Stumps drawn 1st, 2nd, 3rd & 4th days at 6.30   5th day at 5.30 or 6
Luncheon Interval 1.30 p.m.—2.10 p.m.
Tea Interval 4.15 p.m.—4.35 p.m. (may be varied according to state of game)

India won the toss

at India's middle order. Nobody was able to stay with Ajit Wadekar, who stood alone in making 57 in two and a quarter hours. England's bowlers were helped immensely by the performance of John Murray behind the stumps. By taking six catches on the first day, including at least one off every bowler, he equalled the Test record then held jointly by Australia's Wally Grout and South Africa's Denis Lindsay.

India's weakness had always been in their opening bowlers. Surti and Subramanya were never the most threatening of pace attacks, and although Surti removed John Edrich soon enough, it was left to the spinners to try to work their way through the rest. But Barrington and then Graveney, between showers and bad light, put the game well out of reach of the visitors. Tom Graveney's 113th century of his career was completed on the Saturday morning, and when he was stumped in the first over after lunch, the last five wickets fell for just 27 runs. But it was enough: Illingworth took 6 for 29 in India's second innings and only Kunderan, who opened in place of the injured Sardesai, offered any resistance. It was all over so quickly that they could not even wait for the Queen to arrive. Both teams were presented to her half an hour after the game was over.

1967: England v Pakistan

(1st Test) July 27, 28, 29, 31, August 1
Match drawn

Another rain-affected Lord's Test nevertheless had several important landmarks. It was, for a start, John Murray's final Test appearance, only five weeks after his record performance against India. Perhaps the most significant achievement, in terms of the match, was Hanif Mohammad's only Test century in England, a mammoth 187 not out in 542 minutes – a day and a half's batting, but still barely half the length of his epic 337 against West Indies almost a decade earlier. Hanif scored over half his side's runs.

The batting performance of the summer, though, was not Hanif's but Ken Barrington's. In his fifteenth Test innings at Lord's the great Surrey batsman finally hit a century, and it was to be followed by two more centuries in the next two matches against Pakistan. Barrington's Test scores in 1967 were 93 (run out), 46, 97, 75, 13, 148, 14, 109 not out, 142 and 13 not out, giving him a Test average of Bradmanesque proportions – 93.75. Even then he had to take second place to Geoff Boycott, who only played three of the Tests, but thanks mainly to his ultra-slow 246 not out (which seemed quite fast when compared to Hanif at Lord's), averaged 97.66.

Pakistan, rather surprisingly, called on no fewer than four players who were not part of the touring party but who were playing professionally in England that summer. Nasim-ul-Ghani (Longton) and Intikhab Alam (West of Scotland) were playing league cricket, and Khalid Ibadulla (Warwickshire) and Mushtaq Mohammad (Northamptonshire) were playing county cricket when they came to the aid of their injury-stricken countrymen, but between them in the first innings they scored just 31 runs.

The leading wicket-taker for Pakistan was HM the Queen. The Test against India in June had ended before the Queen arrived. Against Pakistan the Queen met the teams after the visitors' first innings had been completed on the fourth day, and by close of play, her handshakes had accounted for four England wickets for just 95 runs. Thanks to a brisk 81 not out by Basil D'Oliveira the next morning, England were able to set Pakistan 257 to win in 210 minutes. In the event, they made just 88 for 3 in 62 overs, a display described by *Wisden* as 'the sort of cricket that has caused attendances to fall so alarmingly at first-class matches in England'.

Hanif Mohammad: small, defiant and prolific.

Match Drawn

 LORD'S **GROUND**

ENGLAND v. PAKISTAN

Thurs., Fri., Sat., Mon. & Tues., July 27, 28, 29, 31 & August 1, 1967   (5-day Match)

ENGLAND

		First Innings		Second Innings	
1 C. Milburn	...Northamptonshire	c Bari b Asif	3	c Asif b Majid	32
2 W. E. Russell	...........Middlesex	b Intikhab	43	b Majid	12
3 K. F. Barrington	............Surrey	c Bari b Asif	148	b Intikhab	14
4 T. W. Graveney	..Worcestershire	b Salim	81	c Ibadulla b Asif	30
5 B. D'Oliveira	......Worcestershire	c Intikhab b Mushtaq	59	not out	81
†6 D. B. Close	................Yorkshire	c sub b Salim	4	st Bari b Nasim	36
*7 J. T. Murray	..........Middlesex	b Salim	0	c and b Nasim	0
8 R. Illingworth	..........Yorkshire	b Asif	4	c and b Nasim	9
9 K. Higgs	................Lancashire	l b w b Mushtaq	14	c Hanif b Intikhab	1
10 J. A. Snow	....................Sussex	b Mushtaq	0	b Mushtaq	7
11 R. N. S. Hobbs	............Essex	not out	1	not out	1
‡ Innings closed		B , l-b **5**, w , n-b **7**,	12	B **12**, l-b **5**, w , n-b **1**,	18
		Total	369	Total	‡241

FALL OF THE WICKETS

1—5   2—82   3—283   4—283   5—287   6—287   7—292   8—352   9—354   10—369
1—33   2—48   3—76   4—95   5—199   6—201   7—215   8—220   9—239   10—

ANALYSIS OF BOWLING

Name	1st Innings						2nd Innings					
	O.	M.	R.	W.	Wd.	N-b	O.	M.	R.	W.	Wd.	N-b
Salim Altaf	33	6	74	3		3	1	0	4	0	...	...
Asif Iqbal	28	10	76	3		4	21	5	50	1	...	1
Khalid Ibadulla	3	0	5	0								
Majid Jahangir	11	2	28	0			10	0	32	2	...	...
Nasim-ul-Ghani	12	1	36	0			13	3	32	3	...	...
Intikhab Alam	29	3	86	1			30	7	70	2	...	...
Mushtaq Mohammad	11.3	3	23	3			16	4	35	1	...	...
Saeed Ahmad	11	3	29	0			...	...	...	...	...	...

PAKISTAN

		First Innings		Second Innings	
1 Khalid Ibadulla	...............Lahore	b Higgs	8	c Close b Illingworth	32
2 Javed Burki	....................Karachi	l b w b Higgs	31	c and b Barrington	13
3 Mushtaq Mohammad	...Karachi	c Murray b Higgs	4	not out	30
†4 Hanif Mohammad	.......P.I.A.	not out	187		
5 Majid Jahangir	..............Lahore	c and b Hobbs	5	c Close b Barrington	5
6 Nasim-ul-Ghani	..........P.W.D.	c D'Oliveira b Snow	2		
7 Saeed Ahmad	...............Karachi	c Graveney b Snow	6	not out	6
8 Intikhab Alam	..............Karachi	l b w b Illingworth	17		
9 Asif Iqbal	.......................Karachi	c Barrington b Illingw'h	76		
*10 Wasim Bari	...................Karachi	c Close b Barrington	13		
11 Salim Altaf	...................Lahore	c Milburn b Snow	2		
		B **1**, l-b **2**, w , n-b ,	3	B **1**, l-b **1**, w , n-b ,	2
		Total	354	Total	88

FALL OF THE WICKETS

1—19   2—25   3—67   4—76   5—91   6—99   7—139   8—269   9—310   10—354
1—27   2—39   3—77   4—   5—   6—   7—   8—   9—   10—

ANALYSIS OF BOWLING

Name	1st Innings						2nd Innings					
	O.	M.	R.	W.	Wd.	N-b	O.	M.	R.	W.	Wd.	N-b
Snow	45.1	11	120		...	...						
Higgs	39	12	81	3	...	...	4	2	6	0	...	...
D'Oliveira	15	7	17	0	...	...	6	3	6	0	...	...
Illingworth	31	14	48	2	...	...						
Hobbs	35	16	46	1	...	...	15	11	10	1	...	...
Barrington	11	1	29	1	...	...	16	9	28	0	...	...
Close	6	3	10	0	...	...	13	2	23	0	...	...
							8	5	13	0	...	...

Umpires—C. S. Elliott & A. Jepson

† Captain   * Wicket-keeper   Scorer—A. Fowler

Play begins 1st, 2nd, 3rd & 4th days at 11.30   5th day at 11
Stumps drawn 1st, 2nd, 3rd & 4th days at 6.30   5th day at 5.30 or 6
Luncheon Interval 1.30 p.m.—2.10 p.m.
Tea Interval 4.15 p.m.—4.35 p.m. (may be varied according to state of game)

England won the toss

1968: England v Australia

(2nd Test) June 20, 21, 22, 24, 25
Match drawn

David Brown and Colin Cowdrey put on a cheerful face as rain
denies England.

The old Tavern had been demolished and the new Tavern Stand put up in its place in time for the arrival of the Australians in 1968. Most people thought it was a pity that the atmosphere of the Tavern had been changed for ever, even John Arlott admitted that the better viewing opportunities afforded by the new Tavern concourse 'may not allay alcoholically nostalgic regrets for the Tavern which is gone'. But in the years since the redevelopment of the site, the consumption of alcohol and the enjoyment of the spectators has not noticeably decreased.

This was the 200th Test between England and Australia (Australia had won the 199th, at Old Trafford two weeks earlier), and Cowdrey's ninety-ninth Test in a career that stretched back to 1954. But the weather was to hold all the cards. England won the toss (103 out of the first 200 went to England, 97 to Australia) and chose to bat. Rain washed out all play after lunch on the first day, when England were 53 for the loss of Edrich. The next morning, Colin Milburn took the Australian attack apart, adding 67 to his total in 80 minutes, before he was caught on the boundary trying to hit the leg spinner Gleeson for another six. The rain then took over the match to such an extent that England had only reached 351 for 7 at the end of the third day, with injuries to Barrington and Jarman (chipped bones in the fingers) along the way. Jarman injured the finger again when he batted and missed the next Test match as a result.

Cowdrey declared on the fourth morning, and the English bowlers then put the Australian batsmen to the sword. David Brown, in particular, bowled with a fire he rarely showed at Test level, and thanks to some brilliant close catching (not otherwise a feature of England's summer), he and Barry Knight dismissed Australia for 78. Cowdrey, who took three catches, established a new record of 111 Test catches when he caught Gleeson. But on the final day, despite conditions which were very much to Underwood's liking (18-15-8-2), the rain returned and Australia escaped with a draw. A few weeks later, at the Oval, the rain could not prevent Underwood and England securing a thrilling last day victory.

At least the rain gave the inmates of the new Tavern concourse a chance to keep on drinking, and reminiscing about the good old days before M.C.C. did away with their most famous amenity.

Match Drawn

 LORD'S GROUND

ENGLAND v. AUSTRALIA
(200th MATCH)
Thurs., Fri., Sat., Mon. & Tues., June 20, 21, 22, 24 & 25, 1968   (5-day Match)

ENGLAND

			First Innings		Second Innings
1	G. Boycott	Yorkshire	c Sheahan b McKenzie.	49	
2	J. H. Edrich	Surrey	c Cowper b McKenzie...	7	
3	C. Milburn	Northamptonshire	c Walters b Gleeson......	83	
†4	M. C. Cowdrey	Kent	c Cowper b McKenzie...	45	
5	K. F. Barrington	Surrey	c Jarman b Connolly ...	75	
6	T. W. Graveney	Worcestershire	c Jarman b Connolly ...	14	
7	B. R. Knight	Leicestershire	not out	27	
*8	A. Knott	Kent	run out	33	
9	J. A. Snow	Sussex	not out	0	
10	D. J. Brown	Warwickshire			
11	D. L. Underwood	Kent	Innings closed		

B 7, l-b 5, w 1, n-b 5, 18   B , l-b , w , n-b ,

Total 351   Total ....

FALL OF THE WICKETS

1—10 2—142 3—147 4—244 5—271 6—330 7—351 8— 9— 10—
1— 2— 3— 4— 5— 6— 7— 8— 9— 10—

ANALYSIS OF BOWLING

Name	1st Innings						2nd Innings					
	O.	M.	R.	W.	Wd.	N-b	O.	M.	R.	W.	Wd.	N-b
McKenzie	45	18	111	3	1							
Hawke	35	7	82	0								
Connolly	26.3	8	55	2		5						
Walters	3	2	2	0								
Cowper	8	2	40	0								
Gleeson	27	11	43	1								

AUSTRALIA

			First Innings		Second Innings
†1	W. M. Lawry	Victoria	c Knott b Brown	0	c Brown b Snow............ 28
2	I. R. Redpath	Victoria	c Cowdrey b Brown......	4	b Underwood 53
3	R. M. Cowper	Victoria	c Graveney b Snow	8	c Underw'd b Barring'tn 32
4	K. D. Walters	N.S.W.	c Knight b Brown......	26	b Underwood.............. 0
5	A. P. Sheahan	Victoria	c Knott b Knight	6	not out 0
6	I. M. Chappell	S. Australia	l b w b Knight	6	not out 12
7	N. J. N. Hawke	S. Australia	c Cowdrey b Knight	7	
8	G. D. McKenzie	W. Australia	b Brown	2	
9	J. W. Gleeson	N.S.W.	c Cowdrey b Brown......	5	
*10	B. N. Jarman	S. Australia	retired hurt..............	14	
11	A. N. Connolly	Victoria	not out	0	

B , l-b 2, w , n-b 4, 6   B , l-b , w , n-b 2, 2

Total 78   Total 127

FALL OF THE WICKETS

1—1 2—12 3—23 4—46 5—52 6—58 7—63 8—78 9—78 10—
1—66 2—93 3—97 4—115 5— 6— 7— 8— 9— 10—

ANALYSIS OF BOWLING

Name	1st Innings						2nd Innings					
	O.	M.	R.	W.	Wd.	N-b	O.	M.	R.	W.	Wd.	N-b
Snow	9	5	14	1		3	12	5	30	1		2
Brown	14	5	42	5		1	19	9	40	0		
Knight	10.4	5	16	3			16	9	35	0		
Underwood							18	15	8	2		
Barrington							2	0	12	1		

Umpires—J. S. Buller & A. E. Fagg

Scorers—E. Solomon & D. Sherwood

† Captain   * Wicket-keeper

Play begins 1st, 2nd, 3rd & 4th days at 11.30   5th day at 11

Stumps drawn 1st, 2nd, 3rd & 4th days at 6.30   5th day at 5.30 or 6

Luncheon Interval 1.30 p.m.—2.10 p.m.

Tea Interval 4.15 p.m.—4.35 p.m. (may be varied according to state of game)

England won the toss

1969: England v West Indies

(2nd Test) June 26, 27, 28, 30, July 1
Match drawn

'The sun shone gloriously all the time.' It is not often that *Wisden* is able to report a Lord's Test so favoured by the weather, but despite the sun no result was possible. Altogether 1,314 runs were scored for the loss of 36 wickets, four centuries were scored, and Gary Sobers had to leave the field because of an injury for only the second time in 75 Tests. Over 100,000 watched the match and gate receipts of £67,700 were only £5,000 short of the record set in 1968 when Australians were the visitors.

Although Charlie Davis made 103 in a little over six hours, the only century by a West Indian in that summer's three Test series, and although John Snow took five wickets in West Indies' total of 380, the match belonged to John Hampshire. Selected because of an injury to Tom Graveney (not to mention Barrington, Cowdrey, Dexter and Milburn who were all also out of action), Hampshire became the first Englishman ever to hit a hundred on Test debut at Lord's. Before this, the 55th Test at the ground, only one man had achieved that feat, Harry Graham of Australia in 1893. Hampshire came to the wicket when England were in real trouble at 37 for 4 (Sobers 2 for 9 in 11 overs), and he stayed until England

Ray Illingworth leads England out for the first time.

LORD'S **GROUND** 6ᴰ

Match Drawn

ENGLAND v. WEST INDIES

Thurs., Fri., Sat., Mon. & Tues., June 26, 27, 28, 30 & July 1, 1969   (5-day Match)

WEST INDIES

			First Innings		Second Innings	
1 G. S. Camacho	Guyana	c Sharpe b Snow	67	b D'Oliveira	45
2 R. C. Fredericks	Guyana	c Hampshire b Knight	63	c Hampshire b Illingw'h	60
3 C. A. Davis	Trinidad	c Knott b Brown	103	c Illingw'h b D'Oliveira	0
4 B. F. Butcher	Guyana	c Hampshire b Brown	29	b Illingworth	24
†5 G. S. Sobers	Barbados	run out	18	not out	50
6 C. H. Lloyd	Guyana	c Illingworth b Brown	32	c Knott b Snow	70
7 J. N. Shepherd	Barbados	c Edrich b Snow	23	c Sharpe b Illingworth	11
*8 T. M. Findlay	Windward Is.	b Snow	6	c Sharpe b Knight	11
9 V. A. Holder	Barbados	l b w b Snow	18	run out	7
10 L. R. Gibbs	Guyana	c Knott b Snow	3	b Knight	5
11 G. Shillingford	Windward Is.	not out	9	Innings closed	
		B 5, l-b 4, w , n-b	9	B 4, l-b 7, w , n-b 1, 12	
		Total	380	Total	295

FALL OF THE WICKETS

1—106 2—151 3—167 4—217 5—247 6—324 7—336 8—343 9—376 10—380
1—73   2—73   3—128 4—135 5—191 6—232 7—263 8—280 9—295 10—

ANALYSIS OF BOWLING

		1st Innings							2nd Innings				
Name	O.	M.	R.	W.	Wd.	N-b		O.	M.	R.	W.	Wd.	N-b
Snow	39	5	114	5	...	...		22	4	69	1	...	1
Brown	38	8	99	3	...	...		9	3	25	0	...	...
Knight	38	11	65	1	...	...		27.5	6	78	2	...	...
D'Oliveira	26	10	46	0	...	...		15	2	45	2	...	...
Illingworth	16	4	39	0	...	...		27	9	66	3	...	...
Parfitt	1	0	8	0	...	...		...	...	...	...	...	...

ENGLAND

			First Innings		Second Innings	
1 G. Boycott	Yorkshire	c Findlay b Shepherd	23	c Butcher b Shillingford	106
2 J. H. Edrich	Surrey	c Fredericks b Holder		c Camacho b Holder	1
3 P. H. Parfitt	Middlesex	c Davis b Sobers	4	c Findlay b Shepherd	39
4 B. D'Oliveira	Worcestershire	c Shepherd b Sobers	0	c Fredericks b Gibbs	18
5 P. J. Sharpe	Yorkshire	b Holder	11	c Davis b Sobers	86
6 J. H. Hampshire	Yorkshire	l b w b Shepherd	107	run out	5
*7 A. Knott	Kent	b Shillingford	53	b Shillingford	11
†8 R. Illingworth	Leicestershire	c and b Gibbs	113	not out	9
9 B. R. Knight	Leicestershire	l b w b Shillingford	0	not out	1
10 D. J. Brown	Warwickshire	c Findlay b Shepherd	1		
11 J. A. Snow	Sussex	not out	9		
		B 1, l-b 5, w , n-b 10, 16		B 9, l-b 5, w , n-b 5, 19	
		Total	344	Total	295

FALL OF THE WICKETS

1—19 2—37 3—37 4—37 5—61 6—189 7—249 8—250 9—261 10—344
1—1   2—94 3—137 4—263 5—271 6—272 7—292 8—   9—   10—

ANALYSIS OF BOWLING

		1st Innings							2nd Innings				
Name	O.	M.	R.	W.	Wd.	N-b		O.	M.	R.	W.	Wd.	N-b
Sobers	26	12	57	2	...	...		29	8	72	1	...	2
Holder	38	16	83	2	...	7		11	4	36	1	...	3
Shillingford	19	4	53	2	...	3		13	4	30	2	...	...
Shepherd	43	14	74	3	...	...		12	3	45	1	...	...
Gibbs	27.4	9	53	1	...	...		41	14	93	1	...	...
Davis	1	1	0	2	...	...		...	...	...	...	...	...
Butcher	3	1	6	0	...	...		...	...	...	...	...	...

Scorers—E. Solomon & W. F. B. Hoyos

Umpires—J. S. Buller & A. E. Fagg

† Captain   * Wicket-keeper

Play begins 1st, 2nd, 3rd & 4th days at 11.30   5th day at 11
Stumps drawn 1st, 2nd, 3rd & 4th days at 6.30   5th day at 5.30 or 6
Luncheon Interval 1.30 p.m.—2.10 p.m.
Tea Interval 4.15 p.m.—4.35 p.m. (may be varied according to state of game)

West Indies won the toss

---

were 249 for 7. Then his captain and fellow Yorkshireman Ray Illingworth, took over and largely unaided by runs off anybody else's bat, took the score up to 344 before he gave a return catch early on the Monday morning to Lance Gibbs. On the Saturday afternoon, when Sobers was off the field, Gibbs had been acting as captain, so he was probably relieved to take the final wicket before England's revival became a first innings' lead.

In the West Indies' second innings, when Sobers came in to bat at number seven it was with a runner, Steve Camacho. He made a quick 50 before declaring, leaving England most of the last day to make 322. They might have made them, but the bowler who did as much as anybody to prevent a home victory was Sobers, who bowled 29 overs, mainly in his faster style, and without a runner. At the pavilion end, Gibbs bowled 41 overs, 40 in succession, and despite Boycott becoming the third Yorkshireman to make a hundred in the match, England finished tantalisingly short.

1969: England v New Zealand

(1st Test) July 24, 25, 26, 28
England won by 230 runs

England won by 230 runs, but even so New Zealand were not outclassed. New Zealand gave three new players their first caps – Ken Wadsworth, the wicketkeeper-batsman who died seven years later of cancer, aged 29, Hedley Howarth, whose younger brother Geoff would have his finest hour at Lord's nine years later, and Dayle Hadlee, whose father had captained New Zealand at Lord's twenty years earlier and whose younger brother Richard would become the greatest New Zealand bowler of all time. England awarded a first Test cap to Derbyshire's fiery bowler Alan Ward, whose Test career was to be disappointingly short.

All the debutants made significant contributions to the game (Hadlee's caught-and-bowled off Alan Knott was a brilliant left-handed effort described by *Wisden* as one 'which only a superbly fit athlete could have reached'), but the match belonged to two scarcely older hands, one Englishman and one New Zealander.

After a pretty equal first two days, England dominated the Saturday thanks to John Edrich's 115 and 'some painful early batting from Boycott'.

Alan Knott caught and bowled by Dayle Hadlee for 8 in England's first innings.

It is noticeable that when Geoffrey Boycott batted slowly, he was castigated for it (sometimes with good reason, it must be said), but when opponents did it, they were praised for their 'calm and skilled defiance', to quote EW Swanton in the *Daily Telegraph*. Glenn Turner was one such. Here at Lord's, at the age of 22 years and 63 days, he carried his bat through the second New Zealand innings, scoring only 43 but staying there for four and a quarter hours while all around him crumbled. He was the youngest batsman ever to achieve the feat, the first New Zealander, and only the fourth man to do so at Lord's. The reason England won, however, was Derek Underwood. Seven for 32 in 31 overs was a brilliant effort, backed up by Illingworth's tactical brain which meant that Turner only faced 79 of the 186 balls 'Deadly Derek' bowled. So England won with half an hour to spare at the end of the fourth day.

England won by 230 runs

LORD'S GROUND 6D.

ENGLAND v. NEW ZEALAND

THURS., FRI., SAT., MON. & TUES., July 24, 25, 26, 28 & 29, 1969 (5-day Match)

ENGLAND

		First Innings		Second Innings	
1 G. Boycott	Yorkshire	c Congdon b Motz	0	c Turner b Pollard	47
2 J. H. Edrich	Surrey	c Motz b Taylor	16	c Wadsworth b Hadlee	115
3 P. J. Sharpe	Yorkshire	c Turner b Taylor	20	c Congdon b Howarth	46
4 K. W. R. Fletcher	Essex	b Motz	9	b Howarth	7
5 B. D'Oliveira	Worcestershire	run out	37	c Wadsworth b Taylor	12
*6 A. Knott	Kent	c and b Hadlee	8	l b w b Howarth	10
†7 R. Illingworth	Leicestershire	c Wadsworth b Howarth	53	c Wadsworth b Taylor	0
8 B. R. Knight	Leicestershire	c Hadlee b Pollard	29	b Motz	49
9 D. J. Brown	Warwickshire	not out	9	b Motz	4
10 D. L. Underwood	Kent	c Pollard b Howarth	11	not out	19
11 A. Ward	Derbyshire	b Taylor	1		
		B 1, l-b 3, w 1, n-b 1,	6	B 4, l-b 15, w , n-b 5,	24
		Total	190	Total	340

FALL OF THE WICKETS

1—0 2—27 3—47 4—47 5—63 6—113 7—158 8—186 9—188 10—190
1—125 2—199 3—234 4—243 5—259 6—259 7—259 8—284 9—300 10—340

ANALYSIS OF BOWLING

Name	1st Innings						2nd Innings					
	O.	M.	R.	W.	Wd.	N-b	O.	M.	R.	W.	Wd.	N-b
Motz	19	5	46	2			39.4	17	78	2		4
Hadlee	14	2	48	1	1		16	5	43	1		1
Taylor	13.5	4	35	3		1	25	4	62	3		
Howarth	19	9	24	2			49	20	102	1		
Pollard	9	1	31	1			8	2	20	1		
Burgess							3	0	11	0		

NEW ZEALAND

		First Innings		Second Innings	
†1 G. T. Dowling	Canterbury	c Illing'th b Underw'd	41	c Knott b Ward	4
2 G. M. Turner	Otago	c Knott b Ward	5	not out	43
3 B. E. Congdon	Central Districts	c Sharpe b Ward	41	c Fletcher b Underwood	17
4 B. F. Hastings	Canterbury	c Ward b Illingworth	23	c Knott b Underwood	0
5 V. Pollard	Central Districts	c Ward b Underwood	8	l b w b Underwood	0
6 M. G. Burgess	Auckland	l b w b Illingworth	10	l b w b Underwood	6
*7 K. J. Wadsworth	C. Districts	l b w b Illingworth	14	b Underwood	5
8 B. R. Taylor	Canterbury	c Brown b Illingworth	3	b Underwood	0
9 R. C. Motz	Canterbury	b Underwood	15	c Knott b Underwood	23
10 D. R. Hadlee	Canterbury	c Illing'th b Underw'd	1	c Sharpe b D'Oliveira	7
11 H. J. Howarth	Auckland	not out	0	b Ward	4
		B 4, l-b 4, w , n-b	8	B 5, l-b 4, w , n-b 1,	10
		Total	169	Total	131

FALL OF THE WICKETS

1—14 2—76 3—92 4—101 5—126 6—137 7—146 8—150 9—168 10—169
1—5 2—27 3—45 4—45 5—67 6—67 7—73 8—101 9—126 10—131

ANALYSIS OF BOWLING

Name	1st Innings						2nd Innings					
	O.	M.	R.	W.	Wd.	N-b	O.	M.	R.	W.	Wd.	N-b
Brown	12	5	17	0								
Ward	14	2	49	2			5	3	6	0		1
Underwood	29.3	16	38	4			10.5	0	48	2		
Knight	10	3	20	0			31	18	32	7		
Illingworth	22	8	37	4			3	1	5	0		
D'Oliveira							18	9	24	0		
							8	3	6	1		

Umpires—J. S. Buller & A. Jepson   Scorers—E. Solomon & R. M. Cairns

† Captain   * Wicket-keeper

Play begins 1st, 2nd, 3rd & 4th days at 11.30 5th day at 11
Stumps drawn 1st, 2nd, 3rd & 4th days at 6.30 5th day at 5.30 or 6
Luncheon Interval 1.30 p.m.—2.10 p.m.
Tea Interval 4.15 p.m.—4.35 p.m. (may be varied according to state of game)

England won the toss

1971: England v Pakistan

(2nd Test) June 17, 18, 19, 21, 22 (no play on third day)
Match drawn

After a year without an official Test at Lord's, it was back to normal service in 1971. The 1970 series against South Africa had been cancelled because of the protests against apartheid in that country, and replaced by a series between England and the Rest of The World, captained by Gary Sobers. At the time they had been billed as official Tests, and caps were awarded, but retrospectively they were downgraded. Pity poor Alan Jones, the Glamorgan opener, whose only appearances in England colours were in 1970.

Back to normal service meant that the weather once again played a major role. Just as on their first appearance at Lord's in 1954, the Pakistanis were given no chance of a result by virtue of the rain that took seventeen hours and seventeen minutes from the allotted total of 30 hours. On the first day, play began at 3.30 pm, and only 23 minutes' play was possible on the second day. The third day, the Saturday, was washed out completely, so it was not until the afternoon of the fourth day (play began at 2.30 pm that day) that Illingworth declared. Geoffrey Boycott had managed to squeeze in a hundred between the downpours, 'not having made a glimmer of an error', as *Wisden* put it.

Geoffrey Boycott at work.

ENGLAND

G Boycott	not out	121	
BW Luckhurst	c Wasim b Salim	46	not out ... 53
JH Edrich	c Asif Masood b Pervez	37	
DL Amiss	not out	19	
RA Hutton	did not bat		not out ... 58
	(B 6, LB 2, W 5, NB 5)	18	(B 1, LB 1, NB 4) ... 6
Totals	(2 wkts dec)	241	(0 wkt) ... 117

Did not bat: BL D'Oliveira, †R Illingworth, *APE Knott, P Lever, N Gifford, JSE Price.

PAKISTAN

Aftab Gul	c Knott b Hutton	33
Sadiq Mohammad	c Knott b d'Oliveira	28
Zaheer Abbas	c Hutton b Lever	40
Mushtaq Mohammad	c Amiss b Hutton	2
Asif Iqbal	c Knott b Gifford	9
Majid J Khan	c Edrich b Price	9
† Intikhab Alam	c Gifford b Lever	18
* Wasim Bari	c Knott b Price	0
Salim Altaf	not out	0
Asif Masood	b Price	0
Pervez Sajjad	absent ill	0
	(LB 5, W 1, NB 3)	9
Total		148

PAKISTAN	O	M	R	W	O	M	R	W
Asif Masood	21	3	60	0	3	1	3	0
Salim	19	5	42	1	5	2	11	0
Asif Iqbal	13	2	24	0	4	1	11	0
Khan	4	0	16	0	6	2	7	0
Intikhab	20	2	64	0	9	1	26	0
Pervez	6	2	17	1				
Mushtaq					11	3	31	0
Sadiq					5	1	17	0
Gul					1	0	4	0
Zaheer					1	0	1	0

ENGLAND	O	M	R	W
Price	11.4	5	29	3
Lever	16	3	38	2
Gifford	12	6	13	1
Illingworth	7	6	1	0
Hutton	16	5	36	2
D'Oliveira	10	5	22	1

FALL OF WICKETS

Wkt	Eng. 1st	Pak. 1st
1st	124	57
2nd	205	66
3rd		97
4th		117
5th		119
6th		146
7th		148
8th		148
9th		148

† Captain   * Wicketkeeper

Richard Hutton, son of Sir Leonard, was making his Test debut, and unlike his father did not fail at the first attempt. His first Test wicket, that of Aftab Gul, was also Alan Knott's one hundredth in Tests, and gave the Kent wicketkeeper the Test double of 1,000 runs and 100 dismissals. He was still some way behind his illustrious Kent and England predecessor, Godfrey Evans (219 victims), but he eventually went on to overtake even him. Aftab Gul was an interesting character. The 33 he scored in this match was his highest Test score, but he combined the role of Test opener with that of student revolutionary. He was arrested for having the component parts of a nuclear bomb in his garage, or some such charge, but still played first-class cricket while out on bail. The only tour he made to England was in 1971, but it was alleged that his power as a student leader meant that, for several seasons the Pakistan authorities dare not pick a Test side to play in Lahore without him.

It was also a memorable game for John Price, the Middlesex fast bowler. He finished off the Pakistan innings with two wickets in two balls, and was denied the chance of a hat-trick by the absence of Pervez Sajjad through illness. During the match, each of the Pakistan team apart from wicketkeeper Wasim Bari bowled at least one over.

1971: England v India

(1st Test) July 22, 23, 24, 26, 27
Match drawn

John Snow and Sunil Gavaskar collide.

For the second time this summer, the weather played the deciding role in the Lord's Test, with rain coming as India needed 38 more to win with two wickets left. This might have given India their first Test victory in England, but in the event they had to wait another month until the Third Test at the Oval. In all, some five hours' play was lost during the match, with no play at all on the fourth morning.

England won the toss and chose to bat, and were soon in trouble against the spinners – all except Boycott who began his odd sequence of failures against Indian medium-pacers when Abid Ali had him caught for just three. The rest of the England side found Venkataraghavan, Bedi and Chandrasekhar just too much of a handful, and only Knott and John Snow, who made his highest first-class score of 73, came to terms with them. Knott's innings was described by *Wisden* as 'an object lesson on how to tackle spin'.

When India batted, it was their captain Wadekar who led from the front, although Viswanath and Solkar also made good scores. They batted very slowly between the showers on the Saturday, which did not satisfy the 20,000 crowd, but they earned India a first innings lead of nine. This seemed crucial when England batted again and, despite Edrich's 62, they were all out for 191 on the last morning, leaving India 260 minutes to make 183 to win.

The innings began sensationally. Sunil Gavaskar, a small man but a brilliantly gifted batsman, was completing a quick single when he was shoulder-charged by the bowler John Snow who appeared to be attempting to field the ball. Gavaskar fell to the ground, and might have been run out had the England fielders attempted to do so. John Snow was asked after the match by Alec Bedser, chairman of selectors, and Billy Griffith, secretary of M.C.C. and thus the T.C.C.B. as well, to apologise to Gavaskar, and he did so. However, he was dropped from the next Test as a disciplinary measure, and replaced by Peter Lever. Bizarrely, Lever made 88 not out in that Test, his highest score in all cricket, and was then dropped to let Snow back in. So in consecutive Tests, England had dropped a fast bowler after he had made his highest first-class score.

Gavaskar seemed unaffected by John Snow's shoulder charge and went on to make 53, putting on 66 in 50 minutes with Farokh Engineer, who was promoted to bat at number four. However, it was just too little too late and the rain won the day.

ENGLAND

G Boycott	c Engineer b Abid Ali	3	c Wadekar b Venkataraghavan	33
BW Luckhurst	c Solkar b Chandrasekhar	30	b Solkar	1
JH Edrich	c Venkataraghavan b Bedi	18	c Engineer b Bedi	62
DL Amiss	c Engineer b Bedi	9	run out	0
BL D'Oliveira	c Sokar b Chandrasekhar	4	b Bedi	30
* APE Knott	c Wadekar b Venkataraghavan	67	c Wadekar b Chandrasekhar	24
† R Illingworth	c Engineer b Bedi	33	c Wadekar b Venkataraghavan	20
RA Hutton	b Venkataraghavan	20	b Chandrasekhar	0
JA Snow	c Abid Ali b Chandrasekhar	73	c Chandrasekhar b Venkataraghavan	9
N Gifford	b Bedi	17	not out	7
JSE Price	not out	5	c Abid Ali b Venkataraghavan	0
	(B 8, LB 12, NB 5)	25	(LB 5)	5
Total		304		191

INDIA

AV Mankad	c Gifford b Snow	1	c Knott b Snow	5
SM Gavaskar	c Amiss b Price	4	c Edrich b Gifford	53
† AL Wadekar	c Illingworth b Gifford	85	c Boycott b Price	5
DN Sardesai	c Illingworth b Gifford	25	b Illingworth	1
GR Viswanath	c Knott b Hutton	68	c Amiss b Gifford	9
* FM Engineer	c Illingworth b Hutton	28	st Knott b Gifford	35
ED Solkar	c Knott b Gifford	67	not out	6
S Abid Ali	c Luckhurst b Snow	6	c Snow b Illingworth	14
S Venkataraghavan	c Hutton b Price	11	c Hutton b Gifford	7
BS Bedi	c Price b Gifford	0	not out	2
BS Chandrasekhar	not out	0		
	(B 7, LB 9, NB 2)	18	(LB 7, NB 1)	8
Total		313	(8 wkts)	145

INDIA	O	M	R	W	O	M	R	W
Abid Ali	15	3	38	1	9	1	20	0
Solkar	8	3	17	0	6	3	13	1
Venkataraghavan	28	8	44	2	30.5	11	52	4
Chandrasekhar	49	10	110	3	23	7	60	2
Bedi	39.3	18	70	4	30	13	41	2

ENGLAND	O	M	R	W	O	M	R	W
Price	25	9	46	2	4	0	26	1
Snow	31	9	64	2	8	0	23	1
Hutton	24	8	38	2	3	0	12	0
Gifford	45.3	14	84	4	19	4	43	4
D'Oliveira	15	7	20	0				
Illingworth	25	12	43	0	16	2	33	2

FALL OF WICKETS

Wkt	Eng. 1st	Ind. 1st	Eng. 2nd	Ind. 2nd
1st	18	1	4	8
2nd	46	29	65	21
3rd	56	108	70	87
4th	61	125	117	101
5th	71	175	145	108
6th	161	267	153	114
7th	183	279	153	135
8th	223	302	174	145
9th	294	311	189	
10th	304	313	191	

† Captain   * Wicketkeeper

1972: England v Australia

(2nd Test) June 22, 23, 24, 26
Australia won by 8 wickets

Massie's Match: that says it all (or nearly all). Bob Massie, a Western Australian right arm fast medium bowler playing in his first Test match, took sixteen England wickets for 137 runs to give Australia their first victory in a Test match against England since the 1968 series, when they won the opening match at Old Trafford. Massie's first innings performance of eight for 84 in 32.5 overs was astonishing enough, but it was his second innings effort of eight for 53 as England crumbled to 116 all out that won the match for Australia. Massie had played a few games for Northampton-shire Second XI two years earlier, with little success and was not offered a contract. He took his revenge on English cricket in no uncertain terms.

In England's first innings, six men reached 30, but only one went on to reach 50. From a score of 28 for 3 (two of the first three wickets falling to Dennis Lillee), a total of 272 might not look too bad, but on what was essentially a good batting wicket, it was not enough. In overcast conditions, Massie produced a wonderful display of con-trolled swing bowling, both over and round the wicket, and the England batsmen could not ever begin to dominate. Australia's batsmen fared little better, but there were two differences: firstly, Greg Chappell played superbly to make 131, more than twice any other score in the match; and secondly, England had nobody who bowled like Bob Massie. The one man who might have done, Surrey's Geoff

Massie, whose sixteen for 137 is unequalled in a Lord's Test.

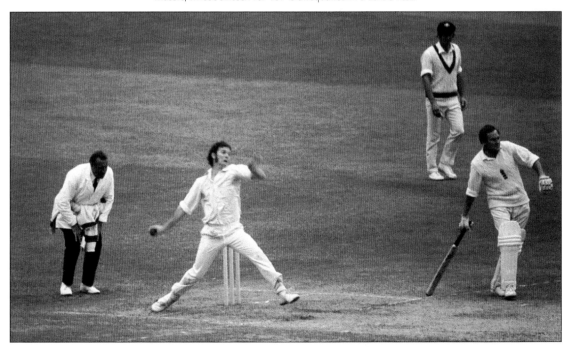

ENGLAND

Batsman	1st innings		2nd innings	
G Boycott	b Massie	11	b Lillee	6
JH Edrich	lbw b Lillee	10	c Marsh b Massie	6
BW Luckhurst	b Lillee	1	c Marsh b Lillee	4
MJK Smith	b Massie	34	c Edwards b Massie	30
BL D'Oliveira	lbw b Massie	32	c GS Chappell b Massie	3
AW Greig	c Marsh b Massie	54	c IM Chappell b Massie	3
* APE Knott	c Colley b Massie	43	c GS Chappell b Massie	12
† R Illingworth	lbw b Massie	30	c Stackpole b Massie	12
JA Snow	b Massie	37	c Marsh b Massie	0
N Gifford	c Marsh b Massie	3	not out	16
JSE Price	not out	4	c GS Chappell b Massie	19
	(LB 6, W 1, NB 6)	13	(W 1, NB 4)	5
Total		272		116

AUSTRALIA

Batsman	1st innings		2nd innings	
KR Stackpole	c Gifford b Price	5	not out	57
BC Francis	b Snow	0	c Knott b Price	9
† IM Chappell	c Smith b Snow	56	c Luckhurst b D'Oliveira	6
GS Chappell	b D'Oliveira	131	not out	7
KD Walters	c Illingworth b Snow	1		
R Edwards	c Smith b Illingworth	28		
JW Gleeson	c Knott b Greig	1		
* RW Marsh	c Greig b Snow	50		
DJ Colley	c Greig b Price	25		
RAL Massie	c Knott b Snow	0		
DK Lillee	not out	2		
	(LB 7, NB 2)	9	(LB 2)	2
Total		308	(2 wkts)	81

AUSTRALIA	O	M	R	W	O	M	R	W
Lillee	28	3	90	2	21	6	50	2
Massie	32.5	7	84	8	27.2	9	53	8
Colley	16	2	42	0	7	1	8	0
GS Chappell	6	1	18	0				
Gleeson	9	1	25	0				

ENGLAND	O	M	R	W	O	M	R	W
Snow	32	13	57	5	8	2	15	0
Price	26.1	5	87	2	7	0	28	1
Greig	29	6	74	1	3	0	17	0
D'Oliveira	17	5	48	1	8	3	14	1
Gifford	11	4	20	0				
Illingworth	7	2	13	1				
Luckhurst					0.5	0	5	0

FALL OF WICKETS

Wkt	Eng. 1st	Aus. 1st	Eng. 2nd	Aus. 2nd
1st	22	1	12	20
2nd	23	7	16	51
3rd	28	82	18	
4th	84	84	25	
5th	97	190	31	
6th	193	212	52	
7th	200	250	74	
8th	260	290	74	
9th	265	290	81	
10th	272	308	116	

† Captain   * Wicketkeeper

Arnold, had dropped out with a hamstring injury on the morning of the match, to be replaced by Middlesex's John Price. Although John Snow, who bowled considerably quicker than Massie, took five wickets in Australia's first innings, there was nobody to support him, and England's policy of going in with two spinners, Ray Illingworth and Norman Gifford, was shown to be a mistake. The fastest bowler on show in the match, though, was Dennis Lillee, and as *Wisden* said, 'he was truly fast ... Massie capitalised on the hostility of his partner.'

England were defeated with plenty of time to spare on the fifth day. Massie's final analysis was, of course, the best ever achieved in a Test at Lord's, and over 100,000 people were there to witness all or part of it over the five days. Receipts of £82,914 were thought to be a world record for a cricket match. Sixteen years later, a similar number of spectators paid over £1 million.

LORD'S GROUND

1973: England v New Zealand

(2nd Test) June 21, 22, 23, 25, 26
Match drawn

A close call for Burgess, one of New Zealand's three century-makers.

The year 1973 was a very good one for New Zealand cricket. In February, in an odd match against Pakistan, Hastings and Collinge put on 151 for the last wicket, a record for all Tests. (In the same match Rodney Redmond, on debut, scored 107 and 56 and was never chosen for New Zealand again). On 31 May their prolific opening bat Glenn Turner became the seventh man, and the first New Zealander, to score 1,000 runs before the end of May, and when they went into the Test series against England, it was almost as equals rather than as perennial underdogs.

England won the First Test, at Trent Bridge, but only by 38 runs after New Zealand were set 479 to win. At Lord's, England were lucky to escape with a draw.

New Zealand won the toss and put England in to bat, only the second time they had ever done that in England, but the decision paid off. England were all out for 253, and New Zealand set about building a substantial lead. At 10 for 2 this did not look likely, but skipper Bev Congdon (who had made 176 in the previous Test), Mark Burgess and Vic Pollard became the first three New Zealanders all to score centuries in the same Test innings, and the total reached 551, a lead of 298.

For Lancashire-born Vic Pollard, his third tour of his native land proved to be by far his most successful. His Test scores that summer were 16 not out, 116, 105 not out, 62 and 3, giving him an average of 100.66, batting at number six or seven. These were the only two centuries of his Test career, as he retired from international cricket at the end of the tour, aged only 28, to concentrate on his career as a teacher and Baptist lay preacher. Pollard was always firmly opposed to playing cricket on Sundays, so his career or his principles would have been severely compromised if he had carried on playing at the top level.

Richard Hadlee, the youngest member of New Zealand's touring party in 1973, played only in the First Test. He and his elder brother Dayle were the first pair of brothers ever to play together for New Zealand when they both played at Trent Bridge, and there were two other men at Lord's – John Parker and Hedley Howarth – who would subsequently play in the same Test sides as their younger brothers.

Match Drawn

LORD'S GROUND

ENGLAND v. NEW ZEALAND

THURS., FRI., SAT., MON. & TUES., JUNE 21, 22, 23, 25 & 26, 1973 (5-day Match)

ENGLAND

			First Innings		Second Innings	
1 G. Boycott	Yorkshire	c Parker b Collinge	61	c and b Howarth	92
2 D. L. Amiss	Warwickshire	c Howarth b Hadlee	9	c and b Howarth	53
3 G. R. J. Roope	Surrey	l b w b Howarth	56	c Parker b Taylor	51
4 K. W. R. Fletcher	Essex	c Hastings b Howarth	25	c Taylor b Collinge	178
5 A. W. Greig	Sussex	c Howarth b Collinge	63	c Wadsworth b Hadlee	12
†6 R. Illingworth	Leicestershire	c Collinge b Hadlee	3	c Turner b Howarth	22
*7 A. P. E. Knott	Kent	b Hadlee	0	c Congdon b Howarth	0
8 C. M. Old	Yorkshire	b Howarth	7	c Congdon b Pollard	7
9 J. A. Snow	Sussex	b Taylor	2	c Hastings b Pollard	0
10 G. G. Arnold	Surrey	not out	8	not out	23
11 N. Gifford	Worcestershire	c Wadsworth b Collinge	8	not out	2
		B , l-b 1, w 1, n-b 9,	11	B 8, l-b 3, w , n-b 12,	23
		Total	253	Total	463

FALL OF THE WICKETS

1—24 2—116 3—148 4—165 5—171 6—175 7—195 8—217 9—237 10—253
1—112 2—185 3—250 4—274 5—335 6—339 7—352 8—368 9—460 10—

ANALYSIS OF BOWLING 1st Innings

| Name | O. | M. | R. | W. | Wd. | N-b | | 2nd Innings | | | | |
							O.	M.	R.	W.	Wd.	N-b
Collinge	31	8	69	3	...	8	19	4	41	1	...	6
Taylor	19	1	54	1	1	...	34	10	90	1	...	6
Hadlee	26	4	70	3	...	1	25	2	79	1	...	
Congdon	5	2	7	0	...	...	8	3	22	0	...	...
Howarth	25	6	42	3	...	...	70	24	144	4	...	...
Pollard	...	...	...	...	...	...	39	11	61	2	...	...
Hastings	...	...	...	...	...	...	1	0	3	0	...	...

NEW ZEALAND

			First Innings		Second Innings
1 G. M. Turner	Otago	c Greig b Arnold	4	
2 J. M. Parker	N. Districts	c Knott b Snow	3	
†3 B. E. Congdon	Otago	c Knott b Old	175	
4 B. F. Hastings	Canterbury	l b w b Snow	86	
5 H. J. Howarth	Auckland	hit wicket b Old	17	
6 M. G. Burgess	Auckland	b Snow	105	
7 V. Pollard	Canterbury	not out	105	
*8 K. J. Wadsworth	Canterbury	c Knott b Old	27	
9 B. R. Taylor	Wellington	b Old	11	
10 D. R. Hadlee	Canterbury	c Fletcher b Old	6	
11 R. O. Collinge	Wellington	Innings closed		
		B , l-b 5, w , n-b 7,	12	B , l-b , w , n-b ,
		Total	551	Total

FALL OF THE WICKETS

1—5 2—10 3—200 4—249 5—330 6—447 7—523 8—535 9—551 10—
1— 2— 3— 4— 5— 6— 7— 8— 9— 10—

ANALYSIS OF BOWLING 1st Innings

| Name | O. | M. | R. | W. | Wd. | N-b | | 2nd Innings | | | | |
							O.	M.	R.	W.	Wd.	N-b
Snow	38	4	109	3	...	3	...	...	...	...	...	...
Arnold	41	6	108	1	...	3	...	...	...	...	...	...
Old	41.5	7	113	5	...	1	...	...	...	...	...	...
Roope	6	1	15	0	...	...	...	...	...	...	...	...
Gifford	39	6	107	0	...	...	...	...	...	...	...	...
Illingworth	39	12	87	0	...	...	...	...	...	...	...	...

Umpires—A. E. Fagg & T. W. Spencer   Scorers—E. Solomon & I. Walter

† Captain   * Wicket-keeper

Play begins 1st, 2nd, 3rd & 4th days at 11.30   5th day at 11

Stumps drawn 1st, 2nd, 3rd & 4th days at 6.30   5th day at 5.30 or 6

In the event of play being suspended, due to weather or ground conditions, for one hour or more on any of the first four days, play may be extended to 7.30 p.m. on that day).

Luncheon Interval 1.30 p.m.—2.10 p.m.

Tea Interval 4.15 p.m.—4.35 p.m. (may be varied according to state of game)

New Zealand won the toss and elected to field

1973: England v West Indies

(3rd Test) August 23, 24, 25, 27
West Indies won by an innings and 226 runs

The sun shone throughout this second Lord's Test of the summer, and the first ever staged at Lord's in August, as record after record was broken. For a start, the West Indies total of 652 for 8 was their highest thus far against England, brought about largely by two great cricketers whose Test careers were nearing the end. Gary Sobers hit his tenth Test hundred against England, his last of a total of 26, a record for West Indies that survived until Brian Lara roared past it in the third millennium. Rohan Kanhai scored his fifteenth and final Test century, and topped 6,000 runs for West Indies. Both had first played in a Lord's Test sixteen years before, when England won by an innings. The wheel had come full circle, and now crushed England absolutely.

With newcomer Bernard Julien, who scored his debut first-class century in only 127 balls, Sobers put on 155 in just 113 minutes before retiring with a stomach disorder. If he had been fully fit, the English bowling would really have come in for some stick. As it was, for the first time in Test history, every bowler used in the innings went for more than 100 runs. Illingworth shared the misery around fairly equally: Geoff Boycott's military medium and Brian Luckhurst's left arm spin were not tried. Tony Greig, especially, must have wished they had been.

All members of the West Indies fielding side surround the batsman.

West Indies won by an innings and 226 runs

LORD'S GROUND

(5p) (5p)

ENGLAND v. WEST INDIES

Thurs., Fri., Sat., Mon. & Tues., August 23, 24, 25, 27 & 28, 1973 (5-day Match)

WEST INDIES		First Innings		Second Innings
1 R. C. Fredericks	Guyana	c Underwood b Willis...	51	
*2 D. L. Murray	Trinidad	b Willis	4	
†3 R. B. Kanhai	Guyana	c Greig b Willis	157	
4 C. H. Lloyd	Guyana	c and b Willis	63	
5 A. I. Kallicharran	Guyana	c Arnold b Illingworth...	14	
6 G. S. Sobers	Barbados	not out	150	
7 M. L. C. Foster	Jamaica	c Willis b Greig	9	
8 B. D. Julien	Trinidad	c and b Greig	121	
9 K. D. Boyce	Barbados	c Amiss b Greig	36	
10 V. A. Holder	Barbados	not out	23	
11 L. R. Gibbs	Guyana	Innings closed		
		B 1, l-b 14, w 1, n-b 8,	24	B , l-b , w , n-b
		Total	652	Total

FALL OF THE WICKETS

1—8   2—87   3—225   4—256   5—339   6—373   7—604   8—610   9—   10—

1—   2—   3—   4—   5—   6—   7—   8—   9—   10—

ANALYSIS OF BOWLING 1st Innings

Name	O.	M.	R.	W.	Wd.	N-b		O.	M.	R.	W.	Wd.	N-b
							2nd Innings						
Arnold	35	6	111	0	...	3		...	...	...	...	...	...
Willis	35	3	118	4	1	5		...	...	...	...	...	...
Greig	33	2	180	3	...	...		...	...	...	...	...	...
Underwood	34	6	105	0	...	...		...	...	...	...	...	...
Illingworth	31.4	3	114	1	...	...		...	...	...	...	...	...

ENGLAND		First Innings		Second Innings	
1 G. Boycott	Yorkshire	c Kanhai b Holder	4	c Kallicharran b Boyce	15
2 D. L. Amiss	Warwickshire	c Sobers b Holder	35	c Sobers b Boyce	10
3 B. W. Luckhurst	Kent	c Murray b Boyce	1	c Sobers b Julien	12
4 F. C. Hayes	Lancashire	c Fredericks b Holder..	8	c Holder b Boyce	0
5 K. W. R. Fletcher	Essex	c Sobers b Gibbs	68	not out	86
6 A. W. Greig	Sussex	c Sobers b Boyce	44	l b w b Julien	13
†7 R. Illingworth	Leicestershire	c Sobers b Gibbs	0	c Kanhai b Gibbs	13
*8 A. P. E. Knott	Kent	c Murray b Boyce	21	c Murray b Boyce	5
9 G. G. Arnold	Surrey	c Murray b Boyce	5	c Fredericks b Gibbs	1
10 R. G. D. Willis	Warwickshire	not out	5	c Fredericks b Julien	0
11 D. L. Underwood	Kent	c Gibbs b Holder	12	b Gibbs	14
		B 6, l-b 4, w 3, n-b 17,	30	B 9, l-b , w 1, n-b 14,	24
		Total	233	Total	193

FALL OF THE WICKETS

1—5   2—7   3—29   4—97   5—176   6—176   7—187   8—205   9—213   10—233

1—32   2—38   3—42   4—49   5—63   6—87   7—132   8—143   9—146   10—193

ANALYSIS OF BOWLING 1st Innings

Name	O.	M.	R.	W.	Wd.	N-b		O.	M.	R.	W.	Wd.	N-b
							2nd Innings						
Holder	15	3	56	4	...	4		14	4	18	0	...	7
Boyce	20	7	50	4	...	12		16	5	49	4	...	4
Julien	11	4	26	0	3	...		18	2	69	3	1	3
Gibbs	18	3	39	2	...	...		13.3	3	26	3	...	...
Sobers	8	0	30	0	...	1		4	1	7	0	...	...
Foster	1	0	2	0	...	...		...	...	...	...	...	...

Scorers—E. Solomon & G. G. A. Saulez

Umpires—H. D. Bird & C. S. Elliott   † Captain   * Wicket-keeper

Play begins 1st, 2nd & 3rd days at 11.30   4th & 5th day at 11

Stumps drawn 1st & 2nd days at 6.30, 3rd day at 7.00 4th day at 6.30 5th day at 5.55 or 6.25
(In the event of play being suspended, due to weather or ground conditions, for one hour or
more on any of the first four days, play may be extended to 7.30 p.m. on that day).

Luncheon Interval 1.30 p.m.—2.10 p.m.

Tea Interval 4.15 p.m.—4.35 p.m. (may be varied according to state of game)

West Indies won the toss

England soon found that the wicket was not the batsman's paradise the West Indies had shown it to be. Sobers, at the age of 37, picked up four catches in the innings, and took two more in the second innings to equal the then Test record. Only Keith Fletcher held out, scoring 154 runs for once out in the match – nearly half of the runs scored off the bat by England.

On Saturday afternoon, 25 August, the IRA sent a coded warning of a bomb at Lord's, and play was suspended from 2.42 pm as a precaution. A few spectators went home, thinking that play would not be resumed, but the majority either stayed where they were or spilled out onto the pitch where umpires Charlie Elliott and Dickie Bird tried to keep them off the square. After 89 minutes, the 'all clear' was given and play was resumed, and one hour of this lost time was made up that evening. It was hardly needed. England capitulated just before 3.00 pm on the fourth afternoon, and it would have required a succession of bomb scares, and perhaps even a few detonations, to have prevented a West Indian victory.

1974: England v India

(2nd Test) June 20, 21, 22, 24
England won by an innings and 285 runs

Geoff Arnold and Chris Old after they had bowled India out for the
lowest total in the first 100 Lord's Test Matches.

The first of 1974's two Lord's Tests gave England their biggest winning margin ever at the ground, beating the innings and 148 run margin by which England had beaten New Zealand in 1958. India's second innings was the lowest recorded Test total at Lord's (although they batted one man short), and England's total of 629 was their highest ever at Lord's and their highest against India until Graham Gooch rewrote the record books in 1990.

Geoff Boycott, who had made only 10 and 6 in the First Test, stood down and England gave a first Test cap to the Lancashire left-hander David Lloyd. Opening the batting that summer against India was not a particularly onerous task – Abid Ali, Solkar and Madan Lal were none of them much above medium pace – so Lloyd's 46 was no more than a promising debut in an innings where three of his colleagues scored centuries and a fourth made 96. Lloyd, who went on to coach England with mixed fortunes, finished his Test career in possession of one unique record: he is the only man to have made a Test double hundred (214 not out in the next Test) without having made any other Test score of 50 or more.

England won by an innings and 285 runs

 LORD'S **GROUND**

(5p) (5p)

ENGLAND v. INDIA

Thurs., Fri., Sat., Mon. & Tues., June 20, 21, 22, 24 & 25, 1974   (5-day Match)

ENGLAND		First Innings		Second Innings
1 D. Lloyd	Lancashire	c Solkar b Prasanna	46	
2 D. L. Amiss	Warwickshire	l b w b Prasanna	188	
3 J. H. Edrich	Surrey	l b w b Bedi	96	
†4 M. H. Denness	Kent	c sub b Bedi	118	
5 K. W. R. Fletcher	Essex	c Solkar b Bedi	15	
6 A. W. Greig	Sussex	c and b Abid Ali	106	
*7 A. P. E. Knott	Kent	c and b Bedi	26	
8 C. M. Old	Yorkshire	b Abid Ali	3	
9 G. G. Arnold	Surrey	b Bedi	5	
10 D. L. Underwood	Kent	c Solkar b Bedi	9	
11 M. Hendrick	Derbyshire	not out	1	
		B 8, l-b 4, w 2, n-b 2,	16	B , l-b , w , n-b ,
		Total	629	Total

FALL OF THE WICKETS

1—116 2—337 3—339 4—369 5—571 6—591 7—604 8—611 9—624 10—629
1—   2—   3—   4—   5—   6—   7—   8—   9—   10—

ANALYSIS OF BOWLING	1st Innings						2nd Innings					
Name	O.	M.	R.	W.	Wd	N-b	O.	M.	R.	W.	Wd	N-b
Abid Ali	22	2	79	2	2	...	...	...	...	...	...	...
Solkar	6	2	16	0	...	2	...	...	...	...	...	...
Madan Lal	30	6	93	0	...	...	...	...	...	...	...	...
Bedi	64.2	8	226	6	...	...	...	...	...	...	...	...
Chandrasekhar	10	1	33	0	...	...	...	...	...	...	...	...
Prasanna	51	6	166	2	...	...	...	...	...	...	...	...

INDIA		First Innings		Second Innings	
1 S. M. Gavaskar	Bombay	c Knott b Old	49	l b w b Arnold	5
*2 F. M. Engineer	Bombay	c Denness b Old	86	l b w b Arnold	0
†3 A. L. Wadekar	Bombay	c Underwood b Hendrick	18	b Old	3
4 G. R. Viswanath	Mysore	b Underwood	52	c Knott b Arnold	5
5 B. P. Patel	Mysore	c Fletcher b Greig	1	c Knott b Arnold	1
6 E. D. Solkar	Bombay	c Underwood b Hendrick	43	not out	18
7 S. Abid Ali	Hyderabad	c Arnold b Old	14	c Knott b Old	3
8 Madan Lal	Delhi & Districts	c Knott b Old	0	c Hendrick b Old	2
9 E. A. S. Prasanna	Mysore	c Denness b Hendrick	0	b Old	5
10 B. S. Bedi	Delhi & Districts	b Arnold	14	b Old	0
11 B. S. Chandrasekhar	Mysore	not out	2	absent hurt	
		B 4, l-b 7, w , n-b 12,	23	B , l-b , w , n-b ,	
		Total	302	Total	42

FALL OF THE WICKETS

1—131 2—149 3—183 4—188 5—250 6—280 7—281 8—286 9—286 10—302
1—5   2—5   3—12   4—14   5—25   6—28   7—30   8—42   9—42   10—

ANALYSIS OF BOWLING	1st Innings						2nd Innings					
Name	O.	M.	R.	W.	Wd	N-b	O.	M.	R.	W.	Wd	N-b
Arnold	24.5	6	81	4	...	11	8	1	19	4	...	...
Old	21	6	67	4	...	1	8	3	21	5	...	...
Hendrick	18	4	46	3	...	...	1	0	2	0	...	...
Greig	21	4	63	1	...	...	...	...	...	...	...	...
Underwood	15	10	18	1	...	...	...	...	...	...	...	...
Lloyd	2	0	4	0	...	...	...	...	...	...	...	...

Scorers—E. Solomon & A. Ruia

Umpires—A. E. Fagg & T. W. Spencer

† Captain   * Wicket-keeper

Play begins 1st, 2nd, 3rd & 4th days at 11.30 5th day at 11
Stumps drawn 1st, 2nd, 3rd & 4th days at 6.30 5th day at 5.30 or 6
(In the event of play being suspended, due to weather or ground conditions, for one hour or more on any of the first four days, play may be extended to 7.30 p.m. on that day).
Luncheon Interval 1.30—2.10
Tea Interval 4.15—4.35 (may be varied according to state of game)

England won the toss

Amiss and Edrich put on a Lord's Test record 221 for the second wicket (beaten twice since in 2004 and 2005), and Denness and Greig made 202 to do the same for the fifth wicket. Bishen Bedi, the great Indian left arm spinner, became the first man to concede 200 runs in a Test innings at Lord's. He took six England wickets in the process, but it was a long hard bowl all the same. India's reply to this massive target began well enough, but in the end they did not even make half England's total.

All the same, what happened next was unexpected. With India 2 for 0 in their second innings overnight, the Monday morning crowd came to Lord's expecting a full and interesting day's play. What they got was an early lunch. Anybody who arrived even a little late missed most of the action, as India capitulated in just over an hour to 42 all out and the match was over. Geoff Arnold and Chris Old bowled straight and to great effect. That was all that was needed.

1974: England v Pakistan

(2nd Test) August 8, 9, 10, 12, 13 (no play on final day)
Match drawn

In 1973, August had been a month of blazing sunshine and high scores, but a year later the rain dominated, to make the second August Lord's Test much less interesting than the first. Unless, that is, you were called Derek Underwood. For this was 'Deadly Derek's' match, and if the rain had not wiped out the final day for the second Test in a row, England would have gone one up in the three-Test series.

Pakistan's first innings featured an opening stand of 71 between Sadiq Mohammad and Majid Khan but then faded into obscurity as Underwood and Tony Greig, bowling off-spinners, took 8 for 43 between them in 22.5 overs. England's batting was scarcely more distinguished, although Alan Knott's 83 was the highest score of the series thus far. By the end of the Saturday's play, Pakistan were 173 for 3, a lead of 33 and hoping for more runs from Mushtaq and Wasim to put them into a strong position.

Unfortunately it rained on Sunday and, what

Zaheer Abbas becomes one of Underwood's thirteen victims.

was worse (for the Pakistanis), water seeped under the covers. The conditions were absolutely perfect for Underwood, and he let nobody down. Mushtaq and Wasim Raja added a further 19 runs before Raja was out to a fine catch at short leg. Underwood then took five more wickets for nine more runs: at one point he had taken 6 for 2 in 8.3 overs. Pakistan were all out for 226, leaving England only 87 to win in over a day. However, the rain returned and the entire final day was wiped out. Match drawn.

This was one of those rare Tests, a match without a single bye. In Tests in England, there have only been eight such Tests, and three of those (at Lord's in 1902 and 1987, and at Trent Bridge in 1926) were almost entirely obliterated by the weather. Of the other five, four have been at Lord's (in 1890, 1958, 1972 and 1974) and one at Trent Bridge, against New Zealand in 1994. Why Lord's should have hosted three-quarters of England's byeless Tests remains a mystery.

PAKISTAN

Sadiq Mohammad	lbw b Hendrick	40	lbw b Arnold	43
Majid Khan	c Old b Greig	48	lbw b Underwood	19
Zaheer Abbas	c Hendrick b Underwood	1	c Greig b Underwood	1
Mushtaq Mohammad	c Greig b Underwood	0	c Denness b Greig	76
Wasim Raja	c Greig b Underwood	24	c Lloyd b Underwood	53
Asif Iqbal	c Amiss b Underwood	2	c Greig b Underwood	0
† Intikhab Alam	b Underwood	5	b Underwood	0
Imran Khan	c Hendrick b Greig	4	c Lloyd b Underwood	0
* Wasim Bari	lbw b Greig	4	lbw b Underwood	1
Sarfraz Nawazq	not out	0	c Lloyd b Underwood	1
Asif Masood	(did not bat)		not out	17
	(NB 2)	2	(LB 8, NB 7)	15
Total	(9 wkts)	130		226

ENGLAND

D Lloyd	c Zaheer b Sarfraz	23	not out	12
DL Amiss	c Sadiq b Masood	2	not out	14
JH Edrich	c Sadiq b Intikhab	40		
† MH Denness	b Imran	20		
KWR Fletcher	lbw b Imran	8		
AW Greig	run out	9		
* APE Knott	c Bari b Masood	83		
CM Old	c Bari b Mushtaq	41		
GG Arnold	c Bari b Masood	10		
DL Underwood	not out	12		
M Hendrick	c Imran b Intikhab	6		
	(LB 14, W 1, NB 1)	16	(NB 1)	1
Total		270	(0 wkt)	27

PAKISTAN	O	M	R	W	O	M	R	W
Arnold	8	1	32	0	15	3	37	1
Old	5	0	17	0	14	1	39	0
Hendrick	9	2	36	1	15	4	29	0
Underwood	14	8	20	5	34.5	17	51	8
Greig	8.5	4	23	3	19	6	55	1

ENGLAND	O	M	R	W	O	M	R	W
Masood	25	10	47	3	4	0	9	0
Sarfraz	22	8	42	1	3	0	7	0
Intikhab	26	4	80	2	1	1	0	0
Raja	2	0	8	0				
Mushtaq	7	3	16	1				
Imran	18	2	48	2				
Iqbal	5	0	13	0				
Majid					2	0	10	0

FALL OF WICKETS

	Ind.	Eng.	Ind.
Wkt	1st	1st	2nd
1st	71	2	55
2nd	91	52	61
3rd	91	90	77
4th	91	94	192
5th	103	100	192
6th	111	118	200
7th	116	187	200
8th	130	231	206
9th	130	254	208
10th		270	226

† Captain   * Wicketkeeper

1975: England v Australia

(2nd Test) July 31, August 1, 2, 4, 5
Match drawn

A high-scoring drawn match usually has little to offer except the memories of some fine but ultimately fruitless batting. The 1975 Lord's Test was an exception. Yes, there was plenty of fine batting, especially from John Edrich, who hit his seventh Test century against Australia, and his second at Lord's. Ross Edwards scored 99 in the Australian first innings and the Chappell brothers batted beautifully in the second. Dennis Lillee hit his highest Test score to date, which included three sixes and eight fours. Tony Greig, England's new captain, hit 96 in 150 minutes and David Steele, in his first Test, made 50 and 45. But there was more

than just good batting and very quick bowling from Lillee, Jeff Thomson (22 no-balls and four wides in the first innings) and John Snow.

When the first England wicket fell, David Steele hurried down from the team dressing room to play his first innings for his country. But he had never been in the Lord's home dressing room before, failed to check his route before setting out and went down one flight of stairs too many. He thus found himself in the Gents rather than in the Long Room. It could be argued that anybody going out to face Lillee and Thomson in full flow would need to visit the Gents first, but Steele had

Michael Angelow, during the Monday afternoon's play.

but one thought: to get out on to the pitch before he became the first Test batsman to be timed out. He made it.

The other event of any note occurred on Monday 4 August and concerned a Mr Michael Angelow of St Albans, who became Lord's first streaker. Angelow ran across the outfield and hurdled the stumps before attempting to make a getaway into the Mound Stand. To John Arlott, commentating on BBC Radio's 'Test Match Special' at the time, he was 'a freaker, we've got a freaker down the wicket now.' *Wisden* did not deign to mention his presence, but to Arlott (and to the cricketers and the vast majority of the crowd) his bravado was welcome light relief on a hot afternoon. 'He's being embraced by a blond policeman,' continued Arlott. 'This may be his last public appearance, but what a splendid one.'

When on the next day Mr Angelow appeared at Marylebone Magistrates Court, charged with insulting behaviour, he told the bench that he had run naked across the pitch for a £20 bet. 'The court will have that twenty pounds,' said the chairman.

Match Drawn

 LORD'S GROUND

ENGLAND v. AUSTRALIA

THURS., FRI., SAT., MON. & TUES., JULY 31 & AUGUST 1, 2, 4 & 5, 1975 (5-day Match)

ENGLAND

#	Batsman	County	First Innings		Second Innings	
1	B. Wood	Lancashire	l b w b Lillee	6	c Marsh b Thomson	52
2	J. H. Edrich	Surrey	l b w b Lillee	9	c Thomson b Mallett	175
3	D. S. Steele	Northamptonshire	b Thomson	50	c and b Walters	45
4	D. L. Amiss	Warwickshire	l b w b Lillee	0	c G. Chappell b Lillee	10
5	G. A. Gooch	Essex	c Marsh b Lillee	6	b Mallett	31
†6	A. W. Greig	Sussex	c I. Chappell b Walker	96	c Walters b I. Chappell	41
*7	A. P. E. Knott	Kent	l b w b Thomson	69	not out	22
8	R. A. Woolmer	Kent	c Turner b Mallett	33	b Mallett	31
9	J. A. Snow	Sussex	c Walker b Mallett	11		
10	D. L. Underwood	Kent	not out	0		
11	P. Lever	Lancashire	l b w b Walker	4	Innings closed	
		Extras	B 3, l-b 1, w 4, n-b 23	31	B , l-b 18, w 2, n-b 9	29
		Total		**315**		**436**

FALL OF THE WICKETS

1—10 2—29 3—31 4—49 5—145 6—222 7—288 8—309 9—310 10—315
1—111 2—215 3—249 4—315 5—380 6—387 7—436 8— 9— 10—

ANALYSIS OF BOWLING

Name	1st Innings						2nd Innings					
	O.	M.	R.	W.	Wd.	N-b	O.	M.	R.	W.	Wd.	N-b
Lillee	20	4	84	4			33	10	80	1		2
Thomson	24	7	92	2	4	17	29	8	73	1	2	2
Walker	21.4	7	52	2		6	37	8	95	0		4
Mallett	22	4	66	2			36.4	10	127	3		
I. Chappell							10	2	26	1		1
Walters							2	0	6	1		

AUSTRALIA

#	Batsman	State	First Innings		Second Innings	
1	R. B. McCosker	N.S.W.	c and b Lever	29	l b w b Steele	79
2	A. Turner	N.S.W.	l b w b Snow	9	c Gooch b Greig	21
†3	I. M. Chappell	S. Australia	c Knott b Snow	2	l b w b Greig	86
4	G. S. Chappell	Queensland	l b w b Snow	4	not out	73
5	R. Edwards	W. Australia	l b w b Woolmer	99	not out	52
6	K. D. Walters	N.S.W.	c Greig b Lever	2		
*7	R. W. Marsh	W. Australia	c Amiss b Greig	3		
8	M. H. N. Walker	Victoria	b Snow	5		
9	J. R. Thomson	Queensland	b Underwood	17		
10	D. K. Lillee	W. Australia	not out	73		
11	A. A. Mallett	S. Australia	l b w b Steele	14		
		Extras	B , l-b 5, w , n-b 6	11	B 4, l-b , w , n-b 14	18
		Total		**268**		**329**

FALL OF THE WICKETS

1—21 2—29 3—37 4—54 5—56 6—64 7—81 8—133 9—199 10—268
1—50 2—169 3—222 4— 5— 6— 7— 8— 9— 10—

ANALYSIS OF BOWLING

Name	1st Innings						2nd Innings					
	O.	M.	R.	W.	Wd.	N-b	O.	M.	R.	W.	Wd.	N-b
Snow	21	4	66	4			19	3	82	0		
Lever	15	0	83	2		3	20	5	55	0		4
Woolmer	13	5	31	1			3	1	3	0		
Greig	15	5	47	1		1	26	6	82	2		2
Underwood	13	5	29	1		2	31	14	64	0		7
Steele	0.4	0	1	1			9	4	19	1		
Wood							1	0	6	0		

Umpires—W. E. Alley & T. W. Spencer

† Captain * Wicket-keeper Scorers—E. Solomon & D. Sherwood

Play begins 1st, 2nd, 3rd & 4th days at 11.30 5th day at 11
Stumps drawn 1st, 2nd, 3rd & 4th days at 6.30 5th day at 5.30 or 6
(In the event of play being suspended, due to weather or ground conditions, for one hour or more on any of the first four days, play may be extended to 7.30 p.m. on that day).
Luncheon Interval 1.30—2.10
Tea Interval 4.15—4.35 (may be varied according to state of game)

England won the toss

1976: England v West Indies

(2nd Test) June 17, 18, 19, 21, 22 (no play on third day)
Match drawn

Once again, a Lord's Test lost a complete day to rain, and the chances of a result became very slim. Despite a wash-out on the Saturday, the match attracted 99,944 paying spectators, and the final hour was very exciting.

After holding their own in the First Test despite a brilliant double century from Viv Richards, England came to Lord's with some confidence. Edrich was unavailable, so Barry Wood opened with Mike Brearley. England had five different opening partnerships in the five Tests of the summer, and it was the lack of a good start as much as anything that would in the end mean that England's challenge

fizzled out over the summer. Edrich, Brearley, Wood, Amiss, Woolmer, Close and Steele were all used as openers during the summer, but only once did any combination pass fifty. Andy Roberts, with able support from Vanburn Holder, was the main destroyer of England's innings, but Underwood and Snow were even more destructive when the West Indians batted. A first innings lead of 68 by the end of the second day would have been even better had not Barry Wood been injured in the closing moments of the day, struck more than once on the hand by Roberts at his most lethal in fading light.

Brian Close, aged 45, under attack from Holding, aged 22.

Match Drawn

5p LORD'S GROUND 5p

ENGLAND v. WEST INDIES

Thurs., Fri., Sat. (no play), Mon. & Tues., June 17, 18, 19, 21 & 22, 1976 (5-day Match)

ENGLAND		First Innings		Second Innings	
1 B. Wood	Lancashire	c Murray b Roberts	6	c Murray b Holding	30
2 J. M. Brearley	Middlesex	b Roberts	40	b Holding	13
3 D. S. Steele	Northamptonshire	l b w b Roberts	7	c Jumadeen b Roberts	64
4 D. B. Close	Somerset	c Holder b Jumadeen	60	c and b Holder	46
5 R. A. Woolmer	Kent	c Murray b Holding	38	c Murray b Roberts	29
†6 A. W. Greig	Sussex	c Lloyd b Roberts	6	c Gomes b Holder	20
*7 A. P. E. Knott	Kent	b Holder	17	l b w b Roberts	4
8 C. M. Old	Yorkshire	b Holder	19	run out	13
9 J. A. Snow	Sussex	b Roberts	0	not out	6
10 D. L. Underwood	Kent	b Holder	31	b Roberts	2
11 P. I. Pocock	Surrey	not out	0	c Jumadeen b Roberts	3
		B 7, l-b 5, w 5, n-b 9,	26	B 7, l-b 7, w , n-b 10,	24
		Total	250	Total	254

FALL OF THE WICKETS

1—15 2—31 3—115 4—153 5—161 6—188 7—196 8—197 9—249 10—250

1—29 2—29 3—112 4—169 5—186 6—207 7—215 8—245 9—249 10—254

ANALYSIS OF BOWLING

Name	1st Innings						2nd Innings					
	O.	M.	R.	W.	Wd.	N-b	O.	M.	R.	W.	Wd.	N-b
Roberts	23	6	60	5		4	29.5	10	63	5	...	...
Holding	19	4	52	1	...	1	27	10	56	2	...	1
Julien	23	6	64	0	1	4	13	5	20	0	...	4
Holder	18.4	7	35	3	...	4	19	2	50	2	...	5
Jumadeen	12	4	23	1	...	...	16	4	41	0	...	...
	...	...	...	...	...	...	...	...	...	...	...	...

WEST INDIES		First Innings		Second Innings	
1 R. C. Fredericks	Guyana	c Snow b Old	0	c Greig b Old	138
2 C. G. Greenidge	Barbados	c Snow b Underwood	84	c Close b Pocock	22
3 H. A. Gomes	Trinidad	c Woolmer b Snow	11	b Underwood	0
4 A. I. Kallicharran	Guyana	c Old b Snow	0	b Greig	34
†5 C. H. Lloyd	Guyana	c Knott b Underwood	50	b Greig	33
*6 D. L. Murray	Trinidad	b Snow	2	not out	7
7 B. D. Julien	Trinidad	l b w b Snow	3	b Underwood	1
8 M. A. Holding	Jamaica	b Underwood	0		
9 V. A. Holder	Barbados	c Woolmer b Underwood	12	not out	0
10 A. M. E. Roberts	Antigua	b Underwood	16		
11 R. R. Jumadeen	Trinidad	not out	0		
		B 2, l-b , w , n-b 2,	4	B 3, l-b 2, w , n-b 1,	6
		Total	182	Total	241

FALL OF THE WICKETS

1—0 2—28 3—40 4—139 5—141 6—145 7—146 8—153 9—178 10—182

1—41 2—154 3—230 4—233 5—238 6—238 7— 8— 9— 10—

ANALYSIS OF BOWLING

Name	1st Innings						2nd Innings					
	O.	M.	R.	W.	Wd.	N-b	O.	M.	R.	W.	Wd.	N-b
Old	10	0	68	1	...	1	14	4	46	1	...	1
Snow	19	3	68	4	...	...	7	2	22	0	...	...
Underwood	18.4	7	39	5	...	1	24.3	8	73	2	...	...
Pocock	3	0	13	0	...	...	27	9	52	1	...	...
Greig	...	...	...	...	...	...	14	3	42	2	...	...
	...	...	...	...	...	...	...	...	...	...	...	...

Umpires—H. D. Bird & D. J. Constant   Scorers—E. Solomon & G. G. A. Saulez

† Captain   * Wicket-keeper

Play begins 1st, 2nd, 3rd & 4th days at 11.30   5th day at 11.00
Stumps drawn 1st, 2nd, 3rd & 4th days at 6.30   5th day at 5.30 or 6.00
(In the event of play being suspended, due to weather or ground conditions, for one hour or more on any of the first four days, play may be extended to 7.30 p.m. on that day).
Luncheon Interval 1.30—2.10
Tea Interval 4.15—4.35 (may be varied according to state of game)

England won the toss

When the game resumed on the fourth day, it was David Steele and Brian Close, two of the toughest characters to have played for England in the second half of the twentieth century, whose batting brought England into a strong position. Despite another five-wicket haul by Roberts, the visitors were set 323 to win in slightly under five hours. West Indies went about their task with caution, and even though Roy Fredericks hit a six and fourteen fours in his hundred, his team still needed 154 more to win in the final 20 overs. Nine overs later, 113 were still needed, but Lloyd, who was then batting with Fredericks, claimed the final half hour. Four overs later Fredericks was out, and in the next, Lloyd went too. At this point, Lloyd motioned to Greig that he was happy to finish the game there, but now Greig scented victory, and insisted they play on. He did not abandon the chase until the fourth ball of the final over when, barring stumpings off wides and run outs off no-balls, victory was an impossibility.

1977: England v Australia

(1st Test) June 16, 17, 18, 20, 21
Match drawn

Wisden Cricketers' Almanack for 1978 did not beat about the bush: 'Although the day should never come when an Australian cricket team is described as colourless, the 1977 party to England took on a very light shade of grey.' The party proved far weaker than the 'good average' England team arrayed against them, and the Ashes returned to England. The underlying reason was Kerry Packer's World Series Cricket. Thirteen of the seventeen Australian tourists had signed for Packer before they arrived in England, and as the summer wore on and the arguments between the cricket authorities and WSC moved ever closer to the law courts it was obvious the players had more on their minds than merely playing cricket. If Packer did nothing in the short term for the health of English cricket, at least he gave us back the Ashes for a while. Of course, he did also force a change in the England captaincy, Mike Brearley taking over from the WSC-bound Tony Greig.

The 1977 Lord's Test was the Jubilee Test, to celebrate the twenty-five years of Queen Elizabeth's reign. As a match, it was a good, close contest which ended with England probably in the dominant position, but with too little time to press home their advantage. Over four hours' play was lost on the second day, which certainly cost one side or the other the match. There were many

First blood to Australia as Thomson bowls Amiss.

Match Drawn

ENGLAND v. AUSTRALIA

THURS., FRI., SAT., MON. & TUES., JUNE 16, 17, 18, 20 & 21, 1977 (5-day Match)

ENGLAND

		First Innings		Second Innings	
1 D. L. Amiss	Warwickshire	b Thomson	4	b Thomson	0
†2 J. M. Brearley	Middlesex	c Robinson b Thomson	9	c Robinson b O'Keeffe	49
3 R. A. Woolmer	Kent	run out	79	c Chappell b Pascoe	120
4 D. W. Randall	Nottinghamshire	c Chappell b Walker	53	c McCosker b Thomson	0
5 A. W. Greig	Sussex	b Pascoe	5	c O'Keeffe b Pascoe	91
6 G. D. Barlow	Middlesex	c McCosker b Walker	1	l b w b Pascoe	5
*7 A. P. E. Knott	Kent	c Walters b Thomson	8	c Walters b Walker	8
8 C. M. Old	Yorkshire	c Marsh b Walker	9	c Walters b Walker	0
9 J. K. Lever	Essex	b Pascoe	8	c Marsh b Thomson	3
10 D. L. Underwood	Kent	not out	11	not out	12
11 R. G. D. Willis	Warwickshire	b Thomson	17	c Marsh b Thomson	0
		B 1, l-b 3, w 1, n-b 7,	12	B 5, l-b 9, w 1, n-b 2,	17
		Total	**216**	**Total**	**305**

FALL OF THE WICKETS

1—12 2—13 3—111 4—121 5—134 6—155 7—171 8—183 9—189 10—216
1—0 2—132 3—224 4—263 5—286 6—286 7—286 8—286 9—305 10—305

ANALYSIS OF BOWLING

Name	1st Innings						2nd Innings					
	O.	M.	R.	W.	Wd.	N-b	O.	M.	R.	W.	Wd.	N-b
Thomson	20.5	5	41	4	1	5	24.4	3	86	4	...	2
Pascoe	23	7	53	2	...	1	26	2	96	3	1	
Walker	30	6	66	3	...	1	35	13	56	2	...	
O'Keeffe	10	3	32	0	...	...	15	7	26	1	...	
Chappell	3	0	12	0	...	...	12	2	24	0	...	...

AUSTRALIA

		First Innings		Second Innings	
1 R. B. McCosker	N.S.W.	b Old	23	b Willis	1
2 R. D. Robinson	Victoria	b Lever	11	c Woolmer b Old	4
‡3 G. S. Chappell	Queensland	c Old b Willis	66	c Lever b Old	24
4 C. S. Serjeant	W. Australia	c Knott b Willis	81	c Amiss b Underwood	3
5 K. D. Walters	N.S.W.	c Brearley b Willis	53	c sub b Underwood	10
6 D. W. Hookes	S. Australia	c Brearley b Old	11	c and b Willis	50
*7 R. W. Marsh	W. Australia	l b w b Willis	1	not out	6
8 K. J. O'Keeffe	N.S.W.	c sub b Willis	12	not out	8
9 M. H. N. Walker	Victoria	c Knott b Willis	4		
10 J. R. Thomson	Queensland	b Willis	6		
11 L. S. Pascoe	N.S.W.	not out	3		
		B , l b 7, w 1, n b 17,	25	B , l-b , w , n-b 8,	8
		Total	**296**	**Total**	**114**

FALL OF THE WICKETS

1—25 2—51 3—135 4—238 5—256 6—264 7—265 8—284 9—290 10—296
1—5 2—5 3—48 4—64 5—71 6—102 7— 8— 9— 10—

ANALYSIS OF BOWLING

Name	1st Innings						2nd Innings					
	O.	M.	R.	W.	Wd.	N-b	O.	M.	R.	W.	Wd.	N-b
Willis	30.1	7	78	7	1	6	10	1	40	4	...	5
Lever	19	5	61	1	...	...	5	2	4	0	...	
Underwood	25	6	42	0	...	11	10	3	16	2	...	3
Old	35	10	70	2	...	...	14	0	46	2	...	
Woolmer	5	1	20	0	...	...	...	...	...	...	...	

Scorers—E. Solomon & D. Sherwood

Umpires—H. D. Bird & W. L. Budd

† Captain * Wicket-keeper

Play begins 1st, 2nd, 3rd & 4th days at 11.30 5th day at 11.00
Stumps drawn 1st, 2nd, 3rd & 4th days at 6.30 5th day at 5.30 or 6.00
(In the event of play being suspended, due to weather or ground conditions, for one hour or more on any of the first four days, play may be extended to 7.30 p.m. on that day).
Luncheon Interval 1.30—2.10
Tea Interval 4.15—4.35 (may be varied according to state of game)

England won the toss

great individual performances: the Bobs, Woolmer and Willis, for England, and Craig Serjeant, Greg Chappell and Jeff Thomson among many for Australia. We should not forget the efforts of Alan Ealham, either. The Kent player was on the field for most of the time that Australia batted, fielding substitute for Derek Randall – hit on the elbow during his first innings 53 – and he proved to be probably the only man in the country at the time who made the England fielding stronger in the absence of Randall. He became the second substitute fielder (after the Australian FA Iredale in 1896) to take a catch in both innings of a Lord's Test, an inconsequential but satisfying statistic for a fine county cricketer who never won a Test cap of his own.

The match was watched by 101,050 people and receipts totalled £220,384, then an English record. The first WSC 'Super Test' between Australia and West Indies six months later began in front of a crowd of 400.

1978: England v Pakistan

(2nd Test) June 15, 16, 17, 19 (no play on first day)
England won by an innings and 120 runs

Enter the Gorilla. Ian Botham made his Test debut in the Third Test of the previous summer, batting at number eight, yet by the time he came to his first Lord's Test, he already had two Test hundreds to his name. He had also taken five wickets a few times, but now his second innings analysis became the best in any Test at Lord's, a record that still stands. As Michael Melford wrote in the *Daily Telegraph* the morning after the game was over, 'Botham has played in seven Test matches. He has made three hundreds and a fifty, and has taken five wickets or more in an innings five times. And he is still only 22.' Nobody before or since has made a hundred and taken eight wickets in an innings in the same Test, anywhere in the world. By the end of his career, Botham would look back on Lord's with mixed feelings, but in 1978 he obviously loved the place.

This was the first match in which four of the major pillars of England's 1980s and early 1990s sides played together. Graham Gooch was playing his first Test since 1975, David Gower was playing only his second Test, and Botham and Willis had only recently earned their places in the team – both had been among *Wisden*'s Five Cricketers of the Year for their exploits the previous summer.

Ian Botham running riot.

The first day was notable only for the drizzle and for the presence of the Queen, who met the teams inside the pavilion rather than on the field of play. The clouds did not really clear away until the Monday morning. When Botham came to the wicket on the Friday, England were 134 for 5, and had only reached that score thanks to fifties from Gooch and Gower. By the end of the day, England were 309 for 8, with Botham 102 not out, his century having come up in 104 balls. Pakistan's first innings reply was a feeble 105, but it was Bob Willis and Phil Edmonds (4 for 6 in eight overs) who caused the collapse. They followed on 259 behind, and reached 96 for 2 by the end of Saturday.

The Monday morning was cloudless. Brearley switched Botham to the Nursery end, and suddenly the ball – a replacement for one that had gone out of shape on the Saturday evening – swung all over the place. Beating the bat three or four times each over, Botham took six wickets for 8 runs in his final 8.5 overs.

ENGLAND

† JM Brearley	lbw b Liaquat	2
GA Gooch	lbw b Wasim Raja	54
CT Radley	c Mohsin b Liaquat	8
DI Gower	b Qasim	56
GRJ Roope	c Mohsin b Qasim	69
G Miller	c Miandad b Qasim	0
IT Botham	b Liaquat	108
* RW Taylor	c Mudassar b Sikander	10
CM Old	c Mohsin b Sikander	0
PH Edmonds	not out	36
RGD Willis	b Mudassar	18
	(LB 2, NB1)	3
Total		364

PAKISTAN

Mudassar Nazar	c Edmonds b Willis	1	c Taylor b Botham		10
Sadiq Mohammad	c Botham b Willis	11	c Taylor b Willis		0
Mohsin Khan	c Willis b Edmonds	31	c Roope b Willis		46
Haroon Rashid	b Old	15	(5) b Botham		4
Javed Miandad	c Taylor b Willis	0	(6) c Gooch b Botham		22
Wasim Raja	b Edmonds	28	(7) c and b Botham		1
Talat Ali	c Radley b Edmonds	2	(4) c Roope b Botham		40
†* Wasim Bari	c Brearley b Willis	0	c Taylor b Botham		2
Iqbal Qasim	b Willis	0	(10) b Botham		0
Sikander Bakht	c Brearley b Edmonds	4	(9) c Roope b Botham		1
Liaquat Ali	not out	4	not out		0
	(NB 9)	9	(B 1, LB 3, W 5, NB 4)		13
Total		105			139

PAKISTAN	O	M	R	W				
Sikander	27	3	115	2				
Liaquat	18	1	80	3				
Mudassar	4.2	0	16	1				
Qasim	30	5	101	3				
Wasim Raja	12	3	49	1				

ENGLAND	O	M	R	W	O	M	R	W
Willis	13	1	47	5	10	2	26	2
Old	10	3	26	1	15	4	36	0
Botham	5	2	17	0	20.5	8	34	8
Edmonds	8	6	6	4	12	4	21	0
Miller					9	3	9	0

FALL OF WICKETS

	Eng.	Pak.	Pak.
Wkt	1st	1st	2nd
1st	5	11	1
2nd	19	22	45
3rd	120	40	100
4th	120	41	108
5th	134	84	114
6th	252	96	119
7th	290	97	121
8th	290	97	130
9th	324	97	130
10th	364	105	139

† Captain   * Wicketkeeper

1978: England v New Zealand

(1st Test) August 24, 25, 26, 28
England won by 7 wickets

England had already won the first two Tests of the three match series when the teams came to Lord's at the end of August, so a victory for the hosts was the expected result. In the event, that was what happened, but not before New Zealand had got themselves into some good positions. They lost it on the third afternoon, undone by some fine fast bowling by Willis and Botham.

For John Emburey, one future England captain, this was his first Test, and for two New Zealand stalwarts it was their last. Bev Congdon extended two New Zealand records: for most Tests, to 61, and for most Test runs, to 3,448 (both

of which have now been surpassed), and Richard Collinge, in only his thirty-fifth Test, extended his New Zealand Test wicket-taking record to 116. One of his team-mates in this Test, Richard Hadlee, was to make mincemeat of that record in due course, but Collinge set the target that Hadlee had to overtake.

New Zealand won the toss and batted. They finally reached 339, well ahead of par on a pitch that favoured bowlers throughout, and they owed much of their success to Geoff Howarth. The score was 65 for 1 when Howarth came in. He was not at his fluent best, mainly because he was

Botham again ... running out Hadlee.

struggling against influenza as well as the England attack. At the end of the first day, when he had made 105 not out, he admitted that he had not slept the night before because of the flu, so his four and a quarter hour effort was all the more praiseworthy. England began cautiously against Hadlee and Collinge, but in the final hour of the second day, Radley and Gower added 75 runs by a series of magnificent shots and some excellent running, and the day ended with England in a strong position at 175 for 2.

On the Saturday, it all changed. Only 151 runs were scored for the loss of fifteen wickets, the lowest number of runs in any day of any Test in England. The home side could not prosper against New Zealand's bowlers, and finished 50 runs behind. Botham and Willis, however, did even better than Hadlee and co. With Howarth still flu-ridden, there was nobody to stand up to bowlers who were making the ball lift alarmingly from what the batsmen were once again calling the Lord's ridge. Botham (5 for 39 and the run out of Hadlee) took the most wickets, but Bob Willis, 4 for 16 in 16 overs, was the one who set up England's victory.

England won by 7 wickets

 LORD'S **GROUND** (10p) (10p)

CORNHILL INSURANCE TEST SERIES
ENGLAND v. NEW ZEALAND

THURS., FRI., SAT., MON. & TUES., AUGUST 24, 25, 26, 28 & 29, 1978 (5-day Match)

NEW ZEALAND

Batsman	County	First Innings		Second Innings	
1 J. G. Wright	N. Districts	c Edmonds b Botham	17	b Botham	12
*2 B. A. Edgar	Wellington	c Edmonds b Emburey	39	b Botham	4
3 G. P. Howarth	N. Districts	c Taylor b Botham	123	not out	14
4 J. M. Parker	N. Districts	l b w b Hendrick	14	c Taylor b Botham	3
†5 M. G. Burgess	Auckland	l b w b Botham	68	c Hendrick b Botham	14
6 B. E. Congdon	Canterbury	c Emburey b Botham	2	c Taylor b Willis	3
7 R. W. Anderson	C. Districts	b Botham	16	c Taylor b Willis	1
8 R. J. Hadlee	Canterbury	c Brearley b Botham	0	run out	5
9 R. O. Collinge	N. Districts	c Emburey b Willis	19	b Botham	0
10 S. L. Boock	Canterbury	not out	4	c Radley b Willis	0
11 B. P. Bracewell	C. Districts	st Taylor b Emburey	4	c Hendrick b Willis	0
		B 4, l-b 18, w 4, n-b 7,	33	B , l-b 3, w , n-b 8,	11
		Total	339	Total	67

FALL OF THE WICKETS

1—65	2—70	3—117	4—247	5—253	6 290	7—290	8—321	9—333	10—339
1—10	2—14	3—20	4—29	5—33	6—37	7—37	8—43	9—57	10—67

ANALYSIS OF BOWLING

Name	1st Innings						2nd Innings					
	O.	M.	R.	W.	Wd.	N b	O.	M.	R.	W.	Wd.	N-b
Willis	29	9	79	1		6	16	8	16	4	...	7
Hendrick	28	14	39	1	1							
Botham	38	13	101	6	2	1	18.1	4	39	5	...	1
Edmonds	12	3	19	0								
Emburey	26.1	12	39	2			3	2	1	0	...	
Gooch	10	0	29	0	1							

ENGLAND

Batsman	County	First Innings		Second Innings	
1 G. Boycott	Yorkshire	c Hadlee b Bracewell	24	b Hadlee	4
2 G. A. Gooch	Essex	c Boock b Hadlee	2	not out	42
3 C. T. Radley	Middlesex	c Congdon b Hadlee	77	b Hadlee	0
4 D. I. Gower	Leicestershire	c Wright b Boock	71	c Congdon b Bracewell	46
†5 J. M. Brearley	Middlesex	c Edgar b Hadlee	33	not out	8
6 I. T. Botham	Somerset	c Edgar b Collinge	21		
*7 R. W. Taylor	Derbyshire	l b w b Hadlee	1		
8 P. H. Edmonds	Middlesex	c Edgar b Hadlee	5		
9 J. E. Emburey	Middlesex	b Collinge	2		
10 M. Hendrick	Derbyshire	b Bracewell	12		
11 R. G. D. Willis	Warwickshire	not out	7		
		B 7, l-b 5, w , n-b 22,	34	B , l-b 3, w 4, n-b 11,	18
		Total	289	Total	118

FALL OF THE WICKETS

1—2	2—66	3—180	4—211	5—249	6—255	7—258	8—263	9—274	10—289
1—14	2—14	3—84	4—	5—	6—	7—	8—	9—	10—

ANALYSIS OF BOWLING

Name	1st Innings						2nd Innings					
	O.	M.	R.	W.	Wd.	N b	O.	M.	R.	W.	Wd.	N b
Hadlee	32	9	84	5		12	13.5	2	31	2	4	4
Collinge	30	9	58	2		5	6	1	26	0	...	2
Bracewell	19.3	1	68	2		5	6	0	32	1	...	5
Boock	25	10	33	1			5	1	11	0	...	
Congdon	6	1	12	0								

Umpires—H. D. Bird & B. J. Meyer   Scorers—E. Solomon & W. N. Larkins

† Captain   * Wicket-keeper

Play begins 1st, 2nd, 3rd & 4th days at 11.30   5th day at 11.00

Stumps drawn 1st, 2nd, 3rd & 4th days at 6.30   5th day at 5.30 or 6.00

(In the event of play being suspended, due to weather or ground conditions, for one hour or more on any of the first four days, play may be extended to 7.30 p.m. on that day).

Luncheon Interval 1.30—2.10

Tea Interval 4.15—4.35 (may be varied according to state of game)

New Zealand won the toss

1979: England v India

(2nd Test) August 2, 3, 4, 6, 7
Match drawn

After the 1979 World Cup, won by West Indies in an easy victory over England in the final, the Indians played four Tests against England. The second of the four was ruined as a contest by rain and bad light, which eliminated about a day and a half's playing time, but there were still some fine individual performances.

India, led by off-spinner Srinavasaraghavan Venkataraghavan who went on to become one of the world's leading umpires, won the toss and decided to bat. It was not a good move. Apart from

Sunil Gavaskar, nobody put together any sort of an innings, and when the dust settled after the final four wickets all fell at the same score, 96, it could be seen that Ian Botham (who else?) had taken five for 35, his fourth five-wicket haul in his three Test appearances at Lord's so far. His overall statistics in Lord's Tests to the end of India's first innings were 101 overs, 32 maidens, 226 runs and 24 wickets, at an average of 9.41 and a strike rate of one wicket every 25 balls. And he had also scored 165 runs at an average of 53. He did not

'Start delayed!' – Lord's on August 3rd.

Match Drawn

 LORD'S GROUND (10p)

CORNHILL INSURANCE TEST SERIES
ENGLAND v. INDIA
Thurs., Fri., Sat., Mon. & Tues., August 2, 3, 4, 6 & 7, 1979 (5-day Match)

INDIA

			First Innings		Second Innings	
1	S. M. Gavaskar	Bombay	c Taylor b Gooch	42	c Brearley b Botham	59
2	C. P. S. Chauhan	Delhi	c Randall b Botham	2	c Randall b Edmonds	31
3	D. B. Vengsarkar	Bombay	c Botham b Hendrick	0	c Boycott b Edmonds	103
4	G. R. Viswanath	Karnataka	c Brearley b Hendrick	13	c Gower b Lever	113
5	A. D. Gaekwad	Baroda	c Taylor b Botham	11	not out	1
6	Yashpal Sharma	Punjab	c Taylor b Botham	11	not out	5
7	Kapil Dev	Haryana	c Miller b Botham	4		
8	K. D. Ghavri	Bombay	not out	3		
*9	B. Reddy	Tamil Nadu	l b w b Botham	0		
†10	S. Venkataraghavan	Tamil Nadu	run out	0		
11	B. S. Bedi	Delhi	b Lever	0	B 2, l-b 2, w 1, n-b 1,	6
			B , l-b , w , n-b			
			Total	**96**	**Total**	**318**

FALL OF THE WICKETS

1—12	2—23	3—51	4—75	5—79	6—89	7—96	8—96	9—96	10—96
1—79	2—99	3—309	4—312	5—	6—	7—	8—	9—	10—

ANALYSIS OF BOWLING

	1st Innings						2nd Innings				
Name	O.	M.	R.	W.	Wd.	N-b	O.	M.	R.	W.	Wd. N-b
Lever	9.5	3	29	1			24	7	69	1	1
Botham	19	9	35	5			35	13	80	1	1
Hendrick	15	7	15	2			25	12	66	0	
Edmonds	2	1	1	0			45	18	62	2	
Gooch	10	5	16	1			2	0	8	0	
Miller							17	6	37	0	

ENGLAND

			First Innings		Second Innings	
†1	J. M. Brearley	Middlesex	c Reddy b Dev	12		
2	G. Boycott	Yorkshire	c Gavaskar b Ghavri	32		
3	G. A. Gooch	Essex	b Dev	10		
4	D. I. Gower	Leicestershire	b Ghavri	82		
5	D. W. Randall	Nottinghamshire	run out	57		
6	I. T. Botham	Somerset	b Venkat	36		
7	G. Miller	Derbyshire	st Reddy b Bedi	62		
8	P. H. Edmonds	Middlesex	c Reddy b Dev	20		
*9	R. W. Taylor	Derbyshire	c Vengsarkar b Bedi	64		
10	J. K. Lever	Essex	not out	6		
11	M. Hendrick	Derbyshire	Innings closed			
			B 11, l-b 21, w 2, n-b 4,	38	B , l-b , w , n-b ,	
			Total	**419**	**Total**	

FALL OF THE WICKETS

1—21	2—60	3—71	4—185	5—226	6—253	7—291	8—394	9—419	10—
1—	2—	3—	4—	5—	6—	7—	8—	9—	10—

ANALYSIS OF BOWLING

	1st Innings						2nd Innings				
Name	O.	M.	R.	W.	Wd.	N-b	O.	M.	R.	W.	Wd. N-b
Kapil Dev	38	11	93	3	2						
Ghavri	31	2	122	2		4					
Bedi	38.5	13	87	2							
Venkataraghavan	22	2	79	1							

Umpires—H. D. Bird & K. E. Palmer
Scorers—E. Solomon & Yashvant Chad
† Captain * Wicket-keeper

Play begins 1st, 2nd, 3rd & 4th days at 11.30 5th day at 11.00
Stumps drawn 1st, 2nd, 3rd & 4th days at 6.30 5th day at 5.30 or 6.00
(In the event of play being suspended, for any reason, for one hour or more on any of the first four days, play may be extended to 7.30 p.m. on that day).
Luncheon Interval 1.30—2.10
Tea Interval 4.15—4.35 (may be varied according to state of game)

India won the toss

---

have to bat twice in a Lord's Test until his infamous pair in 1981, in his last Test as England captain.

Between the showers (which all but wiped out the second day), there were other heroes too. For India, Vengsarkar hit the first of his three Lord's Test centuries, as he and Viswanath made the game safe on the final day. That was after Botham had dismissed Gavaskar to take his hundredth Test wicket (and his twenty-fifth at Lord's), at the time the fastest hundred Test wickets ever. He took only two years and nine days to reach that mark, a record that stood until India's Kapil Dev got there even faster during the following winter.

Vengsarkar and Viswanath put on 210 for the third wicket, just one short of the record for India against England. A few seasons later, they broke the record, with the help of Yashpal Sharma who was making his debut in this game. At Madras in 1981/82, Vengsarkar and Viswanath put on 99 for the third wicket before Vengsarkar retired hurt, but then Viswanath and Sharma added another 316 before they were parted – a three-man total of 415 between the fall of the second and third wickets.

1980: England v West Indies

(2nd Test) June 19, 20, 21, 23, 24
Match drawn

The previous Lord's Test had lost eight hours and 54 minutes to rain, but this one exceeded that total by one hour and one minute, most of the time being washed away for the final two days. Ian Botham was now captain, having taken over from Mike Brearley at the start of the season, and he began his captaincy at headquarters by winning the toss and deciding to bat. This was a wise decision. Despite the early dismissal of Boycott, Graham Gooch at last proved his talent at Test level by hitting a magnificent century. Ably assisted by Chris Tavaré, Gooch made 123 out of 165 in 211 minutes. In light of his subsequent achievements, it is astonishing to recall that this was Gooch's first Test century in his twenty-second Test match over five years. The selectors were prepared to stick with a man in whom class was permanent even if form was temporary, and their faith in him paid off. In the team with Gooch was another man who took a long while to hit a Test century, and who never made one at his home ground of Lord's – Mike Gatting. Also Gatting never made a Test century against West Indies.

Two men who took the chance to hit a century on their first Test appearance at Lord's were Viv Richards and Desmond Haynes. Richards

Graham Gooch turns a ball to the off-side during his score of 123.

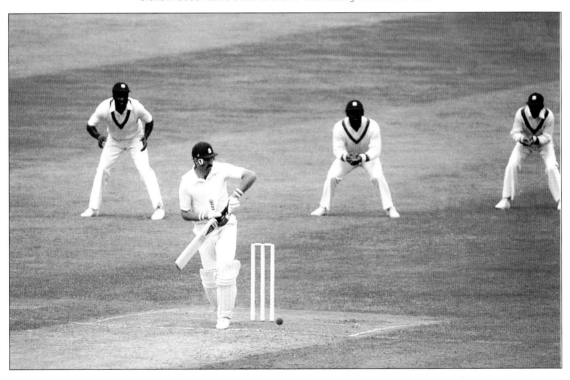

dominated in their partnership of 223 in 296 minutes, before he was caught by the twelfth man, Graham Dilley. 'Richards, c Dilley b Willey' is not quite as satisfying as the 'Lillee, c Willey b Dilley' that occurred the previous winter, but any dismissal of the greatest batsman of his time was welcome to the hard-pressed England team. This was already Richards' tenth Test hundred, and he topped 1,000 runs against England in only six Tests. Haynes' even bigger hundred was the highest score for West Indies at Lord's, until his opening partner Gordon Greenidge beat it four years later. Michael Holding's 6 for 67 in the first innings was also the best analysis by a West Indian at Lord's until Malcolm Marshall beat it in 1988. The West Indies were a very strong side indeed throughout the 1980s.

Having conceded a first innings lead of 249, England had only the draw to play for. The weather helped them achieve this modest goal.

ENGLAND

GA Gooch	lbw b Holding	123	b Garner	47
G Boycott	c Murray b Holding	8	not out	49
CJ Tavaré	c Greenidge b Holding	42	lbw b Garner	6
RA Woolmer	c Kallicharran b Garner	15	not out	19
MW Gatting	b Holding	18		
† IT Botham	lbw b Garner	8		
DL Underwood	lbw b Garner	3		
P Willey	b Holding	4		
* APE Knott	c Garner b Holding	9		
RGD Willis	b Garner	14		
M Hendrick	not out	10		
	(B 4, LB 1, W 4, NB 6)	15	(LB 1, NB 11)	12
Total		269	(2 wkts)	133

WEST INDIES

CG Greenidge	lbw b Botham	25
DL Haynes	lbw b Botham	184
IVA Richards	c sub (GR Dilley) b Willey	145
CEH Croft	run out	0
AI Kallicharran	c Knott b Willis	15
SFAF Bacchus	c Gooch b Willis	0
† CH Lloyd	b Willey	56
* DL Murray	c Tavaré b Botham	34
AME Roberts	b Underwood	24
J Garner	c Gooch b Willis	15
MA Holding	not out	0
	(B 1, LB 9, W 1, NB 9)	20
Total		518

WEST INDIES	O	M	R	W	O	M	R	W
Roberts	18	3	50	0	13	3	24	0
Holding	28	11	67	6	15	5	51	0
Garner	24.3	8	36	4	15	6	21	2
Croft	20	3	77	0	8	2	24	0
Richards	5	1	24	0	1	0	1	0

ENGLAND	O	M	R	W
Willis	31	12	103	3
Botham	37	7	145	3
Underwood	29.2	7	108	1
Hendrick	11	2	32	0
Gooch	7	1	26	0
Willey	25	8	73	2
Boycott	7	2	11	0

FALL OF WICKETS

	Eng.	WI	Eng.
Wkt	1st	1st	2nd
1st	20	37	71
2nd	165	260	96
3rd	190	275	
4th	219	326	
5th	220	330	
6th	231	437	
7th	232	469	
8th	244	486	
9th	245	518	
10th	269	518	

† Captain * Wicketkeeper

1980: England v Australia

(Centenary Test) August 28, 29, 30, September 1, 2
Match drawn

Over eight hours lost in the Lord's Test against India in 1979, over nine hours lost against West Indies earlier in the 1980 summer and now, in the Centenary Test to celebrate the anniversary of the first Test Match ever staged in England, over ten hours lost to bad light and rain. The fact that this was the only Lord's Test ever staged in September may have had something to do with the bad weather. It was held in September because the first Test Match in England had been held in September 1880. That original match had, of course, been staged at the Oval, but a hundred years on it was decided that Lord's was the only proper place to stage the Centenary Test.

The Test itself was inevitably drawn. Gubby Allen's opinion was that neither team looked a very good side. He was most impressed by Greg Chappell and Kim Hughes, who scored 201 runs in the match. He described Hughes' straight six off Chris Old as 'possibly the most remarkable straight six I have seen. To . . . hit a flat skimmer onto the top of the pavilion at Lord's takes some beating.' There were also centuries for Wood and Boycott, but it was two events off the field that attracted most attention.

On the Saturday afternoon, as the two captains, Botham and Chappell, and the umpires returned from a fifth inspection of the pitch and

Kim Hughes batting during his 117 with Hendrick and Gooch in the slips.

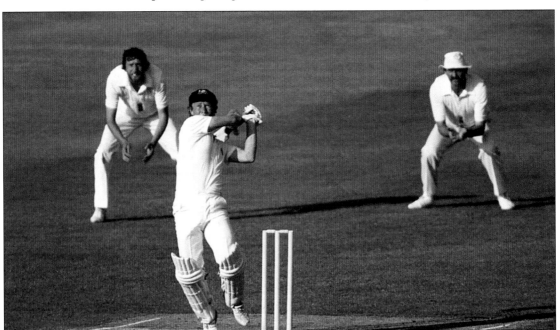

Match Drawn

 LORD'S GROUND

CORNHILL INSURANCE CENTENARY TEST MATCH
ENGLAND v. AUSTRALIA

Thurs., Fri., Sat., Mon. & Tues., August 28, 29, 30, Sept. 1 & 2, 1980 (5-day Match)

AUSTRALIA

		First Innings		Second Innings	
1 B. M. Laird	W. Australia	c Bairstow b Old	24	c Bairstow b Old	6
2 G. M. Wood	W. Australia	st Bairstow b Emburey	112	l b w b Old	8
†3 G. S. Chappell	Queensland	c Gatting b Old	47	b Old	59
4 K. J. Hughes	W. Australia	c Athey b Old	117	l b w b Botham	84
5 G. N. Yallop	Victoria	l b w b Hendrick	2	not out	21
6 A. R. Border	New South Wales	not out	56		
*7 R. W. Marsh	W. Australia	not out	16		
8 D. K. Lillee	W. Australia				
9 A. A. Mallett	S. Australia				
10 R. J. Bright	Victoria	Innings closed		Innings closed	
11 L. S. Pascoe	New South Wales				
		B 1, l-b 8, w , n-b 2,	11	B 1, l-b 8, w , n-b 2,	11
		Total	**385**	**Total**	**189**

FALL OF THE WICKETS

1—64 2—150 3—260 4—267 5—320 6— 7— 8— 9— 10—

1—15 2—28 3—139 4—189 5— 6— 7— 8— 9— 10—

ANALYSIS OF BOWLING

Name	1st Innings						2nd Innings					
	O.	M.	R.	W.	Wd.	N-b	O.	M.	R.	W.	Wd.	N-b
Old	35	9	91	3			20	6	47	3		
Hendrick	30	6	67	1			15	4	53	0		
Botham	22	2	89	0			9.2	1	43	1		1
Emburey	38	9	104	1		2	9	2	35	0		
Gooch	8	3	16	0								
Willey	1	0	7	0								

ENGLAND

		First Innings		Second Innings	
1 G. A. Gooch	Essex	c Bright b Lillee	8	l b w b Lillee	16
2 G. Boycott	Yorkshire	c Marsh b Lillee	62	not out	128
3 C. W. J. Athey	Yorkshire	b Lillee	9	c Laird b Pascoe	1
4 D. I. Gower	Leicestershire	b Lillee	45	b Mallett	35
5 M. W. Gatting	Middlesex	l b w b Pascoe	12	not out	51
†6 I. T. Botham	Somerset	c Wood b Pascoe	0		
7 P. Willey	Northamptonshire	l b w b Pascoe	5		
*8 D. L. Bairstow	Yorkshire	l b w b Pascoe	6		
9 J. E. Emburey	Middlesex	l b w b Pascoe	3		
10 C. M. Old	Yorkshire	not out	24		
11 M. Hendrick	Derbyshire	c Border b Mallett	5		
		B 6, l-b 8, w , n-b 12,	26	B 3, l-b 2, w , n-b 8,	13
		Total	**205**	**Total**	**244**

FALL OF THE WICKETS

1—10 2—41 3—137 4—151 5—158 6—163 7—164 8—173 9—200 10—205

1—19 2—43 3—124 4— 5— 6— 7— 8— 9— 10—

ANALYSIS OF BOWLING

Name	1st Innings						2nd Innings					
	O.	M.	R.	W.	Wd.	N-b	O.	M.	R.	W.	Wd.	N-b
Lillee	15	4	43	4		4	19	5	53	1		2
Pascoe	18	5	59	5		4	17	1	73	1		3
Chappell	2	0	2	0								
Bright	21	6	60	0		2	25	9	44	0		
Mallett	7.2	3	25	1		2	21	2	61	1		3

Umpires—H. D. Bird & D. J. Constant   Scorers—E. Solomon & D. K. Sherwood

† Captain   * Wicket-keeper

Play begins 1st, 2nd & 3rd days at 11.30 4th & 5th days at 11.00
Stumps drawn 1st, 2nd & 3rd days at 6.30 4th day at 7.00 5th day at 6.30 or 7.00
Luncheon Interval 1st, 2nd & 3rd days 1.30—2.10 4th & 5th days 1.20—2.00
Tea Interval 1st, 2nd & 3rd days 4.10—4.30 4th & 5th days 4.20—4.40
(may be varied according to state of game)

Australia won the toss

decided that the ground was still not fit for play, umpire David Constant was reportedly grabbed by the tie and 'shoved and jostled' by members of M.C.C. in front of the Long Room. Botham was hit on the back of the head, and Chappell complained that 'intimidatory and abusive language was being used.' The sledger sledged. There was much made of it all in the press, and M.C.C. conducted an official investigation, the outcome of which was never made public. As *The Times* put it, 'Has civilisation as we know it ended with the disgraceful scenes in the Members' Enclosure at Lord's?'

No, but some would suggest that cricket civilisation ended later in the game when John Arlott made his final broadcast for 'Test Match Special'. With the words, 'and after Trevor Bailey, it'll be Christopher Martin-Jenkins,' he signed off a unique broadcasting career. A public address announcement confirmed the sad event, and the entire ground, including the Australian fielders and Boycott and Gower, who were batting, joined in the spontaneous applause.

A great gathering of the clans.

1. F J Bryant (ACB)
2. T C J Caldwell (ACB)
3. L V Maddocks
4. A N Connolly
5. M H N Walker
6. A E Moss
7. P E Richardson
8. C R Ingamells (ACB)
9. K R Stackpole
10. R A L Massie
11. R B Simpson
12. R T Simpson
13. W M Lawry
14. A Turner
15. R Tattersall
16. R A Gaunt
17. M J McInnes (ACB)
18. A W Walsh (ACB)
19. J W Gleeson
20. A C Smith
21. G B Hole
22. D L Richards (ACB)
23. D A Allen
24. R M Prideaux
25. H W H Rigg (ACB)
26. R Subba Row
27. T R Veivers
28. F J Titmus
29. F W C Bennett (ACB)
30. K D Mackay
31. T W Cartwright
32. R Edwards
33. J T Murray
34. W Watson
35. R M Cowper
36. C S Serjeant
37. J S E Price
38. M J K Smith
39. J M Parks
40. C C McDonald
41. B L D'Oliveira
42. A S M Oakman
43. J A Flavell
44. J A Ledward (ACB)
45. L J Coldwell
46. R Benaud
47. I R Redpath
48. G R A Langley
49. P H Edmonds
50. G A R Lock
51. F E Rumsey
52. J H de Courcy
53. K V Andrew
54. R B McCosker
55. H B Taber
56. J H Hampshire
57. F M Misson
58. T W Graveney
59. A K Davidson
60. K D Walters
61. G D McKenzie
62. P J Loader
63. E W Freeman
64. G D Watson
65. G E Corling
66. A J W McIntyre
67. D B Close
68. G J Gilmour
69. I M Chappell
70. F H Tyson
71. R Illingworth
72. D J Colley
73. J B Statham
74. K Taylor
75. P H Parfitt
76. R Appleyard
77. P J Sharpe
78. C G Howard (M.C.C.)
79. I J Jones
80. E R Dexter
81. A R Barnes (ACB)
82. I D Craig
83. C S Elliott (T.C.C.B.)
84. V J W M Lawrence (M.C.C.)
85. K F Barrington
86. J H Wardle
87. W E Bowes
88. J G Dewes
89. A G Chipperfield
90. C J Barnett
91. T G Evans
92. E W CLark
93. J A Young
94. W Voce.
95. J C Laker
96. Sir L Hutton
97. E R H Toshack
98. E L McCormick
99. W A Johnston
100. K E Rigg
101. A R Morris
102. D T Ring
103. F R Brown
104. S J E Loxton
105. K R Miller
106. D V P Wright
107. A V Bedser
108. K Cranston
109. M G Waite
110. C Washbrook
111. C L Badcock
112. N W D Yardley
113. A L Hassett
114. H E Dollery
115. W A Brown
116. J T Ikin
117. L G James (M.C.C.)
118. W E Hollies
119. J A Bailey (M.C.C. Secretary)
120. A R Border
121. J Dyson
122. G Dymock
123. R J Bright
124. B M Laird
125. G M Wood
126. G N Yallop
127. K J Hughes
128. R W Marsh
129. L S Pascoe
130. J R Thomson
131. A A Mallett
132. D K Lillee
133. P M Lush (T.C.C.B.)
134. J R Stephenson (M.C.C.)
135. D B Carr (T.C.C.B. Secretary)
136. D J Constant (umpire)
137. P M Willey
138. J Emburey
139. C W J Athey
140. R D Jackman
141. D L Bairstow
142. M W Gatting
143. C M Old
144. M Hendrick
145. G Boycott
146. G A Gooch
147. D I Gower
148. H D Bird (umpire)
149. W J O'Reilly
150. L S Darling
151. E L a'Beckett
152. W H Ponsford
153. A Sandham
154. R C Steele (ACB)
155. P B H May
156. G S Chappell
157. S C Griffith (M.C.C. President)
158. I T Botham
159. R J Parish (ACB Chairman)
160. F G Mann (T.C.C.B. Chairman)
161. H S T L Hendry
162. G O B Allen
163. R E S Wyatt
164. P G H Fender

ACB: Australian Cricket Board
T.C.C.B.: Test and County Cricket Board (now E.C.B.)

1980: ENGLAND v AUSTRALIA (CENTENARY TEST)

1981: England v Australia

(2nd Test) July 2, 3, 4, 6, 7
Match drawn

The Second Test of 1981 marked the nadir of Ian Botham's Test career, and was the last of his twelve matches as captain. Although England finished the match in the stronger position, they could not press home their advantage, which meant that when Botham resigned as captain he had never led England to victory. Different people will remember the match for different reasons – for Geoffrey Boycott it was his one hundredth Test, and for Bob Woolmer it was his last – but most people will remember it for the silence that greeted Ian Botham as he returned to the pavilion after his second innings duck. Members looked away in embarrassment as Botham, head down,

walked back to the England dressing room. We all thought then that Botham's summer was over.

This was the first time since 1905, and the final time to date, that two consecutive Lord's Tests had been against the same opponents (although in 2010 Pakistan played consecutive Tests at Lord's first as the home side then as the visitors). Australia, with what in retrospect can be seen as no more than an average team, had won the first Test of the summer by four wickets, thanks mainly to their bowling attack of Dennis Lillee – still a force as he approached his thirty-second birthday – Terry Alderman and Geoff Lawson. Nothing much changed at Lord's, with Geoff Lawson

A pair for Botham and the end of his captaincy.

taking most advantage of the conditions and England's uncertain batting to take 7 for 81 and earn himself the Man of the Match award. Peter Willey and John Emburey put on 97 together in the middle of the innings, but England then lost their last six wickets in under an hour, four of them to Lawson. When Australia batted, they really only gained an edge by virtue of 55 extras, the highest number conceded in an England v Australia match to that date, and useful tail-end runs from Marsh, Bright and Lillee. Australia's last five wickets added 178 runs compared with England's 27.

England's second innings included Boycott's sixtieth half century for England, Botham's first pair and a useful indication that Graham Dilley could bat. Australia, set 232 to win, could only reach 90 for 4 in 48.5 overs, and were thankful for the draw. In the next match, Mike Brearley came back as captain in place of the injured Woolmer, and Botham proved what a great player he is. Australia, lulled into a false sense of security after two Tests, never knew what hit them.

Match Drawn

 LORD'S **GROUND**

CORNHILL INSURANCE TEST SERIES
ENGLAND v. AUSTRALIA

Thurs., Fri., Sat., Mon. & Tues., July 2, 3, 4, 6 & 7, 1981   (5-day Match)

ENGLAND

			First Innings		Second Innings	
1 G. A. Gooch	Essex	c Yallop b Lawson	44	l b w b Lawson	20
2 G. Boycott	Yorkshire	c Alderman b Lawson	17	c Marsh b Lillee	60
3 R. A. Woolmer	Kent	c Marsh b Lawson	21	l b w b Alderman	9
4 D. I. Gower	Leicestershire	c Marsh b Lawson	27	c Alderman b Lillee	89
5 M. W. Gatting	Middlesex	l b w b Bright	59	c Wood b Bright	16
6 P. Willey	Northamptonshire	c Border b Alderman	82	c Chappell b Bright	12
7 J. E. Emburey	Middlesex	run out	31		
†8 I. T. Botham	Somerset	l b w b Lawson	0	b Bright	0
*9 R. W. Taylor	Derbyshire	c Hughes b Lawson	0	b Lillee	9
10 G. R. Dilley	Kent	not out	7	not out	27
11 R. G. D. Willis	Warwickshire	c Wood b Lawson	5	Innings closed	
		B 2, l-b 3, w 3, n-b 10,	18	B 2, l-b 8, w , n-b 13,	23
		Total	311	Total	265

FALL OF THE WICKETS
1—60 2—65 3—134 4—187 5—284 6—293 7—293 8—293 9—298 10—311
1—31 2—55 3—178 4—217 5—217 6—217 7—242 8—265 9— 10—

ANALYSIS OF BOWLING

Name	1st Innings						2nd Innings					
	O.	M.	R.	W.	Wd.	N-b	O.	M.	R.	W.	Wd.	N-b
Lillee	35.4	7	102	0			26.4	8	82	3		1
Alderman	30.2	7	79	1		5	17	2	42	1		8
Lawson	43.1	14	81	7	3	5	19	6	51	1		3
Bright	15	7	31	1			36	18	67	3		1

AUSTRALIA

			First Innings		Second Innings	
1 G. M. Wood	W. Australia	c Taylor b Willis	44	not out	62
2 J. Dyson	New South Wales	c Gower b Botham	7	l b w b Dilley	1
3 G. N. Yallop	Victoria	b Dilley	1	c Botham b Willis	3
†4 K. J. Hughes	W. Australia	c Willis b Emburey	42	l b w b Dilley	4
5 T. M. Chappell	New South Wales	c Taylor b Dilley	2	c Taylor b Botham	5
6 A. R. Border	Queensland	c Gatting b Botham	64	not out	12
*7 R. W. Marsh	W. Australia	l b w b Dilley	47		
8 R. J. Bright	Victoria	l b w b Emburey	33		
9 G. F. Lawson	New South Wales	l b w b Willis	5		
10 D. K. Lillee	W. Australia	not out	40		
11 T. M. Alderman	W. Australia	c Taylor b Willis	5		
		B 6, l-b 11, w 6, n-b 32,	55	B , l-b , w 1, n-b 2,	3
		Total	345	Total	90

FALL OF THE WICKETS
1—62 2—62 3—69 4—81 5—167 6—244 7—257 8—268 9—314 10—345
1—2 2—11 3—17 4—62 5— 6— 7— 8— 9— 10—

ANALYSIS OF BOWLING

Name	1st Innings						2nd Innings					
	O.	M.	R.	W.	Wd.	N-b	O.	M.	R.	W.	Wd.	N-b
Willis	27.4	9	50	3		24	12	3	35	1		2
Dilley	30	8	106	3	4	8	7.5	1	18	2		
Botham	26	8	71	2	2		8	3	10	1	1	
Gooch	10	4	28	0								
Emburey	25	9	35	2			21	10	24	0		

Umpires—D. O. Oslear & K. E. Palmer

Scorers—E. Solomon & D. K. Sherwood

† Captain   * Wicket-keeper

Play begins 1st, 2nd, 3rd & 4th days at 11.30   5th day at 11.00
Stumps drawn 1st, 2nd, 3rd & 4th days at 6.30   5th day at 5.30 or 6.00
(In the event of play being suspended, for any reason, for one hour or more on any of the first four days, play may be extended to 7.30 p.m. on that day).
Luncheon Interval 1st, 2nd, 3rd & 4th days 1.30—2.10   5th day 1.00—1.40
Tea Interval 1st, 2nd, 3rd & 4th days 4.10—4.30   5th day 3.40—4.00
(may be varied according to state of game)

Australia won the toss and elected to field

LORD'S GROUND

1982: England v India

(1st Test) June 10, 11, 12, 14, 15
England won by 7 wickets

Following the Centenary Test two years earlier, Lord's now celebrated the Golden Jubilee of Test matches against India, and as in that first Test, there was a man playing for India whose entire Test career would be this one outing at Lord's. In 1932 it was Lall Singh, and in 1982 it was GA Parkar. No other non-English players have played their entire Test cricket careers at Lord's.

England had a new captain. Bob Willis was the fourth Warwickshire player to lead England, and their fourth captain in twelve months after Botham, Brearley and Fletcher (on the winter tour). England had to do without fifteen players including Geoff Boycott, Graham Gooch, John

Emburey and Wayne Larkins, all of whom had taken part in the rebel South African tour in March of that year. To fill the gaps England capped two new players, the Kenyan-born captain of Cambridge University Derek Pringle, and the South African-born Allan Lamb, who had been scoring runs by the hatful in county cricket while waiting for his Test qualification to mature. With Zambian Phil Edmonds in the side as well, England had an African look even without the rebels.

For Lamb the match began poorly. As he wrote in his autobiography, 'We won the toss and I was in and out inside the first hour – lbw to Kapil for

Randall – stationary for once.

     1982: ENGLAND v INDIA

England won by 7 wickets

 LORD'S **GROUND**

CORNHILL INSURANCE TEST SERIES
ENGLAND v. INDIA
GOLDEN JUBILEE MATCH

Thurs., Fri., Sat., Mon. & Tues., June 10, 11, 12, 14 & 15, 1982   (5-day Match)

ENGLAND

		First Innings		Second Innings	
1 G. Cook	Northamptonshire	l b w b Kapil Dev	4	l b w b Kapil Dev	10
2 C. J. Tavare	Kent	c Viswanath b Kapil Dev	4	b Kapil Dev	3
3 A. J. Lamb	Northamptonshire	l b w b Kapil Dev	9	not out	37
4 D. I. Gower	Leicestershire	c Viswanath b Kapil Dev	37	not out	14
5 I. T. Botham	Somerset	c Malhotra b Madan Lal	67		
6 D. W. Randall	Nottinghamshire	c Parkar b Kapil Dev	126		
7 D. R. Pringle	Cambridge Univ.	c Gavaskar b Doshi	7		
8 P. H. Edmonds	Middlesex	c Kirmani b Madan Lal	64		
*9 R. W. Taylor	Derbyshire	c Viswanath b Doshi	31	c Malhotra b Kapil Dev	1
10 P. J. W. Allott	Lancashire	not out	41		
†11 R. G. D. Willis	Warwickshire	b Madan Lal	28		
		B 1, l-b 5, w , n-b 9,	15	B , l-b 2, w , n-b	2
		Total	433	Total	67

FALL OF THE WICKETS

1—5	2—18	3—37	4—96	5—149	6—166	7—291	8—363	9—363	10—433
1—11	2—13	3—18	4—	5—	6—	7—	8—	9—	10—

ANALYSIS OF BOWLING

	1st Innings						2nd Innings					
Name	O.	M.	R.	W.	Wd.	N-b	O.	M.	R.	W.	Wd.	N-b
Kapil Dev	43	8	125	5	...	6	10	1	43	3	...	...
Madan Lal	28.1	6	99	3	...	3	2	1	2	0	...	...
Shastri	34	10	73	0	...		2	0	9	0	...	...
Doshi	40	7	120	2	...		5	3	11	0	...	...
Yashpal Sharma	3	2	1	0	...		...	...	...	...	...	...

INDIA

		First Innings		Second Innings	
†1 S. M. Gavaskar	Bombay	b Botham	48	c Cook b Willis	24
2 G. A. Parkar	Bombay	l b w b Botham	6	b Willis	1
3 D. B. Vengsarkar	Bombay	l b w b Willis	2	c Allott b Willis	157
4 G. R. Viswanath	Karnataka	b Botham	1	c Taylor b Pringle	3
5 Yashpal Sharma	Punjab	l b w b Pringle	4	b Willis	37
6 A. Malhotra	Haryana	l b w b Pringle	5	c Taylor b Willis	0
7 Kapil Dev	Haryana	c Cook b Willis	41	c Cook b Botham	89
8 R. J. Shastri	Bombay	c Cook b Willis	4	b Allott	23
*9 S. M. H. Kirmani	Karnataka	not out	6	c Gower b Willis	3
10 S. Madan Lal	Delhi	c Tavare b Botham	6	l b w b Pringle	15
11 D. R. Doshi	Bengal	c Taylor b Botham	0	not out	0
		B , l-b 1, w , n-b 4,	5	B , l-b 2, w , n-b 11,	13
		Total	128	Total	369

FALL OF THE WICKETS

1—17	2—21	3—22	4—31	5—45	6—112	7—116	8—116	9—128	10—128
1—6	2—47	3—107	4—110	5—252	6—252	7—254	8—275	9—341	10—369

ANALYSIS OF BOWLING

	1st Innings						2nd Innings					
Name	O.	M.	R.	W.	Wd.	N-b	O.	M.	R.	W.	Wd.	N-b
Botham	19.4	3	46	5	...	4	31.5	7	103	1	...	9
Willis	16	2	41	3	...		28	3	101	6	...	1
Pringle	9	4	16	2	...		19	4	58	2	...	1
Edmonds	2	1	5	0	...		15	6	39	0	...	1
Allott	4	1	15	0	...		17	3	51	1	...	
Cook							1	0	4	0	...	

Umpires—D. G. L. Evans & B. J. Meyer   Scorers—E. Solomon & G. G. A. Saulez

† Captain   * Wicket-keeper

Play begins each day at 11.00

Stumps drawn each day at 6.00, or after 96 overs have been bowled, whichever is the later.

Luncheon Interval each day 1.00—1.40

Tea Interval each day 3.40—4.00, or when 35 overs remain to be bowled, whichever is the later. (May be varied according to state of game)

England won the toss

---

nine runs with no movement of my feet.' Fortunately for England, the minor crisis he left behind – 37 for 3 – was overcome by Ian Botham, Derek Randall and the tail. The fifth wicket went down at 149, but England finished on 433, with Randall's first Test century in England the mainstay of the innings. England's tenth wicket stand in this innings – 70 between Allott and Willis - survives as the record for all Tests between England and India.

When India batted, 45 for 5 became 128 all out, and but for their captain Sunil Gavaskar and their future captain Kapil Dev, they would have been all out for under 40. Every batsman was out bowled, lbw or caught close to the wicket as Botham, Willis and Pringle raced through the card. The follow-on was a much better affair, with Dilip Vengsarkar scoring his usual Lord's Test century, but it was not quite enough. Lamb was able to record that 'rain threatened us on the final morning, but I hit the winning boundary off Kapil.'

1982: England v Pakistan

(2nd Test) August 12, 13, 14, 16
Pakistan won by 10 wickets

Two months can be a long time. Under their fifth captain in a little over a year, and with a team showing four changes from the side that beat India in June, England were beaten by a Pakistan side that outplayed them on almost all counts. England were led by David Gower because Bob Willis dropped out at the last minute with a stiff neck. Willis had batted with Bob Taylor for so long in England's victorious First Test (they put on 79 for the last wicket in England's second innings), wearing the then still unfamiliar helmet,

that two weeks later he could still barely move his head. Robin Jackman took his place.

Pakistan's opener Mohsin Khan scored the first Test double hundred at Lord's since Martin Donnelly's 206 for New Zealand in 1949: no Englishman scored a Test double hundred at Lord's between Denis Compton in 1947 and Graham Gooch's 333 in 1990. When England batted in response to Pakistan's 428, extras top-scored with 46 (including a Test record 13 wides), and no Englishman got more than Mike Gatting's

Mohsin Khan, unchallenged as Man of the Match.

Pakistan won by 10 wickets

LORD'S GROUND 15p

CORNHILL INSURANCE TEST SERIES
ENGLAND v. PAKISTAN

THURS., FRI., SAT., SUN. & MON., AUGUST 12, 13, 14, 15 & 16, 1982 (5-day Match)

PAKISTAN		First Innings		Second Innings	
1 Mudassar Nazar	...United Bank	c Taylor b Jackman	20	not out	39
2 Mohsin Khan	...Habib Bank	c Tavare b Jackman	200		
3 Mansoor Akhtar	...United Bank	c Lamb b Botham	57	not out	26
4 Javed Miandad	...Habib Bank	run out	6		
5 Zaheer Abbas	...P.I.A.	b Jackman	75		
6 Haroon Rashid	...United Bank	l b w b Botham	1		
†7 Imran Khan	...Lahore	c Taylor b Botham	12		
8 Tahir Naqqash	...M.C.B.	c Gatting b Jackman	2		
*9 Wasim Bari	...P.I.A.	not out	24		
10 Abdul Qadir	...Habib Bank	not out	18		
11 Sarfraz Nawaz	...Lahore	Innings closed			
		B 3, l-b 8, w , n-b 2, 13		B 1, l-b 10, w 1, n-b , 12	
		Total	**428**	**Total**	**77**

FALL OF THE WICKETS
1—53 2—197 3—208 4—361 5—364 6—380 7—382 8—401 9— 10—
1— 2— 3— 4— 5— 6— 7— 8— 9— 10—

ANALYSIS OF BOWLING	1st Innings					2nd Innings					
Name	O.	M.	R.	W.	Wd	N-b	O.	M.	R.	W.	Wd	N-b
Botham	44	8	148	3	...	1	7	0	30	0	1	
Jackman	36	5	110	4	...	1	4	0	22	0		
Pringle	26	9	62	0	...	...						
Greig	13	2	42	0	...	...	2.1	0	13	0		
Hemmings	20	3	53	0	...	...	...	...	...	...		

ENGLAND		First Innings		Second Innings	
1 D. W. Randall	...Nottinghamshire	b Sarfraz	29	b Mudassar	9
2 C. J. Tavare	...Kent	b Sarfraz	8	c Miandad b Imran	82
3 A. J. Lamb	...Northamptonshire	c Haroon b Tahir	33	l b w b Mudassar	0
†4 D. I. Gower	...Leicestershire	c Mansoor b Imran	29	c W.-Bari b Mudassar	0
5 I. T. Botham	...Somerset	c Mohsin b Qadir	31	c Sarfraz b Mudassar	69
6 M. W. Gatting	...Middlesex	not out	32	c W.-Bari b Mudassar	7
7 D. R. Pringle	...Essex	c Haroon b Qadir	5	c Miandad b Qadir	14
8 I. A. Greig	...Sussex	l b w b Qadir	3	l b w b Mudassar	2
9 E. E. Hemmings	...Notts.	b Sarfraz	6	c Wasim Bari b Imran	14
*10 R. W. Taylor	...Derbyshire	l b w b Qadir	5	not out	24
11 R. D. Jackman	...Surrey	l b w b Imran	0	c Haroon b Qadir	17
		B 11, l-b 12, w 13, n-b 10, 46		B 10, l-b 19, w 5, n-b 4, 38	
		Total	**227**	**Total**	**276**

FALL OF THE WICKETS
1—16 2—69 3—89 4—157 5—173 6—187 7—197 8—217 9—226 10—227
1—9 2—9 3—9 4—121 5—132 6—171 7—180 8—224 9—235 10—276

ANALYSIS OF BOWLING	1st Innings					2nd Innings					
Name	O.	M.	R.	W.	Wd	N-b	O.	M.	R.	W.	Wd	N-b
Imran	23	4	55	2	10		42	13	84	2	1	
Sarfraz	23	4	56	3	1	5	14	5	22	0	...	4
Tahir	12	4	25	1	1	3	7	5	6	0	...	
Qadir	24	3	39	4	1	2	37.5	15	94	2	...	
Mudassar	4	1	6	0	1	...	19	7	32	6	4	

Umpires—H. D. Bird & D. J. Constant   Scorers—E. Solomon & R. M. Costan
† Captain   * Wicket-keeper

Play begins 1st, 2nd, 3rd & 5th days at 11.00, 4th day at 12.00
Luncheon Interval 1st, 2nd, 3rd & 5th days 1.00—1.40, 4th day 2.00—2.40
Tea Interval 1st, 2nd, 3rd & 5th days 3.40—4.00, 4th day 4.40—5.00; or when 35 overs remain to be bowled on any day, whichever is the later. (May be varied according to state of game).
Stumps drawn 1st, 2nd, 3rd & 5th days at 6.00, 4th day at 7.00; or after 96 overs have been bowled on any day, whichever is the later. In the event of play being suspended, for any reason, for one hour or more on any of the first four days, play may continue on that day until 7.00 (1st, 2nd & 3rd days) or 8.00 (4th day).

Pakistan won the toss

32 not out. At stumps on the third day, England had reached 226 for 9, with Gatting and Jackman the not out batsmen. That evening Gower, Lamb and Jackman went out for dinner together and all chose duck. The next morning, Jackman was out for a duck and England followed on 201 behind. Within a few overs, Lamb and Gower were both also out, for ducks, and England were 9 for 3. At this stage, the game was lost, but nobody told Chris Tavaré, who had not eaten the duck the night before. His 82 was the highest score by an Englishman in the match, and it took him 404 minutes. His fifty came up in 350 minutes, at that time the second slowest fifty in cricket history. He took 67 minutes to get off the mark, and spent another hour with his score on 24, thus becoming the first player ever to spend at least an hour becalmed twice in the same innings. The jokes about his slow batting were legion, but his value to a generally dashing but sometimes unreliable batting line-up should not be underestimated.

His efforts were not quite enough to save the match. Pakistan won with barely five overs left to play. Bob Willis came back for the Third Test, and normal service was resumed. England won.

LORD'S GROUND

1983: England v New Zealand

(3rd Test) August 11, 12, 13, 15
England won by 127 runs

This was the 75th Test Match at Lord's, an achievement which meant the ground ranked first equal with the Melbourne Cricket Ground in terms of the number of Tests staged. Lord's was then, and still is, behind the MCG in the number of limited overs internationals staged, but is now equal in the number of Olympic Games hosted, but in Test matches, Lord's has moved ahead to become the clear leader.

Lord's still also leads in World Cup Finals staged. The 1983 World Cup Final, won by the underdogs India, took place there on 25 June, which put the rest of the summer's cricket a little later than was usual. This was the Third Test of the series, only the second (and to date the last)

time that Lord's had been the venue of a Third Test. The score in the series so far was one all, so this was the deciding match.

New Zealand must have thought they had made the right decision to put England in when Chris Smith was out lbw to the first ball he faced in Test cricket. Smith was one of three debutants in the England team, the first time three new England caps (Smith, Foster and Cook) had been awarded at the same time since 1964 in Bombay. However, Tavaré, Gower and Gatting repaired the damage, David Gower helped by Lance Cairns dropping a very simple catch off Martin Crowe's bowling when he had only made 21. It would have been Crowe's first wicket in Test cricket, but

The tools of a groundsman's trade.

he had to wait another three hours for that.

In 1983, the New Zealand attack was the world class Richard Hadlee at one end, and any one of five lesser bowlers at the other. England made the most of their time away from Hadlee's end. When New Zealand batted, Nick Cook exploited the New Zealand batsmen's weakness against spin to take 5 for 35 in 26 overs on debut, while Ian Botham exploited their batsmen's weakness against Botham by taking four for 50. Allan Lamb equalled the record set in the Tests of 1963 (by Cowdrey) and 1973 (by Sobers) by taking six catches in the match. Nobody managed six catches in 1993.

There were no pairs of brothers playing in this Test, although five of the players had brothers who had been, or would also be Test cricketers. Jeff Crowe, Hedley Howarth, Brendon Bracewell and Dayle Hadlee of New Zealand and Robin Smith of England are the brothers in question. Lance Cairns' son Chris also became a Test cricketer.

15p **LORD'S GROUND** 15p

CORNHILL INSURANCE TEST SERIES

ENGLAND v. NEW ZEALAND

THURS., FRI., SAT., MON. & TUES., AUGUST 11, 12, 13, 15 & 16, 1983 (5-day Match)

ENGLAND		First Innings		Second Innings	
1 C. J. Tavare	Kent	b Crowe	51	c Crowe b Hadlee	16
2 C. L. Smith	Hampshire	l b w b Hadlee	0	c Coney b Hadlee	43
3 D. I. Gower	Leicestershire	l b w b Crowe	108	c Crowe b Gray	34
4 A. J. Lamb	Northamptonshire	c sub b Chatfield	17	c Hadlee b Gray	4
5 M. W. Gatting	Middlesex	c Wright b Hadlee	81	b Gray	15
6 I. T. Botham	Somerset	l b w b Cairns	8	c Coney b Chatfield	61
*7 R. W. Taylor	Derbyshire	b Hadlee	16	c and b Coney	7
8 N. A. Foster	Essex	c Smith b Hadlee	10	c Wright b Hadlee	3
9 N. G. B. Cook	Leicestershire	b Chatfield	16	c Bracewell b Chatfield	5
†10 R. G. D. Willis	Warwickshire	c Smith b Hadlee	7	not out	2
11 N. G. Cowans	Middlesex	not out	1	c Smith b Chatfield	1
		B 3, l-b 3, w 2, n-b 3,	11	B 5, l-b 6, w 9, n-b ,	20
		Total	326	Total	211

FALL OF THE WICKETS

1—3	2—152	3—174	4—191	5—218	6—288	7—290	8—303	9—318	10—326
1—26	2—79	3—87	4—119	5—147	6—195	7—199	8—208	9—210	10—211

ANALYSIS OF BOWLING

	1st Innings						2nd Innings					
Name	O.	M.	R.	W.	Wd.	N-b	O.	M.	R.	W.	Wd.	N-b
Hadlee	40	15	93	5	1	3	26	7	42	3	8	...
Cairns	23	8	65	1	...	...	3	0	9	0	...	...
Chatfield	36.3	8	116	2	...	...	13.3	4	29	3	...	...
Crowe	13	1	35	2	1	...	...	...	...	...	...	...
Coney	8	7	6	0	...	...	6	4	9	1	1	...
Bracewell	...	...	...	...	...	...	11	4	29	0	...	...
Gray	...	...	...	...	...	...	30	8	73	3	...	...

NEW ZEALAND		First Innings		Second Innings	
1 B. A. Edgar	Wellington	c Willis b Cook	70	c Lamb b Cowans	27
2 J. G. Wright	Northern Districts	c Lamb b Willis	11	c Taylor b Botham	12
†3 G. P. Howarth	Northern Districts	b Cook	25	c Taylor b Willis	0
4 M. D. Crowe	Auckland	b Botham	46	c Foster b Cowans	12
5 J. V. Coney	Wellington	b Cook	7	c Gatting b Foster	68
6 E. J. Gray	Wellington	c Lamb b Botham	11	c Lamb b Cook	17
7 J. G. Bracewell	Auckland	c Gower b Cook	0	l b w b Willis	4
8 R. J. Hadlee	Canterbury	c Botham b Cook	0	b Willis	30
9 B. L. Cairns	Northern Districts	c Lamb b Botham	5	b Cook	16
*10 I. D. S. Smith	Central Districts	c Lamb b Botham	3	not out	17
11 E. J. Chatfield	Wellington	not out	5	c and b Cook	2
		B , l-b 5, w , n-b 3,	8	B 3, l-b 4, w , n-b 7,	14
		Total	191	Total	219

FALL OF THE WICKETS

1—18	2—49	3—147	4—159	5—176	6—176	7—176	8—183	9—184	10—191
1—15	2—17	3—57	4—61	5—108	6—154	7—158	8—190	9—206	10—219

ANALYSIS OF BOWLING

	1st Innings						2nd Innings					
Name	O.	M.	R.	W.	Wd.	N-b	O.	M.	R.	W.	Wd.	N-b
Willis	13	6	28	1	...	3	12	5	24	3	...	7
Foster	16	5	40	0	...	...	12	0	35	1	...	...
Cowans	9	1	30	0	...	...	11	1	36	2	...	...
Botham	20.4	6	50	4	...	...	7	2	20	1	...	...
Cook	26	11	35	5	...	...	27.2	9	90	3	...	...

Umpires—D. J. Constant & D. G. L. Evans Scorers—E. Solomon & J. O'Sullivan

† Captain * Wicket-keeper

Play begins each day at 11.00

Luncheon Interval each day 1.00—1.40

Tea Interval each day 3.40—4.00, or when 35 overs remain to be bowled, if later.

Stumps drawn each day at 6.00, or after 96 overs have been bowled, whichever is the later. In the event of play being suspended, for any reason, for one hour or more on any of the first four days, play may continue on that day until 7.00.

(Timings may be varied according to state of game)

New Zealand won the toss and elected to field

England won by 127 runs

1984: England v West Indies

(2nd Test) June 28, 29, 30, July 2, 3
West Indies won by 9 wickets

One hundred years, less about three weeks, since the first Test match was played at Lord's, the West Indians brought to headquarters what many consider their finest team ever, and duly demolished England. Having already overwhelmed their hosts at Edgbaston in the First Test, they went on to win the next three as well, to become the first touring team ever to win all five Tests in an English summer. Although it does not look like it, the Lord's Test was probably the closest fought of the series, with West Indies owing their victory mainly to a quite superb double hundred by Gordon Greenidge on the final day.

That summer, England were still not at full strength, because of the bans imposed on those who had participated in the rebel tour of South Africa. Without Graham Gooch, Peter Willey, Derek Underwood and John Emburey, for example, the selectors could not choose the best and had to make do with the best available. All the same, England have fielded plenty of weaker sides even when they had all the options, so too many

Gordon Greenidge hooks Neil Foster for six during his brilliant second innings.

(15p) LORD'S GROUND (15p)

CORNHILL INSURANCE TEST SERIES
ENGLAND v. WEST INDIES

Thurs., Fri., Sat., Mon. & Tues., June 28, 29, 30 & July 2, 3, 1984 (5-day Match)

ENGLAND

		First Innings		Second Innings	
1 G. Fowler	Lancashire	c Harper b Baptiste	106	l b w b Small	11
2 B. C. Broad	Nottinghamshire	c Dujon b Marshall	55	c Harper b Garner	0
†3 D. I. Gower	Leicestershire	l b w b Marshall	3	c Lloyd b Small	21
4 A. J. Lamb	Northamptonshire	l b w b Marshall	23	c Dujon b Marshall	110
5 M. W. Gatting	Middlesex	l b w b Marshall	1	l b w b Marshall	29
6 I. T. Botham	Somerset	c Richards b Baptiste	30	l b w b Garner	81
*7 P. R. Downton	Middlesex	not out	23	l b w b Small	4
8 G. Miller	Derbyshire	run out	0	b Harper	9
9 D. R. Pringle	Essex	l b w b Garner	2	l b w b Garner	8
10 N. A. Foster	Essex	c Harper b Marshall	6	not out	9
11 R. G. D. Willis	Warwickshire	b Marshall	2	Innings closed	
		B 4, l-b 14, w 2, n-b 15	35	B 4, l-b 7, w 1, n-b 6	18
		Total	**286**	**Total**	**300**

FALL OF THE WICKETS

1—101 2—106 3—183 4—185 5—243 6—248 7—251 8—255 9—264 10—286

1—5 2—33 3—36 4—88 5—216 6—230 7—273 8—290 9—300 10—

ANALYSIS OF BOWLING

	1st Innings						2nd Innings					
Name	O.	M.	R.	W.	Wd.	N-b	O.	M.	R.	W.	Wd.	N-b
Garner	32	10	67	1	...	1	30.3	3	91	3	...	1
Small	9	0	38	0	...	...	12	2	40	3	...	5
Marshall	36.5	10	85	6	1	4	22	6	85	2	1	...
Baptiste	20	6	36	2	1	...	26	8	48	0	...	...
Harper	8	0	25	0	...	2	8	1	18	1	...	...

WEST INDIES

		First Innings		Second Innings	
1 C. G. Greenidge	Barbados	c Miller b Botham	1	not out	214
2 D. L. Haynes	Barbados	l b w b Botham	12	run out	17
3 H. A. Gomes	Trinidad & Tobago	c Gatting b Botham	10	not out	92
4 I. V. A. Richards	Antigua	l b w b Botham	72		
†5 C. H. Lloyd	Guyana	l b w b Botham	39		
*6 P. J. Dujon	Jamaica	c Fowler b Botham	8		
7 M. D. Marshall	Barbados	c Pringle b Willis	29		
8 E. A. E. Baptiste	Antigua	c Downton b Willis	44		
9 R. A. Harper	Guyana	c Gatting b Botham	8		
10 J. Garner	Barbados	c Downton b Botham	6		
11 M. A. Small	Barbados	not out	3		
		B , l-b 5, w 1, n-b 7	13	B 4, l-b 4, w , n-b 13	21
		Total	**245**	**Total**	**344**

FALL OF THE WICKETS

1—1 2—18 3—35 4—138 5—147 6—177 7—213 8—231 9—241 10—245

1—57 2— 3— 4— 5— 6— 7— 8— 9— 10—

ANALYSIS OF BOWLING

	1st Innings						2nd Innings					
Name	O.	M.	R.	W.	Wd.	N-b	O.	M.	R.	W.	Wd.	N-b
Willis	19	5	48	2	...	4	15	5	48	0	...	9
Botham	27.4	6	103	8	1	...	20.1	2	117	0	...	4
Pringle	11	0	54	0	...	3	8	0	44	0	...	...
Foster	6	2	13	0	...	...	12	0	69	0	...	...
Miller	2	0	14	0	...	...	11	0	45	0	...	...

Scorers—E. Solomon & A. E. Weld

Umpires—D. G. L. Evans & B. J. Meyer
† Captain   * Wicket-keeper

Play begins each day at 11.00
Luncheon Interval 1.00—1.40
Tea Interval 3.40—4.00 (may be varied according to state of game)
Stumps drawn 1st, 2nd, 3rd & 4th days at 6.00, 5th day at 5.30 or 6.00. (In the event of play being suspended for any reason for one hour or more in aggregate on any of the first four days, play may be extended to 7.00 on that day).

West Indies won the toss and elected to field

West Indies won by 9 wickets

rebel tourists is not an excuse for defeat. And anyway, this match was the first Test in their last seven in which the West Indies had even lost a wicket in their second innings. A win by nine wickets was a close run thing by their standards.

Apart from the magnificent savagery of Greenidge's second innings' display, the game featured many other individual achievements. Ian Botham even won a share in the Man of the Match award, adjudicated by Godfrey Evans, for his eight for 103 in the West Indies' first innings, although if you add it to his 0 for 117 when it mattered in the second innings you might think him a little lucky on this occasion to get a share of the champagne. Allan Lamb batted for at least part of each of the five days of the Test, taking all of the fourth day to move from 30 to 109 in his second innings. And David Gower became the first England captain since Norman Yardley in 1948 to lose a match after declaring his second innings. 'It was exciting to be able to declare at Lord's, and pretend we had a chance of winning,' was how he later described it.

1984: England v Sri Lanka

(only Test) August 23, 24, 25, 27, 28
Match drawn

England went into the inaugural Test Match against Sri Lanka having lost all five Tests to West Indies, and hoping for some light relief against a team described by one county coach as 'not much better than Cambridge University'. That would have been a wonderful tribute if the comment had been made in, for example, 1950, when May, Sheppard, Dewes and Doggart were at the heart of a batting line-up that could challenge any county. But in 1984 it was less of a compliment.

England got no light relief at all. Sri Lanka's batsmen, with the single exception of Madugalle, piled up the runs against England's flimsy bowling attack in at least one innings, and their captain, Duleep Mendis, fell only six short of becoming the only batsman to hit two hundreds in his Lord's Test debut. Their first innings total of 491 for 7 declared was their highest in Tests thus far, and Sidath Wettimuny's Man of the Match-winning twelve and a half hour 190 was the rock around which the total was built. It was the longest innings ever played at Lord's. When England batted, Allan Lamb scored his second Lord's Test century of the summer, and his fourth on all grounds, but still England were bowled out 121 runs behind their visitors. Pat Pocock provided the main statistical highlight of the innings. The Surrey off-spinner, who had been recalled to the team two Tests earlier, had made four consecutive ducks against the West Indies, so when he scored his first Test run for eight years Allan Lamb (already with a century to his name) walked down the pitch to shake him by the hand.

The teams. *L-r, standing*: DGL Evans (umpire), G Fowler, ADA Samaranayaka, RM Ellison, ALF de Mel, PJW Allott, JR Ratnayeke, JP Agnew, VB John, PA de Silva, PR Downton, SAR Silva, BC Broad, A Ranatunga, HD Bird (umpire). Seated: N Chanmugam (Sri Lanka's manager), CJ Tavaré, RS Madugalle, PI Pocock, LRD Mendis (Sri Lanka's captain), DI Gower (England's captain), RL Dias, IT Botham, DS de Silva, AJ Lamb, S Wettimuny.

In Sri Lanka's second innings, Pocock the official off-spinner was upstaged by another man bowling off-spin for a change: Ian Botham took six for 90 as the game meandered to a draw and the certainty that England would never underestimate Sri Lanka again.

The whole game was played in front of only average crowds. The fourth day was Bank Holiday Monday, and remarkably hot for a public holiday, but still only around 7,000 turned up. While it might give some pleasure to the English crowds to see their team winning – even against rather feeble underdogs – it is very hard to persuade people to come along to watch an already very unsuccessful side being shown to be even more inept against a team 'not much better than Cambridge University'.

LORD'S GROUND

(15p) **(15p)**

CORNHILL INSURANCE TEST MATCH
ENGLAND v. SRI LANKA

THURS., FRI., SAT., MON. & TUES., AUGUST 23, 24, 25, 27 & 28, 1984   (5-day Match)

SRI LANKA

			First Innings		Second Innings	
1	S. Wettimuny	Singhalese	c Downton b Allott	190	c Gower b Botham	13
*2	S. A. R. Silva	Nondescripts	l b w b Botham	8	not out	102
3	R. S. Madugalle	Nondescripts	b Ellison	5	b Botham	3
4	R. L. Dias	Singhalese	c Lamb b Pocock	32	l b w b Botham	38
5	A. Ranatunga	Singhalese	b Agnew	84	l b w b Botham	0
†6	L. R. D. Mendis	Singhalese	c Fowler b Pocock	111	c Fowler b Botham	94
7	P. A. de Silva	Nondescripts	c Downton b Agnew	16	c Downton b Pocock	3
8	A. L. F. de Mel	Singhalese	not out	20	c Ellison b Botham	14
9	J. R. Ratnayeke	Nondescripts	not out	5	not out	7
10	D. S. de Silva	Moratuwa				
11	V. B. J. John	Bloomfield				

Innings closed   Innings closed

B 2, l-b 8, w 2, n-b 8, 20   B 5, l-b 4, w , n-b 11, 20

Total 491   Total 294

FALL OF THE WICKETS

1—17   2—43   3—144   4—292   5—442   6—456   7—464   8—   9—   10—

1—19   2—27   3—111   4—115   5—118   6—256   7—276   8—   9—   10—

ANALYSIS OF BOWLING

Name	1st Innings						2nd Innings					
	O.	M.	R.	W.	Wd.	N-b	O.	M.	R.	W.	Wd.	N-b
Agnew	32	3	123	2		8	11	3	54	0		11
Botham	29	6	114	1	1		27	6	90	6		
Ellison	28	6	70	1	1		7	0	36	0		
Pocock	41	17	75	1			29	10	78	1		
Allott	36	7	89	1			1	0	2	0		
Lamb							1	0	6	0		
Tavare							3	3	0	0		
Fowler							1	0	8	0		

ENGLAND

			First Innings		Second Innings
1	G. Fowler	Lancashire	c Madugalle b John	25	
2	B. C. Broad	Nottinghamshire	c Silva b de Mel	86	
3	C. J. Tavare	Kent	c Ranatunga b S de Silva	14	
†4	D. I. Gower	Leicestershire	c Silva b de Mel	55	
5	A. J. Lamb	Northamptonshire	c Dias b John	107	
6	I. T. Botham	Somerset	c sub b John	6	
7	R. M. Ellison	Kent	c Ratnayeke b S de Silva	41	
*8	P. R. Downton	Middlesex	c Dias b de Mel	10	
9	P. J. W. Allott	Lancashire	b de Mel	0	
10	P. I. Pocock	Surrey	c Silva b John	2	
11	J. P. Agnew	Leicestershire	not out	1	

B 5, l-b 7, w 5, n-b 6, 23   B , l-b , w , n-b ,

Total 370   Total ....

FALL OF THE WICKETS

1—49   2—105   3—190   4—210   5—218   6—305   7—354   8—354   9—369   10—370

1—   2—   3—   4—   5—   6—   7—   8—   9—   10—

ANALYSIS OF BOWLING

Name	1st Innings						2nd Innings					
	O.	M.	R.	W.	Wd.	N-b	O.	M.	R.	W.	Wd.	N-b
de Mel	37	10	110	4	1	2						
John	39.1	12	98	4	1	4						
Ratnayeke	22	5	50	0	2							
D. S. de Silva	45	16	85	2								
Ranatunga	1	1	0	0								
Madugalle	3		4	0								

Umpires—H. D. Bird & D. G. L. Evans   Scorers— E. Solomon & G. G. A. Saulez

† Captain   * Wicket-keeper

Play begins each day at 11.00

Luncheon Interval 1.00—1.40

Tea Interval 3.40—4.00 (may be varied according to state of game)

Stumps drawn 1st, 2nd, 3rd & 4th days at 6.00, 5th day at 5.30 or 6.00. (In the event of play being suspended for any reason for one hour or more in aggregate on any of the first four days, play may be extended to 7.00 on that day).

England won the toss and elected to field

Match Drawn

LORD'S GROUND

1985: England v Australia

(2nd Test) June 27, 28, 29, July 1, 2
Australia won by 4 wickets

England spent much of the 1980s establishing for themselves the reputation of a team that could always summon defeat from the jaws of victory, especially at Lord's. Never was this truer than in 1985. For most of the very hot summer England were masters of the Australian tourists, and won the six Test series by three matches to one. Lord's was the one.

David Gower lost the toss for the sixth consecutive time (but then won the next four of the summer), and Allan Border invited England to bat. The Australian team included South African-born

Kepler Wessels who nine years later would come back to Lord's as captain of the South African side, thus emulating AH Kardar of India and Pakistan in playing Tests at Lord's for two different countries.

For the only time that year, England were dismissed for a first innings total below 400, as their opening partnership of Gooch and Robinson for once failed while Gatting, Lamb and Botham made only minor contributions. Craig McDermott was the main destroyer, with six for 70. Australia's innings was a monument to their captain Allan

Three cheers for Her Majesty, led by George Mann, then President of M.C.C.

LORD'S GROUND

CORNHILL INSURANCE TEST SERIES
ENGLAND v. AUSTRALIA

THURS., FRI., SAT., MON. & TUES., JUNE 27, 28, 29 & JULY 1, 2, 1985   (5-day Match)

ENGLAND

			First Innings		Second Innings	
1 G. A. Gooch	....................Essex	l b w b McDermott	 30	c Phillips b McDermott	17
2 R. T. Robinson	..Nottinghamshire	l b w b McDermott	 6	b Holland	 12
†3 D. I. Gower	.... Leicestershire	c Border b McDermott..	86	c Phillips b McDermott	22
4 M. W. Gatting	............Middlesex	l b w b Lawson	 14	not out	 75
5 A. J. Lamb	...Northamptonshire	c Phillips b Lawson.....	47	c Holland b Lawson.....	9
6 I. T. Botham	............Somerset	c Ritchie b Lawson	5	c Border b Holland	 85
*7 P. R. Downton	...........Middlesex	c Wessels b McDermott	21	c Boon b Holland	 0
8 J. E. Emburey	............Middlesex	l b w b O'Donnell........	33	b Lawson	 20
9 P. H. Edmonds	............Middlesex	c Border b McDermott..	21	c Boon b Holland	 1
10 N. A. Foster	....................Essex	c Wessels b McDermott	3	c Border b Holland	 0
11 P. J. W. Allott	........Lancashire	not out	 1	b Lawson	 0
		B 1, l-b 4, w 1, n-b 17,	23	B 1, l-b 12, w 4, n-b 3,	20
		Total	290	Total	261

FALL OF THE WICKETS

1—26	2—51	3—99	4—179	5—184	6—211	7—241	8—273	9—283	10—290
1—32	2—34	3—38	4—57	5—77	6—98	7—229	8—229	9—261	10—261

ANALYSIS OF BOWLING

	1st Innings						2nd Innings					
Name	O.	M.	R.	W.	Wd.	N-b	O.	M.	R.	W.	Wd.	N-b
Lawson	25	2	91	3	...	15	23	0	86	3	...	1
McDermott	29.2	5	70	6	1	2	20	2	84	2	4	2
O'Donnell	22	3	82	1	1	...	5	0	10	0	...	...
Holland	23	6	42	0	...	...	32	12	68	5	...	...

AUSTRALIA

			First Innings		Second Innings	
1 A. M. J. Hilditch	......S. Australia	b Foster	 14	c Lamb b Botham	 0
2 G. M. Wood	...Western Australia	c Emburey b Allott	8	c Lamb b Botham	 6
3 K. C. Wessels	............Queensland	l b w b Botham.........	11	run out	 28
†4 A. R. Border	............Queensland	c Gooch b Botham	196	not out	 41
5 D. C. Boon	..............Tasmania	c Downton b Botham...	4	b Edmonds	 1
6 G. M. Ritchie	............Queensland	l b w b Botham.........	94	b Allott	 2
*7 W. B. Phillips	...South Australia	c Edmonds b Botham..	21	c Edmonds b Emburey	29
8 S. P. O'Donnell	............Victoria	c Lamb b Edmonds	48	not out	 9
9 G. F. Lawson	..New South Wales	not out	 5		
10 C. J. McDermott	......Queensland	run out	 9		
11 R. G. Holland	..New South Wales	b Edmonds	 0		
		B , l-b 10, w 1, n-b 4,	15	B , l-b 11, w , n-b ,	11
		Total	425	Total	127

FALL OF THE WICKETS

1—11	2—24	3—80	4—101	5—317	6—347	7—398	8—414	9—425	10—425
1—0	2—9	3—22	4—63	5—65	6—116	7—	8—	9—	10—

ANALYSIS OF BOWLING

	1st Innings						2nd Innings					
Name	O.	M.	R.	W.	Wd.	N-b	O.	M.	R.	W.	Wd.	N-b
Foster	23	1	83	1	1	...	7	4	8	1	...	...
Allott	30	4	70	1	...	...	15	0	49	2	...	...
Botham	24	2	109	5	...	4	16	5	35	1	...	...
Edmonds	25.4	5	85	2	...	...						
Gooch	3	1	11	0	...	...	8	4	24	1	...	...
Emburey	19	3	57	0	...	...						

Umpires—H. D. Bird & D. G. L. Evans   Scorers—E. Solomon & M. P. Ringham

† Captain   * Wicket-keeper

Play begins each day at 11.00

Luncheon Interval 1.00—1.40

Tea Interval 3.40—4.00 (may be varied according to state of game)

Stumps drawn at 6.00, or after 90 overs have been bowled, whichever is the later. (In the event of play being suspended for any reason for one hour or more in aggregate on any of the first four days, play may be extended to 7.00 on that day). The captains may agree to stop play at 5.30 on the 5th day if there is no prospect of a result.

Australia won the toss and elected to field

Australia won by 4 wickets

Border who made the highest score by a visiting Test captain at Lord's (beating Hanif Mohammad's 187 not out in 1967, but beaten again by Graeme Smith in 2003). He came in with the score at 24 for 2 and immediately took control. During the course of his seven and a half-hour innings he clocked up 5,000 Test runs, and few watching him bat would have been surprised to learn that there were over 6,000 more to come.

England had chosen Edmonds and Emburey to play in the same Test for the first time since Emburey's Test debut, also at their home ground, against New Zealand in 1978, but the Middlesex spin twins were no more successful this time than seven years earlier. It was left to Ian Botham to achieve his 25th five-wicket haul in Tests, then a record but which has since been beaten by Hadlee, Muralitharan, Warne, Kumble and McGrath. When Wood was caught by Lamb in the second innings, Botham also established an England record of 326 Test match victims. His final career total of 383 wickets remains the record for England.

1986: England v India

(1st Test) June 5, 6, 7, 9, 10
India won by 5 wickets

This was the 79th Lord's Test, one more than had been played at the Melbourne Cricket Ground, to give Lord's the record for most Tests played, a record it still holds. It was also the earliest start to any Lord's Test, but that record stood only until 2000, when the first ever May Lord's Test was staged. And once again, Lord's proved a grave-yard for the England captaincy. David Gower, who had led England in four previous Lord's Tests without recording a win, found that his fifth game in charge at headquarters was to be his last, at least for the time being. His final outing as Eng-

land captain at Lord's would come in 1989 – another defeat, to give him a final record there of played 6, lost 5, drawn 1, an unfair reflection of his captaincy skills.

This was only India's second Test victory in England, and their first ever at Lord's. If the England selectors thought that David Gower's leadership was not producing results, the Indian selectors could be forgiven for wondering about Kapil Dev's captaincy. This was his twenty-first Test as captain, and his first experience of victory. He won the toss and put England in to bat, but

Right: The Grand Stand scoreboard during India's second innings of 136.
Below: Vengsarkar, the first visiting player to make three hundreds at Lord's.

England got off to a good start facing an attack that looked to rely on Kapil Dev and pretty well nobody else of any talent. Gooch was by this time one of the best batsmen in the world, and his second Test hundred at Lord's was his sixth in all Tests. But apart from Gooch only Derek Pringle was able to build a score and England's final total of 294 was disappointing. Chetan Sharma took five for 64 and was the pick of the bowlers.

Looking back, it is surprising to find that England's opening bowlers in this Test were Graham Dilley and Richard Ellison. Both bowlers played for Kent, but even for the county they were rarely the opening pair. Dilley was genuinely quick at his peak, but Ellison was a medium fast swing bowler – an ideal first or second change but never the spearhead of a Test attack. And so it proved: the England attack had no real edge and the Indian batsmen were able slowly but surely to build a lead. On the second day, when some time was lost to the weather, only 132 runs were scored in 83 overs, but on the Saturday Dilip Vengsarkar became the first batsman to score three Test hundreds against England at Lord's.

LORD'S GROUND

CORNHILL INSURANCE TEST SERIES
ENGLAND v. INDIA

THURS., FRI., SAT., MON. & TUES., JUNE 5, 6, 7, 9 & 10, 1986   (5-day Match)

ENGLAND

			First Innings		Second Innings	
1 G. A. Gooch	Essex	b Sharma	114	l b w b Kapil Dev	8
2 R. T. Robinson	Nottinghamshire	c Az'ruddin b Maninder	35	c Amarnath b Kapil Dev	11
†3 D. I. Gower	Leicestershire	c More b Sharma	18	l b w b Kapil Dev	8
4 M. W. Gatting	Middlesex	b Sharma	0	b Sharma	40
5 A. J. Lamb	Northamptonshire	c Srikkanth b Sharma	6	c More b Shastri	39
6 D. R. Pringle	Essex	b Binny	63	c More b Kapil Dev	6
7 J. E. Emburey	Middlesex	c Amarnath b Kapil Dev	7	c and b Maninder	1
*8 P. R. Downton	Middlesex	l b w b Sharma	5	c Shastri b Maninder	29
9 R. M. Ellison	Kent	c Kapil Dev b Binny	12	c More b Binny	19
10 G. R. Dilley	Kent	c More b Binny	4	not out	2
11 P. H. Edmonds	Middlesex	not out	7	c Binny b Maninder	7
		B , l-b 15, w 1, n-b 7,	23	B , l-b 6, w 1, n-b 3,	10
		Total	294	Total	180

FALL OF THE WICKETS

1—66　2—92　3—92　4—98　5—245　6—264　7—269　8—271　9—287　10—294
1—18　2—23　3—35　4—108　5—113　6—121　7—164　8—170　9—170　10—180

ANALYSIS OF BOWLING

Name	1st Innings						2nd Innings					
	O.	M.	R.	W.	Wd.	N-b	O.	M.	R.	W.	Wd.	N-b
Kapil Dev	31	8	67	1	...	...	22	7	52	4	...	...
Binny	18.2	4	55	3	...	...	15	3	44	1	1	1
Sharma	32	10	64	5	1	5	17	4	48	1	...	2
Maninder	30	15	45	1	...	...	20.4	12	9	3	...	...
Amarnath	7	1	18	0	...	2	2	2	0	0	...	...
Shastri	10	3	30	0	...	...	20	8	21	1	...	...

INDIA

			First Innings		Second Innings	
1 S. M. Gavaskar	Bombay	c Emburey b Dilley	34	c Downton b Dilley	22
2 K. Srikkanth	Tamil Nadu	c Gatting b Dilley	20	c Gooch b Dilley	0
3 M. B. Amarnath	Baroda	c Pringle b Edmonds	69	l b w b Pringle	8
4 D. B. Vengsarkar	Bombay	not out	126	b Edmonds	33
5 M. Azharuddin	Hyderabad	c and b Dilley	33	run out	14
6 R. J. Shastri	Bombay	c Edmonds b Dilley	1	not out	20
7 R. M. H. Binny	Karnataka	l b w b Pringle	9		
†8 Kapil Dev	Haryana	c Lamb b Ellison	1	not out	23
9 C. J. Sharma	Haryana	b Pringle	1		
*10 K. S. More	Baroda	l b w b Pringle	2		
11 Maninder Singh	Delhi	c Lamb b Emburey	25		
		B , l-b 5, w 1, n-b 9,	15	B 1, l-b 9, w 1, n-b 5,	16
		Total	341	Total	136

FALL OF THE WICKETS

1—31　2—90　3—161　4—232　5—238　6—252　7—253　8—264　9—303　10—341
1—10　2—31　3—76　4—78　5—110　6—　7—　8—　9—　10—

ANALYSIS OF BOWLING

Name	1st Innings						2nd Innings					
	O.	M.	R.	W.	Wd.	N-b	O.	M.	R.	W.	Wd.	N-b
Dilley	34	7	146	4	...	7	10	3	28	2	...	4
Ellison	29	11	63	1	1	...	6	0	17	0	1	...
Emburey	27	13	28	1	...	...	...	...	...	...	...	...
Edmonds	22	7	41	1	...	1	11	2	51	1	...	1
Pringle	25	7	58	3	...	...	15	5	30	1	...	...
	...	...	...	...	...	...	...	...	...	...	...	...

Umpires—K. E. Palmer & D. R. Shepherd

Scorers—E. Solomon & Yashvant Chad

† Captain　　* Wicket-keeper

Play begins each day at 11.00
Luncheon Interval 1.00—1.40
Tea Interval 3.40—4.00 (may be varied according to state of game)
Stumps drawn at 6.00, or after 90 overs have been bowled, whichever is the later. (In the event of play being suspended for any reason for one hour or more in aggregate on any of the first four days, play may be extended to 7.00 on that day). The captains may agree to stop play at 5.30 on the 5th day if there is no prospect of a result.

India won the toss and elected to field

India won by 5 wickets

1986: England v New Zealand

(1st Test) July 24, 25, 26, 28, 29
Match drawn

Moxon is given out lbw by Dickie Bird to Hadlee.

Injuries in Test matches are common enough, but the way that England solved the problem of their injured wicketkeeper Bruce French was unique. Early on the second day, the England score was 259 for 6, and French had only just come in when he failed to pick up the line of a Richard Hadlee delivery. He turned away and the ball hit him on the back of the head, and part of the inside of his helmet jagged into his skull, causing a wound that needed three stitches. The injury looked far worse than it proved to be, but it meant that French was not fit to keep wicket.

When the New Zealand innings began, Bill Athey, 'a perfectly serviceable keeper' according to

the *Daily Telegraph*'s correspondent at the time, came out wearing the pads and gloves. However, Mike Gatting had already asked his opposite number Jeremy Coney whether the recently retired Bob Taylor could keep wicket as substitute. Taylor was at Lord's in his capacity as Press Relations Officer for the sponsors, Cornhill, and Coney sportingly agreed. An announcement went out over the public address system, and to everybody's delight and astonishment (not least his own) Bob Taylor emerged to take over the gloves from Athey after just two overs. For the rest of the day, 74 overs, Taylor kept wicket immaculately. On the third day, Taylor's place was taken by Bobby Parks

LORD'S **GROUND**

CORNHILL INSURANCE TEST SERIES
ENGLAND v. NEW ZEALAND

Thurs., Fri., Sat., Mon. & Tues., July 24, 25, 26, 28 & 29, 1986   (5-day Match)

ENGLAND

		First Innings		Second Innings	
1 G. A. Gooch	.................Essex	c Smith b Hadlee	18	c Watson b Bracewell	183
2 M. D. Moxon	...............Yorkshire	l b w b Hadlee	74	l b w b Hadlee	5
3 C. W. J. Athey	...Gloucestershire	c J. Crowe b Hadlee	44	b Gray	16
4 D. I. Gower	........Leicestershire	c M. Crowe b Bracewell	62	b Gray	3
†5 M. W. Gatting	........Middlesex	b Hadlee	2	c M. Crowe b Gray	26
6 P. Willey	.........Leicestershire	l b w b Watson	44	b Bracewell	42
7 P. H. Edmonds	........Middlesex	c M. Crowe b Hadlee	6	not out	9
*8 B. N. French	...Nottinghamshire	retired hurt	0		
9 G. R. Dilley	......................Kent	c Smith b Hadlee	17	Innings closed	
10 N. A. Foster	................Essex	b Watson	8		
11 N. V. Radford	...Worcestershire	not out	12		
		B 6, l-b 7, w , n-b 7,	20	B , l-b 6, w 1, n-b 4,	11
		Total	**307**	**Total**	**295**

FALL OF THE WICKETS

1—27   2—102   3—196   4—198   5—237   6—258   7—271   8—285   9—307   10—

1—9   2—68   3—72   4—136   5—262   6—295   7—   8—   9—   10—

ANALYSIS OF BOWLING

Name	1st Innings						2nd Innings					
	O.	M.	R.	W.	Wd.	N-b	O.	M.	R.	W.	Wd.	N-b
Hadlee	37.5	11	80	6	...	6	27	3	78	1	...	4
Watson	30	7	70	2	...	1	17	2	50	0	...	...
M. Crowe	8	1	38	0	...	...	4	0	13	0	...	...
Coney	4	0	12	0	...	...	23.4	7	57	2	...	...
Bracewell	26	8	65	1	...	...	46	14	83	3	...	...
Gray	13	9	29	0	...	...	3	0	8	0	...	...
Rutherford												

NEW ZEALAND

		First Innings		Second Innings	
1 J. G. Wright	...........Canterbury	b Dilley	0	c Gower b Dilley	0
2 B. A. Edgar	.............Wellington	c Gatting b Gooch	83	c Gower b Foster	0
3 K. R. Rutherford	...........Otago	c Gooch b Dilley	0	not out	24
4 M. D. Crowe	...Central Districts	c and b Edmonds	106	not out	11
5 J. J. Crowe	............Auckland	c Gatting b Edmonds	18		
†6 J. V. Coney	............Wellington	c Gooch b Radford	51		
7 E. J. Gray	.............Wellington	c Gower b Edmonds	11		
8 R. J. Hadlee	............Canterbury	b Edmonds	19		
*9 I. D. S. Smith	...Central Districts	c Edmonds b Dilley	18		
10 J. G. Bracewell	............Auckland	not out	1		
11 W. Watson	...............Auckland	l b w b Dilley	1		
		B 4, l-b 9, w 6, n-b 15,	34	B , l-b 4, w , n-b 2,	6
		Total	**342**	**Total**	**41**

FALL OF THE WICKETS

1—2   2—5   3—215   4—218   5—274   6—292   7—310   8—340   9—340   10—342

1—0   2—8   3—   4—   5—   6—   7—   8—   9—   10—

ANALYSIS OF BOWLING

Name	1st Innings						2nd Innings					
	O.	M.	R.	W.	Wd.	N-b	O.	M.	R.	W.	Wd.	N-b
Dilley	35.1	9	82	4	...	9	6	3	5	1	...	2
Foster	25	6	56	0	6	...	3	1	13	1	...	...
Radford	25	4	71	1	...	6	5	0	18	0	...	...
Edmonds	42	10	97	4	...	1	1	0	1	0	...	...
Gooch	13	6	23	1	...	...						
Gower												

Scorers—E. Solomon & B. Curgenven

Umpires—H. D. Bird & A. G. T. Whitehead

† Captain   * Wicket-keeper

Play begins each day at 11.00

Luncheon Interval 1.00—1.40

Tea Interval 3.40—4.00 (may be varied according to state of game)

Stumps drawn at 6.00, or after 90 overs have been bowled, whichever is the later. (In the event of play being suspended for any reason for one hour or more in aggregate on any of the first four days, play may be extended to 7.00 on that day). The captains may agree to stop play at 5.30 on the 5th day if there is no prospect of a result.

England won the toss

Match Drawn

of Hampshire (who did not have a county match that day), by the end of which Martin Crowe had scored an 'almost flawless' hundred and New Zealand had advanced to 342 for 9. On the fourth morning, Bruce French was fit again to keep wicket, but the innings ended with the first ball of the morning, with Graham Dilley trapping Watson lbw. England had used four wicketkeepers in one innings, certainly a Lord's Test record, and possibly a first-class record. The use of substitutes in this match was not limited to the men behind the stumps. There were moments when England had three substitutes on the field, and as for New Zealand, Coney himself was off the field for some time with a strain.

In among all this excitement, some of the original selections prospered too. Richard Hadlee took five wickets in an innings for the twenty-sixth time, equalling Ian Botham's Test record (Botham was missing, undergoing a temporary ban after admitting he had smoked cannabis), and Graham Gooch made 183 in the second England innings, the highest ever Test score against New Zealand at Lord's.

LORD'S GROUND

1987: England v Pakistan

(2nd Test) June 18, 19, 20, 22, 23 (no play on 2nd, 4th and 5th days)
Match drawn

For the first time since Pakistan's first tour of England in 1954, three complete days of a Test Match were lost to the rain. It meant that no result was remotely likely and the insurance policy taken out by the T.C.C.B. to refund those who had bought their tickets in advance was activated. Some £230,000 was paid out, but the total receipts were £670,000, which was not bad for a match limited to barely a day and a half. The match was also notable as the first Test match played since the completion of the new Mound Stand, which despite the grey and gloomy weather was adjudged to be a fine addition to the architecture of the ground.

For England, only Bill Athey prospered. In his fifteenth Test he scored his first (and in the event, only) Test century. He was the first Gloucestershire player to hit a hundred for England since Arthur Milton in 1958, and many Gloucestershire members would point out that the main cause of the long wait was that the county has long seemed 'unfashionable' to the England selectors.

Groundsmen mopping up rainwater after lunch, with the new Mound Stand in the background.

Some ex-Gloucestershire players, including Tom Graveney and Chris Broad, Athey's partner in a second-wicket stand of 89, had scored Test hundreds in the interim, and of course Bill Athey was not really a Gloucester man, having only moved to Gloucestershire from Yorkshire three seasons earlier. It would be a season or two longer before a player born in Gloucestershire, Jack Russell, would score a Test hundred. On the county theme, the Nottinghamshire partnership of Broad and Tim Robinson became the first county pair to open for England since John Edrich and Ken Barrington, of Surrey, had opened against India at Lord's twenty years earlier.

Apart from Athey's hundred, the only images that remain of the Test are Mike Gatting's good fortune in surviving an lbw decision early in his innings, and umpire David Constant running off even more quickly than the players when rain began to fall (again!) on the Saturday evening.

 LORD'S GROUND

CORNHILL INSURANCE TEST SERIES
ENGLAND v. PAKISTAN
THURS., FRI., SAT., MON. & TUES., JUNE 18, 19, 20, 22 & 23, 1987
(no play on Friday, Monday & Tuesday) (5-day Match)

ENGLAND

		First Innings		Second Innings
1 R. T. Robinson	Nottinghamshire	c Yousuf b Kamal	7	
2 B. C. Broad	Nottinghamshire	b Mudassar	55	
3 C. W. J. Athey	Gloucestershire	b Imran	123	
4 D. I. Gower	Leicestershire	c Yousuf b Mudassar	8	
†5 M. W. Gatting	Middlesex	run out	43	
*6 B. N. French	Nottinghamshire	b Akram	42	
7 I. T. Botham	Worcestershire	c Miandad b Akram	6	
8 J. E. Emburey	Middlesex	run out	12	
9 N. A. Foster	Essex	b Qadir	21	
10 P. H. Edmonds	Middlesex	not out	17	
11 G. R. Dilley	Worcestershire	c Yousuf b Imran	17	
		B , l-b 12, w 1, n-b 4,	17	B , l-b , w , n-b ,
		Total	368	Total

FALL OF THE WICKETS

1—29 2—118 3—128 4—230 5—272 6—294 7—305 8—329 9—340 10—368
1— 2— 3— 4— 5— 6— 7— 8— 9— 10—

ANALYSIS OF BOWLING

Name		1st Innings					2nd Innings				
	O.	M.	R.	W.	Wd.	N-b	O.	M.	R.	W.	Wd.	N-b
Imran	34.5	7	90	2	1	1					
Akram	28	1	98	2	...	2					
Kamal	9	2	42	1	...	...					
Qadir	25	1	100	1	...	...					
Mudassar	16	6	26	2	...	1					

PAKISTAN

		First Innings	Second Innings
1 Mudassar Nazar	United Bank		
2 Shoaib Mohammad	P.I.A.		
3 Mansoor Akhtar	United Bank		
4 Javed Miandad	Habib Bank		
5 Saleem Malik	Habib Bank		
6 Ijaz Ahmed	Habib Bank		
†7 Imran Khan	Lahore		
*8 Saleem Yousuf	Allied Bank		
9 Wasim Akram	Lahore		
10 Abdul Qadir	Habib Bank		
11 Mohsin Kamal	Lahore		
		B , l-b , w , n-b ,	B , l-b , w , n-b ,
		Total	Total

FALL OF THE WICKETS

1— 2— 3— 4— 5— 6— 7— 8— 9— 10—
1— 2— 3— 4— 5— 6— 7— 8— 9— 10—

ANALYSIS OF BOWLING

Name		1st Innings					2nd Innings				
	O.	M.	R.	W.	Wd.	N-b	O.	M.	R.	W.	Wd.	N-b

Umpires—D. J. Constant & A. G. T. Whitehead   Scorers—E. Solomon & W. A. Powell
† Captain   * Wicket-keeper
Play begins each day at 11.00
Luncheon Interval 1.00—1.40
Tea Interval 3.40—4.00 (may be varied according to state of game)
Stumps drawn at 6.00, or after 90 overs have been bowled, whichever is the later. (In the event of play being suspended for any reason for one hour or more in aggregate on any of the first four days, play may be extended to 7.00 on that day). The captains may agree to stop play at 5.30 on the 5th day if there is no prospect of a result.

England won the toss

Match Abandoned

1988: England v West Indies

(2nd Test) June 16, 17, 18, 20, 21
West Indies won by 134 runs

This was not a happy Test for England. It began with Mike Gatting being stripped of the captaincy for 'damaging cricket's image' through his activities at the team hotel during the Trent Bridge Test match two weeks earlier. In his place, John Emburey was appointed captain, another Middlesex man – the eleventh to captain his country. Many thought Emburey was lucky not to have been dropped, let alone made captain, an opinion with which the selectors finally agreed two Tests later. Chris Broad, opening the innings for England at the end of the first day, was dismissed in poor light by a quick delivery from Malcolm Marshall which kept low, and his expression of unhappiness at the lbw decision was caught so well by the television cameras that it was no surprise when he was left out of the next Test. Gladstone Small managed to aggravate a thigh strain on the third day, which kept him out of Test cricket for the rest of the summer, so that by the end of the match England's selectors had an even smaller pool of talent to call upon than at the start of the season.

John Emburey lost the toss, but in every other way his first two hours of Test captaincy went wonderfully well. At lunch, West Indies were 66 for 5, with Graham Dilley enjoying bowling figures of four for 35 in 13 overs on the trot. After lunch, it all began to slip away. Gus Logie and Jeff Dujon added 130 for the sixth wicket, and the West Indies edged above 200. In reply, England subsided to 165 all out, against Malcolm Marshall at his very best. All summer Marshall was the spearhead of the West Indies attack, and his six for 32 was just one of three hauls of six wickets or more in Tests that summer. It was also the best bowling analysis by a West Indian in Tests at Lord's, beating his own six for 85 four years earlier. Only Gooch and Gower stood firm, but neither reached 50.

When the West Indies' second innings reached 397, it was clear that England had little chance of avoiding defeat. The weather was never good, but nor was it ever bad enough to save the home side. Nor was the England batting good enough, Allan Lamb always excepted. Lamb scored his third Test hundred at Lord's, his second against West Indies, taking 25 minutes on the final morning to move from 99 not out overnight to 100. Apart from that, the only good news for the authorities was that the match receipts topped the £1 million mark for the first time in England.

LORD'S **GROUND**

CORNHILL INSURANCE TEST SERIES
ENGLAND v. WEST INDIES
(5-day Match)

THURS., FRI., SAT., MON. & TUES., JUNE 16, 17, 18, 20 & 21, 1988

WEST INDIES		First Innings		Second Innings	
1 C. G. Greenidge	Barbados	c Downton b Dilley	22	c Emburey b Dilley	103
2 D. L. Haynes	Barbados	c Moxon b Dilley	12	c Downton b Dilley	5
3 R. B. Richardson	Leeward Is.	c Emburey b Dilley	5	l b w b Pringle	26
†4 I. V. A. Richards	Leeward Is.	c Downton b Dilley	6	b Pringle	72
5 C. L. Hooper	Guyana	c Downton b Small	3	c Downton b Jarvis	11
6 A. L. Logie	Trinidad & Tobago	c Emburey b Small	81	not out	95
*7 P. J. L. Dujon	Jamaica	b Emburey	53	b Jarvis	52
8 M. D. Marshall	Barbados	c Gooch b Dilley	11	b Jarvis	6
9 E. L. C. Ambrose	Leeward Is.	c Gower b Small	0	b Dilley	0
10 C. A. Walsh	Jamaica	not out	9	b Dilley	0
11 B. P. Patterson	Jamaica	b Small	0	c Downton b Jarvis	2
		B , l-b 6, w , n-b 1,	7	B , l-b 19, w 1, n-b 5,	25
		Total	209	Total	397

FALL OF THE WICKETS
1—21 2—40 3—47 4—50 5—54 6—184 7—199 8—199 9—199 10—209
1—32 2—115 3—198 4—226 5—240 6—371 7—379 8—380 9—384 10—397

ANALYSIS OF BOWLING

	1st Innings						2nd Innings					
Name	O.	M.	R.	W.	Wd.	N-b	O.	M.	R.	W.	Wd.	N-b
Dilley	23	6	55	5	...	...	27	6	73	4	...	...
Jarvis	13	2	47	0	...	...	26	3	107	4	...	1
Small	18	5	64	4	...	...	19	1	76	0	1	3
Pringle	7	3	20	0	...	··	21	4	60	2	...	2
Emburey	6	2	17	1	...	1	15	1	62	0	...	...

ENGLAND		First Innings		Second Innings	
1 G. A. Gooch	Essex	b Marshall	44	l b w b Marshall	16
2 B. C. Broad	Nottinghamshire	l b w b Marshall	0	c Dujon b Marshall	1
3 M. D. Moxon	Yorkshire	c Richards b Ambrose	26	run out	14
4 D. I. Gower	Leicestershire	c sub b Walsh	46	c Rich'son b Patterson	1
5 A. J. Lamb	Northamptonshire	l b w b Marshall	10	run out	113
6 D. R. Pringle	Essex	c Dujon b Walsh	1	l b w b Walsh	0
*7 P. R. Downton	Middlesex	l b w b Marshall	11	l b w b Marshall	27
†8 J. E. Emburey	Warwickshire	b Patterson	7	b Ambrose	30
9 G. C. Small	Warwickshire	not out	5	c Richards b Marshall	7
10 P. W. Jarvis	Yorkshire	c Haynes b Marshall	7	not out	29
11 G. R. Dilley	Worcestershire	b Marshall	0	c Rich'son b Patterson	28
		B , l-b 6, w , n-b 2,	8	B 5 l-b 20 w 2 n-b 14,	41
		Total	165	Total	307

FALL OF THE WICKETS
1—13 2—58 3—112 4—129 5—134 6—140 7—153 8—157 9—165 10—165
1—27 2—29 3—31 4—104 5—105 6—161 7—212 8—232 9—254 10—307

ANALYSIS OF BOWLING

	1st Innings						2nd Innings					
Name	O.	M.	R.	W.	Wd.	N-b	O.	M.	R.	W.	Wd.	N-b
Marshall	18	5	32	6	...	1	25	5	60	4	2	1
Patterson	13	3	52	1	...	··	21.5	2	100	2	...	7
Ambrose	12	1	39	1	...	··	20	1	75	1	...	6
Walsh	16	6	36	2	...	1	20	4	47	1	...	...

Umpires—K. E. Palmer & D. R. Shepherd

Scorers—E. Solomon & A. Weld

† Captain   * Wicket-keeper

Play begins each day at 11.00   Luncheon Interval 1.00—1.40

Tea Interval 3.40—4.00 (may be varied according to state of game)

Stumps drawn 1st, 2nd, 3rd & 4th days at 6.00, or after 90 overs have been bowled, whichever is the later - 5th day at 6.00, or after a minimum of 75 overs for playing time other than the last hour, when Law of Cricket 17.6 and 17.7 shall apply (20 overs). (In the event of play being suspended for any reason for one hour or more in aggregate on any of the first four days, play may be extended to 7.00 on that day). The captains may agree to stop play at 5.30 on the 5th day if there is no prospect of a result.

West Indies won the toss

West Indies won by 134 runs

Right: Viv Richards with a powerful drive through the off side.

1988: England v Sri Lanka

(only Test) August 25, 26, 27, 29, 30
England won by 7 wickets

This was England's sixth Test match in a remarkably unsuccessful summer, and even a victory against Sri Lanka – England's first Test victory in their past eighteen attempts – was greeted with some scorn in the media as just a mismatch against a much weaker team. During the six matches of the summer, England had used four captains (and Derek Pringle as substitute captain for a few overs) and 28 players: only Graham Gooch, the fourth of those captains, played in all six Tests.

In this match, England capped four new players. The one who would go on to the greatest things was Jack Russell, who proved his temperament for Test cricket by scoring his highest first-class score to date, 94, when batting at number three as England's nightwatchman. This is the highest score ever made by an England nightwatchman at Lord's, and despite England's intensive use of this tactic it is still the fourth highest nightwatchman score made anywhere for England, after Alex Tudor (99 not out), Harold Larwood (98) and Eddie Hemmings (95). The other three debutants, Kim Barnett, David 'Syd' Lawrence and Philip Newport, were not destined to have distinguished Test careers, but all contributed to England's victory in this Test.

The fixture list in 1988 had arranged a round of county matches to start on the last day of the Test match, and because it was so late in the season several of these matches were crucial for the final outcome of the Championship. Many of the players were hoping that the game would finish a day early so that they could get back to their county dressing rooms in time. It was therefore a little bizarre to see England, needing just 89 more runs to win on the final morning, failing to finish the game off before lunch. Tim Robinson played out the final three balls of the last over before lunch

with the scores level, so everybody had to hang on for another forty minutes before they could get back to what many of them considered the main business of the day – county cricket. In the event, only England's captain Graham Gooch succeeded in playing two matches in one day. Essex were away to Surrey, just across the Thames, and he got there in time to spend the afternoon fielding as Alec Stewart hit a century for Surrey. Gooch replied with one of his own the next day, but his Essex and England team-mates Neil Foster and Derek Pringle did not play.

Jack Russell on Test debut.

LORD'S **GROUND**

(20p) (20p)

CORNHILL INSURANCE TEST MATCH
ENGLAND v. SRI LANKA

THURS., FRI., SAT., MON. & TUES., AUGUST 25, 26, 27, 29 & 30, 1988 (5-day Match)

SRI LANKA

			First Innings		Second Innings	
*1	S. A. R. Silva	Nondescripts	c Russell b Foster	1	c Russell b Newport	16
2	D. S. B. P. Kuruppu	Bloomfield	c Gooch b Newport	46	c Barnett b Foster	25
3	M. A. R. Samarasekera	Colombo	c Russell b Foster	0	l b w b Emburey	57
4	P. A. De Silva	Nondescripts	c Gooch b Newport	3	l b w b Lawrence	18
†5	R. S. Madugalle	Nondescripts	l b w b Foster	3	b Foster	20
6	A. Ranatunga	Sinhalese	l b w b Newport	5	b Newport	78
7	L. R. D. Mendis	Sinhalese	c Smith b Lawrence	21	l b w b Pringle	66
8	J. R. Ratnayeke	Nondescripts	not out	59	c Lamb b Lawrence	32
9	W. R. Madurasinghe	Kurunegala	run out	4	b Newport	2
10	H. C. P. Ramanayake	Tamil U.	l b w b Pringle	0	c Gooch b Newport	2
11	G. F. Labrooy	Colombo	l b w b Pringle	42	not out	9
			B 1, l-b 7, w , n-b 2,	10	B , l-b 8, w , n-b 8,	16
			Total	194	Total	331

FALL OF THE WICKETS
1—7   2—44   3—52   4—53   5—61   6—63   7—122   8—127   9—130   10—194
1—43   2—51   3—96   4—145   5—147   6—251   7—309   8—311   9—323   10—331

ANALYSIS OF BOWLING

Name	1st Innings					2nd Innings				
	O.	M.	R.	W.	Wd. N-b	O.	M.	R.	W.	Wd. N-b
Foster	21	5	51	3	... ...	33	10	98	2	... ...
Lawrence	15	4	37	1	... ...	21	4	74	2	... 8
Newport	21	4	77	3	... 2	26.3	7	87	4	... ...
Pringle	6.5	1	17	2	... ...	11	2	30	1	... ...
Emburey	2	1	4	0	... ...	18	9	34	1	... ...

ENGLAND

			First Innings		Second Innings	
†1	G. A. Gooch	Essex	l b w b Ratnayeke	75	c Silva b Samarasekera	36
2	R. T. Robinson	Nottinghamshire	c Sam'kera b Ratnayeke	19	not out	34
*3	R. C. Russell	Gloucestershire	c Sam'kera b Labrooy	94		
4	K. J. Barnett	Derbyshire	c Ranatunga b Labrooy	66	c Silva b Samarasekera	0
5	A. J. Lamb	Northamptonshire	b Labrooy	63	c De Silva b Ranatunga	8
6	R. A. Smith	Hampshire	b Ranatunga	31	not out	8
7	D. R. Pringle	Essex	c Silva b Labrooy	14		
8	J. E. Emburey	Middlesex	c De Silva b Sam'kera	0		
9	P. J. Newport	Worcestershire	c De Silva b R'anayake	26		
10	N. A. Foster	Essex	not out	14		
11	D. V. Lawrence	Gloucestershire	c Mendis b R'anayake	4		
			B 1, l-b 3, w 2, n-b 17,	23	B , l-b 8, w 2, n-b 4,	14
			Total	429	Total	100

FALL OF THE WICKETS
1—40   2—171   3—233   4—320   5—358   6—373   7—378   8—383   9—420   10—429
1—73   2—73   3—82   4—   5—   6—   7—   8—   9—   10—

ANALYSIS OF BOWLING

Name	1st Innings					2nd Innings				
	O.	M.	R.	W.	Wd. N-b	O.	M.	R.	W.	Wd. N-b
Ratnayeke	32	3	107	2	... 4	7	1	16	0	... ...
Labrooy	40	7	119	3	... 10	9	0	24	0	... 1 4
Ramanayake	27.2	3	86	2	... 1 3	...	...	...	...	... ...
Madurasinghe	16	4	41	0	... ...	...	...	...	...	... ...
Samarasekera	22	5	66	1	... ...	10	0	38	2	... 1
Ranatunga	6	3	6	1	... ...	8.4	4	14	1	... ...

Umpires—D. J. Constant & J. W. Holder

Scorers—E. Solomon & W. A. Powell

† Captain   * Wicketkeeper

Play begins each day at 11.00
Luncheon Interval 1.00—1.40
Tea Interval 3.40—4.00 (may be varied according to state of game)
Stumps drawn 1st, 2nd, 3rd & 4th days at 6.00, or after 90 overs have been bowled, whichever is the later - 5th day at 6.00, or after a minimum of 75 overs for playing time other than the last hour, when Law of Cricket 17.6 and 17.7 shall apply (20 overs). (In the event of play being suspended for any reason for one hour or more in aggregate on any of the first four days, play may be extended to 7.00 on that day). The captains may agree to stop play at 5.30 on the 5th day if there is no prospect of a result.

England won the toss and elected to field

England won by 7 wickets

1989: England v Australia

(2nd Test) June 22, 23, 24, 26, 27
Australia won by 6 wickets

The road that led David Gower back to the captaincy of England is too complicated to bear description here, but it involved a change in the England management and the cancellation of a tour of India because of Graham Gooch's South African connections. However, by the end of the summer, Gower might well have been wishing he had not been given back the captaincy, because

Australia were just too good. The change between 1985 and 1989 was complete, except of course for the fact that Australia won at Lord's yet again.

The weather, most unusually, was perfect: glorious sunshine throughout, which encouraged about 97,000 people to come to St John's Wood and to pay £1,250,000 for the privilege. They got their money's worth. Steve Waugh, who had made 177 not out in the First Test, hit 152 and 21, both not out, at Lord's. He had taken 393 runs off the England attack before they finally dismissed him in the Third Test, and his series average was 126.50. David Boon also hit 152 runs for once out, and Geoff Lawson made the highest first-class score of his life, batting at number 10. Waugh and Lawson put on 130 in under two hours, the second highest for the ninth wicket in Australian Test history. It is interesting to note, in passing, that after 34 Ashes Tests at Lord's, none of the series wicket partnership records by either side have been set there. On the other hand four have been set at the Oval, where 35 England v Australia Tests have so far been played.

England were 242 behind on first innings, and at 28 for three in their second innings must have been looking up the train timetables for an early

Australia get their first view of the new Mound Stand and the new electronic scoreboard.

LORD'S **GROUND**

(20p) (20p)

CORNHILL INSURANCE TEST SERIES
ENGLAND v. AUSTRALIA
(5-day Match)

THURS., FRI., SAT., MON. & TUES., JUNE 22, 23, 24, 26 & 27, 1989

ENGLAND

			First Innings		Second Innings	
1	G. A. Gooch	Essex	c Healy b Waugh	60	l b w b Alderman	0
2	B. C. Broad	Nottinghamshire	l b w b Alderman	18	b Lawson	20
3	K. J. Barnett	Derbyshire	c Boon b Hughes	14	c Jones b Alderman	3
4	M. W. Gatting	Middlesex	c Boon b Hughes	0	l b w b Alderman	22
†5	D. I. Gower	Leicestershire	b Lawson	57	c Border b Hughes	106
6	R. A. Smith	Hampshire	c Hohns b Lawson	32	b Alderman	96
7	J. E. Emburey	Middlesex	b Alderman	0	not out	36
*8	R. C. Russell	Gloucestershire	not out	64	c Boon b Lawson	29
9	N. A. Foster	Essex	c Jones b Hughes	16	l b w b Alderman	4
10	P. W. Jarvis	Yorkshire	c Marsh b Hughes	6	l b w b Alderman	5
11	G. R. Dilley	Worcestershire	c Border b Alderman	7	c Boon b Hughes	24
			B , l-b 9, w , n-b 3,	12	B 6, l-b 6, w , n-b 2,	14
			Total	286	Total	359

FALL OF THE WICKETS

1—31 2—52 3—58 4—131 5—180 6—185 7—191 8—237 9—253 10—286
1—0 2—18 3—28 4—84 5—223 6—274 7—300 8—304 9—314 10—359

ANALYSIS OF BOWLING

Name	1st Innings						2nd Innings					
	O.	M.	R.	W.	Wd.	N-b	O.	M.	R.	W.	Wd.	N-b
Alderman	20.5	4	60	3	...	1	38	6	128	6	...	2
Lawson	27	8	88	2	...	...	39	10	99	2	...	...
Hughes	23	6	71	4	...	...	24	8	44	2	...	...
Waugh	9	3	49	1	...	2	7	2	20	0	...	...
Hohns	7	3	9	0	...	...	13	6	33	0	...	...
Border	...	...	...	...	...	...	9	3	23	0	...	...

AUSTRALIA

			First Innings		Second Innings	
1	G. R. Marsh	W. Australia	c Russell b Dilley	3	b Dilley	1
2	M. A. Taylor	N.S.W.	l b w b Foster	62	c Gooch b Foster	27
3	D. C. Boon	Tasmania	c Gooch b Dilley	94	not out	58
†4	A. R. Border	Queensland	c Smith b Emburey	35	c sub b Foster	1
5	D. M. Jones	Victoria	l b w b Foster	27	c Russell b Foster	0
6	S. R. Waugh	N.S.W.	not out	152	not out	21
*7	I. A. Healy	Queensland	c Russell b Jarvis	3		
8	M. G. Hughes	Victoria	c Gooch b Foster	30		
9	T. V. Hohns	Queensland	b Emburey	21		
10	G. F. Lawson	N.S.W.	c Broad b Emburey	74		
11	T. M. Alderman	W. Australia	l b w b Emburey	8		
			B , l-b 11, w , n-b 8,	19	B 3, l-b 4, w , n-b 4,	11
			Total	528	Total	119

FALL OF THE WICKETS

1—6 2—151 3—192 4—221 5—235 6—265 7—331 8—381 9—511 10—528
1—9 2—51 3—61 4—67 5— 6— 7— 8— 9— 10—

ANALYSIS OF BOWLING

Name	1st Innings						2nd Innings					
	O.	M.	R.	W.	Wd.	N-b	O.	M.	R.	W.	Wd.	N-b
Dilley	34	3	141	2	...	7	10	2	27	1	...	4
Foster	45	7	129	3	...	...	18	3	39	3	...	...
Jarvis	31	3	150	1	...	1	9.2	0	38	0	...	...
Emburey	42	12	88	4	...	...	3	0	8	0	...	...
Gooch	6	2	9	0	...	...						

Umpires—H. D. Bird & N. T. Plews Scorers—E. Solomon & M. Walsh
† Captain * Wicket-keeper

Play begins each day at 11.00 Luncheon Interval 1.00—1.40
Tea Interval 3.40—4.00 (may be varied according to state of game)
Stumps drawn 1st, 2nd, 3rd & 4th days at 6.00, or after 90 overs have been bowled, whichever is the later - 5th day at 6.00, or after a minimum of 75 overs for playing time other than the last hour, when Law of Cricket 17.6 and 17.7 shall apply (20 overs). (In the event of play being suspended for any reason for one hour or more in aggregate on any of the first four days, play may be extended to 7.00 on that day). The captains may agree to stop play at 5.30 on the 5th day if there is no prospect of a result.

England won the toss

Australia won by 6 wickets

---

departure home. But David Gower and Robin Smith, due to become Hampshire colleagues the following season, added 139 for the fourth wicket, and brought England some way back into the match. This was after Gower, 15 not out overnight, had left the end of day press conference early, and not a little irritated by the questions he was being asked, to go to a performance of the West End production of *Anything Goes*. He may have appeared 'laid back', but his seventh Test hundred against Australia proved how much he cared.

LORD'S   GROUND

1990: England v New Zealand

(2nd Test) June 21, 22, 23, 25, 26
Match drawn

By 1990, England were beginning to believe that things were improving a little. The top order was looking good, with Atherton and Gooch beginning a fruitful partnership as openers, and Alec Stewart (more than just the son of the England manager), Allan Lamb and Robin Smith in the next three slots. Jack Russell was proving himself England's best wicketkeeper-batsman for many years (until his place was lost to Alec Stewart), and the bowling attack included a genuine fast bowler in Devon Malcolm. England had got the better of the First Test, a rain-affected draw at Trent Bridge, and came to Lord's with an unchanged team and a great deal of confidence.

But so did New Zealand. Nine days before the match began, the world's leading Test wicket-taker Richard Hadlee, now almost 39 years old, was knighted in the Birthday Honours for his services to cricket. He thus became only the second knight to play Test cricket, after the Maharajah of Vizianagram in 1936. Sir Timothy O'Brien had also played Test cricket, but he, of course, was a baronet, not a knight. And no knight before Hadlee had ever won a Man of the Match award in a Test.

It was one of those Tests where there was enough time lost to rain – 118 overs in all – to make a draw almost inevitable. It was also one of those Tests where things almost happened but didn't quite. Seven people made fifties, but only one man turned his into a century. For Trevor Franklin, it was his only century in 21 Tests for New Zealand, but the highlight of the tourists' innings was Hadlee's 86 in 84 balls. When Hemmings finally bowled him, the sighs of disappointment around the ground were not only from the New Zealand supporters. Everybody there wanted him to score those final 14 runs.

The electronic scoreboard showing Sir Richard Hadlee's name. He had just been knighted in the Queen's Birthday Honours.

The year 1990 was also one for hard hats and tarpaulins at Lord's. The Edrich and Compton stands were under construction, very slowly indeed, and there was some danger of the Nursery End becoming permanently rechristened the Building Site End.

LORD'S GROUND

(20p) (20p)

CORNHILL INSURANCE TEST SERIES
ENGLAND v. NEW ZEALAND

THURS., FRI., SAT., MON. & TUES., JUNE 21, 22, 23, 25 & 26, 1990 (5-day Match)

ENGLAND

			First Innings		Second Innings	
†1	G. A. Gooch	Essex	c and b Bracewell	85	b Hadlee	37
2	M. A. Atherton	Lancashire	b Morrison	0	c Bracewell b Jones	54
3	A. J. Stewart	Surrey	l b w b Hadlee	54	c sub b Bracewell	42
4	A. J. Lamb	Northamptonshire	l b w b Snedden	39	not out	84
5	R. A. Smith	Hampshire	c Bracewell b Morrison	64	hit wicket b Bracewell	0
6	N. H. Fairbrother	Lancashire	c Morrison b Bracewell	2	not out	33
*7	R. C. Russell	Gloucestershire	b Hadlee	13		
8	P. A. J. DeFreitas	Lancashire	c Franklin b Morrison	38		
9	G. C. Small	Warwickshire	b Morrison	3		
10	E. E. Hemmings	Notts.	b Hadlee	0	Innings closed	
11	D. E. Malcolm	Derbyshire	not out	0		
			B , l-b 13, w 1, n-b 22,	36	B 8, l-b 8, w , n-b 6,	22
			Total	334	Total	272

FALL OF THE WICKETS

1—3 2—151 3—178 4—216 5—226 6—255 7—319 8—322 9—332 10—334
1—68 2—135 3—171 4—175 5— 6— 7— 8— 9— 10—

ANALYSIS OF BOWLING

	1st Innings						2nd Innings				
Name	O.	M.	R.	W.	Wd.	N-b	O.	M.	R.	W	Wd.	N-b
Sir Richard Hadlee	29	5	113	3	...	10	13	2	32	1	...	3
Morrison	18.4	4	64	4	...	7	16	0	81	0	...	3
Snedden	21	4	72	1	1	5	...					
Bracewell	21	3	72	2	...		34	13	85	2	...	...
Jones	...	...	...	...	...		12	3	40	1	...	...
Rutherford	...	...	...	...	...		3	0	18	0	...	...

NEW ZEALAND

			First Innings		Second Innings
1	T. J. Franklin	Auckland	c Russell b Malcolm	101	
†2	J. G. Wright	Auckland	c Stewart b Small	98	
3	A. H. Jones	Wellington	c Stewart b Malcolm	49	
4	M. D. Crowe	Central Districts	c Russell b Hemmings	1	
5	M. J. Greatbatch	C. Districts	b Malcolm	47	
6	K. R. Rutherford	Otago	c Fairbrother b Malcolm	0	
7	Sir Richard Hadlee	Canterbury	b Hemmings	86	
8	J. G. Bracewell	Auckland	run out	4	
*9	I. D. S. Smith	Auckland	c Small b Malcolm	27	
10	M. C. Snedden	Auckland	not out	13	
11	D. K. Morrison	Auckland	not out	2	
			B 12, l-b 15, w 2, n-b 5,	34	B , l-b , w , n-b
			Total	‡462	Total

‡ Innings closed

FALL OF THE WICKETS

1—185 2—278 3—281 4—284 5—285 6—408 7—415 8—425 9—448 10—
1— 2— 3— 4— 5— 6— 7— 8— 9— 10—

ANALYSIS OF BOWLING

	1st Innings						2nd Innings				
Name	O.	M.	R.	W.	Wd.	N-b	O.	M.	R.	W.	Wd.	N-b
Malcolm	43	14	94	5	...	1	...					
Small	35	4	127	1	1		...					
DeFreitas	35.4	1	122	0	...	4	...					
Hemmings	30	13	67	2	...		...					
Gooch	13	7	25	0	1		...					
Atherton	1	1	0	0	...		...					

Umpires—M. J. Kitchen & D. R. Shepherd Scorers—E. Solomon & P. N. Culpan

† Captain * Wicket-keeper

Play begins each day at 11.00
Luncheon Interval 1.00—1.40
Tea Interval 3.40—4.00 (may be varied according to state of game)
Stumps drawn 1st, 2nd, 3rd & 4th days at 6.00, or after 90 overs have been bowled, whichever is the later - 5th day at 6.00, or after a minimum of 75 overs for playing time other than the last hour, when Law of Cricket 17.6 and 17.7 shall apply (20 overs). (In the event of play being suspended on any of the first four days for any reason other than normal intervals, the timing for cessation of play on that day will be extended by an amount of time equal to the aggregate time lost prior to 6.00. However, play shall not continue on any of the first four days after 7.00). The captains may agree to stop play at 5.30 on the 5th day if there is no prospect of a result.

New Zealand won the toss and elected to field

Match Drawn

1990: England v India

(1st Test) July 26, 27, 28, 30, 31
England won by 247 runs

It is difficult to know where to start with this match. Beyond the rubble and the tarpaulin that once had been the Nursery End, one of the great cricket matches of all time was played out. It was never a close match, and England's final margin of victory was huge, but it was full of such individual brilliance that the spectators were gripped throughout.

Towering over everything was Graham Gooch and his two innings of 333 and 123. His 333 was the highest score in any match at Lord's, the highest score by an England captain, the third highest Test score for England and the second highest score of the season (after Neil Fairbrother's 366 for Lancashire against Surrey). His total of 456 runs in one Test was the highest

Kapil Dev hits Eddie Hemmings, the spinner, for his fourth consecutive six.

LORD'S GROUND

CORNHILL INSURANCE TEST SERIES
ENGLAND v. INDIA

Thurs., Fri., Sat., Mon. & Tues., July 26, 27, 28, 30 & 31, 1990   (5-day Match)

ENGLAND		First Innings		Second Innings	
†1 G. A. Gooch	Essex	b Prabhakar	333	c Azharuddin b Sharma	123
2 M. A. Atherton	Lancashire	b Kapil Dev	8	c Vengsarkar b Sharma	72
3 D. I. Gower	Hampshire	c Manjrekar b Hirwani	40	not out	32
4 A. J. Lamb	Northamptonshire	c Manjrekar b Sharma	139	c Tendulkar b Hirwani	19
5 R. A. Smith	Hampshire	not out	100	b Prabhakar	15
6 J. E. Morris	Derbyshire	not out	4		
*7 R. C. Russell	Gloucestershire				
8 C. C. Lewis	Leicestershire	Innings closed		Innings closed	
9 E. E. Hemmings	Notts.				
10 A. R. C. Fraser	Middlesex				
11 D. E. Malcolm	Derbyshire	B 2, l-b 21, w 2, n-b 4,	29	B , l-b 11, w , n-b ,	11
		Total	653	Total	272

FALL OF THE WICKETS

1—14 2—141 3—449 4—641 5— 6— 7— 8— 9— 10—
1—204 2—207 3—250 4—272 5— 6— 7— 8— 9— 10—

ANALYSIS OF BOWLING	1st Innings						2nd Innings					
Name	O.	M.	R.	W.	Wd.	N-b	O.	M.	R.	W.	Wd.	N-b
Kapil Dev	34	5	120	1	1	...	10	0	53	0	...	...
Prabhakar	43	6	187	1	...	2	11.2	2	45	1	...	...
Sharma	33	5	122	1	1	2	15	0	75	2	...	...
Shastri	22	0	99	0	...	...	7	0	38	0	...	...
Hirwani	30	1	102	1	...	...	11	0	50	1	...	...

INDIA		First Innings		Second Innings	
1 R. J. Shastri	Bombay	c Gooch b Hemmings	100	c Russell b Malcolm	12
2 N. S. Sidhu	Punjab	c Morris b Fraser	30	c Morris b Fraser	1
3 S. V. Manjrekar	Bombay	c Russell b Gooch	18	c Russell b Malcolm	33
4 D. B. Vengsarkar	Bombay	c Russell b Fraser	52	c Russell b Hemmings	35
†5 M. Azharuddin	Hyderabad	b Hemmings	121	c Atherton b Lewis	37
6 S. R. Tendulkar	Bombay	b Lewis	10	c Gooch b Fraser	27
7 M. Prabhakar	Delhi	c Lewis b Malcolm	25	l b w b Lewis	8
8 Kapil Dev	Haryana	not out	77	c Lewis b Hemmings	7
*9 K. S. More	Baroda	c Morris b Fraser	8	l b w b Fraser	16
10 S. K. Sharma	Delhi	c Russell b Fraser	0	run out	38
11 N. D. Hirwani	Madhya Pradesh	l b w b Fraser	0	not out	0
		B , l-b 1, w 4, n-b 8,	13	B 3, l-b 1, w , n-b 6,	10
		Total	454	Total	224

FALL OF THE WICKETS

1—63 2—102 3—191 4—241 5—288 6—348 7—393 8—430 9—430 10—454
1—9 2—23 3—63 4—114 5—127 6—140 7—158 8—181 9—206 10—224

ANALYSIS OF BOWLING	1st Innings						2nd Innings					
Name	O.	M.	R.	W.	Wd.	N-b	O.	M.	R.	W.	Wd.	N-b
Malcolm	25	1	106	1	...	1	10	0	65	2	...	2
Fraser	39.1	9	104	5	...	3	22	7	39	2	...	1
Lewis	24	3	108	1	4	4	8	1	26	2	...	3
Gooch	6	3	26	1	...	...						
Hemmings	20	3	109	2	...	...	21	2	79	2	...	...
Atherton	...	...	...	...	...	...	1	0	11	0	...	...

Umpires—H. D. Bird & N. T. Plews

Scorers—E. Solomon & Yashvant Chad

† Captain   * Wicket-keeper

Play begins each day at 11.00   Luncheon Interval 1.00—1.40

Tea Interval 3.40—4.00 (may be varied according to state of game)

Stumps drawn 1st, 2nd, 3rd & 4th days at 6.00, or after 90 overs have been bowled, whichever is the later - 5th day at 6.00, or after a minimum of 75 overs for playing time other than the last hour, when Law of Cricket 17.6 and 17.7 shall apply (20 overs). (In the event of play being suspended on any of the first four days for any reason other than normal intervals, the timing for cessation of play on that day will be extended by an amount of time equal to the aggregate time lost prior to 6.00. However, play shall not continue on any of the first four days after 7.00). The captains may agree to stop play at 5.30 on the 5th day if there is no prospect of a result.

India won the toss and elected to field

England won by 247 runs

Four more for Graham Gooch.

ever: only Hanif Mohammad and, later, Brian Lara exceeded that in any first-class match. Gooch also became the first Englishman to score three hundreds against the same Test opponents at Lord's, emulating the feat of Dilip Vengsarkar. There were more runs scored in the match (1,603) and more hundreds (6) than in any previous Test at Lord's.

In any other match, Azharuddin's 121 would have been the batting highlight. According to Tony Lewis in the *Daily Telegraph*, 'Azharuddin made good length straight balls into blitzing boundaries by meeting them with a flowing bat on the up.' It was a brilliant attacking innings by one of the most accomplished strokemakers of his generation. But when he was out, India still had work to do to save the follow-on. Azharuddin, as captain, had put England in and

fielded through the highest Test score ever made by a team put in by the opposition, but it fell to Kapil Dev to avoid the follow-on. With India needing 24 to make England bat again, and with the ninth wicket down, Kapil Dev hit four consecutive sixes off Eddie Hemmings, and the deed was done. Off the first ball of the next over, Fraser trapped Hirwani, and Gooch put his pads back on.

The feature of England's second innings, apart from Gooch continuing run-getting, was the catch by the seventeen-year-old Sachin Tendulkar to dismiss Allan Lamb. He ran a full 30 yards to take a perfectly middled hit by Lamb with outstretched arms almost directly behind the bowler. Only a very young and very fit man could have taken that catch, one of the best ever seen at Lord's.

1991: England v West Indies

(2nd Test) June 20, 21, 22, 23, 24 (no play on fourth day)
Match drawn

Robin Smith at his best.

Yet again – this is becoming a litany of down-pours – the rain had the final say. After three days' engrossing cricket in which England got them-selves into trouble and then out again, the rain came down, washing out all play on the Sunday and limiting it to less than half an hour on the final day.

England had an international look about them, with only four of the side born in England. The rest consisted of four born in Africa, two in the West Indies and one in Wales. But this was the same eleven that had just won the First Test, so hopes were high. The most significant of the 'overseas' stars that summer was Graeme Hick, at long last qualified for England. In county cricket he had already scored 57 hundreds at a career average of around 60, and he was expected to step up to Test cricket with no difficulty whatsoever. It is easy in retrospect to see that the expectations of an impatient English cricketing public were far too high. Still, it was sad to see him out of the side by the end of the summer, with a series average of under 11, even though subsequently, he was again selected by England.

ENGLAND v. WEST INDIES

Thursday, Friday, Saturday, Sunday & Monday, June 20, 21, 22, 23 & 24, 1991
(no play on Sunday - rain)   (5-day Match)

WEST INDIES		First Innings		Second Innings	
1 P. V. Simmons	Trinidad/Tobago	c Lamb b Hick	33	l b w b DeFreitas	2
2 D. L. Haynes	Barbados	c Russell b Pringle	60	not out	4
3 R. B. Richardson	Leeward Is.	c DeFreitas b Hick	57	c Hick b Malcolm	1
4 C. L. Hooper	Guyana	c Lamb b Pringle	111	not out	1
†5 I. V. A. Richards	Leeward Is.	l b w b DeFreitas	63		
6 A. L. Logie	Trinidad & Tobago	b DeFreitas	5		
*7 P. J. L. Dujon	Jamaica	c Lamb b Pringle	20		
8 M. D. Marshall	Barbados	l b w b Pringle	25		
9 C. E. L. Ambrose	Leeward Is.	c and b Malcolm	5		
10 C. A. Walsh	Jamaica	c Atherton b Pringle	10		
11 I. B. A. Allen	Windward Islands	not out	1		
		B 3, l-b 7, w , n-b 19,	29	B , l-b 2, w , n-b 2,	4
		Total	419	Total	12

FALL OF THE WICKETS

1—90 2—102 3—198 4—322 5—332 6—366 7—382 8—402 9—410 10—419
1—9   2—10   3—   4—   5—   6—   7—   8—   9—   10—

ANALYSIS OF BOWLING

Name	1st Innings						2nd Innings					
	O.	M.	R.	W.	Wd.	N-b	O.	M.	R.	W.	Wd.	N-b
DeFreitas	31	6	93	2	...	2	3	2	1	1	...	2
Malcolm	19	3	76	1	...	3	2.5	0	9	1	...	
Watkin	15	2	60	0	...	14						
Pringle	35.1	6	100	5	...							
Hick	18	4	77	2	...							
Gooch	2	0	3	0	...							

ENGLAND		First Innings		Second Innings	
†1 G. A. Gooch	Essex	b Walsh	37		
2 M. A. Atherton	Lancashire	b Ambrose	5		
3 G. A. Hick	Worcestershire	c Richardson b Ambrose	0		
4 A. J. Lamb	Northamptonshire	c Haynes b Marshall	1		
5 M. R. Ramprakash	Middlesex	c Richards b Allen	24		
6 R. A. Smith	Hampshire	not out	148		
*7 R. C. Russell	Gloucestershire	c Dujon b Hooper	46		
8 D. R. Pringle	Essex	c Simmons b Allen	35		
9 P. A. J. DeFreitas	Lancashire	c Dujon b Marshall	29		
10 S. L. Watkin	Glamorgan	b Ambrose	6		
11 D. E. Malcolm	Derbyshire	b Ambrose	0		
		B , l-b 1, w , n-b 22,	23	B , l-b , w , n-b ,	
		Total	354	Total	

FALL OF THE WICKETS

1—5   2—6   3—16   4—60   5—84   6—180 7—269 8—316 9—353 10—354
1—   2—   3—   4—   5—   6—   7—   8—   9—   10—

ANALYSIS OF BOWLING

Name	1st Innings						2nd Innings					
	O.	M.	R.	W.	Wd.	N-b	O.	M.	R.	W.	Wd.	N-b
Ambrose	34	10	87	4	...	6						
Marshall	30	4	78	2	...	13						
Walsh	26	4	90	1	...							
Allen	23	2	88	2	...	3						
Hooper	5	2	10	1	...							

Umpires—B. J. Meyer & K. E. Palmer   Scorers—E. Solomon & A. Weld

† Captain   * Wicket-keeper

Play begins each day at 11.00   Luncheon Interval 1.00—1.40

Tea Interval 3.40—4.00 (may be varied according to state of game)

Stumps drawn 1st, 2nd, 3rd & 4th days at 6.00, or after 90 overs have been bowled, whichever is the later - 5th day at 6.00, or after a minimum of 75 overs for playing time other than the last hour, when Law of Cricket 17.6 and 17.7 shall apply (20 overs). (In the event of play being suspended on any of the first four days for any reason other than normal intervals, the timing for cessation of play on that day will be extended by an amount of time equal to the aggregate time lost prior to 6.00. However, play shall not continue on any of the first four days after 7.00). The captains may agree to stop play at 5.30 on the 5th day if there is no prospect of a result.

West Indies won the toss

Match Abandoned

The West Indies made 419, thanks in particular to Carl Hooper, who in many ways can be compared with Graeme Hick: full of natural talent, but so rarely fulfilling it. At Lord's he showed his true class, taking a little over four hours over his first century against England. At the end of the first day, West Indies stood at 317 for 3, with Hooper and Richards both going strongly, but a great bowling performance the next morning by Derek Pringle kept the score within range for England. But when England slumped to 84 for 5 towards the end of the Friday, a quick defeat seemed very possible.

The Saturday was a personal triumph for Robin Smith. He moved from 23 not out overnight to 148 not out, his highest Test score, when England's innings finally ended only 65 behind West Indies. It was a much slower century than Hooper's, partly because the West Indian over rate was much slower, but it was also a match-saving innings, watchful and sometimes pugnacious. The Robin Smith square cut was much in evidence – one of the most devastating strokes played by any batsman of his time. Not surprisingly, he was named Man of the Match.

1991: England v Sri Lanka

(only Test) August 22, 23, 24, 26, 27
England won by 137 runs

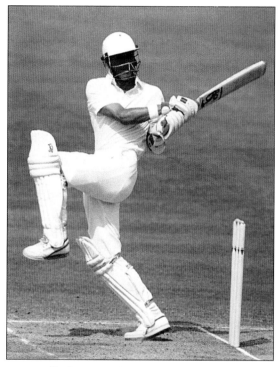

Alec Stewart during his first Test hundred.

In 1991, England still did not feel that Sri Lanka merited a full tour – or even half a tour – so instead they gave them a one-off Test at Lord's at the end of a busy summer. The attitude was summed up in the *Cricketer*, which began its report of the Test with the words, 'For the first two days of this entertaining match, Sri Lanka acquitted themselves very favourably.' It would not be long before England were to be jolted out of this condescending attitude, but 1991 was not the year for that.

Gooch won the toss and batted. He and Hugh Morris immediately set a record opening partnership for England against Sri Lanka (it was only

the fourth Test between the countries), which remained a record until England's second innings. Gooch's departure at 70 let in Alec Stewart, who dominated the rest of the England innings, scoring 113 of the final 212 runs of the innings. Nobody stayed with him for long, although Ian Botham hit a brisk 22. The innings, timed at 308 minutes, actually lasted from the first morning until late on the Friday, a day which was much curtailed by the rain. Rumesh Ratnayake, in his twentieth Test, became the first Sri Lankan to take five wickets in a Test innings against England, but 282 seemed a solid enough score.

MARYLEBONE CRICKET CLUB

ENGLAND v. SRI LANKA

Thursday, Friday, Saturday, Monday & Tuesday, August 22, 23, 24, 26 & 27, 1991
(5-day Match)

ENGLAND		First Innings		Second Innings	
†1 G. A. Gooch	Essex	c and b Ramanayake...	38	b Anurasiri	174
2 H. Morris	Glamorgan	l b w b Ratnayake	42	c Mah'ama b Anurasiri.	23
3 A. J. Stewart	Surrey	not out	113	c de Silva b Anurasiri...	43
4 R. A. Smith	Hampshire	c Till'ratne b Ratnayake	4	not out	63
5 M. R. Ramprakash	Middlesex	c Mah'ama b Hat'singhe	0		
6 I. T. Botham	Worcestershire	c Mah'ama b Ram'yake	22		
7 C. C. Lewis	Leicestershire	c de Silva b Anurasiri.	11	not out	12
*8 R. C. Russell	Gloucestershire	b Anurasiri	17		
9 P. A. J. DeFreitas	Lancashire	b Ratnayake	1		
10 D. V. Lawrence	Gloucestershire	c and b Ratnayake	3		
11 P. C. R. Tufnell	Middlesex	l b w b Ratnayake	0	Innings closed	
		B 9, l-b 8, w , n-b 14,	31	B 15, l-b 23, w 1, n-b 10,	49
		Total	282	Total	364

FALL OF THE WICKETS

1—70 2—114 3—119 4—120 5—160 6—183 7—246 8—258 9—276 10—282

1—78 2—217 3—322 4— 5— 6— 7— 8— 9— 10—

ANALYSIS OF BOWLING

Name		1st Innings						2nd Innings				
	O.	M.	R.	W.	Wd.	N-b	O.	M.	R.	W.	Wd.	N-b
Ratnayake	27	4	69	5	...	1	26	4	91	0	1	4
Ramanayake	24	5	75	2	...	3	20	2	86	0		2
Wijegunawardene	10	1	36	0	...	2	2	0	13	0		
Hathurusinghe	17	6	40	1	...	2						
Anurasiri	17	4	45	2	...	6	36.1	8	135	3		4
Jayasuriya	...	...	...	...	...	...	1	0	1	0		

SRI LANKA		First Innings		Second Innings	
1 D. S. B. P. Kuruppu	Burgher	b DeFreitas	5	l b w b Lewis	21
2 U. C. Hathurusinghe	Tamil U.	c Tufnell b DeFreitas	66	c Morris b Tufnell	25
3 A P. Gurusinha	Nondescripts	l b w b DeFreitas	4	b Tufnell	34
†4 P. A. de Silva	Nondescripts	c Lewis b DeFreitas	42	c Russell b Lawrence	18
5 R. S. Mahanama	C.C.C.	c Russell b Botham	2	c Botham b Tufnell	15
6 S. T. Jayasuriya	C.C.C.	c Smith b DeFreitas	11	c Russell b Lewis	66
*7 H. P. Tillekeratne	Nondescripts	c Morris b Lawrence	20	b Tufnell	16
8 R. J. Ratnayake	Nondescripts	c de Silva b DeFreitas	52	c sub b Lawrence	17
9 C P. Ramanayake	Tamil Union	l b w b DeFreitas	0	not out	34
10 K. I. W. Wijegunawardene	C.C.C.	not out	6	c Botham b DeFreitas	4
11 S. D. Anurasiri	Panadura	b Lawrence	1	l b w b Tufnell	16
		B , l-b 15, w , n-b ,	15	B 1, l-b 16, w , n-b 2,	19
		Total	224	Total	285

FALL OF THE WICKETS

1—12 2—22 3—75 4—86 5—105 6—139 7—213 8—213 9—220 10—224

1—50 2—50 3—111 4—119 5—159 6—212 7—212 8—241 9—253 10—285

ANALYSIS OF BOWLING

Name		1st Innings						2nd Innings				
	O.	M.	R.	W.	Wd.	N-b	O.	M.	R.	W.	Wd.	N-b
DeFreitas	26	8	70	7	...	...	22	8	45	1	...	2
Lawrence	15.1	3	61	2	...	...	23	7	83	2	...	
Lewis	10	5	29	0	...	...	18	4	31	2	...	
Botham	10	3	26	1	...	...	6	2	15	0	...	
Tufnell	7	2	23	0	...	...	34.3	14	94	5	...	

Umpires—H. D. Bird & J. H. Hampshire

† Captain

Scorers—E. Solomon & G. G. A. Saulez

* Wicket-keeper

Play begins each day at 11.00

Luncheon Interval 1.00—1.40

Tea Interval 3.40—4.00 (may be varied according to state of game)
Stumps drawn 1st, 2nd, 3rd & 4th days at 6.00, or after 90 overs have been bowled, whichever is the later - 5th day at 6.00, or after a minimum of 75 overs for playing time other than the last hour, when Law of Cricket 17.6 and 17.7 shall apply (20 overs). (In the event of play being suspended on any of the first four days for any reason other than normal intervals, the timing for cessation of play on that day will be extended by an amount of time equal to the aggregate time lost prior to 6.00. However, play shall not continue on any of the first four days after 7.00). The captains may agree to stop play at 5.30 on the 5th day if there is no prospect of a result.

England won the toss

England won by 137 runs

One thing that must be said about Sri Lankan cricket is that it is unpredictable. After Kuruppu (one of only three men with four initials to have hit a Test double century) and Gurusinha were out cheaply, the Sri Lankan captain Aravinda de Silva came out in the murky Friday evening light and proceeded to hit 42 off 30 balls, including seven fours. Overnight the Sri Lankan total stood at 75 for 2, and Saturday seemed set fair for a full house crowd to enjoy some dashing batting. But off the second ball of the morning, de Silva was brilliantly caught by Lewis in the gully and the day went quiet. Only Ratnayeke, batting at number 8, livened up the Saturday crowd with a belligerent 52 off 55 balls, the second half of an all round performance which won him Sri Lanka's Man of the Match award. His partnership of 74 with Hathurusinghe for the seventh wicket was a series record.

The Sri Lankans, it was reported, 'played their cricket with enthusiasm, wreathed in smiles and with no little skill.' But even with all that and an England victory, only 43,000 people watched the match over the five days. What more did the public want?

1992: England v Pakistan

(2nd Test) June 18, 19, 20, 21
Pakistan won by 2 wickets

Of all the Tests playedat Lord's, this one had the narrowest margin of victory, equalled only when England beat West Indies by the same margin in 2000. It was also one of the most enthralling of all Tests, and could have gone either way until the final ball. In what proved to be Ian Botham's 102nd and final Test for England, his 15th at Lord's, the Lord's hoodoo struck. England, who should have won when Pakistan were 18 for 3 and then 95 for 8 in their second innings, lost again. England were certainly hampered by injuries to DeFreitas and Botham which meant neither of

them bowled in Pakistan's second innings, but there were no excuses: this was a game Pakistan won rather than England lost.

When Gooch and Stewart put on 123 for the first wicket, it seemed that a high scoring game was in prospect. But as the ball got older and Waqar in particular exploited the opportunities for reverse swing, England more than struggled, they collapsed. The pitch too, showed signs of deterioration quite early on, and by the first afternoon, it was clear that this was to be a bowlers' match. So it was, and in Pakistan's case the bowlers did the

Wasim Akram hits the winning run.

batting as well, with Wasim and Waqar putting together a stand of 46 for the ninth wicket which won the game late on the fourth evening. Despite England's appalling over rate of 12 an hour (with England debutant leg-spinner Ian Salisbury bowling one third of the overs), Wasim managed to hit the winning runs a few moments before the day's play was due to end. The regulations did not allow for the extra half hour to be claimed on the fourth day, so the match might have slipped into a fifth day if Wasim had not cover driven the first ball of Salisbury's fifteenth over to the boundary.

Before all that happened, Alec Stewart had grabbed a little slice of Lord's Test history by becoming the first – and to date only – Englishman to carry his bat through the innings there: he joined a list already containing three Australians and a New Zealander. Ian Botham also took his 119th and 120th Test match catches, to draw level with Colin Cowdrey as England's leading fielder in Tests. Only five men – Botham, Gary Sobers, Jacques Kallis, Shane Warne and Carl Hooper – have scored 1,000 runs, taken 100 wickets and pouched 100 catches in Test cricket.

MARYLEBONE CRICKET CLUB

ENGLAND v. PAKISTAN

THURSDAY, FRIDAY, SATURDAY, SUNDAY & MONDAY, JUNE 18, 19, 20, 21 & 22, 1992
(5 day Match completed in first 4 days)

ENGLAND

		First Innings		Second Innings	
†1 G. A. Gooch	Essex	b Wasim Akram	69	l b w b Aqib Javed	13
2 A. J. Stewart	Surrey	c Javed b Asif Mujtaba	74	not out	69
3 G. A. Hick	Worcestershire	c Javed b Waqar	13	c Moin Khan b Mushtaq	11
4 R. A. Smith	Hampshire	c sub b Wasim Akram	9	b Mushtaq Ahmed	8
5 A. J. Lamb	Northamptonshire	b Waqar Younis	30	b Mushtaq Ahmed	12
6 I. T. Botham	Durham	b Waqar Younis	2	l b w b Waqar Younis	6
7 C. C. Lewis	Nottinghamshire	l b w b Waqar Younis	2	b Waqar Younis	15
*8 R. C. Russell	Gloucestershire	not out	22	b Wasim Akram	1
9 P. A. J. DeFreitas	Lancashire	c Inzamam b Waqar	3	c Inzamam b Wasim	0
10 I. D. K. Salisbury	Sussex	hit wicket b Mushtaq	4	l b w b Wasim Akram	12
11 D. E. Malcolm	Derbyshire	l b w b Mushtaq Ahmed	0	b Wasim Akram	0
		B 6, l-b 12, w , n-b 9,	27	B 5, l-b 8 , w , n-b 15 ,	28
		Total	255	Total	175

FALL OF THE WICKETS

1—123 2—153 3—172 4—197 5—213 6—221 7—232 8—242 9—247 10—255
1—40 2—73 3—108 4—120 5—137 6—148 7—174 8—175 9—175 10—175

ANALYSIS OF BOWLING

Name	1st Innings						2nd Innings					
	O.	M.	R.	W.	Wd.	N-b	O.	M.	R.	W.	Wd.	N-b
Wasim Akram	19	5	49	2	...	8	17.4	2	66	4	...	12
Aqib Javed	14	3	40	0	...	1	12	3	23	1	...	3
Waqar Younis	21	4	91	5	...		13	3	40	2	...	
Mushtaq Ahmed	19.1	5	57	2	...		9	1	32	3	...	
Asif Mujtaba	3	3	0	1	...		1	0	1	0	...	

PAKISTAN

		First Innings		Second Innings	
1 Aamir Sohail	Habib Bank	c Russell b DeFreitas	73	b Salisbury	39
2 Ramiz Raja	P.N.S.C.	b Lewis	24	c Hick b Lewis	0
3 Asif Mujtaba	P.I.A.	c Smith b Malcolm	59	c Russell b Lewis	0
†4 Javed Miandad	Habib Bank	c Botham b Salisbury	9	c Russell b Lewis	0
5 Salim Malik	Habib Bank	c Smith b Malcolm	55	c Lewis b Salisbury	12
6 Inzamam Ul-Haq	United Bank	c and b Malcolm	0	run out	8
7 Wasim Akram	P.I.A.	b Salisbury	24	not out	45
*8 Moin Khan	P.I.A.	c Botham b DeFreitas	12	c Smith b Salisbury	3
9 Mushtaq Ahmed	United Bank	c Russell b DeFreitas	4	c Hick b Malcolm	5
10 Waqar Younis	United Bank	b Malcolm	14	not out	20
11 Aqib Javed	P.A.C.O.	not out	5		
		B 4, l-b 3, w , n-b 7,	14	B 2, l-b 5, w 1, n-b 1,	9
		Total	293	Total	141

FALL OF THE WICKETS

1—43 2—123 3—143 4—228 5—228 6—235 7—263 8—271 9—276 10—293
1—6 2—10 3—18 4—41 5—62 6—68 7—81 8—95 9— 10—

ANALYSIS OF BOWLING

Name	1st Innings						2nd Innings					
	O.	M.	R.	W.	Wd.	N-b	O.	M.	R.	W.	Wd.	N-b
DeFreitas	26	8	58	3	...	6						
Malcolm	15.5	1	70	4	...							
Lewis	29	7	76	1	...	1	15	2	42	1	...	1
Salisbury	23	3	73	2	...		16	3	43	3	...	1
Botham	5	2	9	0	...		14.1	0	49	3	...	

Umpires—B. Dudleston & J. H. Hampshire   Scorers—E. Solomon & A. Weld

† Captain   * Wicket-keeper

Play begins each day at 11.00   Luncheon Interval 1.00—1.40

Tea Interval 3.40—4.00 (may be varied according to state of game)

Stumps drawn - 1st, 2nd, 3rd & 4th days at 6.00, or after 90 overs have been bowled, whichever is the later - 5th day at 6.00, or after a minimum of 75 overs for playing time other than the last hour, when Law of Cricket 17.6 and 17.7 shall apply (except a minimum of 15 overs). Except in the last hour of the match, in the event of play being suspended for any reason other than normal intervals or one or more changes of innings, the playing time on that day shall be extended by the amount of time lost up to a maximum of one hour. The captains may agree to stop play at 5.30 on the 5th day if there is no prospect of a result.

England won the toss

Pakistan won by 2 wickets

1993: England v Australia

(2nd Test) June 17, 18, 19, 20, 21
Australia won by an innings and 62 runs

It was Lord's, so England lost yet another Test they should at least have managed to draw. There was never any realistic chance of victory, at least not after the first day which finished with Australia on 292 for 2, but on a very good batting wicket and with Craig McDermott in hospital after emergency surgery for a twisted bowel, England should have been able to hold out for a draw.

There are a lot of 'should haves' in England's Test cricket, especially at Lord's. Throughout the summer, Australia were clearly the better side, so it was no disgrace to lose the series, but 2–1 or 3–1 might have been a fairer reflection of the relative strengths of the sides rather than the actual result of 4–1.

The match was notable for many statistical oddities. None were quite as bizarre as Graham Gooch's dismissal 'handled the ball' in the First Test that summer, but the Lord's Test had its moments, too. Taylor and Slater put on 260 for the first wicket, not quite as many as the record 329 that Taylor and Geoff Marsh had compiled four years earlier, but still a very solid start. By the time Border declared on 632 for 4, their second highest total ever at Lord's, no Australian batsman had been dismissed for less than 50, and none of England's first three bowlers had taken a wicket. Alec Stewart had not conceded a bye, either, creating a record for the highest Test total in England that does not include any byes. Mark Waugh was out for 99, as was Michael Atherton, whose 179 runs in the match without scoring a century (he never did in a Lord's Test) are the most since Frank Woolley scored 95 and 93 (188 in all) in 1921. This was the only Lord's Test in which two batsmen were out for 99.

It was also the match in which Robin Smith and Ian Healy made cricket history. When Smith

Slater and Taylor on their way to making 260 together for Australia's first wicket.

was stumped by Healy, square leg umpire Mervyn Kitchen referred to the third umpire, Chris Balderstone, for the first time in English Test history. It took Balderstone three close looks at the video replay to decide that Smith was out, so in the end he went, the first of a kind.

ENGLAND v. AUSTRALIA

THURSDAY, FRIDAY, SATURDAY, SUNDAY & MONDAY, JUNE 17, 18, 19, 20 & 21, 1993
(5-day Match)

AUSTRALIA

			First Innings		Second Innings
1	M. A. Taylor	New South Wales	st Stewart b Tufnell	111	
2	M. J. Slater	New South Wales	c sub b Lewis	152	
3	D. C. Boon	Tasmania	not out	164	
4	M. E. Waugh	New South Wales	b Tufnell	99	
†5	A. R. Border	Queensland	b Lewis	77	
6	S. R. Waugh	New South Wales	not out	13	
*7	I. A. Healy	Queensland			
8	T. B. A. May	South Australia			
9	M. G. Hughes	Victoria	Innings closed		
10	S. K. Warne	Victoria			
11	C. J. McDermott	Queensland			

B , l-b **1**, w **1**, n-b **14, 16**   B , l-b , w , n-b ,

Total .... **632**   Total ....

FALL OF THE WICKETS

1—260 2—277 3—452 4—591 5— 6— 7— 8— 9— 10—
1— 2— 3— 4— 5— 6— 7— 8— 9— 10—

ANALYSIS OF BOWLING

Name	1st Innings						2nd Innings					
	O.	M.	R.	W.	Wd.	N-b	O.	M.	R.	W.	Wd.	N-b
Caddick	38	5	120	0			...	...	...	...	...	...
Foster	30	4	94	0		4	...	...	...	...	...	...
Such	38	6	90	0			...	...	...	...	...	...
Tufnell	39	3	129	2		4	...	...	...	...	...	...
Lewis	36	5	151	2		6	...	...	...	...	...	...
Gooch	9	1	26	0	1		...	...	...	...	...	...
Hick	8	3	21	0			...	...	...	...	...	...

ENGLAND

			First Innings		Second Innings	
†1	G. A. Gooch	Essex	c May b Hughes	12	c Healy b Warne	29
2	M. A. Atherton	Lancashire	b Warne	80	run out	99
3	M. W. Gatting	Middlesex	b May	5	l b w b Warne	59
4	R. A. Smith	Hampshire	st Healy b May	22	c sub b May	5
5	G. A. Hick	Worcestershire	c Healy b Hughes	20	c Taylor b May	64
*6	A. J. Stewart	Surrey	l b w b Hughes	3	l b w b May	62
7	C. C. Lewis	Nottinghamshire	l b w b Warne	0	st Healy b May	0
8	N. A. Foster	Essex	c Border b Warne	16	c M. Waugh b Border	20
9	A. R. Caddick	Somerset	c Healy b Hughes	21	not out	0
10	P. M. Such	Essex	c Taylor b Warne	7	b Warne	4
11	P. C. R. Tufnell	Middlesex	not out	2	b Warne	0

B , l-b **8**, w , n-b **9, 17**   B **10**, l-b **13**, w , n-b **23**

Total .... **205**   Total **365**

FALL OF THE WICKETS

1—33 2—50 3—84 4—123 5—131 6—132 7—167 8—174 9—189 10—205
1—71 2—175 3—180 4—244 5—304 6—312 7—361 8—361 9—365 10—365

ANALYSIS OF BOWLING

Name	1st Innings						2nd Innings					
	O.	M.	R.	W.	Wd.	N-b	O.	M.	R.	W.	Wd.	N-b
Hughes	20	5	52	4			31	9	75	0	...	...
M. Waugh	6	1	16	0	...	5	17	4	55	0	...	...
S. Waugh	4	1	5	0	...	1	2	0	13	0	...	...
May	31	12	64	2	...		51	23	81	4	...	...
Warne	35	12	57	4	...	3	48.5	17	102	4	...	...
Border	3	1	3	0			16	9	16	1	...	...

Umpires—M. J. Kitchen & D. R. Shepherd   Scorers—E. Solomon & M. Walsh

† Captain   * Wicket-keeper

Play begins each day at 11.00   Luncheon Interval 1.00—1.40

Tea Interval 3.40—4.00 (may be varied according to state of game)

Stumps drawn 1st, 2nd, 3rd & 4th days at 6.00, or after 90 overs have been bowled, whichever is the later - 5th day at 6.00, or after a minimum of 75 overs for playing time other than the last hour, when Law of Cricket 17.6 and 17.7 shall apply (except a minimum of 15 overs). Except in the last hour of the match, in the event of play being suspended for any reason other than normal intervals or one or more changes of innings, the playing time on that day shall be extended by the amount of time lost up to a maximum of one hour. The captains may agree to stop play at 5.30 on the 5th day if there is no prospect of a result.

Australia won the toss

Australia won by an innings and 62 runs

1994: England v New Zealand

(2nd Test) June 16, 17, 18, 19, 20
Match drawn

What happens to touring sides when they come to Lord's? There is clear evidence that they do better at headquarters than at other grounds in England, and New Zealand in 1994 were another case in point. They did not win, but England were left with over 150 still to make with only two wickets standing when the match came to an end. This was a side that had lost the First Test by an innings and plenty, and should have been mere cannon fodder for England. But in the person of 22-year-old Dion Nash, in his fifth Test, they found an unlikely hero. Nash took 11 wickets for 169 runs and scored 56 to make his selection as Man of the Match a mere formality.

By batting first, New Zealand certainly had the best of the wicket. It was never a true batting surface, as the eleven lbw decisions in the game testify. Seven of those eleven came in the third and fourth innings of the game, when only thirteen wickets fell in total. New Zealand also had the best

Martin Crowe during his 142.

batsman, Martin Crowe, who scored his second Test hundred at Lord's, his sixteenth in all. With a solid middle order – the 180 he and Thomson added for the fifth wicket is a New Zealand record against England – he guided his side to 476, not far short of their record score, made also at Lord's in 1973. England, thanks to bits and pieces from almost everybody but a big score from nobody, limped past the follow-on mark, but five runs later gave up the ghost.

By close of play on the fourth day, England had reached 56 without loss, and an unlikely England win was on the cards. Only 351 more to make. But early the next morning, Nash removed Atherton and Gooch in the same over, and from then on it was a matter of saving the game. Alec Stewart, almost as prolific at Lord's as at his home ground across the river, hit another century, and Steve Rhodes, preferred to Jack Russell as a wicketkeeper-batsman, proved his worth by defending for 129 minutes with such batting worthies as Gus Fraser (2 in 35 minutes) and Paul Taylor (0 not out in 23 minutes) to save the day. Rhodes batted for five hours and 40 minutes in the match for 56 runs without being dismissed. In the end, it was the lack of another bowler to back up Dion Nash that cost New Zealand the game.

MARYLEBONE CRICKET CLUB

ENGLAND v. NEW ZEALAND

THURSDAY, FRIDAY, SATURDAY, SUNDAY & MONDAY, JUNE 16, 17, 18, 19 & 20, 1994
(5-day Match)

NEW ZEALAND

			First Innings		Second Innings	
1 B. A. Young	Northern Districts	l b w b Fraser	0	c Hick b Such	94
2 B. A. Pocock	Northern Districts	c Smith b Such	10	l b w b DeFreitas	2
†3 K. R. Rutherford	Otago	c Stewart b DeFreitas	37	l b w b DeFreitas	0
4 M. D. Crowe	Wellington	c Smith b DeFreitas	142	b DeFreitas	9
5 S. P. Fleming	Canterbury	l b w b Fraser	41	l b w b Taylor	39
6 S. A. Thomson	N. Districts	run out	69	not out	38
*7 A. C. Parore	Auckland	c Rhodes b Taylor	40	not out	15
8 M. N. Hart	Northern Districts	b Such	25		
9 D. J. Nash	Otago	b White	56		
10 C. Pringle	Auckland	c Hick b DeFreitas	14		
11 M. B. Owens	Canterbury	not out	2	Innings closed	
		B 3, l-b 15, w 1, n-b 21,	40	B , l-b 4, w , n-b 10,	14
		Total	476	Total	211

FALL OF THE WICKETS

1—0 2—39 3—67 4—138 5—318 6—350 7—391 8—397 9—434 10—476
1—9 2—9 3—29 4—144 5—170 6— 7— 8— 9— 10—

ANALYSIS OF BOWLING

		1st Innings						2nd Innings				
Name	O.	M.	R.	W.	Wd.	N-b	O.	M.	R.	W.	Wd.	N-b
Fraser	36	9	102	2	...	9	15	0	60	0	...	4
DeFreitas	35	8	102	3	...	9	16	0	63	3	...	6
Taylor	20	4	64	1	...	6	6	2	18	1	...	...
Such	30	8	84	2	...		25	5	55	1	...	...
White	21.1	5	84	1	1		4	1	21	0	...	...
Gooch	5	1	13	0	...							
Hick	2	0	9	0	...		2	2	0	0	...	...

ENGLAND

			First Innings		Second Innings	
†1 M. A. Atherton	Lancashire	l b w b Hart	28	c Young b Nash	33
2 A. J. Stewart	Surrey	c Parore b Nash	45	c Crowe b Nash	119
3 G. A. Gooch	Essex	l b w b Nash	13	l b w b Nash	0
4 R. A. Smith	Hampshire	c and b Nash	6	c Parore b Nash	23
5 G. A. Hick	Worcestershire	c Young b Pringle	58	l b w b Pringle	37
6 C. White	Yorkshire	run out		c Thomson b Nash	9
*7 S. J. Rhodes	Worcestershire	not out	51	not out	24
8 P. A. J. DeFreitas	Derbyshire	c Parore b Thomson	11	l b w b Owens	3
9 A. R. C. Fraser	Middlesex	c and b Nash	10	l b w b Hart	2
10 J. P. Taylor	Northamptonshire	c Parore b Nash	0	not out	0
11 P. M. Such	Essex	c Parore b Nash	4		
		B 4, l-b 12, w , n-b 7,	23	B 2, l-b 1, w , n-b 1,	4
		Total	281	Total	254

FALL OF THE WICKETS

1—65 2—95 3—95 4—101 5—193 6—225 7—241 8—265 9—271 10—281
1—60 2—60 3—136 4—210 5—217 6—240 7—244 8—250 9— 10—

ANALYSIS OF BOWLING

		1st Innings						2nd Innings				
Name	O.	M.	R.	W.	Wd.	N-b	O.	M.	R.	W.	Wd.	N-b
Owens	7	0	34	0	...	2	10	3	35	1	...	1
Nash	25	6	76	6	...	2	29	8	93	5	...	...
Pringle	23	5	65	1	...	3	16	5	41	1	...	...
Hart	44	21	50	1	...		41	23	55	1	...	...
Thomson	22	8	40	1	...		12	4	27	0	...	...

Umpires—N. T. Plews & S. U. Bucknor

Scorers—E Solomon & M. Jones

† Captain   * Wicket-keeper

Play begins each day at 11.00

Luncheon Interval 1.00—1.40

Tea Interval 3.40—4.00 (may be varied according to state of game)

Stumps drawn 1st, 2nd, 3rd & 4th days at 6.00, or after 90 overs have been bowled, whichever is the later - 5th day at 6.00, or after a minimum of 75 overs for playing time other than the last hour, when Law of Cricket 17.6 and 17.7 shall apply (except a minimum of 15 overs). Except in the last hour of the match, in the event of play being suspended for any reason other than normal intervals or one or more changes of innings, the playing time on that day shall be extended by the amount of time lost up to a maximum of one hour. The captains may agree to stop play at 5.30 on the 5th day if there is no prospect of a result.

New Zealand won the toss

Match Drawn

1994: England v South Africa

(1st Test) July 21, 22, 23, 24
South Africa won by 356 runs

England had not played South Africa at Lord's since 1965, and South Africa had not won at Lord's since 1935. In this first Test in England since South Africa's return to the active list of Test-playing countries, Kepler Wessels led his team to the biggest victory, in terms of runs, that the Springboks had ever achieved against any opposition. Wessels became only the second person, after AH Kardar, to play Test cricket at Lord's for two different countries, having already played for Australia in 1985. More importantly, he became the only man ever to score a century on Test debut against England twice: he hit 162 as an Australian at Brisbane in the 1982/83 series, and

now 105 at Lord's a dozen years later. Opener Andrew Hudson, however, was the first South African ever to score a century on his Test debut, but at Lord's he was out of luck.

Even though the opening partnerships were undistinguished (all under 20, for the first time at Lord's since India visited in 1982) two of the openers had significant matches. Gary Kirsten made two good scores in building South Africa's domination with the bat, and he was also half of a unique combination: with his elder brother Peter, they became the first pair of half-brothers to play Test cricket at Lord's, a curiosity that was matched by Pedro Collins and Fidel Edwards for

South Africa, welcomed back.

MARYLEBONE CRICKET CLUB
ENGLAND v. SOUTH AFRICA

THURSDAY, FRIDAY, SATURDAY, SUNDAY & MONDAY, JULY 21, 22, 23, 24 & 25, 1994
(5-day Match)

SOUTH AFRICA

			First Innings		Second Innings	
1	A. C. Hudson	Natal	c Gooch b Gough	6	l b w b Fraser	3
2	G. Kirsten	Western Province	c DeFreitas b Hick	72	st Rhodes b Hick	44
3	W. J. Cronje	Orange Free State	c Crawley b Fraser	7	c Fraser b Gough	32
†4	K. C. Wessels	Eastern Province	c Rhodes b Gough	105	c Crawley b Salisbury	28
5	P. N. Kirsten	Border	c Rhodes b Gough	8	b Gough	42
6	J. N. Rhodes	Natal	b White	32	b Gough	32
7	B. M. McMillan	W. Province	c Rhodes b Fraser	29	not out	39
*8	D. J. Richardson	E. Province	l b w b Gough	26	c Rhodes b Fraser	3
9	C. R. Matthews	W. Province	b White	41	b Gough	25
10	P. S. de Villiers	N. Transvaal	c Rhodes b Fraser	8	Innings closed	
11	A. A. Donald	Orange Free State	not out	5		
			B , l-b 9, w , n-b 9,	18	B 8, l-b 10, w , n-b 12,	30
			Total	357	Total	278

FALL OF THE WICKETS

1—18 2—35 3—141 4—164 5—239 6—241 7—281 8—334 9—348 10—357
1—14 2—73 3—101 4—141 5—208 6—209 7—220 8—278 9— 10—

ANALYSIS OF BOWLING

Name	1st Innings						2nd Innings					
	O.	M.	R.	W.	Wd.	N-b	O.	M.	R.	W.	Wd.	N-b
DeFreitas	18	5	67	0	...	5	14	3	43	0	...	...
Gough	28	6	76	4	...		19.3	5	46	4	...	6
Salisbury	25	2	68	0	...	4	19	4	53	1	...	6
Fraser	24.5	7	72	3	...		23	5	62	2	...	...
Hick	10	5	22	1	...		23	14	38	1	...	...
White	13	2	43	2	...		3	0	18	0	...	...

ENGLAND

			First Innings		Second Innings	
†1	M. A. Atherton	Lancashire	c Wessels b Donald	20	c McMillan b de Villiers	8
2	A. J. Stewart	Surrey	b Donald	12	c Rich'son b Matthews	27
3	J. P. Crawley	Lancashire	c Hudson b de Villiers	9	c Hudson b McMillan	7
4	G. A. Hick	Worcestershire	c Rich'son b de Villiers	38	l b w b Donald	11
5	G. A. Gooch	Essex	l b w b de Villiers	20	l b w b Donald	28
6	C. White	Yorkshire	c Richardson b Donald	10	c Wessels b Matthews	0
*7	S. J. Rhodes	Worcestershire	b McMillan	15	not out	14
8	I. D. K. Salisbury	Sussex	not out	6	l b w b Donald	0
9	P. A. J. DeFreitas	Derbyshire	c Wessels b Donald	20	c G. Kirston b Matthews	1
10	D. Gough	Yorkshire	c and b Donald	12	retired hurt	0
11	A. R. C. Fraser	Middlesex	run out	3	l b w b McMillan	1
			B 2, l-b 5, w , n-b 8,	15	B 1, l-b 1, w , n-b ,	2
			Total	180	Total	99

FALL OF THE WICKETS

1—19 2—41 3—68 4—107 5—119 6—136 7—141 8—161 9—176 10—180
1—16 2—29 3—45 4—74 5—74 6—82 7—85 8—88 9—99 10—

ANALYSIS OF BOWLING

Name	1st Innings						2nd Innings					
	O.	M.	R.	W.	Wd.	N-b	O.	M.	R.	W.	Wd.	N-b
Donald	19.3	5	74	5	...	7	12	5	29	2	...	...
de Villiers	16	5	28	3	...	1	12	4	26	1	...	...
Matthews	16	6	46	0	...		14	6	25	3	...	...
McMillan	10	1	25	1	...		6.5	2	16	3	...	...
Cronje							1	0	1	0	...	...

Umpires—H. D. Bird & S. G. Randell

Scorers—E Solomon & A. W. Weld

† Captain   * Wicket-keeper

Play begins each day at 11.00   Luncheon Interval 1.00—1.40

Tea Interval 3.40—4.00 (may be varied according to state of game)
Stumps drawn 1st, 2nd, 3rd & 4th days at 6.00, or after 90 overs have been bowled, whichever is the later - 5th day at 6.00, or after a minimum of 75 overs for playing time other than the last hour, when Law of Cricket 17.6 and 17.7 shall apply (except a minimum of 15 overs). Except in the last hour of the match, in the event of play being suspended for any reason other than normal intervals or one or more changes of innings, the playing time on that day shall be extended by the amount of time lost up to a maximum of one hour. The captains may agree to stop play at 5.30 on the 5th day if there is no prospect of a result.

South Africa won the toss

South Africa won by 356 runs

West Indies in 2004. For Mike Atherton, England's captain and opening bat, it was a match he will never forget, however much he would like to. During South Africa's second innings, he was seen on television clearly taking dirt from his pocket and applying it to the ball in an attempt to help his bowlers achieve some reverse swing. This caused a great deal of fuss in the press and around the ground at Lord's, but in the end Peter Burge the match referee found Atherton not guilty of contravening Law 42.5, regarding 'action to alter the condition of the ball'. Despite this, he was fined £2,000 by the England management for failing to disclose the true facts to the referee when first asked. A messy business, and the only thing to be said in its favour is that the alleged ball-tampering did not work. South Africa declared on the fourth day, leaving England over 450 to win. They never even got close, being all out for their lowest total at Lord's for 106 years. In 1997, they would do even worse.

1995: England v West Indies

(2nd Test) June 22, 23, 24, 25, 26
England won by 72 runs

After their first defeat by South Africa at Lord's in 59 years, nobody was expecting England's first victory against the West Indies at Lord's in 38 years, just twelve months on. The First Test of the summer had resulted in a nine-wicket win for West Indies, and all the selectors did for the Second Test was to replace DeFreitas and Malcolm with Fraser and Cork. It was Dominic Cork's Test debut, and he launched himself into Test cricket in style. The selectors also adjusted the batting order, allowing Robin Smith, who had opened in the First Test, to slip back down to his preferred number five slot, and gambling that Alec Stewart could both open and keep wicket. He could.

England had first go on a pitch that the West Indies coach Andy Roberts later described as one of the worst he had seen for a Test match in England, but in reality it was not a bad pitch, just a slower one than the West Indians had been expecting. Graham Thorpe was put in hospital by the first ball he received from Courtney Walsh in the second innings, but that was nothing to do with the pitch. It was a high, fast full toss that hit him on the helmet. He returned the following day

Campbell, the most tenacious of Cork's seven second innings victims.

to make 42, adding 95 with Robin Smith in a partnership that gave England the edge, but then retired to the pavilion with a throat infection. Paul Weekes took two catches as substitute in his place.

The England matchwinners were Robin Smith and Dominic Cork. Smith scored 151 runs in the match, and Cork took 7 for 43 in the second innings to make sure that West Indies did not threaten the target of 296 to win. When Campbell and Lara were together at the end of the fourth day, and there were only another 228 to make, the match was still very much in the balance. But when Alec Stewart took a brilliant diving one-handed catch to get rid of Lara off Darren Gough, the tables turned finally towards England. Cork's second innings analysis was the best ever by an England bowler on Test debut, beating John Lever's 7 for 46 against India in 1976/77. It was the best analysis by an England bowler at Lord's since Ian Botham's 8 for 103 in 1984, and the fourteenth instance of seven or more wickets by an England bowler at Lord's.

MARYLEBONE CRICKET CLUB
ENGLAND v. WEST INDIES
THURSDAY, FRIDAY, SATURDAY, SUNDAY & MONDAY, JUNE 22, 23, 24, 25 & 26, 1995
(5-day Match)

ENGLAND

		First Innings		Second Innings	
†1 M. A. Atherton	Lancashire	b Ambrose	21	c Murray b Walsh	9
*2 A. J. Stewart	Surrey	c Arthurton b Gibson	34	c Murray b Walsh	36
3 G. A. Hick	Worcestershire	c Lara b Bishop	13	b Bishop	67
4 G. P. Thorpe	Surrey	c Lara b Ambrose	52	c Richardson b Ambrose	42
5 R. A. Smith	Hampshire	b Hooper	61	l b w b Ambrose	90
6 M. R. Ramprakash	Middlesex	c Campbell b Hooper	0	c sub b Bishop	0
7 D. G. Cork	Derbyshire	b Walsh	30	c Murray b Bishop	23
8 P. J. Martin	Lancashire	c Campbell b Gibson	11	b Ambrose	20
9 D. Gough	Yorkshire	b Walsh	29	c Arthurton b Ambrose	1
10 R. K. Illingworth	Worcestershire	not out	16	l b w b Walsh	4
11 A. R. C. Fraser	Middlesex	l b w b Walsh	1	not out	2
		B 1, l-b 10, w , n-b 4,	15	B 6, l-b 27, w 2, n-b 7,	42
		Total	283	Total	336

FALL OF THE WICKETS
1—29 2—70 3—74 4—185 5—187 6—191 7—205 8—255 9—281 10—283
1—32 2—51 3—150 4—155 5—240 6—290 7—320 8—329 9—334 10—336

ANALYSIS OF BOWLING

		1st Innings					2nd Innings				
Name	O.	M.	R.	W.	Wd.	N-b	O.	M.	R.	W.	Wd.	N-b
Ambrose	26	6	72	2	...	2	24	5	70	4	1	2
Walsh	22.4	6	50	3	...	1	28.1	10	91	3	...	2
Gibson	20	2	81	2	...	1	14	1	51	0	...	...
Bishop	17	4	33	1	...	...	22	5	56	3	1	3
Hooper	14	3	36	2	...	...	9	1	31	0	...	...
Adams	...	...	...	...	...	...	2	0	4	0	...	...

WEST INDIES

		First Innings		Second Innings	
1 S. L. Campbell	Barbados	c Stewart b Gough	5	c Stewart b Cork	93
2 C. L. Hooper	Guyana	b Martin	40	c Martin b Gough	14
3 B. C. Lara	Trinidad & Tobago	l b w b Fraser	6	c Stewart b Gough	54
4 J. C. Adams	Jamaica	l b w b Fraser	54	c Hick b Cork	13
†5 R. B. Richardson	Leeward Is.	c Stewart b Fraser	49	l b w b Cork	0
6 K. L. T. Arthurton	Leeward Is.	c Gough b Fraser	75	c sub b Cork	0
*7 J. R. Murray	Windward Islands	c and b Martin	16	c sub b Gough	9
8 O. D. Gibson	Barbados	l b w b Gough	29	l b w b Cork	14
9 I. R. Bishop	Trinidad & Tobago	b Cork	8	not out	10
10 C. E. L. Ambrose	Leeward Is.	c Ramprakash b Fraser	12	c Illingworth b Cork	11
11 C. A. Walsh	Jamaica	not out	11	c Stewart b Cork	0
		B 8, l-b 11, w , n-b ,	19	B , l-b 5, w , n-b ,	6
		Total	324	Total	223

FALL OF THE WICKETS
1—6 2—23 3—88 4—166 5—169 6—197 7—246 8—272 9—305 10—324
1—15 2—99 3—124 4—130 5—138 6—177 7—198 8—201 9—223 10—223

ANALYSIS OF BOWLING

		1st Innings					2nd Innings				
Name	O.	M.	R.	W.	Wd.	N-b	O.	M.	R.	W.	Wd.	N-b
Gough	27	2	84	2	...	...	20	0	79	3	...	...
Fraser	33	13	66	5	...	...	9	9	57	0	...	...
Cork	22	4	72	1	...	...	25	6	43	7	...	...
Martin	23	5	65	2	...	...	19.3	5	43	7	...	...
Illingworth	7	2	18	0	...	...	7	0	30	0	...	...
							7	4	9	0	...	...

Umpires—D. R. Shepherd & S. Venkataraghavan   Scorers—D. Kendix & A. Weld

† Captain   * Wicket-keeper

Play begins each day at 11.00   Luncheon Interval 1.00—1.40

Tea Interval 3.40—4.00 (may be varied according to state of game)

Stumps drawn 1st, 2nd, 3rd & 4th days at 6.00, or after 90 overs have been bowled, whichever is the later - 5th day at 6.00, or after a minimum of 75 overs for playing time other than the last hour, when Law of Cricket 17.6 and 17.7 shall apply (except a minimum of 15 overs). Except in the last hour of the match, in the event of play being suspended for any reason other than normal intervals or one or more changes of innings, the playing time on that day shall be extended by the amount of time lost up to a maximum of one hour. The captains may agree to stop play at 5.30 on the 5th day if there is no prospect of a result.

England won the toss

England won by 72 runs

1996: England v India

(2nd Test) June 20, 21, 22, 23, 24
Match drawn

The Second Test of 1996 was an odd, up-and-down match, with the most unexpected heroes. In the end it was a draw, but for much of the game the bookmakers would have been giving long odds against the stalemate. A total of 1,051 runs were scored, of which three left handers – Jack Russell, Graham Thorpe and Saurav Ganguly – scored 403 and extras another 104. Ganguly became only the third player to score a century at Lord's on his Test debut, after Harry Graham of Australia in 1983 and John Hampshire of England in 1969. A short while later, Rahul Dravid fell only five short of adding his name to that list.

The match began with the players ceding centre stage to an umpire. And not just any umpire, but *the* umpire, Harold 'Dickie' Bird, whose 66th and final Test this was. The Indian fielders formed a guard of honour as Dickie walked out to the middle, waving to the crowd and making frequent use of his handkerchief. His eyes were not too misty, however, to give England's captain Michael Atherton out lbw in the first over of the innings and get England off to a terrible start. Azharuddin must have been pleased with his decision to put England in. By the time England had reached 107 for five, with only

'That's out', says Dickie Bird for the last time in his 66 Test matches as an umpire, Russell being the batsman.

MARYLEBONE CRICKET CLUB
ENGLAND v. INDIA

THURSDAY, FRIDAY, SATURDAY, SUNDAY & MONDAY, JUNE 20, 21, 22, 23 & 24, 1996
(5-day Match)

ENGLAND

			First Innings		Second Innings	
†1	M. A. Atherton	Lancashire	l b w b Srinath	0	b Kumble	17
2	A. J. Stewart	Surrey	b Srinath	20	b Srinath	66
3	N. Hussain	Essex	c Rathore b Ganguly	36	c Dravid b Srinath	28
4	G. P. Thorpe	Surrey	b Srinath	89	c Rathore b Kumble	21
5	G. A. Hick	Worcestershire	c Srinath b Ganguly	1	c Mongia b Prasad	6
6	R. C. Irani	Essex	b Prasad	1	b Mhambrey	41
*7	R. C. Russell	Gloucestershire	c Tendulkar b Prasad	124	l b w b Ganguly	38
8	C. C. Lewis	Surrey	c Mongia b Prasad	31	not out	26
9	D. G. Cork	Derbyshire	c Mongia b Prasad	0	c Azharuddin b Kumble	1
10	P. J. Martin	Lancashire	c Tendulkar b Prasad	4	c Rathore b Prasad	23
11	A. D. Mullally	Leicestershire	not out	0	not out	0
			B 13, l-b 11, w , n-b 14,	38	B 1, l-b 5, w , n-b 5,	11
			Total	344	Total	‡278

‡ Innings closed

FALL OF THE WICKETS
1—0 2—67 3—98 4—102 5—107 6—243 7—326 8—337 9—343 10—344
1—49 2—109 3—114 4—154 5—167 6—168 7—228 8—274 9—275 10—

ANALYSIS OF BOWLING

	1st Innings						2nd Innings					
Name	O.	M.	R.	W.	Wd.	N-b	O.	M.	R.	W.	Wd.	N-b
Srinath	33	9	76	3	...	3	29	8	76	2	...	3
Prasad	33.3	10	76	5	...	1	24	8	54	2	...	1
Mhambrey	19	3	58	0	...	1	14	3	47	1	...	
Kumble	28	9	60	0	...	3	51	14	90	3	...	1
Ganguly	15	2	49	2	...		3	0	5	1	...	
Tendulkar	2	1	1	0	...							

INDIA

			First Innings		Second Innings	
1	V. Rathore	Punjab	c Hussain b Cork	15		
*2	N. R. Mongia	Baroda	l b w b Lewis	24		
3	S. Ganguly	Bengal	b Mullally	131		
4	S. R. Tendulkar	Bombay	b Lewis	31		
†5	M. Azharuddin	Hyderabad	c Russell b Mullally	16		
6	A. D. Jadeja	Haryana	b Irani	10		
7	R. S. Dravid	Karnataka	c Russell b Lewis	95		
8	A. Kumble	Karnataka	l b w b Martin	14		
9	J. Srinath	Karnataka	b Mullally	19		
10	P. L. Mhambrey	Bombay	not out	15		
11	B. K. V. Prasad	Karnataka	c Stewart b Cork	4		
			B 11, l-b 25, w 10, n-b 9,	55	B , l-b , w , n-b ,	
			Total	429	Total	

FALL OF THE WICKETS
1—25 2—59 3—123 4—154 5—202 6—296 7—351 8—388 9—419 10—429
1— 2— 3— 4— 5— 6— 7— 8— 9— 10—

ANALYSIS OF BOWLING

	1st Innings						2nd Innings					
Name	O.	M.	R.	W.	Wd.	N-b	O.	M.	R.	W.	Wd.	N-b
Lewis	40	11	101	3	...		...	...	...	...	...	...
Cork	42.3	10	112	2	2	6	...	...	...	...	...	...
Mullally	39	14	71	3	8	3	...	...	...	...	...	...
Martin	34	10	70	1	...		...	...	...	...	...	...
Irani	12	3	31	1	...		...	...	...	...	...	...
Hick	2	0	8	0	...		...	...	...	...	...	...

Scorers—D. Kendix & J. Blondel

Umpires—H. D. Bird & D. B. Hair

† Captain — * Wicket-keeper

Play begins each day at 11.00

Luncheon Interval 1.00—1.40

Tea Interval 3.40—4.00 (may be varied according to state of game)

Stumps drawn 1st, 2nd, 3rd & 4th days at 6.00, or after 90 overs have been bowled, whichever is the later - 5th day at 6.00, or after a minimum of 75 overs for playing time other than the last hour, when Law of Cricket 17.6 and 17.7 shall apply (except a minimum of 15 overs). Except in the last hour of the match, in the event of play being suspended for any reason other than normal intervals or one or more changes of innings, the playing time on that day shall be extended by the amount of time lost up to a maximum of one hour. The captains may agree to stop play at 5.30 on the 5th day if there is no prospect of a result.

India won the toss and elected to field

Match Drawn

Graham Thorpe showing any form, he must have been even more pleased. But that was the cue for Jack Russell, restored if only briefly as England's preferred wicketkeeper, to make his second Test hundred, and in partnership first with Thorpe and then with Chris Lewis, to take England to a respectable total.

On the Saturday afternoon, as Dravid and Ganguly piled on the runs, the biggest cheer of the session came when England won a game of football a few miles away in Wembley. Most of the 20,000-plus Lord's crowd had radios, and although it may be sacrilegious to admit it, the excitement generated when the footballers of England won their Euro '96 quarter-final against Spain on a penalty shoot-out was greater than anything the England Test team could provide at the same time. It must have been unnerving for the bowlers to have their run-ups interrupted by a huge cheer from the crowd as a penalty was scored or missed, but it was far from the oddest happening of Dickie Bird's Test umpiring career.

LORD'S GROUND

1996: England v Pakistan

(1st Test) July 25, 26, 27, 28, 29
Pakistan won by 164 runs

Over the years, England's selectors have brought in horses for courses, and there are many players who have ended their careers with just one Test cap. One Test cap is better than none, of course, and if you are going to win only one cap, where better to win it than at Lord's? In 1996, Simon Brown became not only the first Durham player to win a Test cap (apart from Ian Botham at the very end of his career), but also the thirteenth England player to win his only Test cap at Lord's. In 1921, the selectors (who had a very bad year) picked three men whose entire Test career was that year's Lord's Test, but nobody had qualified for the one-cap wonder club from Lord's since Alec Coxon in 1948, who also finished his career with Durham.

Brown began his only Test well. In only his second over, he brought one back to have Sohail lbw, and a little later Ijaz Ahmed was bowled by Cork. Inzamam-ul-Haq, a brilliant batsman but one of the worst judges of a run in Test cricket since Denis Compton, shared a stand of 130 with Saeed Anwar, but when Saeed went to his first ball from Graeme Hick, Inzamam promptly ran out Salim Malik and gave England a chance to get back into the game. But that never quite happened.

England got within striking distance of the visitor's first innings total, but then let it slip away as Pakistan batted England out of it in their second innings. Inzamam's two innings of 148 and 70 lifted him to second place above Brian Lara in the then Coopers and Lybrand (now I.C.C. rankings) ratings, and made the world realise that here was a batsman to rank with Pakistan's greatest. If only he could run between the wickets a little more effectively!

Already established as one of Pakistan's greatest bowlers was Waqar Younis, who with Mushtaq Ahmed reduced England from the comparative security of 168 for 1 to 243 all out. After Atherton and Stewart were removed by the leg-spin of Mushtaq, only England's leg-spinner Ian Salisbury seemed to know what to do, but his 40 was in a losing cause. The rest of the batsmen produced 33 between them. Left-handers and leg-spinners have been England's nemeses for too long.

Inzamam in command.

MARYLEBONE CRICKET CLUB

ENGLAND v. PAKISTAN

THURSDAY, FRIDAY, SATURDAY, SUNDAY & MONDAY, JULY 25, 26, 27, 28 & 29, 1996
(5-day Match)

PAKISTAN

			First Innings		Second Innings	
1	Aamir Sohail	Lahore	l b w b Brown	2		
2	Saeed Anwar	A.D.B.P.	c Russell b Hick	74	c Russell b Mullally	88
3	Ijaz Ahmed	Allied Bank	b Cork	1	l b w b Cork	76
4	Inzamam-ul-Haq	United Bank	b Mullally	148	c Ealham b Cork	70
5	Salim Malik	Habib Bank	run out	7	not out	27
6	Shadab Kabir	Karachi	l b w b Cork	17	c Russell b Cork	33
†7	Wasim Akram	P.I.A.	l b w b Ealham	10	not out	34
*8	Rashid Latif	United Bank	c Hick b Salisbury	45		
9	Mushtaq Ahmed	United Bank	c Russell b Mullally	11	c Thorpe b Brown	5
10	Waqar Younis	United Bank	c Brown b Mullally	4		
11	Atta-ur-Rehman	Allied Bank	not out	10		
			B 3, l-b 5, w , n-b 3,	11	Innings closed	
					B 4, l-b 14, w , n-b 1,	19
			Total	340	Total	352

FALL OF THE WICKETS

1—7 2—12 3—142 4—153 5—209 6—257 7—267 8—280 9—290 10—340
1—136 2—136 3—161 4—279 5—308 6— 7— 8— 9— 10—

ANALYSIS OF BOWLING

Name	1st Innings						2nd Innings				
	O.	M.	R.	W.	Wd.	N-b	O.	M.	R.	W.	Wd. N-b
Cork	28	6	100	2	...	2	24	4	86	3	... 1
Brown	17	2	78	1	...	...	16	2	60	1	...
Mullally	24	8	44	3	...	...	30.2	9	70	1	...
Salisbury	12.2	1	42	1	...	...	20	4	63	0	...
Ealham	21	4	42	1	...	1	16	4	39	0	...
Hick	6	0	26	1	...	...	7	2	16	0	...

ENGLAND

			First Innings		Second Innings	
1	N. V. Knight	Warwickshire	l b w b Waqar Younis	51	l b w b Waqar Younis	1
†2	M. A. Atherton	Lancashire	l b w b Wasim Akram	12	c sub b Mushtaq Ahmed	64
3	A. J. Stewart	Surrey	l b w b Mushtaq Ahmed	39	c sub b Mushtaq Ahmed	89
4	G. P. Thorpe	Surrey	b Atta-ur-Rehman	77	l b w b Mushtaq Ahmed	3
5	G. A. Hick	Worcestershire	b Waqar Younis	4	b Waqar Younis	4
6	M. A. Ealham	Kent	c Rashid b Rehman	25	b Mushtaq Ahmed	5
*7	R. C. Russell	Gloucestershire	not out	41	c Rashid b Waqar	1
8	D. G. Cork	Derbyshire	c Anwar b Rehman	3	b Waqar Younis	3
9	I. D. K. Salisbury	Sussex	l b w b Waqar Younis	5	c Rashid b Wasim	40
10	A. D. Mullally	Leicestershire	b Waqar Younis	0	c sub b Mushtaq Ahmed	6
11	S. J. E. Brown	Durham	b Atta-ur-Rehman	1	not out	10
			B 9, l-b 13, w 1, n-b 4,	27	B 6, l-b 7, w , n-b 4,	17
			Total	285	Total	243

FALL OF THE WICKETS

1—27 2—107 3—107 4—116 5—180 6—260 7—264 8—269 9—269 10—285
1—14 2—168 3—171 4—176 5—181 6—182 7—186 8—186 9—208 10—243

ANALYSIS OF BOWLING

Name	1st Innings						2nd Innings				
	O.	M.	R.	W.	Wd.	N-b	O.	M.	R.	W.	Wd. N-b
Wasim Akram	22	4	49	1	...	1	21.1	5	45	1	... 3
Waqar Younis	24	6	69	4	...	...	25	3	85	4	...
Mushtaq Ahmed	38	5	92	1	...	...	38	15	57	5	...
Atta-ur-Rehman	15.4	3	50	4	1	3	11	2	33	0	... 1
Aamir Sohail	3	1	3	0	...	...					
Salim Malik	...	...	...	...	...	...	1	0	1	0	...
Shadab Kabir	...	...	...	...	...	...	1	0	9	0	...

Umpires—S. A. Bucknor & P. Willey

Scorers—D. Kendix & A. Weld

† Captain

* Wicket-keeper

Play begins each day at 11.00

Luncheon Interval 1.00—1.40

Tea Interval 3.40—4.00 (may be varied according to state of game)

Stumps drawn 1st, 2nd, 3rd & 4th days at 6.00, or after 90 overs have been bowled, whichever is the later - 5th day at 6.00, or after a minimum of 75 overs for playing time other than the last hour, when Law of Cricket 17.6 and 17.7 shall apply (except a minimum of 15 overs). Except in the last hour of the match, in the event of play being suspended for any reason other than normal intervals or one or more changes of innings, the playing time on that day shall be extended by the amount of time lost up to a maximum of one hour. The captains may agree to stop play at 5.30 on the 5th day if there is no prospect of a result.

Pakistan won the toss

Pakistan won by 164 runs

1997: England v Australia

(2nd Test) June 19, 20, 21, 22, 23 (no play on first day)
Match drawn

The rain had the final say in a match that began with England defending a lead in the series (they had won at Edgbaston), but between the showers, it included several performances of statistical interest, at least. The rain also had the first say: no play was possible at all on the Thursday for the first time in an Ashes Test since 1964, and for the first time in a Test at Lord's since 1991. The capacity crowd sheltered under their gaudy umbrellas, or drank champagne in the corporate hospitality boxes, but there was no cricket to watch. On the Friday, too, only ninety minutes play was possible, but it was a ninety minutes which took the game away from England. Michael Atherton was captaining England for a record forty-second time, but Mark Taylor won the toss and had no hesitation in putting England in. The conditions were perfect for swinging the ball and the wicket was cracked and treacherous. Glenn McGrath took full advantage: three wickets for two runs in thirteen balls. It could have been four, because with England at 12 for 3 there was a vociferous appeal against Thorpe for a catch behind, but Ian Healy let umpire David Shepherd know that the ball had reached him on the half-volley, and Thorpe survived overnight. Even so, McGrath carried on the next day in the same form, and ended with 8 for 38 in a pitiful England total of 77. At Edgbaston, Thorpe and Hussain had shared a partnership of 288. Here theirs was still the best partnership of the innings, but it only yielded

Glenn McGrath, only the second Australian to take eight wickets in a Test innings at Lord's. Bob Massie was the other.

34 runs. McGrath's was the best analysis ever in an Ashes Test at Lord's, surpassing Bob Massie's figures in the 1972 Test. Massie would have been there to witness his record being broken, but unfortunately arrived at the ground with the wrong tickets. The gatekeeper, in keeping with the traditions of 'they shall not pass' Lord's gatemen over the generations, refused to let him in, and by the time Massie had returned to his hotel and got the right tickets McGrath had finished the job.

When Australia batted Stewart was suffering back spasms, so his place behind the stumps was taken by John Crawley. Matthew Elliott dominated the Australian innings, with a brilliant 112 on his Lord's debut, but the rain intervened so much that by the time Taylor declared 136 runs ahead, there was only one day left to play. Luckily for England, the sun shone, the pitch eased, and England batted themselves out of a big hole. Not that the relief was very long-lasting, though. Australia won the next three Tests by large margins to retain the Ashes.

MARYLEBONE CRICKET CLUB

ENGLAND v. AUSTRALIA

THURSDAY, FRIDAY, SATURDAY, SUNDAY & MONDAY, JUNE 19, 20, 21, 22 & 23, 1997
(5-day Match)

ENGLAND

			First Innings		Second Innings	
1 M. A. Butcher	Surrey	c Blewett b McGrath	5	b Warne	87
†2 M. A. Atherton	Lancashire	c Taylor b McGrath	1	hit wicket b Kasprowicz	77
*3 A. J. Stewart	Surrey	b McGrath	1	c Kasprowicz b McGrath	13
4 N. Hussain	Essex	lbw b McGrath	19	c and b Warne	0
5 G. P. Thorpe	Surrey	c Blewett b Reiffel	21	not out	30
6 J. P. Crawley	Lancashire	c Healy b McGrath	1	not out	29
7 M. A. Ealham	Kent	c Elliott b Reiffel	7		
8 R. D. B. Croft	Glamorgan	c Healy b McGrath	2		
9 D. Gough	Yorkshire	c Healy b McGrath	10		
10 A. R. Caddick	Somerset	lbw b McGrath	1		
11 D. E. Malcolm	Derbyshire	not out	0		

B 4, l-b , w , n-b 5, 9   B 8, l-b 14, w 1, n-b 7, 30

Total ....(42.3 overs) 77   Total ...(4 wkts, 79 overs) 266

FALL OF THE WICKETS

1—11 2—12 3—13 4—47 5—56 6—62 7—66 8—76 9—77 10—77
1—162 2—189 3—197 4—202 5— 6— 7— 8— 9— 10—

ANALYSIS OF BOWLING

Name	1st Innings						2nd Innings					
	O.	M.	R.	W.	Wd.	N-b	O.	M.	R.	W.	Wd.	N-b
McGrath	20.3	8	38	8			20	5	65	1		2
Reiffel	15	9	17	2		3	13	5	29	0		2
Kasprowicz	5	1	9	0		2	15	3	54	1		3
Warne	2	0	9	0			19	4	47	2	1	
Bevan							8	1	29	0		
S. Waugh							4	0	20	0		

AUSTRALIA

			First Innings		Second Innings	
†1 M. A. Taylor	N.S.W.	b Gough	1		
2 M. T. G. Elliott	Victoria	c Crawley b Caddick	112		
3 G. S. Blewett	S. Australia	c Hussain b Croft	45		
4 M. E. Waugh	N.S.W.	c Malcolm b Caddick	33		
5 S. K. Warne	Victoria	c Hussain b Gough	0		
6 S. R. Waugh	N.S.W.	lbw b Caddick	0		
7 M. G. Bevan	N.S.W.	c Stewart b Caddick	4		
*8 I. A. Healy	Queensland	not out	13		
9 P. R. Reiffel	Victoria	not out	1		
10 M. S. Kasprowicz	Queensland				
11 G. D. McGrath	N.S.W.				

B 1, l-b 3, w , n-b 4   B , l-b , w , n-b ,

Total ....(7 wkts dec.) 213   Total ....

FALL OF THE WICKETS

1—4 2—73 3—147 4—147 5—147 6—159 7—212 8— 9— 10—
1— 2— 3— 4— 5— 6— 7— 8— 9— 10—

ANALYSIS OF BOWLING

Name	1st Innings						2nd Innings					
	O.	M.	R.	W.	Wd.	N-b	O.	M.	R.	W.	Wd.	N-b
Gough	20	4	82	2								
Caddick	22	6	71	4								
Malcolm	7	1	26	0								
Croft	12	5	30	1								

Umpires—S. Venkataraghavan & D. R. Shepherd   Scorers—M. Walsh & D. Kendix
†Captain   *Wicket-keeper

Play begins each day at 11.00   Luncheon Interval 1.00—1.40
Tea Interval 3.40—4.00 (may be varied according to state of game)
Stumps drawn 1st, 2nd 3rd & 4th days at 6.00, or after 90 overs have been bowled, whichever is the later - 5th day at 6.00, or after a minimum of 75 overs for playing time other than the last hour, when Law of Cricket 17.6 and 17.7 shall apply (except a minimum of 15 overs). Except in the last hour of the match, in the event of play being suspended for any reason other than normal intervals or one or more changes of innings, the playing time on that day shall be extended by the amount of time lost up to a maximum of one hour. The captains may agree to stop play at 5.30 on the 5th day if there is no prospect of a result.

Australia won the toss and elected to field

Match drawn

1998: England v South Africa

(2nd Test) June 18, 19, 20, 21
South Africa won by 10 wickets

Four years after their first Test victory at Lord's for 59 years the South Africans did it again, and in scarcely less convincing style than in 1994. Only four of the players who beat England then were still in the South African side, but only three of the team they beat were chosen to come back for more of the same. Lord's itself was no longer the same, either. Before the match began, the Duke of Edinburgh officially opened the new Grand Stand which provided a much greater seating capacity and significantly improved views, thus completing the major ground development work which had seen the Mound Stand, the Edrich and Compton Stands and the Grand Stand all rebuilt.

The beginnings of the new Media Centre were visible in 1998, too, but the press were still at the back of the Warner Stand for this match.

England won the toss and asked South Africa to bat, on a damp wicket and in the knowledge that time would probably be lost to rain and poor light. At 46 for four after 17 overs, it looked as though Atherton had made the right decision. But in the next 17, Cronje and Rhodes added 89 runs to take South Africa to 135 for 4 at the end of the first day: honours even. On the second day, the sun came out to give Cronje and Rhodes the chance to add a further 95 in comparative comfort, and for Jonty Rhodes to complete a popular

The view from the pavilion after the end of the match, with the new Grand Stand and the new NatWest Media Centre as symbols of progress at Lord's.

MARYLEBONE CRICKET CLUB

ENGLAND v. SOUTH AFRICA

THURSDAY, FRIDAY, SATURDAY, SUNDAY & MONDAY, JUNE 18, 19, 20, 21 & 22, 1998
(5-day Match)

SOUTH AFRICA

		First Innings		Second Innings	
1 A. M. Bacher	Transvaal	c Stewart b Cork	22	not out	9
2 G. Kirsten	Western Province	b Cork	4		
3 J. H. Kallis	Western Province	b Cork	0	not out	5
4 D. J. Cullinan	Gauteng	c Stewart b Cork	16		
†5 W. J. Cronje	Natal	c Ramprakash b Ealham	81		
6 J. N. Rhodes	Natal	c Stewart b Fraser	117		
7 S. M. Pollock	Natal	c Hussain b Cork	14		
*8 M. V. Boucher	Border	c Stewart b Headley	35		
9 L. Klusener	Natal	b Headley	34		
10 A. A. Donald	Free State	not out	7		
11 P. R. Adams	Western Province	c Stewart b Cork	3		
		B 1, l-b 20, w , n-b 6,	27	B , l-b , w , n-b 1,	1
		Total	360	Total	15

FALL OF THE WICKETS

1—8 2—16 3—43 4—46 5—230 6—273 7—283 8—340 9—359 10—360
1— 2— 3— 4— 5— 6— 7— 8— 9— 10—

ANALYSIS OF BOWLING

Name	1st Innings						2nd Innings					
	O.	M.	R.	W.	Wd.	N-b	O.	M.	R.	W.	Wd.	N-b
Fraser	31	8	78	1	...		1	0	10	0	...	
Cork	31.1	5	119	6	...	6	0.1	0	5	0	...	1
Headley	22	2	69	2	...	2	...	...	...	...	...	
Ealham	15	2	50	1	...		...	...	...	...	...	
Croft	9	3	23	0	...		...	...	...	...	...	

ENGLAND

		First Innings		Second Innings	
1 S. P. James	Glamorgan	c Boucher b Donald	10	c Kallis b Pollock	0
2 M. A. Atherton	Lancashire	c Kirsten b Pollock	0	c Kallis b Adams	44
3 N. Hussain	Essex	c Boucher b Donald	15	lbw b Klusener	105
*†4 A. J. Stewart	Kent	lbw b Pollock	14	c Boucher b Kallis	56
5 D. W. Headley	Surrey	c Boucher b Donald	2	c Cronje b Adams	1
6 G. P. Thorpe	Middlesex	c Bacher b Kallis	10	lbw b Kallis	0
7 M. R. Ramprakash	Kent	c Boucher b Donald	12	b Klusener	0
8 M. A. Ealham	Derbyshire	run out	8	b Kallis	4
9 D. G. Cork	Glamorgan	c Klusener b Pollock	12	c Boucher b Kallis	2
10 R. D. B. Croft	Middlesex	not out	6	not out	16
11 A. R. C. Fraser	Middlesex	c Boucher b Donald	1	c Pollock b Adams	17
		B 8, l-b 10, w , n-b 2,	20	B 1, l-b 6, w 5, n-b 7,	19
		Total	110	Total	264

FALL OF THE WICKETS

1—15 2—15 3—40 4—48 5—49 6—64 7—74 8—97 9—109 10—110
1—8 2—102 3—106 4—222 5—224 6—224 7—225 8—228 9—233 10—264

ANALYSIS OF BOWLING

Name	1st Innings						2nd Innings					
	O.	M.	R.	W.	Wd.	N-b	O.	M.	R.	W.	Wd.	N-b
Donald	15.3	5	32	5	...	...	24	6	82	0	2	2
Pollock	18	5	42	3	...	2	27	16	29	1	...	2
Klusener	8	5	10	0	...	...	23	5	54	2	...	...
Kallis	5	3	8	1	...	...	19	9	24	4	...	...
Adams	...	...	...	...	...	...	23	7	62	3	...	...
Cronje	...	...	...	...	...	...	4	2	6	0	...	...

Scorers—A. E. Weld & D. Kendix

Umpires—G. Sharp & D. B. Hair (3rd Umpire—B. Dudleston)
†Captain   *Wicket-keeper

Play begins each day at 11.00   Luncheon Interval 1.00—1.40
Tea Interval 3.40—4.00 (may be varied according to state of game)
Stumps drawn 1st, 2nd 3rd & 4th days at 6.00, or after 90 overs have been bowled, whichever is the later - 5th day at 6.00, or after a minimum of 75 overs for playing time other than the last hour, when Law of Cricket 17.6 and 17.7 shall apply (except a minimum of 15 overs).
Except in the last hour of the match, in the event of play being suspended for any reason other than normal intervals or one or more changes of innings, the playing time on that day shall be extended by the amount of time lost up to a maximum of one hour. The captains may agree to stop play at 5.30 on the 5th day if there is no prospect of a result.

England won the toss and elected to field
South Africa won by 10 wickets

century. Rhodes will leave his mark on cricket history for his fielding, but in this game he showed why his country picked him as a batsman too.

England's first innings was notable for two things: the fact that extras top-scored for only the third time in a Test at Lord's, and for Mark Ramprakash's reaction to his dismissal. When given out caught behind off what he thought was his elbow, he went over to umpire Hair as he walked back to the pavilion, and had a brief word with him. For this sin he was fined £850 and given a suspended one-match ban. England's second innings was notable for a combative century from Nasser Hussain and the last wicket stand of 31 between Fraser and Croft, which saved the innings defeat, if not the game. In the next Test, this same batting partnership would save the match.

1999: England v New Zealand

(2nd Test) July 22, 23, 24, 25
New Zealand won by 9 wickets

When New Zealand came to England in 1999 they were underrated by most pundits. But they made it to the semi-finals of the World Cup six weeks before the Lord's Test by dint of excellent team spirit and a shrewd understanding of the tactics

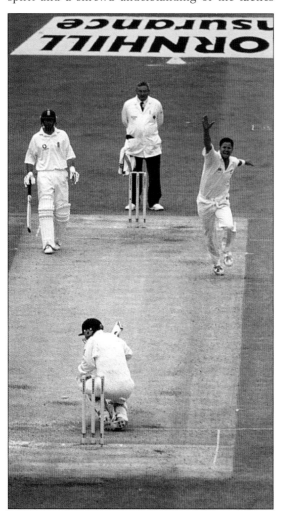

Read is fooled by Cairns's slower ball.

required. They brought these skills, as well as the natural talents of several players maturing into world class cricketers, to Lord's, and for the first time in thirteen attempts they won a Lord's Test.

The media, perched for the first time in the new Media Centre high above the Nursery End, had a field day, giving England even more abuse to add to the acres of newsprint devoted to their ignominious exit from the World Cup. As *Wisden* reported, rather more mildly than most, England finished the match 'in something approaching disarray', and without a captain, as Hussain had broken his finger fielding at gully early on the third morning. Until then, Hussain had done one good thing and one bad thing. The bad thing was deciding to bat on winning the toss (although the weather forecast was wildly inaccurate and the cloud cover never went away as expected). The good thing was his innings of 61 when almost all around him fell apart.

The image that remains most clearly of this Test is the dismissal of Chris Read in the first innings to Chris Cairns' slower ball. The criticism of the young wicket-keeper was unfair, as Cairns had not been known for his use of the slower ball, and poor Read, like a rabbit caught in the headlights, attempted quite sensibly to duck what looked like a beamer but unfortunately turned out to be a yorker. Many other batsmen have been dismissed as feebly and with less excuse, notably many of the England batsmen in their second innings. In that innings Read made a much more confident 37 and with Andy Caddick gave their side a little hope as they put on 78 together on the Sunday.

New Zealand's victory was a personal triumph not only for Cairns, who established himself over the next twelve months as the world's leading all-rounder, but also for Matthew Horne, who scored a century despite batting with an injured elbow for most of the innings. Daniel Vettori also showed what potential he has as a batsman as well as a left arm spinner, and Roger Twose, English born and bred, made up for his pair in the First Test by hitting a fine half century for his adopted country.

ENGLAND v. NEW ZEALAND

Thursday, Friday, Saturday, Sunday & Monday, July 22, 23, 24, 25 & 26, 1999
(5-day Match)

ENGLAND

			First Innings		Second Innings	
1	M. A. Butcher	Surrey	c Parore b Cairns	8	c Astle b Vettori	20
2	A. J. Stewart	Surrey	c Fleming b Nash	50	b Vettori	35
†3	N. Hussain	Essex	c Parore b Cairns	61	absent hurt	
4	G. P. Thorpe	Surrey	c Astle b Cairns	7	b Cairns	7
5	M. R. Ramprakash	Middlesex	lbw b Nash	4	b Cairns	7
6	A. Habib	Leicestershire	b Nash	6	c Parore b Astle	24
*7	C. M. W. Read	Nottinghamshire	b Cairns	0	c Astle b Allott	19
8	A. R. Caddick	Somerset	run out	18	lbw b Nash	37
9	D. W. Headley	Kent	lbw b Cairns	4	c Fleming b Allott	45
10	A. D. Mullally	Leicestershire	c Astle b Cairns	0	c Fleming b Allott	12
11	P. C. R. Tufnell	Middlesex	not out	1	c Twose b Cairns	10
					not out	5
			B 5, l-b 8, w , n-b 14,	27	B 5, l-b 3, w , n-b 7,	15
			Total	186	Total	229

FALL OF THE WICKETS

1—35 2—79 3—102 4—112 5—123 6—125 7—150 8—165 9—170 10—186
1—55 2—71 3—78 4—97 5—123 6—127 7—205 8—216 9—229 10—

ANALYSIS OF BOWLING

Name	1st Innings						2nd Innings					
	O.	M.	R.	W.	Wd.	N-b	O.	M.	R.	W.	Wd.	N-b
Allott	10	1	37	0	...	3	16.4	6	36	3	...	3
Cairns	21.1	1	77	6	...	11	25	6	67	2	...	1
Nash	23	11	50	3	...		25	9	50	1	...	3
Astle	7	3	9	0	...		4	2	6	1	...	
Vettori	...	...	...	...	...	...	31	12	62	2	...	...

NEW ZEALAND

			First Innings		Second Innings	
1	M. J. Horne	Otago	c Hussain b Headley	100	lbw b Caddick	26
2	M. D. Bell	Northern Districts	lbw b Headley	15	not out	26
†3	S. P. Fleming	Canterbury	c Read b Mullally	1	not out	5
4	N. J. Astle	Canterbury	c Read b Mullally	43		
5	R. G. Twose	Wellington	c Caddick b Headley	52		
6	C. D. McMillan	Canterbury	c Read b Caddick	3		
7	D. L. Vettori	Northern Districts	c Thorpe b Tufnell	54		
*8	A. C. Parore	Auckland	b Caddick	12		
9	C. L. Cairns	Canterbury	b Caddick	31		
10	D. J. Nash	Auckland	c Mullally b Tufnell	6		
11	G. I. Allott	Canterbury	not out	1		
			B 1, l-b 24, w 2, n-b 13,	40	B 2, l-b , w , n-b 1,	3
			Total	358	Total	60

FALL OF THE WICKETS

1—43 2—45 3—112 4—232 5—239 6—242 7—275 8—345 9—351 10—
1—31 2— 3— 4— 5— 6— 7— 8— 9— 10—

ANALYSIS OF BOWLING

Name	1st Innings						2nd Innings					
	O.	M.	R.	W.	Wd.	N-b	O.	M.	R.	W.	Wd.	N-b
Mullally	27	7	98	2	2	...						
Caddick	34	11	92	3	...	2	5	0	21	0	...	...
Headley	27	7	74	3	...	8	10	4	18	1	...	...
Tufnell	27.1	7	61	2	...	3	8	2	19	0	...	1
Butcher	3	0	7	0	...	...						
Ramprakash	1	0	1	0	...	...						

Umpires—M. J. Kitchen & R. E. Koertzen (3rd Umpire—N. T. Plews)

Scorers—D. Kendix & A. E. Weld

†Captain   *Wicket-keeper

Play begins each day at 11.00   Luncheon Interval 1.00—1.40

Tea Interval 3.40—4.00 (may be varied according to state of game)

Stumps drawn 1st, 2nd 3rd & 4th days at 6.00, or after 90 overs have been bowled, whichever is the later – 5th day at 6.00, or after a minimum of 75 overs for playing time other than the last hour, when Law of Cricket 17.6 and 17.7 shall apply (except a minimum of 15 overs). Except in the last hour of the match, in the event of play being suspended for any reason other than normal intervals or one or more changes of innings, the playing time on that day shall be extended by the amount of time lost up to a maximum of one hour.

England won the toss

New Zealand won by 9 wickets

2000: England v Zimbabwe

(1st Test) May 18, 19, 20, 21
England won by an innings and 209 runs

Zimbabwe's first Test visit to Lord's, almost eight years after their elevation to Test status, was also the first ever Lord's Test held in May. In 2000, England played seven home Tests, so the first one had to begin a little earlier. The experiment was not wholly successful, as the weather in May turned out to be as awful as it had been in June, July, August and September in previous Lord's Tests, and the opening overs, an hour late thanks to the weather, were played out in front of a crowd of no more than 10,000. The Zimbabweans had plenty of problems as they came into the game, not least the political upheavals at home, a pay dispute with their cricket authorities, and an injury to their opening bowler Henry Olonga. They had a very fine captain, Andy Flower, who would later become the coach who took England to the top of the Test rankings, but perhaps no more than five of his side could be described as Test class. The perceived weakness of the Zimbabweans, along with the known weakness of the England side, did not make for good box office.

England won at a canter. They bowled Zimbabwe out twice within 70 overs, and Alec Stewart and England's own Zimbabwean Graeme Hick between them scored enough runs for England's innings victory. Nine of the side were under central contracts from the E.C.B., the first year that these had been in place, but it was the uncontracted fast bowler Ed Giddins who won the Man of the Match award. He briefly established a record bowling analysis for England v Zimbabwe Tests (this was only the third one ever), and although it was surpassed by Heath Streak in England's innings, Giddins took another two wickets in Zimbabwe's second innings to help win the game. Alec Stewart had a good game too. He scored his third Lord's Test century, and his second

century against Zimbabwe, and while he was at the crease on the Saturday his team Chelsea won the FA Cup Final. He also went through the match without conceding a bye. Debutant Chris Schofield, on the other hand, did not bowl any of the leg-spin he was picked for, and was out third ball for a duck.

England's two century-makers, Stewart and Hick.

ENGLAND v. ZIMBABWE

THURSDAY, FRIDAY, SATURDAY, SUNDAY & MONDAY, MAY 18, 19, 20, 21 & 22, 2000
(5-day Match)

ZIMBABWE

			First Innings		Second Innings	
1	G. W. Flower	Mashonaland	b Caddick	4	lbw b Gough	2
2	T. R. Gripper	Mashonaland	c Stewart b Caddick	1	c Knight b Gough	5
3	M. W. Goodwin	Mashonaland	c Knight b Gough	18	lbw b Caddick	11
4	A. D. R. Campbell	Mashonaland	c Stewart b Caddick	0	lbw b Gough	4
†*5	A. Flower	Mashonaland	c Atherton b Giddins	24	lbw b Gough	2
6	N. C. Johnson	Matabeleland	c Gough b Giddins	14	c Hick b Caddick	9
7	G. J. Whittall	Manicaland	b Giddins	15	c Hick b Caddick	22
8	H. H. Streak	Matabeleland	c Atherton b Giddins	4	c Knight b Giddins	0
9	B. C. Strang	Mashonaland	c Ramprakash b Giddins ..	0	not out	37
10	B. A. Murphy	Mashonaland	c Stewart b Gough	0	lbw b Giddins	14
11	M. Mbangwa	Matabeleland	not out	1	b Caddick	8
			B , l-b 2, w , n-b ,	2	B 2 , l-b 1, w , n-b 7,	8
			Total	83	Total	123

FALL OF THE WICKETS

1—5	2—8	3—8	4—46	5—48	6—67	7—77	8—79	9—82	10—83
1—2	2—7	3—18	4—33	5—36	6—49	7—74	8—74	9—92	10—123

ANALYSIS OF BOWLING

Name	1st Innings O.	M.	R.	W.	Wd.	N-b	2nd Innings O.	M.	R.	W.	Wd.	N-b
Gough	12.3	1	36	2	...	...	15	3	57	4	...	3
Caddick	8	3	28	3	...	...	16.2	5	38	4	...	4
Flintoff	3	2	2	0	...	...	...	...	...	...	...	...
Giddins	7	2	15	5	...	...	7	3	27	2	...	...

ENGLAND

			First Innings		Second Innings
1	M. A. Atherton	Lancashire	lbw b Streak	55	
2	M. R. Ramprakash	Middlesex	lbw b Streak	15	
†3	N. Hussain	Essex	c Murphy b Streak	10	
4	G. A. Hick	Worcestershire	lbw b Streak	101	
*5	A. J. Stewart	Surrey	not out	124	
6	N. V. Knight	Warwickshire	c Johnson b Whittall	44	
7	A. Flintoff	Lancashire	c Streak b Whittall	1	
8	C. P. Schofield	Lancashire	c Johnson b Whittall	0	
9	A. R. Caddick	Somerset	c A. Flower b Streak	13	
10	D. Gough	Yorkshire	c Campbell b Murphy	5	
11	E. S. H. Giddins	Warwickshire	c Strang b Streak	7	
			B 5, l-b 29, w 1, n-b 5,	40	B , l-b , w , n-b ,
			Total	415	Total

FALL OF THE WICKETS

1—29	2—49	3—113	4—262	5—376	6—378	7—378	8—398	9—407	10—415
1—	2—	3—	4—	5—	6—	7—	8—	9—	10—

ANALYSIS OF BOWLING

Name	1st Innings O.	M.	R.	W.	Wd.	N-b	2nd Innings O.	M.	R.	W.	Wd.	N-b
Streak	35.5	12	87	6	1	1	...	...	...	...	...	...
Strang	27	4	86	0	...	...	...	...	...	...	...	...
Mbangwa	21	5	69	0	...	1	...	...	...	...	...	...
Johnson	20	5	55	0	...	2	...	...	...	...	...	...
Whittall	7	0	27	3	...	...	...	...	...	...	...	...
Murphy	25	6	57	1	...	...	...	...	...	...	...	...

Umpires—P. Willey & D. L. Orchard (3rd Umpire—J. W. Holder)

Scorers—V. H. Isaacs & M. Snook

†Captain   *Wicket-keeper

Play begins each day at 11.00   Luncheon Interval 1.00—1.40

Tea Interval 3.40—4.00 (may be varied according to state of game)

Stumps drawn 1st, 2nd 3rd & 4th days at 6.00, or after 90 overs have been bowled, whichever is the later – 5th day at 6.00, or after a minimum of 75 overs for playing time other than the last hour, when Law of Cricket 17.6 and 17.7 shall apply (except a minimum of 15 overs).

Except in the last hour of the match, in the event of play being suspended for any reason other than normal intervals or one or more changes of innings, the playing time on that day shall be extended by the amount of time lost up to a maximum of one hour.

England won the toss and elected to field

England won by an innings and 209 runs

The crowds, especially on the Friday, became impatient with what they saw as unnecessary delays in restarting the game after rain. Lord's at the time had a fine Hover drier, but also still relied on brooms, drainage pipes and tarpaulins which did not give the impression that the latest technology was being applied to the problem. Lord's has finally got close to a solution with its underground drainage system installed in 2002/03, but many other grounds continue to struggle to find ways of getting back to the middle far more quickly after a shower

2000: England v West Indies

(2nd Test) June 29, 30, July 1
England won by 2 wickets

What a match to celebrate the one hundredth Lord's Test! It may have been over in three days, but the second and third days were two of the most enthralling ever seen at Lord's. The West Indies were weaker than for very many years, but under their new captain Jimmy Adams they had shown a determination and team spirit during the previous winter that made them hard to beat. England came to Lord's already one down in the series.

England were captained by Alec Stewart in the absence of Nasser Hussain, whose broken finger a year earlier had now been replaced by a broken thumb, and Stewart took the modern course of putting his opponents in to bat. Just before tea on the first day, West Indies were 162 for 1, and even that wicket was a run out. England seemed to be heading for the wrong end of another severe beating. But then Dominic Cork, recalled to the Test side for the first time in two years, got going, and by the end of the day West Indies were 267 for 9.

The Friday produced a bizarre record: it was the first time in Test match history that some part of all four innings was played on the one day. The first innings occupied the briefest possible portion of the day – one ball. England then produced the kind of batting performance all England followers have learned to dread: 9 for 3 in no time

A sight to warm English hearts.

at all became 134 all out as the old maestros Walsh and Ambrose tore England apart. The pens in the Media Centre were dipped into large pots of acid in preparation for the next morning's obituary notices for English cricket.

In the next 26.4 overs, an amazing thing happened. English cricket came alive and support for English cricket became fashionable again. Andy Caddick, England's second innings specialist, took five wickets for 16 runs in an unchanged spell of 13 overs from the Nursery End, the first one by means of a truly brilliant catch at third man by Darren Gough. Cork and Gough got rid of the rest. West Indies all out 54 – their lowest total to date against England. Only Jacobs, the wicketkeeper, reached double figures. England, who less than four years later would dismiss West Indies for 47 in Jamaica, then faced seven balls before bad light intervened leaving them to score 188 to win on the final day.

The builders of the match-winning total were the two Mancunians, Atherton (45) and Vaughan (41). But with eight wickets down, England still needed over 30 to win. The final flourish was provided by Cork. His six into the Grand Stand off Franklyn Rose was the defining moment, and he stayed until the end, the best 33 runs he ever made for England.

ENGLAND v. WEST INDIES

THURSDAY, FRIDAY, JUNE 29, 30 & SATURDAY, SUNDAY & MONDAY JULY 1, 2, 3, 2000
(5-day Match)

WEST INDIES

			First Innings		Second Innings	
1	S. L. Campbell	Barbados	c Hoggard b Cork	82	c Gough b Caddick	4
2	A. F. G. Griffith	Barbados	run out	27	c Stewart b Gough	1
3	W. W. Hinds	Jamaica	c Stewart b Cork	59	c Ramprakash b Caddick	0
4	B. C. Lara	Trinidad & Tobago	c Stewart b Gough	6	c Cork b Caddick	5
5	S. Chanderpaul	Guyana	b Gough	22	c Ramprakash b Gough	9
†6	J. C. Adams	Jamaica	lbw b Gough	1	lbw b Cork	3
*7	R. D. Jacobs	Leewards Islands	c Stewart b Cork	10	c Atherton b Caddick	12
8	C. E. L. Ambrose	Leewards Islands	c Ramprakash b Cork	5	c Ramprakash b Caddick	0
9	F. A. Rose	Jamaica	lbw b Gough	29	c and b Cork	1
10	R. D. King	Guyana	not out	12	lbw b Cork	7
11	C. A. Walsh	Jamaica	lbw b Caddick	1	not out	3
			B 1, l-b 8, w 2, n-b 2,	13	B , l-b 8, w , n-b 1,	9
			Total	267	Total	54

FALL OF THE WICKETS

1—80   2—162   3—175   4—185   5—186   6—207   7—216   8—253   9—258   10—267
1—6   2—6   3—10   4—24   5—24   6—39   7—39   8—39   9—41   10—54

ANALYSIS OF BOWLING

Name	1st Innings						2nd Innings					
	O.	M.	R.	W.	Wd.	N-b	O.	M.	R.	W.	Wd.	N-b
Gough	21	5	72	4	...	2	8	3	17	2	...	1
Caddick	20.3	3	58	1	...	...	13	8	16	5	...	...
Hoggard	13	3	49	0	1	...	...	...	...	...	...	...
Cork	24	8	39	4	...	...	5.4	2	13	3	...	...
White	8	1	30	0	...	...	...	...	...	...	...	...
Vaughan	3	1	10	0	...	...	...	...	...	...	...	...

ENGLAND

			First Innings		Second Innings	
1	M. A. Atherton	Lancashire	c Lara b Walsh	1	lbw b Walsh	45
2	M. R. Ramprakash	Middlesex	c Lara b Ambrose	0	b Walsh	2
3	M. P. Vaughan	Yorkshire	b Ambrose	4	c Jacobs b Walsh	41
4	G. A. Hick	Worcestershire	b Ambrose	25	c Lara b Walsh	15
†*5	A. J. Stewart	Surrey	c Jacobs b Walsh	28	lbw b Walsh	18
6	N. V. Knight	Warwickshire	c Campbell b King	6	c Jacobs b Rose	2
7	C. White	Yorkshire	run out	27	c Jacobs b Walsh	0
8	D. G. Cork	Derbyshire	c Jacobs b Walsh	4	not out	33
9	A. R. Caddick	Somerset	c Campbell b Walsh	6	lbw b Ambrose	7
10	D. Gough	Yorkshire	lbw b Walsh	13	not out	4
11	M. J. Hoggard	Yorkshire	not out	12		
			B , l-b 5, w , n-b 3,	8	B 3, l-b 8, w 1, n-b 12,	24
			Total	134	Total	191

FALL OF THE WICKETS

1—1   2—1   3—9   4—37   5—50   6—85   7—100   8—100   9—118   10—134
1—3   2—95   3—119   4—120   5—140   6—140   7—149   8—160   9—   10—

ANALYSIS OF BOWLING

Name	1st Innings						2nd Innings					
	O.	M.	R.	W.	Wd.	N-b	O.	M.	R.	W.	Wd.	N-b
Ambrose	14.2	8	30	4	...	...	22	11	22	1	...	...
Walsh	17	6	43	4	...	1	23.5	5	74	6	...	7
Rose	7	2	32	0	...	2	16	3	67	1	1	5
King	10	3	24	1	...	...	8	2	17	0	...	...

Umpires—J. H. Hampshire & S. Venkataraghavan (3rd Umpire—R. Julian)

Match Referee—G. T. Dowling   Scorers—D. Kendix & B. Hewes

†Captain   *Wicket-keeper

Play begins each day at 11.00   Luncheon Interval 1.00—1.40

Tea Interval 3.40—4.00 (may be varied according to state of game)

Stumps drawn 1st, 2nd 3rd & 4th days at 6.00, or after 90 overs have been bowled, whichever is the later – 5th day at 6.00, or after a minimum of 75 overs for playing time other than the last hour, when Law of Cricket 17.6 and 17.7 shall apply (except a minimum of 15 overs). Except in the last hour of the match, in the event of play being suspended for any reason other than normal intervals or one or more changes of innings, the playing time on that day shall be extended by the amount of time lost up to a maximum of one hour.

England won the toss and elected to field

England won by 2 wickets

LORD'S   GROUND

2001: England v Pakistan

(1st Test) May 17 (no play), 18, 19, 20
England won by an innings and 9 runs

The 101st Test at Lord's was England's one hundredth Test at the ground, the extra one being the match between Australia and South Africa, in the triangular tournament of 1912. As this was England's first Test match to count towards the newly inaugurated World Test Championship the result was particularly satisfying for them. England included two new caps in their side. Ian Ward of Surrey was one and Ryan Sidebottom of Yorkshire the other. The latter followed his father Arnie to become the tenth father/son pairing for their country.

England won the game because of the bowling of Darren Gough and Andrew Caddick who between them took 16 of the 20 wickets, (Dominic Cork took the other four), and because the weather restricted the match to such an extent that the follow-on law was varied so a lead of 150 runs, rather than 200, was sufficient for it to be invoked. As Pakistan fell 188 runs short of England's first innings' total, they were invited to follow on.

At this time Gough and Caddick were as good an opening attack as England had had for many seasons, and followers of the game feared there

England's match winners, Andrew Caddick (right) and Darren Gough.

would be a lack of suitable replacements once their careers had ended. In fact the two bowlers were the first in a golden era for English fast bowling, and by the end of the decade England had almost an embarrassment of riches from which to choose.

The first day was completely lost to the rain. When the game finally began and Pakistan won the toss, Waqar Younis took the gamble and put England in to bat. For a while it looked as if his strategy would work, but though Pakistan's front line bowlers tested the English batsmen, they struggled to take the wickets that the captain had been hoping for. After cameo knocks from the first three in the order, Nasser Hussain and Graham Thorpe added 132 for the fourth wicket, a partnership that began to take the game away from

LORD'S GROUND
ENGLAND v. PAKISTAN

THURSDAY, FRIDAY, SATURDAY, SUNDAY & MONDAY, MAY 17, 18, 19, 20 & 21, 2001
(5-day Match)

ENGLAND

			First Innings		Second Innings
1	M. A. Atherton	Lancashire	b Mahmood	42	
2	M. E. Trescothick	Somerset	c Mahmood b Razzaq	36	
3	M. P. Vaughan	Yorkshire	c Latif b Mahmood	32	
†4	N. Hussain	Essex	c Latif b Mahmood	64	
5	G. P. Thorpe	Surrey	c Razzaq b Younis	80	
6	R. J. Sidebottom	Yorkshire	c Inzamam b Akram	4	
*7	A. J. Stewart	Surrey	lbw b Akhtar	44	
8	I. J. Ward	Surrey	c Razzaq b Younis	39	
9	D. G. Cork	Derbyshire	c Khan b Akram	25	
10	A. R. Caddick	Somerset	b Mahmood	5	
11	D. Gough	Yorkshire	not out	5	
			B 1, l-b 5, w 1, n-b 8,	15	B , l-b , w , n-b ,
			Total	391	Total

FALL OF THE WICKETS

1—60 2—105 3—114 4—246 5—254 6—307 7—317 8—365 9—385 10—391
1— 2— 3— 4— 5— 6— 7— 8— 9— 10—

ANALYSIS OF BOWLING

Name		1st Innings						2nd Innings				
	O.	M.	R.	W.	Wd.	N-b		O.	M.	R.	W.	Wd. N-b
Wasim Akram	34	9	99	2	1	2						
Waqar Younis	25	5	77	2	...	1						
Shoaib Akhtar	19	4	64	1								
Abdur Razzaq	21	2	68	1		5						
Younis Khan	5	0	27	0								
Azhar Mahmood	26	12	50	4								

PAKISTAN

			First Innings		Second Innings	
1	Saeed Anwar	ADBP	c Atherton b Gough	12	c Thorpe b Caddick	0
2	Salim Elahi	Habib Bank	c Atherton b Caddick	0	c Thorpe b Caddick	0
3	Abdur Razzaq	PIA	c Stewart b Caddick	22	c Atherton b Caddick	53
4	Inzamam-ul-Haq	Faisalabad	c Stewart b Caddick	13	c Stewart b Cork	20
5	Yousuf Youhana	PIA	lbw b Gough	26	c Vaughan b Gough	6
6	Younis Khan	Habib Bank	b Cork	58	lbw b Cork	1
7	Azhar Mahmood	PIA	c Trescothick b Caddick	14	c Stewart b Caddick	24
*9	Rashid Latif	Allied Bank	c Stewart b Gough	18	c Stewart b Gough	20
8	Wasim Akram	PIA	not out	19	c Thorpe b Gough	12
†10	Waqar Younis	Redco	c Thorpe b Gough	0	c Stewart b Cork	21
11	Shoaib Akhtar	KRL	b Gough	0	not out	2
			B 1, l-b 7, w , n-b 13,	21	B , l-b 6, w , n-b 6,	12
			Total	203	Total	179

FALL OF THE WICKETS

1—4 2—21 3—37 4—60 5—116 6—153 7—167 8—203 9—203 10—203
1—2 2—30 3—67 4—84 5—87 6—121 7—122 8—147 9—167 10—179

ANALYSIS OF BOWLING

Name		1st Innings						2nd Innings					
	O.	M.	R.	W.	Wd.	N-b		O.	M.	R.	W.	Wd.	N-b
Gough	16	5	61	5	...	3		16	4	40	3	...	2
Caddick	17	3	52	4	...	7		18	3	54	4	...	2
Sidebottom	11	0	38	0				9	2	26	0	...	2
Cork	11	3	42	1	...	3		15.3	3	41	3	...	4
Trescothick	2	1	2	0									
Vaughan								1	0	12	0	...	...

Umpires—P. Willey & D. B. Hair (3rd Umpire—B. Dudleston)
Match Referee—B. F. Hastings   Scorers—B. Hewes & B. T. Denning
†Captain   *Wicket-keeper
Play begins each day at 11.00   Luncheon Interval 1.00—1.40
Tea Interval 3.40—4.00 (may be varied according to state of game)
Stumps drawn 1st, 2nd 3rd & 4th days at 6.00, or after 90 overs have been bowled, whichever
is the later – 5th day at 6.00, or after a minimum of 75 overs for playing time other than the
last hour, when Law of Cricket 16.6, 16.7 and 16.8 shall apply (except a minimum of 15 overs).
Except in the last hour of the match, in the event of play being suspended for any reason
other than normal intervals or one or more changes of innings, the playing time on that day
shall be extended by the amount of time lost up to a maximum of one hour.

Pakistan won the toss and elected to field

England won by an innings and 9 runs

Pakistan. Hussain's brittle fingers proved his downfall in the end – on the third morning a ball from Shoaib Akhtar broke his right thumb, just as two years earlier (and also on the third morning) he had broken a finger fielding against New Zealand. But Stewart, Ward and Cork all added useful runs, by which time England had built a total of 391 and Pakistan needed 242 to avoid the follow on.

The feature of both Pakistan's innings, apart from the bowling of Gough and Man of the Match Caddick, was the brilliant catching by England's close fielders. Stewart keeping wicket took seven catches, Thorpe four and Atherton three. Thorpe's one-handed catch, diving full length to his right from third slip to dismiss Salim Elahi for a 'pair' was one of the catches of the season. Only Younis Khan in the first innings, and Abdur Razzaq in the second, offered any serious resistance, and by the time Pakistan were reduced to 87 for five in their second innings, it was obvious that not even the weather would save them. England took sixteen wickets on the fourth day while Pakistan scored 265 of the 274 they needed to avoid the innings defeat, their first at Lord's since Ian Botham's one-man demolition of Wasim Bari's side in 1978.

LORD'S GROUND

2001: England v Australia

(2nd Test) July 19, 20, 21, 22
Australia won by eight wickets

The Australian tourists of 2001, captained by Steve Waugh, were a great side. With twin brother Mark and including other world-class players like Hayden, Ponting, Gilchrist, Warne and McGrath, it was not surprising that England assembled for the second Test of the series already one down, thumped by an innings at Edgbaston two weeks earlier. What was worse, their captain, Nasser Hussain, had broken yet another finger and could not be considered for selection. The Yorkshire pair, Michael Vaughan and Matthew Hoggard, were also unfit.

The main story before the match concerned the England captaincy; it seemed that in Hussain's

Gilchrist in typically aggressive form.

LORD'S GROUND

ENGLAND v. AUSTRALIA

THURSDAY, FRIDAY, SATURDAY, SUNDAY & MONDAY, JULY 19, 20, 21, 22 & 23, 2001
(5-day Match)

ENGLAND

			First Innings		Second Innings	
†1 M. A. Atherton	Lancashire	lbw b McGrath	37	b Warne	20
2 M. E. Trescothick	Somerset	c Gilchrist b Gillespie	15	c Gilchrist b Gillespie	3
3 M. A. Butcher	Surrey	c M. Waugh b McGrath	21	c Gilchrist b Gillespie	83
4 G. P. Thorpe	Surrey	c Gilchrist b McGrath	20	lbw b Lee	2
5 M. R. Ramprakash	Surrey	b Lee	14	lbw b Gillespie	40
*6 A. J. Stewart	Surrey	c Gilchrist b McGrath	0	lbw b McGrath	28
7 I. J. Ward	Surrey	not out	23	c Ponting b McGrath	0
8 C. White	Yorkshire	c Hayden b McGrath	0	not out	27
9 D. G. Cork	Derbyshire	c Ponting b Gillespie	24	c Warne b McGrath	2
10 A. R. Caddick	Somerset	b Warne	0	c Gilchrist b Gillespie	7
11 D. Gough	Yorkshire	b Warne	5	c M. Waugh b Gillespie	1
		B 7, l-b 8, w 2, n-b 11,	28	B , l-b 3, w 2, n-b 9,	14
		Total	187	Total	227

FALL OF THE WICKETS

1—33	2—75	3—96	4—121	5—126	6—129	7—131	8—178	9—181	10—187
1—8	2—47	3—50	4—146	5—188	6—188	7—188	8—193	9—225	10—227

ANALYSIS OF BOWLING

Name		1st Innings					2nd Innings				
	O.	M.	R.	W.	Wd.	N-b	O.	M.	R.	W.	Wd.	N-b
McGrath	24	9	54	5	0	0	19	4	60	3	...	...
Gillespie	18	6	56	2	0	4	16	4	53	5	1	2
Lee	16	3	46	1	1	7	9	1	41	1	...	4
Warne	5.3	0	16	2	1	0	20	4	58	1	1	3
M. Waugh	...	...	...	...	...	...	2	1	12	0	...	...

AUSTRALIA

			First Innings		Second Innings	
1 M. J. Slater	N.S.W.	c Stewart b Caddick	25	c Butcher b Caddick	4
2 M. L. Hayden	Queensland	c Butcher b Caddick	0	not out	6
3 R. T. Ponting	Tasmania	c Thorpe b Gough	14	lbw b Gough	4
4 M. E. Waugh	N.S.W.	run out	108	not out	0
†5 S. R. Waugh	N.S.W.	c Stewart b Cork	45		
6 D. R. Martyn	W. Australia	c Stewart b Caddick	52		
*7 A. C. Gilchrist	W. Australia	c Stewart b Gough	90		
8 S. K. Warne	Victoria	c Stewart b Caddick	5		
9 B. Lee	N.S.W.	b Caddick	20		
10 J. N. Gillespie	S. Australia	b Gough	9		
11 G. D. McGrath	N.S.W.	not out	0		
		B , l-b 9, w 1, n-b 23,	33	B , l-b , w , n-b ,	0
		Total	401	Total	14

FALL OF THE WICKETS

1—5	2—27	3—105	4—212	5—230	6—308	7—322	8—387	9—401	10—401
1—6	2—13	3—	4—	5—	6—	7—	8—	9—	10—

ANALYSIS OF BOWLING

Name		1st Innings					2nd Innings				
	O.	M.	R.	W.	Wd.	N-b	O.	M.	R.	W.	Wd.	N-b
Gough	25	3	115	3	...	6	2	0	5	1	...	...
Caddick	32.1	4	101	5	...	11	1.1	0	9	1	...	...
White	18	1	80	1	...	1						
Cork	23	3	84	1	...	5						
Butcher	3	0	12	0	...	1						

Umpires—J. W. Holder & S. A. Bucknor (3rd Umpire—J. W. Lloyds)
Match Referee—Talat Ali   Scorers—D. Kendix & A. E. Weld
†Captain   *Wicket-keeper
Play begins each day at 11.00   Luncheon Interval 1.00—1.40
Tea Interval 3.40—4.00 (may be varied according to state of game)
Stumps drawn 1st, 2nd 3rd & 4th days at 6.00, or after 90 overs have been bowled, whichever
is the later – 5th day at 6.00, or after a minimum of 75 overs for playing time other than the
last hour, when Law of Cricket 16.6, 16.7 and 16.8 shall apply (except a minimum of 15 overs).
Except in the last hour of the match, in the event of play being suspended for any reason
other than normal intervals or one or more changes of innings, the playing time on that day
shall be extended by the amount of time lost up to a maximum of one hour.

Australia won the toss and elected to field

Australia won by eight wickets

Mark Waugh on his way to another hundred.

Ramprakash, Stewart and Ward batting at numbers 3 to 7, for the first time in English Test history players from the same county (Surrey) filled five consecutive positions in the order. It was also the first time that five players from the same county had appeared in an England eleven since the 1949 Lord's Test against New Zealand, when five Middlesex players had been in the side.

The end result was depressingly familiar. England's first innings did not go well. Put in by Steve Waugh under cloudy skies, nobody made more than Atherton's 37 at the top of the order, and McGrath wrote his name on the honours board again with five for 54 as England crumbled to 187 all out. In Australia's reply, Mark Waugh, who had been bowled by Tufnell for 99 eight years earlier, this time reached his century, and with the aid of a typically pugnacious 90 from Gilchrist and a good half century from Martyn, they finished on 401, a lead of 214.

In England's second innings, Gillespie was the bowler to take five wickets, with only Butcher (83) and Ramprakash (40) putting up much resistance. When Mark Waugh caught Gough to end England's innings, it was his 158th Test catch, a new world record. And it left Australia needing 14 to win, a target they reached despite the loss of Slater and Ponting on the way, with well over a day to spare.

In the three most recent Lord's Tests, against West Indies, Pakistan and Australia, only three English bowlers took wickets – Cork with 12, Gough 17 and Caddick 19. All the rest (White, Butcher, Hoggard, Vaughan, Trescothick and Sidebottom) toiled for 68 overs, conceding 259 runs for no reward. This fact is almost as bizarre as the moment when BBC Radio's Test Match Special team were presented with a Dundee cake by Her Majesty the Queen, on her visit to Lord's on the first day of the match.

enforced absence, nobody wanted to take on the job. Stewart and Butcher both made it very clear they did not want to be considered, however temporary it may have been, and in the end a reluctant Michael Atherton was persuaded to take up the reins one more time.

As the second collision with the Australian juggernaut grew ever closer, the selectors shuffled the pack in the England dressing room. Back came Ramprakash, Thorpe and Cork in place of Hussain, Ufzaal and Giles. And with Butcher, Thorpe,

2002: England v Sri Lanka

(1st Test), May 16, 17, 18, 19, 20
Match drawn

Facing a Sri Lankan side that had conceded first innings lead to all three counties they had played on tour to date, and who were without Muralitharan, who was recovering from a dislocated shoulder, England were expected to record a straightforward victory in the first Test of the summer with a minimum of fuss. Perhaps the commentators and fans should have taken notice of the fact that Sri Lanka had won each of their previous ten Tests before this game, against Bangladesh, Pakistan, West Indies and Zimbabwe.

Nasser Hussain lost the toss and Jayasuriya had no hesitation in batting on a balmy spring day. England managed to take a couple of wickets cheaply, but the third wicket pair of Atapattu (the man who had started his Test career with an appalling succession of ducks) and Jayawardene added 206 without any serious alarms, apart from a bad bruise on the hip from a Flintoff delivery which forced Atapattu to call for a runner when he had scored 47. England's experienced bowling attack was made to look toothless. When Sri Lanka finally declared on 555 for eight late on the second day, they had time to capture Trescothick's wicket and leave England in deep trouble.

Things did not improve on the third day, despite the absence of Muralitharan and the fact that a change in the weather meant that the start of play was delayed by about twenty minutes. Sri Lanka relied on four seamers, three of whom bowled left handed, and one of whom – Ruchira Perera – boasted an action that even to the casual observer seemed to stretch the laws against throwing to the very limit. This proved to be almost Perera's international swansong. He played no more Tests on this tour and after one more Test in South Africa later in the year, he was not seen again at the highest level.

England duly failed to avoid the follow-on, for the first time at Lord's since 1998, but in their second innings batted much better. On the fourth day, from 53 without loss overnight, they moved to 321 for two against bowling that was just the same as it had been in the first innings – not particularly threaten-ing. One difference in the Sri Lankan performance was in their catching; Jayasuriya dropped Vaughan twice within the first twenty minutes of the day. Vaughan went on to

Marvan Atapattu guides a ball from Caddick for four.

MARYLEBONE CRICKET CLUB
LORD'S GROUND
(50p)   (50p)
ENGLAND v. SRI LANKA
THURSDAY, FRIDAY, SATURDAY, SUNDAY & MONDAY, MAY 16, 17, 18, 19 & 20, 2002
(5-day Match)

SRI LANKA		First Innings		Second Innings	
†1 S. T. Jayasuriya	Bloomfield	run out	18	c Butcher b Caddick	7
2 M. S. Atapattu	Singhalese	c Trescothick b Cork	185	not out	6
*3 K. C. Sangakkara	Nondescripts	c Flintoff b Hoggard	10	not out	14
4 D. P. M. D. Jayawardene	Singhalese	c Trescothick b Flintoff	107		
5 P. A. de Silva	Nondescripts	c Stewart b Cork	88		
6 R. P. Arnold	Nondescripts	c Trescothick b Hoggard	50		
7 H. P. Tillekeratne	Colts	not out	17		
8 W. P. U. J. C. Vaas	Singhalese	c Trescothick b Cork	6		
9 D. N. T. Zoysa	Singhalese	c Stewart b Flintoff	28		
10 T. C. B. Fernando	Panaduna S.C.	not out	6		
11 P. D. R. L. Perera	Singhalese				
		B 1, l-b 13, w 1, n-b 25,	40	B 5, l-b 2, w , n-b 8,	15
		Total......(8 wkts. Dec.)	555	Total	42

FALL OF THE WICKETS
1—38 2—55 3—261 4—407 5—492 6—492 7—505 8—540 9— 10—
1—16 2— 3— 4— 5— 6— 7— 8— 9— 10—

ANALYSIS OF BOWLING

Name	1st Innings						2nd Innings					
	O.	M.	R.	W.	Wd.	N-b	O.	M.	R.	W.	Wd.	N-b
Caddick	38.3	6	135	0	...	3	7	2	10	1	...	1
Hoggard	39	4	160	2	1	8	1	0	7	0	...	...
Cork	35.3	11	93	3	...	6	...	...	...	...	...	...
Flintoff	39	8	101	2	...	4	5	0	18	0	...	7
Butcher	3	0	17	0	...	...						
Vaughan	14	2	35	0	...	...						

ENGLAND		First Innings		Second Innings	
1 M. E. Trescothick	Somerset	c Jayasuriya b Zoysa	13	lbw b Zoysa	76
2 M. P. Vaughan	Yorkshire	c Zoysa b Perera	64	c Sangakkara b Perera	115
3 M. A. Butcher	Surrey	c Jaya'dene b Fernando	17	run out	105
†4 N. Hussain	Essex	c Sangakkara b Zoysa	57	lbw b Perera	68
5 G. P. Thorpe	Surrey	lbw b Perera	27	c Fernando b de Silva	65
6 J. P. Crawley	Hampshire	c Sangakkara b Vaas	31	not out	41
*7 A. J. Stewart	Surrey	run out	7	not out	26
8 A. Flintoff	Lancashire	c Sangakkara b Fernando	12		
9 D. G. Cork	Derbyshire	c Sangakkara b Fernando	0		
10 A. R. Caddick	Somerset	c Sangakkara b Perera	13		
11 M. J. Hoggard	Yorkshire	not out	0		
		B 4, l-b 7, w 9, n-b 14,	34	B 1, l-b 9, w 1, n-b 22,	33
		Total	275	Total ....(5 wkts. Dec.)	529

FALL OF THE WICKETS
1—17 2—43 3—149 4—203 5—203 6—214 7—237 8—237 9—267 10—275
1—168 2—213 3—372 4—432 5—483 6— 7— 8— 9— 10—

ANALYSIS OF BOWLING

Name	1st Innings						2nd Innings					
	O.	M.	R.	W.	Wd.	N-b	O.	M.	R.	W.	Wd.	N-b
Vaas	21.1	4	51	1	...	2	44	8	113	0	...	1
Zoysa	19	3	82	2	3	6	34	6	84	1	1	8
Fernando	22	5	83	3	1	3	26	1	96	0	...	4
Perera	11	0	48	3	1	3	30	4	90	2	...	8
de Silva	...	...	...	...	...	...	27	7	63	1	...	...
Jayasuriya	...	...	...	...	...	...	25	6	66	0	...	...
Arnold	...	...	...	...	...	...	4	1	7	0	...	...
Tillekeratne	...	...	...	...	...	...	1	1	0	0	...	...

Umpires—D. J. Harper & S. Venkataraghavan (3rd Umpire—J. W. Lloyds)
Match Referee—G. R. Viswanath   Scorers—D. Kendix & J. C. Foley
†Captain   *Wicket-keeper

Play begins each day at 11.00   Luncheon Interval 1.00—1.40
Tea Interval 3.40—4.00 (may be varied according to state of game)
Stumps drawn 1st. 2nd 3rd & 4th days at 6.00, or after 90 overs have been bowled, whichever is the later – 5th day at 6.00, or after a minimum of 75 overs for playing time other than the last hour, when Law of Cricket 16.6, 16.7 and 16.8 shall apply (except a minimum of 15 overs).

Sri Lanka won the toss

Match Drawn

complete his century as he and Trescothick put on 168 for the first wicket. By the time England declared with only a handful of overs left in the match, each of the first five batsmen had made at least 50, and numbers 6 and 7 were batting fluently. The match was saved and England came away feeling the more confident of the two sides.

A fortnight later, the hosts comfortably won the second Test at Edgbaston by an innings and 111 runs.

2002: England v India

(1st Test). July 25, 26, 27, 28, 29
England won by 170 runs

John Crawley, one of his best Test innings.

India proved a tougher proposition – in the end – than Sri Lanka but to judge by the results of the two Lord's Tests of 2002, India seemed to be the softer touch. The Indian middle order batsmen of Dravid, Ganguly, Tendulkar and Laxman, whose combined runmaking powers would propel India to number one in the Test rankings, were all on display, not to mention the brilliantly belligerent Virender Sehwag, whose first Test as an opening bat this was. Their bowling attack was led by Anil Kumble, one of only two men ever to take all ten wickets in a Test innings, and the seamer Zaheer

Khan, although for some reason they left out Harbhajan Singh. England, beset by injuries to Gough and Caddick, gave a Test debut to Glamorgan's Simon Jones, son of Jeff Jones who had played for England at Lord's in 1966.

Nasser Hussain won the toss, but with Butcher, Vaughan and Thorpe all out by the time England had scored 78, it seemed that India held all the cards. However, this was the cue for Hussain to play his best Test innings at Lord's and in partnership with John Crawley, to post a competitive total. When Crawley was out for 64 late on the first day,

England had reached 223, and the next morning Flintoff, White and the debutant Jones all hit cleanly and hard to bring England's final total to 487 at a rate of nearly 3.5 an over. Jones in particular, enjoyed himself, hitting 44 out of the 62 he added with White, an innings in which, according to *Wisden*, he "slogged like the village blacksmith".

India at first took their cue from 'Jones the Smith', with Sehwag and Dravid adding 126 for the second wicket at a rapid rate. But once Sehwag was out, heaving at Giles, the innings slowed down and disciplined bowling from Flintoff, Jones and Hoggard wore through the Indians. England gained a first innings lead of almost 250, but Hussain did not enforce the follow-on. Instead, he allowed his team to pile on the runs. Vaughan and Crawley both hit fluent centuries as England reached 305 in 64.4 overs before Hussain declared, leaving India the best part of two days to make 568 to win, 224 more runs than had ever been chased successfully at Lord's. It was a fascinating contest, in which India batted well at the start and with a flourish at the end, but the middle order let them down. Laxman and Agarkar put on 126 for the seventh wicket, and Agarkar, batting at number eight, hit the first Lord's hundred by an Indian so low down the order. However, with Tendulkar, Ganguly and Nehra together scoring only 52 runs in the match, the end result was inevitable. India made the highest fourth innings score in a Test match at Lord's to that time (since exceeded by Australia in 2009), but still went down by 170 runs.

ENGLAND

			First Innings		Second Innings	
1	M. A. Butcher	Surrey	c Wasim b Kumble	29	lbw b Kumble	18
2	M. P. Vaughan	Yorkshire	lbw b Zaheer	0	c Wasim b Nehra	100
†3	N. Hussain	Essex	c Ratra b Agarkar	155	c Ratra b Agarkar	12
4	G. P. Thorpe	Surrey	b Zaheer	4	c Ganguly b Kumble	1
5	J. P. Crawley	Hampshire	c Dravid b Sehwag	64	not out	100
*6	A. J. Stewart	Surrey	lbw b Zaheer	19	st Ratra b Kumble	33
7	A. Flintoff	Lancashire	c Ratra b Agarkar	59	c Tendulkar b Nehra	7
8	C. White	Yorkshire	st Ratra b Kumble	53	not out	6
9	A. F. Giles	Warwickshire	b Nehra	19		
11	S. P. Jones	Glamorgan	c Dravid b Kumble	44		
10	M. J. Hoggard	Yorkshire	not out	10		
			B 11, l-b 11, w 2, n-b 7,	31	B 5, l-b 14, w , n-b 5,	24
			Total	487	Total ....(6 wkts. dec.)	301

FALL OF THE WICKETS

1—0	2—71	3—78	4—223	5—263	6—356	7—357	8—390	9—452	10—487
1—32	2—65	3—76	4—213	5—228	6—287	7—	8—	9—	10—

ANALYSIS OF BOWLING

Name		1st Innings						2nd Innings				
	O.	M.	R.	W.	Wd.	N-b		O.	M.	R.	W.	Wd.	N-b
Nehra	30	4	101	1	2	5		14	1	80	2	...	4
Zaheer	36	13	90	3	...	...		11	1	41	0	...	1
Agarkar	21	3	98	2	...	...		11.4	1	53	1	...	...
Kumble	42.2	9	128	3	...	...		24	1	84	3	...	...
Ganguly	3	1	16	0	...	1							
Sehwag	10	0	32	1	...	1		2	0	10	0	...	...
Tendulkar								2	0	14	0	...	...

INDIA

			First Innings		Second Innings	
1	Wasim Jaffer	Mumbai	b Hoggard	1	c Hussain b Vaughan	53
2	V. Sehwag	Delhi	b Giles	84	b Jones	27
3	R. Dravid	Karnataka	c Vaughan b Hoggard	46	b Giles	63
4	A. Nehra	Delhi	lbw b Flintoff	0	c Thorpe b White	19
5	S. R. Tendulkar	Mumbai	c Stewart b White	16	b Hoggard	12
†6	S. C. Ganguly	Bengal	c Vaughan b Flintoff	5	lbw b Hoggard	0
7	V. V. S. Laxman	Hyderabad	not out	43	c Vaughan b Jones	74
*8	A. Ratra	Haryana	c Stewart b Jones	1	c Butcher b Hoggard	1
9	A. B. Agarkar	Mumbai	c Flintoff b Jones	2	not out	109
10	A. Kumble	Karnataka	b White	0	c & b Hoggard	15
11	Zaheer Khan	Baroda	c Thorpe b Hoggard	3	c Stewart b White	7
			B 4, l-b 8, w , n-b 8,	20	B 4, l-b 3, w 2, n-b 8,	17
			Total	221	Total	397

FALL OF THE WICKETS

1—2	2—128	3—130	4—162	5—168	6—177	7—191	8—196	9—209	10—221
1—61	2—110	3—140	4—140	5—165	6—170	7—296	8—320	9—334	10—397

ANALYSIS OF BOWLING

Name		1st Innings						2nd Innings				
	O.	M.	R.	W.	Wd.	N-b		O.	M.	R.	W.	Wd.	N-b
Hoggard	16.5	4	33	3	...	...		24	7	87	4	...	...
Flintoff	19	9	22	2	...	1		17	2	87	0	1	2
Giles	9	1	47	1	...	...		29	7	75	1	...	...
Jones	21	2	61	2	...	6		17	1	68	2	1	2
White	16	3	46	2	...	1		16.4	2	61	2	...	4
Vaughan	...	...	...	...	...	...		6	2	12	1	...	...

Umpires—R. E. Koertzen & R. B. Tiffin (3rd Umpire—P. Willey)
Match Referee—M. J. Procter   Scorers—D. Kendix & A. P. Scarlett

†Captain   *Wicket-keeper

Play begins each day at 11.00   Luncheon Interval 1.00—1.40
Tea Interval 3.40—4.00 (may be varied according to state of game)
Stumps drawn 1st, 2nd 3rd & 4th days at 6.00, or after 90 overs have been bowled, whichever is the later – 5th day at 6.00, or after a minimum of 75 overs for playing time other than the last hour, when Law of Cricket 16.6, 16.7 and 16.8 shall apply (except a minimum of 15 overs).

England won the toss

England won by 170 runs

2003: England v Zimbabwe

(1st Test), May 22, 23, 24
England won by an innings and 92 runs

Mark Butcher hits out on his way to a big score.

Zimbabwe have yet to prove themselves to be of Test class at Lord's. There might have been excuses - this was the first Test of the summer and the weather conditions were as unlike Zimbabwe as they could possibly be. On top of that, Zimbabwe's selection had been compromised by the events of the previous winter when Andy Flower and Henry Olonga, two of their best players, had worn black armbands when playing in the World Cup match against Namibia in protest against "the death of democracy in our beloved Zimbabwe" and were forced into retirement if not exile.

All the same, with probably only one player, their captain Heath Streak, who would have broken into the England team, Zimbabwe put up a feeble fight. On the first day, play did not start until half the morning session was gone, and tickets were so hard to sell that around 6,000 schoolchildren had been let in free of charge to swell the gate. The final attendance figure of just over 60,000 was about three quarters of the number who came to see South Africa later in the summer, but receipts were barely one third of the South African game's £2.9 million. Average gate receipts per spectator were about £15.20 for this game, but more than £36 for the South Africans.

Zimbabwe won the toss and opted to field. Vaughan was dismissed comparatively early and if Butcher had been given out to a confident lbw appeal when he had scored only 10, Streak's gamble might have paid off. As it was, Butcher hit a careful century, opening out rather more on the second day when the debutant McGrath and Ashley Giles both hit aggressive half-centuries. England were finally all out for 472, a challenging total.

Zimbabwe were undone in their first innings by James Anderson, on his debut. His bowling was a mixture of the awful and the unplayable, a combination that was to be a feature of his bowling for much of his early Test career, but after giving away 17 runs in his very first over, he recovered to take five for 73, wasting no time in getting his name on the honours board. He became the twelfth player to take five wickets at Lord's on his Test debut, the seventh Englishman and the first since Dominic Cork against the West Indies in 1995.

Zimbabwe batted lamentably in both innings, losing nineteen wickets in a day, and at one stage it even looked as though Anthony McGrath, a part time bowler at best, would join Anderson in taking five wickets. His three for 16, alongside Mark Butcher's four for 60 with gentle medium pace, cleaned up the Zimbabwean second innings to give England an innings victory with two days to spare. For both bowlers it was their best analysis of the season.

MARYLEBONE CRICKET CLUB
LORD'S GROUND
ENGLAND v. ZIMBABWE
THURSDAY, FRIDAY, SATURDAY, SUNDAY & MONDAY, MAY 22, 23, 24, 25 & 26, 2003
(5-day Match)

ENGLAND		First Innings		Second Innings
1 M. E. Trescothick	Somerset	c Ervine b Blignaut	59	
2 M. P. Vaughan	Yorkshire	b Streak	8	
3 M. A. Butcher	Surrey	c Vermeulen b Price	137	
†4 N. Hussain	Essex	c Hondo b Friend	19	
5 R. W. T. Key	Kent	c Taibu b Streak	18	
*6 A. J. Stewart	Surrey	c Taibu b Streak	26	
7 A. McGrath	Yorkshire	b Ervine	69	
8 A. F. Giles	Warwickshire	b Blignaut	52	
9 S. J. Harmison	Durham	c Ebrahim b Ervine	0	
10 M. J. Hoggard	Yorkshire	c Ebrahim b Blignaut	19	
11 J. M. Anderson	Lancashire	not out	4	
		B 14, l-b 27, w 3, n-b 17,	61	B , l-b , w , n-b ,
		Total	472	Total

FALL OF THE WICKETS
1—45 2—121 3—165 4—204 5—274 6—342 7—408 8—408 9—465 10—472
1— 2— 3— 4— 5— 6— 7— 8— 9— 10—

ANALYSIS OF BOWLING	1st Innings						2nd Innings					
Name	O.	M.	R.	W.	Wd.	N-b	O.	M.	R.	W.	Wd.	N-b
Streak	37	9	99	3	1	3	...	...	...	...	...	...
Blignaut	26.1	4	96	3	1	1	...	...	...	...	...	...
Hondo	14	4	45	0	1	6	...	...	...	...	...	...
Ervine	22	5	95	2	...	6	...	...	...	...	...	...
Friend	13	2	49	1	...	1	...	...	...	...	...	...
Price	20	6	44	1	...	...	...	...	...	...	...	...
Flower	1	0	3	0	...	...	...	...	...	...	...	...

ZIMBABWE		First Innings		Second Innings	
1 D. D. Ebrahim	Mashonaland	c McGrath b Butcher	68	c Key b Harmison	6
2 M. A. Vermeulen	Mashonaland	b Anderson	1	c Trescothick b Butcher	61
3 S. V. Carlisle	Mashonaland	c Tresothick b Hoggard	11	lbw b Butcher	24
4 G. W. Flower	Mashonaland	c Key b Hoggard	3	c Trescothick b Harmison	26
*5 T. Taibu	Midlands	lbw b Hoggard	25	c Butcher b McGrath	16
6 S. M. Ervine	Midlands	b Anderson	4	c Trescothick b McGrath	4
†7 H. H. Streak	Matabeleland	b Anderson	10	lbw b McGrath	11
8 A. M. Blignaut	Mashonaland	c Butcher b Anderson	3	b Butcher	6
9 T. J. Friend	Midlands	b Anderson	0	c Giles b Butcher	43
10 R. W. Price	Midlands	not out	7	c Trescothick b Giles	26
11 D. T. Hondo	Mashonaland	b Anderson	0	not out	0
		B 5, l-b 1, w 1, n-b 8,	15	B 1, l-b 6, w 3, n-b ,	10
		Total	147	Total	233

FALL OF THE WICKETS
1—20 2—64 3—79 4—104 5—109 6—129 7—133 8—133 9—147 10—147
1—11 2—91 3—95 4—128 5—132 6—150 7—158 8—168 9—219 10—233

ANALYSIS OF BOWLING	1st Innings						2nd Innings					
Name	O.	M.	R.	W.	Wd.	N-b	O.	M.	R.	W.	Wd.	N-b
Hoggard	18	8	24	3	...	1	15	5	35	0	...	...
Anderson	16	4	73	5	...	3	15	4	65	0	...	...
Harmison	16	0	36	1	...	3	12	4	35	2	1	...
Butcher	5	2	8	1	1	...	12.5	0	60	4	2	...
Giles	...	...	...	...	...	...	8	2	15	1	...	...
McGrath	...	...	...	...	...	...	6	1	16	3	...	...

Umpires—S. A. Bucknor & D. L. Orchard (3rd Umpire—N. A. Mallender)
Match Referee—C. H. Lloyd, C.B.E.   Scorers—D. Kendix & A. P. Scarlett
†Captain   *Wicket-keeper
Play begins each day at 10.45   Luncheon Interval 12.45—1.25
Tea Interval 3.25—3.45 (may be varied according to state of game)
Stumps drawn 1st, 2nd 3rd & 4th days at 5.45, or after 90 overs have been bowled, whichever is the later – 5th day at 5.45, or after a minimum of 75 overs for playing time other than the last hour, when Law of Cricket 16.6, 16.7 and 16.8 shall apply (except a minimum of 15 overs). Up to a maximum of 1 hour of time lost, from either the actual day or from previous days due to play being suspended, shall be made up at the end of the scheduled days play. The close of play shall be re-scheduled accordingly.

Zimbabwe won the toss and elected to field

England won by an innings and 92 runs

2003: England v South Africa

(2nd Test), July 31, August 1, 2, 3
South Africa won by an innings and 92 runs

For the second time in Lord's history, and for the first time since 1947, consecutive Test matches were won and lost by exactly the same margin. But whereas England had beaten Zimbabwe by an innings and 92 runs ten weeks earlier, here it was England who were on the receiving end of a similar defeat.

In the first Test at Edgbaston in the previous week, England had escaped with a draw after Graeme Smith and Herschelle Gibbs put on 338 for the first wicket, but the failure of England's attack to get on top of the South Africans there had been one of the factors in Nasser Hussain's decision to give up the captaincy. The Lord's Test was the first under his successor, Michael Vaughan. The change of leadership did not make matters any better. Smith became only the fourth player, after Bradman, Hammond and Vinod Kambli to score a

double century in consecutive Tests, as South Africa racked up the second highest total ever made in a Lord's Test, 682 for six, in reply to England's pitiful 174 all out. Even that small total owed much to a last wicket stand of 55 between Gough and Anderson, which spared the worst of England's blushes.

Smith's 259 beat Donald Bradman's record score by an overseas player in a Test at Lord's, with only Graham Gooch's monumental 333 ahead of him on the list. The second wicket partnership of 257 between Smith and Gary Kirsten was at the time the seventh highest partnership in a Test at Lord's, but such has been the dominance of bat over ball in recent seasons that this total has been beaten three more times since. Dippenaar and Boucher also tucked into some less than threatening England bowling, until England were

Makhaya Ntini took the bowling honours for South Africa with five wickets in each innings.

MARYLEBONE CRICKET CLUB

LORD'S GROUND

ENGLAND v. SOUTH AFRICA

THURSDAY, JULY 31 & FRIDAY, SATURDAY, SUNDAY & MONDAY, AUGUST 1, 2, 3, 4, 2003
(5-day Match)

ENGLAND

			First Innings		Second Innings	
1	M. E. Trescothick	Somerset	b Ntini	6	c Adams b Ntini	23
†2	M. P. Vaughan	Yorkshire	c sub b Ntini	33	c Pollock b Hall	29
3	M. A. Butcher	Surrey	c Hall b Pollock	19	c Kirsten b Hall	70
4	N. Hussain	Essex	b Hall	14	c Boucher b Ntini	61
5	A. McGrath	Yorkshire	c Kirsten b Hall	4	c Boucher b Pollock	13
*6	A. J. Stewart	Surrey	c Adams b Ntini	7	c Hall b Ntini	0
7	A. Flintoff	Lancashire	c Adams b Ntini	11	st Boucher b Adams	142
8	A. F. Giles	Warwickshire	c Pollock b Hall	7	c Pollock b Ntini	23
9	D. Gough	Yorkshire	c Adams b Pollock	34	c Adams b Pollock	14
10	S. J. Harmison	Durham	b Ntini	0	c Hall b Ntini	7
11	J. M. Anderson	Lancashire	not out	21	not out	4
			b 5, l-b 3, w 1, n-b 3, p 5,	17	b 6, l-b 5, w 3, n-b17, p ,	31
			Total ....(48.4 overs)	173	Total ....(107.1 overs)	417

FALL OF THE WICKETS

1—11 2—35 3—73 4—77 5—85 6—96 7—109 8—112 9—118 10—173
1—52 2—60 3—186 4—208 5—208 6—208 7—297 8—344 9—371 10—417

ANALYSIS OF BOWLING

Name	1st Innings						2nd Innings					
	O.	M.	R.	W.	Wd.	N-b	O.	M.	R.	W.	Wd.	N-b
Pollock	14.4	5	28	2	...	1	29	7	105	2	...	9
Ntini	17	3	75	5	1	...	31	5	145	5	1	6
Pretorius	4	0	20	0	...	2	3	0	16	0	...	...
Hall	10	4	18	3	...	...	24	6	66	2	1	...
Adams	3	0	19	0	...	...	20.1	1	74	1	...	1

SOUTH AFRICA

			First Innings		Second Innings	
†1	G. C. Smith	Western Province	b Anderson	259		
2	H. H. Gibbs	Western Province	b Harmison	49		
3	G. Kirsten	Western Province	b McGrath	108		
4	H. H. Dippenaar	Free State	c Butcher b Giles	92		
5	J. A. Rudolph	Northerns	c Stewart b Flintoff	26		
*6	M. V. Boucher	Border	b Anderson	68		
7	S. M. Pollock	KwaZulu-Natal	not out	10		
8	A. J. Hall	Easterns	not out	6		
9	P. R. Adams	Western Province				
10	D. Pretorius	Free State				
11	M. Ntini	Border				
			b25, l-b21, w 5, n-b13, p ,	64	b , l-b , w , n-b , p ,	
			Total ....(6wkts. dec.)	682	Total	

FALL OF THE WICKETS

1—133 2—390 3—513 4—580 5—630 6—672 7— 8— 9— 10—
1— 2— 3— 4— 5— 6— 7— 8— 9— 10—

ANALYSIS OF BOWLING

Name	1st Innings						2nd Innings					
	O.	M.	R.	W.	Wd.	N-b	O.	M.	R.	W.	Wd.	N-b
Gough	28	3	127	0	1	9	...	...	...	...	...	...
Anderson	27	6	90	2	...	...	...	...	...	...	...	...
Harmison	22	3	103	1	1	...	...	...	...	...	...	...
Flintoff	40	10	115	1	...	4	...	...	...	...	...	...
Giles	43	5	142	1	...	...	...	...	...	...	...	...
Butcher	6	1	19	0	3	...	...	...	...	...	...	...
McGrath	11	0	40	1	...	...	...	...	...	...	...	...

Umpires—S. A. Bucknor & D. B. Hair (3rd Umpire—P. Willey)
Match Referee—R. S. Madugalle   Scorers—D. Kendix & G. Lewis

†Captain   *Wicket-keeper
Play begins each day at 10.45   Luncheon Interval 12.45—1.25
Tea Interval 3.25—3.45 (may be varied according to state of game)
Stumps drawn 1st, 2nd 3rd & 4th days at 5.45, or after 90 overs have been bowled, whichever is the later – 5th day at 5.45, or after a minimum of 75 overs for playing time other than the last hour, when Law of Cricket 16.6, 16.7 and 16.8 shall apply (except a minimum of 15 overs).
Up to a maximum of 1 hour of time lost, from either the actual day or from previous days due to play being suspended, shall be made up at the end of the scheduled days play. The close of play shall be re-scheduled accordingly. The Umpires may agree to play a further 30 minutes of extra time at the end of any of the first four days if a definite result can be obtained.

South Africa won the toss and elected to field

South Africa won by an innings and 92 runs

---

left to score 509 just to make South Africa bat again. And South Africa gave themselves two and a half days to get through England's batting line-up.

It proved a harder struggle than they might have expected. Butcher and Hussain both made half centuries, but when Stewart was dismissed for a duck, England were 208 for five, and staring a massive defeat in the face. Enter Flintoff, who for the first time in England (but not the last) played the sort of innings that only a really strong, superbly coordinated athlete could hope to achieve. He hit 142 in 146 balls, and, with a little help from Giles and Gough, guided England to a total of 417 – not enough to save the match, but enough to tilt the balance of domination a little away from the tourists. Darren Gough, after conceding 127 runs from 28 overs without reward, decided to call a halt to his Test career, after 58 Tests and 229 wickets. Perhaps he had been comparing his match figures with those of Makhaya Ntini, who took ten wickets for 220 in the match, five wickets in each innings.

2004: England v New Zealand

(1st Test), May 20, 21, 22, 23, 24
England won by seven wickets

This match had a little bit of everything, and a lot of some things – drama, sentiment and some thrilling cricket. England's final margin of seven wickets seems comfortable enough, but the result was in doubt until late in the match, and in the end England owed their victory to one former England captain playing in what would be his final Test, and another future England captain making his debut.

The debutant, Andrew Strauss, was not in the original thirteen for the match, but a knee injury to Michael Vaughan in the nets before the game started meant that Trescothick took over the captaincy and Andrew Strauss was called in to take Vaughan's place. He seized the opportunity, emulating John Hampshire to become only the second Englishman to make a century on debut at Lord's.

New Zealand won the toss and batted first. Mark Richardson played a typically obdurate innings of 93 to set the tone for his side. The England bowling attack was the one that would narrowly win the Ashes a year later, but after Richardson was unluckily given out lbw, Astle, Oram and most notably Chris Cairns treated them with something approaching disdain. Astle hit 64 in 77 balls, Oram's 62 took only 82 balls, and Cairns, who at one stage hit four sixes in ten balls, smote 82 from only 47 balls, very acceptable in Twenty20 cricket.

England replied forcefully. Andrew Strauss became England's first man to hit a hundred on debut anywhere since Graham Thorpe in 1993, and with Trescothick put on 190 for the first wicket. A middle order wobble was repaired by Flintoff and Geraint Jones, who added 105 for the seventh wicket, and England reached the halfway stage with a lead of 55. Richardson, whose batting is New

Zealand's best known cure for insomnia, this time got the hundred he deserved, but Brendon McCullum, in at number three because Astle had flu, narrowly missed out, done by the Joneses for 96. With just over one day to go, England were left

Nasser Hussain – a century maker in his last Test match.

MARYLEBONE CRICKET CLUB

LORD'S GROUND

(50p) (50p)

ENGLAND v. NEW ZEALAND

THURSDAY, FRIDAY, SATURDAY, SUNDAY & MONDAY, MAY 20, 21, 22, 23 & 24, 2004
(5-day Match)

	NEW ZEALAND		First Innings		Second Innings	
1	M. H. Richardson	Auckland	lbw b Harmison	93	c G. Jones b Harmison	101
†2	S. P. Fleming	Wellington	c Strauss b S. Jones	34	c Hussain b Harmison	4
3	N. J. Astle	Canterbury	c G. Jones b Flintoff	64	c G. Jones b Harmison	49
4	S. B. Styris	Northern Districts	c G. Jones b S. Jones	0	c Hussain b Giles	4
5	C. D. McMillan	Canterbury	lbw b Hoggard	6	c Hussain b Giles	0
6	J. D. P. Oram	Central Districts	c G. Jones b Harmison	67	run out	4
7	D. R Tuffey	Northern Districts	b Harmison	8	not out	14
8	C. L. Cairns	Canterbury	c Harmison b Flintoff	82	c Butcher b Giles	14
*9	B. B. McCullum	Canterbury	b S. Jones	5	c G. Jones b S. Jones	96
10	D. L. Vettori	Northern Districts	b Harmison	2	c G. Jones b Harmison	5
11	C. S. Martin	Canterbury	not out	1	b Flintoff	7
			b 9, l-b 6, w 2, n-b 7, p ,	24	b14, l-b16, w , n-b 8, p ,	38
			Total ....(102.4 overs)	386	Total ....(121.1 overs)	336

FALL OF THE WICKETS

1—58 2—161 3—162 4—174 5—280 6—287 7—324 8—329 9—338 10—386
1—7 2—180 3—187 4—187 5—203 6—287 7—290 8—304 9—310 10—336

ANALYSIS OF BOWLING	1st Innings						2nd Innings					
Name	O.	M.	R.	W.	Wd.	N-b	O.	M.	R.	W.	Wd.	N-b
Hoggard	22	7	68	1	1	3	14	3	39	0	...	5
Harmison	31	7	126	4	...	...	29	8	76	4	...	...
Flintoff	21.4	7	63	2	...	2	16.1	4	40	1	...	3
S. Jones	23	8	82	3	...	2	23	5	64	1	...	...
Giles	5	0	32	0	1	...	39	8	87	3	...	...

	ENGLAND		First Innings		Second Innings	
†1	M. E. Trescothick	Somerset	c McCullum b Oram	86	c and b Tuffey	2
2	A. J. Strauss	Middlesex	c Richardson b Vettori	112	run out	83
3	M. A. Butcher	Surrey	c McCullum b Vettori	26	c Fleming b Martin	6
4	M. J. Hoggard	Yorkshire	c McCullum b Oram	15	b Martin	
5	N. Hussain	Essex	b Martin	34	not out	103
6	G. P. Thorpe	Surrey	b Cairns	3	not out	51
7	A. Flintoff	Lancashire	c Richardson b Martin	63		
*9	G. O. Jones	Kent	c Oram b Styris	46		
9	A. F. Giles	Warwickshire	c Oram b Styris	11		
10	S. P. Jones	Glamorgan	b Martin	4		
11	S. J. Harmison	Durham	not out	0		
			b 4, l-b18, w , n-b19, p ,	41	b 7, l-b12, w 5, n-b13, p ,	37
			Total ....(124.3 overs)	441	Total ...(3 wkts, 87 overs)	282

FALL OF THE WICKETS

1—190 2—239 3—254 4—288 5—297 6—311 7—416 8—428 9—441 10—441
1—18 2—35 3—143 4— 5— 6— 7— 8— 9— 10—

ANALYSIS OF BOWLING	1st Innings						2nd Innings					
Name	O.	M.	R.	W.	Wd.	N-b	O.	M.	R.	W.	Wd.	N-b
Tuffey	26	4	98	0	...	6	10	3	32	1	...	...
Martin	27	6	94	3	...	1	18	1	75	1	1	5
Oram	30	8	76	2	...	3	15	4	39	0	...	5
Cairns	16	2	71	1	...	7	6	0	27	0	...	2
Vettori	21	1	69	2	...	1	25	5	53	0	...	...
Styris	4.3	0	11	2	...	...	13	5	37	0	...	1

Umpires—D. B. Hair & R. E. Koertzen (3rd Umpire—M. R. Benson)
Match Referee—C. H. Lloyd C.B.E.   Scorers—K. T. Gerrish & D. Kendix

†Captain   *Wicket-keeper

Play begins each day at 10.30   Luncheon Interval 12.30—1.10
Tea Interval 3.10—3.30 (may be varied according to state of game)
Stumps drawn 1st, 2nd 3rd & 4th days at 5.30, or after 90 overs have been bowled, whichever
is the later – 5th day at 5.30, or after a minimum of 75 overs for playing time other than the
last hour, when Law of Cricket 16.6, 16.7 and 16.8 shall apply (except a minimum of 15 overs).
Up to a maximum of 1 hour of time lost, from either the actual day or from previous days
due to play being suspended, shall be made up at the end of the scheduled days play. The close of play
shall be re-scheduled accordingly. The Umpires may agree to play a further 30 minutes of extra time at
the end of any of the first four days if a definite result can be obtained.

New Zealand won the toss

England won by 7 wickets

---

to chase 282 to win, a target higher than they had ever achieved at Lord's.

England's innings began hesitantly. At 35 for two some pundits were already advocating playing for the draw. Then Hussain, scratchy to begin with but increasingly fluent, and Strauss advanced the score to 143 before Hussain called Strauss for a suicidal run. Strauss was gone for 83, and his chance of becoming the first man to score twin centuries on debut at Lord's had gone with it. Hussain, mortified, realized the only thing to do was to win the game off his own bat. In partnership with his long time colleague Thorpe, he not only won the match but also hit his fourteenth Test century in the process. A day or two later he settled the selectors' problems by announcing his immediate retirement from cricket, and as far as is known, he has not strapped on a pad for anything other than display purposes from that day to this.

2004: England v West Indies

(1st Test), July 22, 23, 24, 25, 26
England won by 210 runs

England's final margin of victory was big enough, but until Brian Lara was dismissed on the final morning, any result was possible. West Indies had been set 478 to win, a huge total, but this Lord's wicket was a batsman's paradise and there was no reason to suppose that a genius like Lara could not have got his team there.

Rob Key, the first Kent batsman to score a double century for England.

Lara won the toss and opted to field first. In retrospect this was not a wise decision. At close of play on the first day England had scored 391 for two. Andrew Strauss and Rob Key put on 291 for the second wicket, a record for Tests at Lord's, and on the second morning, Key went on to become the first ever Kent player to score a double hundred for England, an astonishing fact when you consider many of the great Kent men – Cowdrey, Woolley, Ames and many more – who have had the opportunity in the past. Vaughan also got to three figures, something that was becoming routine for the England captain whenever his knee was in working order. But England somehow contrived to collapse from 527 for 3 to 568 all out, and West Indies set about chasing that huge total, knowing that the pitch was made for batting on.

Gayle and Smith hit a lusty 118 for the first wicket, but Sarwan failed and Lara, given out caught behind when replays suggested the ball only brushed his pad, showed his annoyance at the decision by lingering awhile before making the long walk back to the pavilion. However, Chanderpaul hit his eleventh Test hundred and with help from the lower middle order managed to bring West Indies up to 416, conceding a first innings lead of 152. England's second innings was a mixed bag: Vaughan ran out Key with a poor call but went on to become only the third player to score a century in both innings of a Lord's Test, Flintoff hit 50 in 38 balls and when he was out, Vaughan declared.

Chris Gayle hit another fifty and Chanderpaul was left stranded at the end on 97 not out, just three runs short of emulating Vaughan in this match, and his great West Indian predecessor George Headley in 1939. But apart from Lara's 44, before he was bowled by a beauty from the underrated Ashley Giles, the rest of the team made 28 between the eight of them. By the end the match had relapsed into Sunday afternoon village cricket stuff. As Tino Best came out to bat, with the score on 200 for seven, Flintoff called out, "Mind the windows, Tino!", knowing that Best would not be able to resist having a heave at Giles. The scorecard tells the story: Best st Jones b Giles 3. The half-brothers Pedro Collins and Fidel Edwards did their very best to stick around until Chanderpaul could reach his hundred, but it was Giles who had the last laugh, ending with five for 81 to add to his first innings haul of four for 129, and giving England a very comfortable victory.

MARYLEBONE CRICKET CLUB
LORD'S GROUND
ENGLAND v. WEST INDIES
THURSDAY, FRIDAY, SATURDAY, SUNDAY & MONDAY, JULY 22, 23, 24, 25 & 26, 2004
(5-day Match)

ENGLAND

			First Innings		Second Innings	
1	M. E. Trescothick	Somerset	c Sarwan b Best	16	b Collins	45
2	A. J. Strauss	Middlesex	c Jacobs b Banks	137	c Sarwan b Collins	35
3	R. W. T. Key	Kent	c Lara b Bravo	221	run out	15
†4	M. P. Vaughan	Yorkshire	c Smith b Collins	103	not out	101
5	G. P. Thorpe	Surrey	c Jacobs b Bravo	19	c and b Gayle	38
6	A. Flintoff	Lancashire	b Banks	6	c Jacobs b Collins	58
*7	G. O. Jones	Kent	c Jacobs b Collins	4		
8	A. F. Giles	Warwickshire	c Smith b Collins	5		
9	M. J. Hoggard	Yorkshire	not out	1		
10	S. P. Jones	Glamorgan	lbw Collins	4		
11	S. J. Harmison	Durham	b Bravo	4		
			b 2, l-b20, w13, n-b13, p	48	b 3, l-b14, w, n-b16, p	33
			Total ....(121.4 overs)	568	Total ....(5 wkts. dec)	325

FALL OF THE WICKETS
1—29 2—320 3—485 4—527 5—534 6—541 7—551 8—557 9—563 10—568
1—86 2—104 3—117 4—233 5—325 6— 7— 8— 9— 10—

ANALYSIS OF BOWLING

Name	1st Innings						2nd Innings					
	O.	M.	R.	W.	Wd.	N-b	O.	M.	R.	W.	Wd.	N-b
Collins	24	2	113	4	1	6	14.4	1	62	3	...	6
Best	21	1	104	1	1	...	3	1	14	0	...	
Edwards	21	2	96	0	3	6	13	0	47	0	...	8
Bravo	24.4	5	74	3	4	...	7	0	28	0	...	
Banks	22	3	131	2	...	1	26	1	92	0	...	
Sarwan	9	0	28	0	...	...	4	0	20	0	...	
Gayle							9	0	45	1	...	2

WEST INDIES

			First Innings		Second Innings	
1	C. H. Gayle	Jamaica	lbw b Giles	66	b Harmison	81
2	D. S. Smith	Windward Islands	b Giles	45	lbw b Giles	6
3	R. R. Sarwan	Guyana	lbw b Hoggard	1	lbw b Hoggard	4
†4	B. C. Lara	Trinidad & Tobago	c G. Jones b Giles	11	b Giles	44
5	S. Chanderpaul	Guyana	not out	128	not out	97
6	D. D. J. Bravo	Trinidad & Tobago	c G. Jones b S. Jones	44	c & b Giles	10
*7	R. D. Jacobs	Leeward Islands	c G. Jones b Hoggard	32	c Thorpe b Hoggard	1
8	O. A. C. Banks	Leeward Islands	b Flintoff	45	b Harmison	0
9	T. L. Best	Barbados	b Flintoff	0	st G. Jones b Giles	3
10	F. H. Edwards	Barbados	b Flintoff	0	c G. Jones b Flintoff	2
11	P. T. Collins	Barbados	b Giles	5	st G. Jones b Giles	2
			b20, l-b11, w 5, n-b 3, p	39	b 5, l-b 9, w, n-b 3, p	17
			Total ....(116.4 overs)	416	Total ....(79.3 overs)	267

FALL OF THE WICKETS
1—118 2—119 3—127 4—139 5—264 6—327 7—399 8—399 9—401 10—416
1—24 2—35 3—102 4—172 5—194 6—195 7—200 8—203 9—247 10—267

ANALYSIS OF BOWLING

Name	1st Innings						2nd Innings					
	O.	M.	R.	W.	Wd.	N-b	O.	M.	R.	W.	Wd.	N-b
Hoggard	28	7	89	2	...	1	14	2	65	2	...	
Harmison	21	6	72	0	...	...	21	2	78	2	...	3
S. Jones	17	3	70	1	1	2	8	3	29	0	...	
Giles	40.4	5	129	4	...	...	35	9	81	5	...	
Flintoff	10	4	25	3	...	...	1.3	1	0	1	...	

Umpires—R. E. Koertzen & D. J. Harper (3rd Umpire—N. J. Llong)
Match Referee—R. S. Madugalle   Scorers—D. Kendix & B. Mulholland

†Captain   *Wicket-keeper
Play begins each day at 10.30   Luncheon Interval 12.30—1.10
Tea Interval 3.10—3.30 (may be varied according to state of game)
Stumps drawn 1st, 2nd 3rd & 4th days at 5.30, or after 90 overs have been bowled, whichever is the later – 5th day at 5.30, or after a minimum of 75 overs for playing time other than the last hour, when Law of Cricket 16.6, 16.7 and 16.8 shall apply (except a minimum of 15 overs). Up to a maximum of 1 hour of time lost, from either the actual day or from previous days due to play being suspended, shall be made up at the end of the scheduled days play. The close of play shall be re-scheduled accordingly. The Umpires may agree to play a further 30 minutes of extra time at the end of any of the first four days if a definite result can be obtained.

West Indies won the toss and elected to field

England won by 210 runs

2005: England v Bangladesh

(1st Test) May 26, 27, 28
England won by an innings and 261 runs

It was an intensely cold morning in late May when Michael Vaughan won the toss and invited his Bangladeshi opponents to bat. This was the visitors' first Test at Lord's and they were obviously keen to do well. Unfortunately, keenness proved to be no substitute for professional skills, and England won in a canter, or perhaps even at a trot.

For England, this was an important match, coming after an arduous and fairly successful tour of South Africa, but immediately before the Ashes encounter with Australia. Even against the minnows of Bangladesh, England needed to perform well as a team, and individuals within the team had to show they had the right killer instincts to earn their places in the side for the latter part of the summer. And England did do well. Bangladesh were far too inexperienced, and far too cold, to put up much of a fight. England had them all out within 40 overs for a mere 108, with Matthew Hoggard taking four for 42. England in response put together a remorseless and rapid 528 for three declared, with Marcus Trescothick enjoying himself at the top of the order with 194, and Michael Vaughan scoring his third consecutive Lord's Test century (120) to equal the somewhat recondite achievement of Jack Hobbs, whose three consecutive hundreds were in 1912, 1924 and 1926. Dilip Vengsarkar of India also scored three centuries in consecutive Lord's Tests, but not in consecutive innings. Bell and Thorpe also made hay before Vaughan declared, and only Strauss, who had to be content with 69, could be described as having failed to take full advantage of the circumstances.

Bangladesh hardly fared better in their second innings, battling their way to 159 in an effort that lasted for nine balls longer than their first attempt. This time it was Simon Jones and Andrew Flintoff

who were the leading wicket-takers. It must have been very satisfying for Duncan Fletcher, England's manager, to see his fast bowling attack firing so well at this stage of the season. In the match, Hoggard took six wickets, Flintoff five, and Jones and Harmison four each. Gareth Batty, the off-spinner deputizing for the injured Ashley Giles, had a quiet match – he neither batted nor bowled,

Marcus Trescothick and Michael Vaughan during their partnership of 255 runs.

BANGLADESH

Javed Omar	c Trescothick b SP Jones	22	c Thorpe b SP Jones	25
Nafis Iqbal	c Trescothick b Harmison	8	c Flintoff b Hoggard	3
† Habibul Bashar	c GO Jones b Hoggard	3	c Hoggard b SP Jones	16
Aftab Ahmed	c Strauss b Flintoff	20	lbw b Hoggard	32
Mohammad Ashraful	lbw b Flintoff	6	c Harmison b Flintoff	2
Mushfiqur Rahim	b Hoggard	19	c GO Jones b Flintoff	3
* Khaled Mashud	lbw b Hoggard	6	c Thorpe b Flintoff	44
Mohammad Rafique	run out	1	c GO Jones b Harmison	0
Mashrafe bin Mortaza	b Harmison	0	b Harmison	0
Anwar Hossain Monir	not out	5	c Trescothick b SP Jones	13
Shahadat Hossain	c GO Jones b Hoggard	4	not out	2
Extras	(B 1, LB 1, NB 12)	14	(B 1, LB 4, NB 14)	19
Total		108		159

ENGLAND

ME Trescothick	c Khaled Mashud b Mohammad Rafique	194
A. J Strauss	lbw b Mashrafe bin Mortaza	69
† MP Vaughan	c Khaled Mashud b Mashrafe bin Mortaza	120
IR Bell	not out	65
GP Thorpe	not out	42
Extras	(B 4, LB 11, W 3, NB 20)	38
Total	(3 wkts dec.)	528

Did not bat A Flintoff, * GO Jones, GJ Batty, MJ Hoggard, SJ Harmison, SP Jones

ENGLAND	O.	M.	R.	W.	WD.	NB.		O.	M.	R.	W.	WD.	NB.
Hoggard	13.2	5	42	4	–	8		9	1	42	2	–	7
Harmison	14	3	38	2	–	4		10	0	39	2	–	5
Flintoff	5	0	22	2	–	–		9.5	0	44	3	–	2
SP Jones	6	4	4	1	–	–		11	3	29	3	–	–

BANGLADESH	O.	M.	R.	W.	WD.	NB.
Mashrafe bin Mortaza	29	6	107	2	–	–
Shahadat Hossain	12	0	101	0	1	10
Anwar Hossain Monir	22	0	110	0	1	9
Mohammad Rafique	41	3	150	1	–	1
Aftab Ahmed	8	1	45	0	1	–

† Captain   * Wicketkeeper

and nor did he hold any catches. Only two Bangladeshi batsmen made double figures in both innings – Javed Omar and Aftab Ahmed. The team was simply outclassed, and not even the weather turned foul enough to save them. The match was over by lunch on the third day.

One of their number did establish a record, however. Mushfiqur Rahim, who made his Test debut in this match largely thanks to a not out hundred against Northamptonshire a few days earlier, was only 16 years and 267 days old when the game began, making him the youngest player ever to play in a Test at Lord's. He scored 19 in Bangladesh's first innings and has gone on to enjoy a lengthy if not massively successful Test career.

2005: England v Australia

(1st Test) July 21, 22, 23, 24
Australia won by 239 runs

The 2005 Ashes series has achieved an almost mythical status, thanks to the massive excitement engendered by a succession of very close finishes in a series between two very evenly matched teams, one of which played above itself while the other had to struggle with injury and some odd selection decisions. The excitement began to build well before the Australians arrived in the country, and by the time of the first Test, at Lord's, it seemed that most of Britain was focused on the match. This may have been in part to take our minds off the terrorist bomb outrage of two weeks earlier, which had killed so many people and forced us to think about more serious matters. But for the first time in years there seemed to be a genuine national excitement about a Test series against Australia.

In the end, the series lived up to all those expectations, but at Lord's, it seemed as though we were in for the same old string of failures. England had not beaten Australia at Lord's for 71 years, and the new millennium seemed to make no difference. The first morning of the Test, though, was as enthralling a session as the summer had to offer. In front of a capacity crowd, Australia won the toss and elected to bat first and England's sometimes unguided missile, Steve Harmison, opened the bowling. This time, his radar was in perfect working order. In the very first over, a ball just short of a length hit Langer on the elbow, and the "Oooh" which went round the ground signalled sympathy for the pain as well as eagerness for the contest.

By lunch on the first day, Australia were 97 for five, with only 23 overs bowled. England's supporters thought the promised land was just around the corner, but as it turned out, this was the high point of the match. By close of play, in reply to Australia's sub-par score of 190 all out,

Ricky Ponting on his way to 7,000 Test runs.

England were reeling at 92 for seven, having been at one stage 21 for five – all five to Glenn McGrath who at the age of 35 was bowling as well as ever and in the process picked up his 500th Test wicket, that of Trescothick who edged to third slip. The next day England limped to 155 all out, thanks in part to Kevin Pietersen's 57 on debut, but Australia's second innings sealed England's fate. Michael Clarke hit 91, numbers 3 to 6 batted solidly around him and Australia were able to set a target of 420, with over 250 overs left in the match to take ten wickets. They needed only 58 of them plus one ball, despite an opening partnership of 80 and a second half century by Pietersen, and England were thoroughly beaten. The margin of defeat in terms of runs was their worst at Lord's since 1994 when they lost to South Africa by 356 runs.

So the two sides moved on to Edgbaston for the second Test with not much optimism being shown by England's fans around the country. That they were proved wrong to have so little faith is now part of the folklore of English cricket.

MARYLEBONE CRICKET CLUB

LORD'S GROUND

ENGLAND v. AUSTRALIA

THURSDAY, FRIDAY, SATURDAY, SUNDAY & MONDAY, JULY 21, 22, 23, 24 & 25, 2005
(5-day Match)

80p   80p

AUSTRALIA

			First Innings		Second Innings	
1	J. L. Langer	(Western Australia)	c Harmison b Flintoff	40	run out	6
2	M. L. Hayden	(Queensland)	b Hoggard	12	b Flintoff	34
†3	R. T. Ponting	(Tasmania)	c Strauss b Harmison	9	c sub b Hoggard	42
4	D. R. Martyn	(Western Australia)	c G. Jones b S. Jones	2	lbw b Harmison	65
5	M. J. Clarke	(New South Wales)	lbw b S. Jones	11	b Hoggard	91
6	S. M. Katich	(New South Wales)	c G. Jones b Harmison	27	c S. Jones b Harmison	67
*7	A. C. Gilchrist	(Western Australia)	c G. Jones b Flintoff	26	b Flintoff	10
8	S. K. Warne	(Victoria)	b Harmison	28	c Giles b Harmison	2
9	B. Lee	(New South Wales)	c G. Jones b Harmison	3	run out	8
10	J. N. Gillespie	(South Australia)	lbw b Harmison	1	b S. Jones	13
11	G. D. McGrath	(New South Wales)	not out	10	not out	20
			b 5, l-b 4, w 1, n-b 11, p ,	21	b 10, l-b 8, w , n-b 8, p ,	26
			Total ....(40.2 overs)	190	Total ....(100.4 overs)	384

FALL OF THE WICKETS

1—35 2—55 3—66 4—66 5—87 6—126 7—175 8—178 9—178 10—190
1—18 2—54 3—100 4—255 5—255 6—274 7—279 8—289 9—341 10—384

ANALYSIS OF BOWLING

Name	1st Innings						2nd Innings					
	O.	M.	R.	W.	Wd.	N-b	O.	M.	R.	W.	Wd.	N-b
Harmison	11.2	0	43	5	...	...	27.4	6	54	3	...	...
Hoggard	8	0	40	1	...	2	16	1	56	2	...	2
Flintoff	11	2	50	2	...	9	27	4	123	2	...	5
S. Jones	10	0	48	2	1	...	18	1	69	1	...	1
Giles	...	...	...	...	...	...	11	1	56	0	...	...
Bell	...	...	...	...	...	...	1	0	8	0	...	...

ENGLAND

			First Innings		Second Innings	
1	M. E. Trescothick	(Somerset)	c Langer b McGrath	4	c Hayden b Warne	44
2	A. J. Strauss	(Middlesex)	c Warne b McGrath	2	c and b Lee	37
†3	M. P. Vaughan	(Yorkshire)	b McGrath	3	b Lee	4
4	I. R. Bell	(Warwickshire)	b McGrath	6	lbw b Warne	8
5	K. P. Pietersen	(Hampshire)	c Martyn b Warne	57	not out	64
6	A. Flintoff	(Lancashire)	b McGrath	0	c Gilchrist b Warne	3
*7	G. O. Jones	(Kent)	c Gilchrist b Lee	30	c Gillespie b McGrath	6
8	A. F. Giles	(Warwickshire)	c Gilchrist b Lee	11	c Hayden b McGrath	0
9	M. J. Hoggard	(Yorkshire)	c Hayden b Warne	0	lbw b McGrath	0
10	S. P. Jones	(Glamorgan)	not out	20	c Warne b McGrath	0
11	S. J. Harmison	(Durham)	c Martyn b Lee	11	lbw b Warne	0
			b 1, l-b 5, w , n-b 5, p ,	11	b 6, l-b 5, w , n-b 3, p ,	14
			Total ....(48.1 overs)	155	Total ....(58.1 overs)	180

FALL OF THE WICKETS

1—10 2—11 3—18 4—19 5—21 6—79 7—92 8—101 9—122 10—155
1—80 2—96 3—104 4—112 5—119 6—158 7—158 8—164 9—167 10—180

ANALYSIS OF BOWLING

Name	1st Innings						2nd Innings					
	O.	M.	R.	W.	Wd.	N-b	O.	M.	R.	W.	Wd.	N-b
McGrath	18	5	53	5	...	...	17.1	2	29	4	...	...
Lee	15.1	5	47	3	...	4	15	3	58	2	...	1
Gillespie	8	1	30	0	...	1	6	0	18	0	...	2
Warne	7	2	19	2	...	...	20	2	64	4	...	...

Umpires—R. E. Koertzen & A. S. Dar (3rd Umpire—M. R. Benson 4th Umpire—N. G. Cowley)
Match Referee—R. S. Madugalle   Scorers—C. K. Mountain & D. Kendix

†Captain   *Wicket-keeper

Play begins each day at 10.30
Tea Interval 3.10—3.30 (may be varied according to state of game)   Luncheon Interval 12.30—1.10

On the first 4 days, stumps will be drawn at 5.30. However, if the minimum of 90 overs has not been bowled by this time, play can be extended by up to 30 minutes to 6.00. On the last day, the final hour will start at 4.30 or after 75 overs have been bowled, whichever is the later. A minimum of 15 overs must then be bowled in the last hour. Up to a maximum of 1 hour of time lost, from either the actual day or from previous days due to play being suspended, shall be made up at the end of the scheduled day's play. The close of play shall be re-scheduled accordingly. The Umpires may agree to play a further 30 minutes of extra time at the end of any of the first four days if a definite result can be obtained.

Australia won the toss

Australia won by 239 runs

2006: England v Sri Lanka

(1st Test) May 11, 12, 13, 14, 15
Match Drawn

For the second time in consecutive Tests at Lord's, between England and Sri Lanka, and for the second time in all Tests at Lord's, one side was forced to follow on, but then hit over 500 runs in their second innings and thus saved themselves from almost certain defeat. In 2002 it was England who managed the great escape, but now it was Sri Lanka's turn to frustrate England's admittedly under-strength seam attack.

England won the toss, and Flintoff, deputizing for the almost permanently crocked Vaughan,

chose to bat. The entire England batting line-up, apart from Matthew Hoggard, who went in as nightwatchman, made the most of the opportunity. Trescothick and Pietersen both hit centuries, while Alastair Cook, on his home debut, scored 89. England declared at 551 for six, made in 143 overs, and then set about the Sri Lanka batsmen. Even with Plunkett and Mahmood in for the injured Harmison and Anderson, there appeared to be no way out for the Sri Lankans, and when the scoreboard showed the visitors on 91 for six at the end

Marcus Trescothick, a century for England.

LORD'S GROUND

ENGLAND v. SRI LANKA

Thursday, Friday, Saturday, Sunday & Monday, May 11, 12, 13, 14 & 15, 2006
(5-day Match)

ENGLAND

			First Innings		Second Innings
1	M. E. Trescothick	(Somerset)	c Jayaw'ne b Muralitharan	106	
2	A. J. Strauss	(Middlesex)	c Jayaw'ne b Muralitharan	48	
3	A. N. Cook	(Essex)	c Sangakkara b Maharoof	89	
4	K. P. Pietersen	(Hampshire)	lbw b Vaas	158	
5	M. J. Hoggard	(Yorkshire)	b Vaas	7	
6	P. D. Collingwood	(Durham)	b Muralitharan	57	
†7	A. Flintoff	(Lancashire)	not out	33	
*8	G. O. Jones	(Kent)	not out	11	
9	L. E. Plunkett	(Durham)			
10	S. I. Mahmood	(Lancashire)			
11	M. S. Panesar	(Northamptonshire)			
			b 16, l-b 7, w 4, n-b 15, p ,	42	b , l-b , w , n-b , p ,
			Total (6 wkts. dec.)	551	Total

FALL OF THE WICKETS

1—86 2—213 3—312 4—329 5—502 6—502 7— 8— 9— 10—

1— 2— 3— 4— 5— 6— 7— 8— 9— 10—

ANALYSIS OF BOWLING

Name	1st Innings						2nd Innings					
	O.	M.	R.	W.	Wd.	N-b	O.	M.	R.	W.	Wd.	N-b
Vaas	36	2	124	2	1							
Maharoof	28	4	125	1	2	14						
Kulasekara	25	3	89	0	1	1						
Muralitharan	48	10	158	3		1						
Dilshan	6	0	32	0								

SRI LANKA

			First Innings		Second Innings	
1	J. Mubarak	(Colombo)	lbw b Hoggard	0	b Hoggard	6
2	W. U. Tharanga	(Nondescripts)	lbw b Hoggard	10	c Jones b Panesar	52
*3	K. C. Sangakkara	(Nondescripts)	c Trescothick b Mahmood	21	c Jones b Panesar	65
†4	D. P. M. D. Jayawardene	(Sinhalese)	c Jones b Flintoff	61	c Jones b Flintoff	119
5	T. T. Samaraweera	(Sinhalese)	lbw b Mahmood	0	c Jones b Mahmood	6
6	T. M. Dilshan	(Bloomfield)	run out	0	c Trescothick b Plunkett	69
7	C. K. Kapugedera	(Colombo)	lbw b Mahmood	0	c Jones b Flintoff	10
8	M. F. Maharoof	(Bloomfield)	c and b Hoggard	22	c Pietersen b Mahmood	59
9	W. P. U. J. C. Vaas	(Colts)	c Trescothick b Hoggard	31	not out	50
10	K. M. D. N. Kulasekara	(Colts)	c Strauss b Flintoff	29	c Pietersen b Hoggard	64
11	M. Muralitharan	(Tamil Union)	not out	0	not out	1
			b , l-b 8, w , n-b 10, p ,	18	b 9, l-b 19, w 3, n-b 5, p ,	36
			Total (55.3 overs)	192	Total (9 wkts, 199 overs)	537

FALL OF THE WICKETS

1—0 2—21 3—81 4—81 5—85 6—85 7—129 8—131 9—192 10—192

1—10 2—119 3—178 4—291 5—303 6—371 7—405 8—421 9—526 10—

ANALYSIS OF BOWLING

Name	1st Innings						2nd Innings					
	O.	M.	R.	W.	Wd.	N-b	O.	M.	R.	W.	Wd.	N-b
Hoggard	14	4	27	4		2	46	11	110	2	...	1
Flintoff	17.3	2	55	2	...	3	51	11	131	2	1	
Plunkett	11	0	52	0	...	5	31	10	85	1	...	2
Mahmood	13	2	50	3			35	5	118	2	1	
Collingwood							9	2	16	0	1	2
Panesar							27	10	49	2	...	

Umpires—R. E. Koertzen & A. S. Dar (3rd Umpire—N. J. Llong; 4th Umpire—P. J. Hartley)

Match Referee—A. G. Hurst Scorers—D. Kendix & G. A. Stickley

†Captain *Wicket-keeper

Play begins each day at 11.00 Luncheon Interval 1.00—1.40

Tea Interval 3.40—4.00 (may be varied according to state of game)

Stumps drawn 1st, 2nd 3rd & 4th days at 6.00, or after 90 overs have been bowled, save that play cannot continue after 6.30 except for the purpose of making up time lost as a result of bad weather. On the 5th day at 5.30, or after a minimum of 75 overs for playing time other than the last hour, when Laws of Cricket 16.6, 16.7 and 16.8 shall apply (except a minimum of 15 overs). Up to a maximum of 1 hour of time lost, from either the actual day or from previous days due to play being suspended, shall be made up at the end of the scheduled day's play. The close of play shall be re-scheduled accordingly. The Umpires may agree to play a further 30 minutes of extra time at the end of any of the first four days if a definite result can be obtained.

England won the toss

Match abandoned as a draw

Trescothick takes a sharp slip catch.

of the second day's play, everybody was starting to make fresh plans for the Sunday and Monday.

The Sri Lankan first innings did indeed fizzle out shortly on the third day, although a ninth wicket stand of 61 between Vaas and Kulasekara delayed the inevitable for a few more overs. When the follow on was enforced, with England's lead a hefty 359, Hoggard soon accounted for Mubarak and it looked as though another quick kill was probable. However, the Sri Lankans had other thoughts, and as they became more obdurate, so England's catching became more and more unreliable. Seven Sri Lankan batsmen hit fifties, a feat that had not been achieved in a home Test since England's effort against Australia at Old Trafford in 1934.

The Sri Lankan captain Jayawardene led the long march to safety, with a six hour innings of 119, but after Mubarak's early dismissal, only Samaraweera and Kapugedera failed to build an innings of substance. Having reduced Sri Lanka to 371 for six, just 12 runs ahead, with plenty of time left to get the remaining wickets and chase down a reasonable target, England must have been mortified to watch as three of the last five Sri Lankan batsmen, at numbers 8, 9 and 10 all scored half centuries and brought their total to 537 for nine. Catches were dropped by most of the England team – Jones behind the stumps, Cook, the usually reliable Collingwood, Strauss and Flintoff were all guilty at least once – and Sri Lanka's batsmen made the most of their good fortune.

When it all ended in a stoppage for bad light around 5.45 on the final afternoon, Sri Lanka had defied the England attack for 199 overs, and questions were being asked about the wisdom of giving the captaincy, even on a temporary basis, to the side's leading all-rounder, who was already doing more than his fair share of batting and bowling.

2006: England v Pakistan

(1st Test) July 13, 14, 15, 16, 17
Match Drawn

For Andrew Strauss this was his first Test match as captain of England. Had either Michael Vaughan or Andrew Flintoff been fit to play, then Strauss would have been one of the team, not as he put it, 'stand-in for the stand-in'.

Strauss failed to steer England to victory as, under a blazing sun, the game eventually petered out to become the second Lord's Test draw of the summer. However he did join a very select group who have scored a century in their first match as England captain, the only others on this list at the time being Archie MacLaren and Allan Lamb. Though notable enough, his achievement came in England's second innings, whereas three of his teammates had scored centuries in the first innings. What's more, Mohammad Yousuf, the batsman formerly known as Yousuf Youhana, scored a double century for Pakistan, thereby virtually ensuring that Pakistan came out of the game with a draw.

England's first innings revolved around the three centurions. Cook and Collingwood took the score from a slightly shaky 88 for three to a very secure 321 for four, and when Cook departed, that merely let in Ian Bell who, after adding a further 120 with Collingwood, then shepherded the tail long enough to get England well past 500 and himself to a first Lord's Test century. It was also England's 100th in all Tests at Lord's. Bell was perhaps fortunate to be in the side at all, as the general expectation was that if Flintoff had been fit, Bell would have had to make way for him, but as it was, the Warwickshire man seized his chance and retained his place in the side for the rest of the summer and beyond.

For Pakistan, it was all Mohammad Yousuf, with a little help from Inzamam. Yousuf's innings was the highest by a Pakistan player at Lord's,

Ian Bell celebrates his first Test century at Lord's.

beating Mohsin Khan's 200 in 1982, and the team total was also their highest ever scored at Lord's. Yet still they had to yield a first innings lead of 83. Inzamam's scores of 69 and 56 not out were his eighth and ninth consecutive fifties against England, a little known but remarkable world record. England were unable to force the pace as much as they might have liked in their second innings, which meant that Strauss had to delay his declaration until well into the fifth day, and Pakistan had no real difficulty in safely playing out time. When the teams shook hands on a draw, England were six wickets short of their target, but Pakistan were still 166 runs away from a very unlikely victory.

Strauss retained the captaincy for the remaining three Tests, and Ian Bell scored two more centuries in the series (which England won 3-0) and finished with an average of 93.75. The effect of the various injuries to key Englishmen did not prove significant, but did allow those players on the fringe of selection to England's team to show their abilities. The strength in depth of the England squad would prove to be the foundation for their successful assault on the number one Test ranking a year or two later.

MARYLEBONE CRICKET CLUB

LORD'S GROUND

ENGLAND v. PAKISTAN

THURSDAY, FRIDAY, SATURDAY, SUNDAY & MONDAY, JULY 13, 14, 15, 16 & 17, 2006
(5-day Match)

ENGLAND		First Innings		Second Innings	
1 M. E. Trescothick	(Somerset)	c Akmal b Gul	16	b Gul	18
†2 A. J. Strauss	(Middlesex)	lbw b Razzaq	30	c Farhat b Kaneria	128
3 A. N. Cook	(Essex)	b Sami	105	c Yousuf b Gul	4
4 K. P. Pietersen	(Hampshire)	lbw b Razzaq	21	st Akmal b Afridi	41
5 P. D. Collingwood	(Durham)	st Akmal b Kaneria	186	c Butt b Kaneria	3
6 I. R. Bell	(Warwickshire)	not out	100	run out	28
*7 G. O. Jones	(Kent)	lbw b Kaneria	18	c Akmal b Kaneria	16
8 L. E. Plunkett	(Durham)	c Farhat b Kaneria	0	c Akmal b Razzaq	28
9 M. J. Hoggard	(Yorkshire)	lbw b Afridi	13	not out	12
10 S. J. Harmison	(Durham)	run out	2		
11 M. S. Panesar	(Northamptonshire)	not out	0		
		b 8,l-b ,w15,n-b14,p ,	37	b 5,l-b 6,w 1,n-b 6,p ,	18
		Total ......(9 wkts. dec.)	528	Total ......(8 wkts. dec.)	296

FALL OF THE WICKETS

1—60 2—60 3—88 4—321 5—441 6—469 7—473 8—515 9—525 10—
1—38 2—64 3—141 4—146 5—203 6—250 7—253 8—296 9— 10—

ANALYSIS OF BOWLING

Name	1st Innings						2nd Innings					
	O.	M.	R.	W.	Wd.	N-b	O.	M.	R.	W.	Wd.	N-b
Sami	28	4	116	1	1	3	6	1	23	0	...	...
Gul	33	6	133	1	6	7	19	4	70	2	1	3
Razzaq	25	2	86	2	...	1	9.5	0	45	1	...	1
Kaneria	52	6	119	3	...	1	30	4	77	3	...	1
Afridi	19.3	0	63	1	...	1	19	1	65	1	2	
Farhat	1	0	3	0	...	...	1	0	5	0	...	

PAKISTAN		First Innings		Second Innings	
1 Salman Butt	(Lahore)	c Strauss b Harmison	10	lbw b Hoggard	0
2 Imran Farhat	(Lahore)	b Plunkett	33	c Coll'wood b Hoggard	18
3 Faisal Iqbal	(Karachi)	c Coll'wood b Harmison	0	c Cook b Panesar	48
4 Mohammad Yousuf	(Lahore)	c Jones b Harmison	202	lbw b Panesar	48
5 Mohammad Sami	(Karachi)	c Jones b Hoggard	0		
†6 Inzamam-ul-Haq	(Multan)	b Plunkett	69	not out	56
7 Abdul Razzaq	(Lahore)	c Jones b Harmison	22	not out	25
*8 Kamran Akmal	(Lahore)	c Jones b Pietersen	58		
9 Shahid Afridi	(Karachi)	c Bell b Hoggard	17		
10 Umar Gul	(Peshawar)	c Jones b Hoggard	0		
11 Danish Kaneria	(Karachi)	not out	1		
		b 7,l-b14,w 7,n-b 5,p ,	33	b 1,l-b 8,w 6,n-b 4,p ,	19
		Total ....(119.3 overs)	445	Total ...(4 wkts, 73 overs)	214

FALL OF THE WICKETS

1—28 2—28 3—65 4—68 5—241 6—300 7—399 8—435 9—436 10—445
1—0 2—22 3—116 4—141 5— 6— 7— 8— 9—

ANALYSIS OF BOWLING

Name	1st Innings						2nd Innings					
	O.	M.	R.	W.	Wd.	N-b	O.	M.	R.	W.	Wd.	N-b
Hoggard	33	3	117	3	1	5	12	3	31	2	...	2
Harmison	29.3	6	94	4	...	...	15	3	43	0	3	2
Panesar	27	3	93	0	...	...	27	7	60	2	...	...
Plunkett	21	3	78	2	4	...	12	2	41	0	3	...
Collingwood	7	1	31	0	2	...	2	1	11	0	...	...
Pietersen	2	0	11	1	...	...	5	1	19	0	...	...

Umpires—S. A. Bucknor & S. J. A. Taufel (3rd Umpire—P. J. Hartley; 4th Umpire—R. K. Illingworth)
Match Referee—R. S. Madugalle   Scorers—D. Kendix & R. W. Clarke

†Captain   *Wicket-keeper

Play begins at 11.00 each day   Luncheon Interval 1.00—1.40
Tea Interval 3.40—4.00 (may be varied according to state of game)
Stumps drawn at 6.00 on the 1st, 2nd, 3rd and 4th days, or after 90 overs have been bowled save that play cannot continue after 6.30 except for the purpose of making up time lost due to bad weather. The Umpires may agree to play a further 30 minutes of extra time at the end of any of the first four days if a definite result can be obtained.
Any alteration to the hours of play will be announced over the public address system.
Stumps drawn on the fifth day at 6.00 or after 90 overs have been bowled, save that at 5.00, or after 75 overs have been bowled on that day, the last hour – during which a minimum of 15 overs shall be bowled, but otherwise Laws of Cricket 16.6, 16.7 and 16.8 shall apply – will commence. If there is no prospect of a definite result, play may cease when a minimum of 15 overs remain to be bowled.

England won the toss

Match drawn

2007: England v West Indies

(1st Test) May 17, 18, 19, 20, 21
Match Drawn

Matthew Prior becomes the first England 'keeper to score a century in his first Test.

England, returning to headquarters after the ignominy of a 5-0 Ashes defeat down under, found themselves with a new coach, Peter Moores, a new batting coach, Andy Flower, an old new temporary stand-in captain, Andrew Strauss and a new wicket-keeper, Matthew Prior. West Indies also had a new temporary coach, David Moore, and a new captain, Ramnaresh Sarwan. However, there was a large dose of the same old weather and the end result was the third consecutive drawn Test at Lord's.

Sarwan won the toss and gave England first go on a wicket that proved much more batsman friendly than the West Indies skipper had anticipated. With the exception of Owais Shah and to a lesser extent the captain Strauss, every England batsman made the most of it. In the first innings, four of them scored hundreds, including Prior, who thus became the first English wicket-keeper to make a century on debut. In the second innings, Kevin Pietersen also reached three figures, which meant that for the first time ever, five English batsmen made centuries in the same Test match.

West Indies responded solidly to England's score of 553 for five declared, with every batsman apart from Collymore at number eleven reaching

LORD'S GROUND

ENGLAND v. WEST INDIES

THURSDAY, FRIDAY, SATURDAY, SUNDAY & MONDAY, MAY 17, 18, 19, 20 & 21, 2007
(5-day Match)

		First Innings		Second Innings	
†1	A. J. Strauss (Middlesex)	c Smith b Powell	33	c Morton b Collymore	24
2	A. N. Cook (Essex)	c Bravo b Taylor	105	c Ramdin b Collymore	65
3	O. A. Shah (Middlesex)	c Smith b Powell	6	c Ramdin b Collymore	4
4	K. P. Pietersen (Hampshire)	c Smith b Collymore	26	lbw b Gayle	109
5	P. D. Collingwood (Durham)	b Bravo	111	c Morton b Bravo	34
6	I. R. Bell (Warwickshire)	not out	109	c Ganga b Bravo	3
*7	M. J. Prior (Sussex)	not out	126	c Bravo b Gayle	21
8	L. E. Plunkett (Durham)			st Ramdin b Gayle	0
9	M. J. Hoggard (Yorkshire)			not out	11
10	S. J. Harmison (Durham)			not out	3
11	M. S. Panesar (Northamptonshire)				
		b 8, l-b17, w 9, n-b 3, p ,	37	b 1, l-b 3, w 1, n-b 5, p ,	10
		Total ....(5 wkts. dec.)	553	Total ....(8 wkts. dec.)	284

FALL OF THE WICKETS

1—88	2—103	3—162	4—219	5—363	6—	7—	8—	9—	10—
1—35	2—51	3—139	4—241	5—248	6—264	7—264	8—271	9—	10—

ANALYSIS OF BOWLING

Name	1st Innings					2nd Innings				
	O.	M.	R.	W.	Wd. N-b	O.	M.	R.	W.	Wd. N-b
Powell	37	9	113	2	2 ...	9	0	44	0	... ...
Taylor	24	4	114	1	... ...	4	0	21	0	... ...
Collymore	32	5	110	1	... 2	15	1	58	3	... 2
Bravo	32	8	106	1	1 1	18	2	91	2	... 2
Gayle	10	0	48	0	... ...	20.5	4	66	3	1 1
Morton	1	0	4	0	2 ...	...	...	...	...	... ...
Sarwan	6	0	33	0	... ...	...	...	...	...	... ...

		First Innings		Second Innings	
WEST INDIES					
1	C. H. Gayle (Jamaica)	b Plunkett	30	not out	47
2	D. Ganga (Trinidad & Tobago)	lbw b Panesar	49	not out	31
3	D. S. Smith (Windward Islands)	b Panesar	21		
†4	R. R. Sarwan (Guyana)	lbw b Panesar	35		
5	S. Chanderpaul (Guyana)	lbw b Panesar	74		
6	R. S. Morton (Leeward Islands)	lbw b Panesar	14		
7	D. J. Bravo (Trinidad & Tobago)	c Cook b Collingwood	56		
*8	D. Ramdin (Trinidad & Tobago)	c Collingwood b Plunkett	60		
9	D. B. Powell (Jamaica)	not out	36		
10	J. E. Taylor (Jamaica)	c sub b Harmison	21		
11	C. D. Collymore (Barbados)	lbw b Panesar	1		
		b 4, l-b17, w16, n-b 3, p ,	40	b 4, l-b 3, w 3, n-b 1,p ,	11
		Total ....(116.1 overs)	437	Total ....(22 overs)	89

FALL OF THE WICKETS

1—38	2—83	3—151	4—165	5—187	6—279	7—362	8—387	9—424	10—437
1—	2—	3—	4—	5—	6—	7—	8—	9—	10—

ANALYSIS OF BOWLING

Name	1st Innings					2nd Innings				
	O.	M.	R.	W.	Wd. N-b	O.	M.	R.	W.	Wd. N-b
Hoggard	10.1	3	29	0	... ...	...	...	...	...	... ...
Harmison	28	2	117	1	4 2	8	1	21	0	2 1
Plunkett	30	7	107	2	4 ...	11	1	48	0	1 ...
Collingwood	11.5	2	34	1	... 1	...	...	...	...	... ...
Panesar	36.1	3	129	6	... ...	3	0	13	0	... ...

Umpires— R. E. Koertzen & Asad Rauf (3rd Umpire—N. J. Llong; 4th Umpire—R. A. Kettleborough)

Match Referee—A. G. Hurst   Scorers— D. Kendix & R. D. Grimes

†Captain   *Wicket-keeper

Play begins at 11.00 each day   Luncheon Interval 1.00—1.40

Tea Interval 3.40—4.00 (may be varied according to state of game)

Stumps drawn at 6.00 on the 1st, 2nd, 3rd and 4th days, or after 90 overs have been bowled save that play cannot continue after 6.30 except for the purpose of making up time lost due to bad weather. The Umpires may agree to play a further 30 minutes of extra time at the end of any of the first four days if a definite result can be obtained.

Any alteration to the hours of play will be announced over the public address system.

Stumps drawn on the fifth day at 6.00 or after 90 overs have been bowled, save that at 5.00, or after 75 overs have been bowled on that day, the last hour – during which a minimum of 15 overs shall be bowled, but otherwise Laws of Cricket 16.6, 16.7 and 16.8 shall apply – will commence. If there is no prospect of a definite result, play may cease when a minimum of 15 overs remain to be bowled.

West Indies won the toss and elected to field

Match abandoned as a draw

---

double figures. In reaching 437, they saved the follow-on but it was very much in doubt when the fifth wicket fell at 187. Hoggard had pulled up lame by this time, which meant that Collingwood had to put in a longer spell than usual, but two partnerships for the sixth and seventh wickets involving Chanderpaul, first with Bravo and then with Ramdin, brought West Indies to safety. The final five wickets added 250 runs. The eventual destroyer of West Indies was Monty Panesar, who took six for 129 in 36.1 overs, with five of his victims adjudged leg before wicket. This was the first time that any bowler had trapped five batsmen lbw in a Lord's Test innings, and only the fifth time in all Tests – all these instances occurring within the past twenty years. The eccentricity of England's bowling attack was further emphasized by Plunkett, who bowled a sackful of wides, two of which so defeated the unfortunate debutant keeper that they went to the boundary for five runs.

England scored at a little better than four an over in their second innings, but Strauss did not feel confident about leaving West Indies any sort of straightforward target (perhaps he had read about David Gower's badly calculated declaration in 1984, and anyway, he was a bowler short), and when he declared just before the end of the fourth day, he set West Indies 401 to win. What might have been a tense final day became something of a damp squib. Rain and cloud meant that only twenty overs were possible, and the match fizzled out into a draw.

2007: England v India

(1st Test) July 19, 20, 21, 22, 23
Match Drawn

A very wet match: the weather took a hand on almost every day, including a torrential downpour on the second morning which soaked many spectators to the skin but which also proved the worth of Lord's comparatively new underground drainage system. What was a lake at lunchtime was playable barely an hour later, and an investment of £1.25 million five years earlier had in one day alone saved MCC having to refund about £1.5 million worth of tickets.

Without interruptions for the weather, England should have won. When shortly before tea on the

fifth day India were offered the light and the match came to a premature end, they were nine wickets down and had already added nineteen runs for the final wicket. What's more, Panesar had had a very strong appeal for lbw against Sreesanth turned down, despite HawkEye's indication that the batsman was out. It was as close a run match as had been seen at Lord's since 1963, but the result in the end was the same – drawn.

Before the downpour, it had been a batsman's wicket. England won the toss and by close of play on the first day had scored 268 for four wickets,

Sachin Tendulkar – master batsman.

thanks mainly to 96 from Strauss and 79 from Vaughan, who wasn't injured for this match. With the downpour came a sea change in conditions, so that England were rolled over by Sreesanth and Zaheer Khan for the addition of only 30 more runs. But when India batted, Anderson and Sidebottom were just as awkward a proposition. Only Wasim Jaffer reached fifty as the legendary middle order struggled in unwelcoming conditions, and England found themselves 97 ahead on first innings.

England's second innings was built around an astonishing century by Kevin Pietersen. When others find the going almost impossible, Pietersen seems to be playing at another level, and his 134 against a testing attack of Zaheer Khan and a man who found the conditions exactly what he had always been looking for, R P Singh, was one of his very best Test innings. Only Prior was able to stay with him for any length of time, and the pair added 119 for the sixth wicket, setting up an eventual target of 380 for India, and four sessions in which to make the runs.

At the start of the final morning, India were already 137 for three, with Tendulkar trapped lbw by Panesar the night before – a wicket that prompted one of Monty's more energetic celebrations over the demise of the master batsman. When Kartik and Ganguly were both dismissed quickly on the final morning, it looked as though England would win easily, but Dhoni and Laxman had other ideas. Although Tremlett, on debut, finally bowled Laxman, Dhoni was still there at the end, and England had failed to press home the advantage they had held practically throughout the whole match.

MARYLEBONE CRICKET CLUB
LORD'S GROUND
ENGLAND v. INDIA

THURSDAY, FRIDAY, SATURDAY, SUNDAY & MONDAY, JULY 19, 20, 21, 22 & 23, 2007
(5-day Match)

ENGLAND

		First Innings		Second Innings	
1	A. J. Strauss (Middlesex)	c Dravid b Kumble	96	c Tendulkar b Khan	18
2	A. N. Cook (Essex)	lbw b Ganguly	36	lbw b Khan	17
†3	M. P. Vaughan (Yorkshire)	c Dhoni b Singh	79	b Singh	30
4	K. P. Pietersen (Hampshire)	c Dhoni b Khan	37	b Singh	134
5	P. D. Collingwood (Durham)	lbw b Kumble	0	c Laxman b Singh	4
6	R. J. Sidebottom (Nottinghamshire)	b Singh	1	c Dravid b Kumble	9
7	I. R. Bell (Warwickshire)	b Khan	20	b Singh	9
*8	M. J. Prior (Sussex)	lbw b Sreesanth	1	c Dhoni b Khan	42
9	C. T. Tremlett (Hampshire)	lbw b Sreesanth	0	b Khan	0
10	M. S. Panesar (Northamptonshire)	lbw b Sreesanth	0	lbw b Singh	3
11	J. M. Anderson (Lancashire)	not out	28	not out	4
		b 9, l-b10, w 7, n-b 2, p		b 9, l-b 1, w 2, n-b , p	12
		Total (91.2 overs)	298	Total (78.3 overs)	282

FALL OF THE WICKETS
1—76 2—218 3—252 4—255 5—272 6—286 7—287 8—287 9—297 10—298
1—40 2—43 3—102 4—114 5—132 6—251 7—251 8—266 9—275 10—282

ANALYSIS OF BOWLING

Name	1st Innings						2nd Innings					
	O.	M.	R.	W.	Wd.	N-b	O.	M.	R.	W.	Wd.	N-b
Khan	18.2	4	62	2	1	2	28	6	79	4	1	...
Sreesanth	22	8	67	3	3	...	16	3	62	0	...	...
Singh	17	6	58	2	2	...	16.3	3	59	5	1	...
Ganguly	9	3	24	1	...	...						
Kumble	23	2	60	2	...	...	17	3	70	1	...	...
Tendulkar	2	0	8	0	...	...	1	0	2	0	...	...

INDIA

		First Innings		Second Innings	
1	K. D. Karthik (Tamil Nadu)	lbw b Sidebottom	5	c Coll'wood b Anderson	60
2	W. Jaffer (Mumbai)	c and b Tremlett	58	c Pietersen b Anderson	8
†3	R. Dravid (Karnataka)	c Prior b Anderson	2	lbw b Tremlett	9
4	S. R. Tendulkar (Mumbai)	lbw b Anderson	37	lbw b Panesar	16
5	S. C. Ganguly (Bengal)	b Anderson	34	lbw b Sidebottom	40
6	R. P. Singh (Uttar Pradesh)	c Anderson b Sidebottom	17	b Panesar	2
7	V. V. S. Laxman (Hyderabad)	c Prior b Sidebottom	15	b Tremlett	39
*8	M. S. Dhoni (Jharkhand)	c Bell b Anderson	0	not out	76
9	A. Kumble (Karnataka)	lbw b Sidebottom	11	lbw b Sidebottom	3
10	Z. Khan (Baroda)	c Strauss b Anderson	7	c Prior b Tremlett	0
11	S. Sreesanth (Kerala)	not out	0	not out	4
		b 4, l-b 7, w , n-b 4, p	15	b13, l-b 5, w 6, n-b 1, p	25
		Total (77.2 overs)	201	Total (96 overs)	282

FALL OF THE WICKETS
1—18 2—27 3—106 4—134 5—155 6—173 7—175 8—192 9—197 10—201
1—38 2—55 3—84 4—143 5—145 6—231 7—247 8—254 9—263 10—

ANALYSIS OF BOWLING

Name	1st Innings						2nd Innings					
	O.	M.	R.	W.	Wd.	N-b	O.	M.	R.	W.	Wd.	N-b
Sidebottom	22	5	65	4	...	...	19	4	42	2	...	...
Anderson	24.2	8	42	5	...	...	25	4	83	2	2	...
Tremlett	20	8	52	1	...	4	21	5	52	3	...	1
Collingwood	3	1	9	0	...	...	1	0	6	0	...	...
Panesar	8	3	22	0	...	...	26	7	63	2	...	...
Vaughan							4	0	18	0	...	...

Umpires—S. A. Bucknor & S. J. A. Taufel (3rd Umpire—I. J. Gould; 4th Umpire—N. G. Cowley)
Match Referee—R. S. Madugalle   Scorers—D. Kendix & C.A. Booth

†Captain   *Wicket-keeper
Play begins at 11.00 each day
Tea Interval 3.40—4.00 (may be varied according to state of game)   Luncheon Interval 1.00—1.40
Stumps drawn at 6.00 on the 1st, 2nd, 3rd and 4th days, or after 90 overs have been bowled save that play cannot continue after 6.30 except for the purpose of making up time lost due to bad weather. The Umpires may agree to play a further 30 minutes of extra time at the end of any of the first four days if a definite result can be obtained.
Any alteration to the hours of play will be announced over the public address system.
Stumps drawn on the fifth day at 6.00 or after 90 overs have been bowled, save that at 5.00, or after 75 overs have been bowled on that day, the last hour – during which a minimum of 15 overs shall be bowled, but otherwise Laws of Cricket 16.6, 16.7 and 16.8 shall apply – will commence. If there is no prospect of a definite result, play may cease when a minimum of 15 overs remain to be bowled.

England won the toss
Match abandoned as a draw

2008: England v New Zealand

(1st Test) May 15, 16, 17, 18, 19
Match Drawn

Mid-May is a dangerous time to play Test matches in England. The weather, which had been delightful in the days preceding the Test, turned damp and unpleasant, although the New Zealanders would be the one touring team who would have been used to such conditions, as anybody who has seen Test cricket in Dunedin would affirm. However, the combination of rain and bad light so restricted the amount of play possible over the five days that a draw was the only likely outcome from around the middle of the second day.

New Zealand's first innings revolved around an innings – one might almost say an assault – by McCullum, who made 97, including thirteen fours and two sixes, but apart from 48 by the captain, Vettori, one of Test cricket's more effective number eights, nobody got going, and the innings folded under pressure from Sidebottom's left arm and reassuringly straight bowling.

The England innings was a stop and start affair as the umpires offered the light five times to the batsmen on the second day, and five times the batsmen accepted the offer. By close of play, England had only reached 68 without loss, and the third day was even more badly affected by the elements, this time the rain which barely let up all afternoon. So it was not until the fourth day, the Sunday, that England were able to complete their first innings, in which Vaughan made his usual Lord's century. He and the openers, Cook and Strauss, made 230 of the 296 runs that came off the bat, the rest of the side being unable to cope with some high class left arm spin from Vettori.

As the final day began, New Zealand were on 40 for no wicket, just two runs short of clearing their deficit on first innings, but all prospects of a definite result had long been washed away. England talked up their chances in overnight press conferences, but they would need to run through the New Zealand batting order far more quickly than they had managed in the first innings, and then still find time to score the necessary runs.

England applied all the pressure they could, and when How was caught by Cook off Broad for a

England's captain Michael Vaughan on the way to another century at Lord's.

MARYLEBONE CRICKET CLUB
LORD'S GROUND
ENGLAND v. NEW ZEALAND

THURSDAY, FRIDAY, SATURDAY, SUNDAY & MONDAY, MAY 15, 16, 17, 18 & 19, 2008
(5-day Match)

NEW ZEALAND

			First Innings		Second Innings	
1	J. M. How	(Central Districts)	c Ambrose b Anderson		c Cook b Broad	68
2	A. J. Redmond	(Otago)	c Cook b Anderson	7	c Strauss b Anderson	17
3	J. A. H. Marshall	(Northern Districts)	c Strauss b Broad	0	lbw b Sidebottom	0
4	L. R. P. L. Taylor	(Central Districts)	c Collingwood b Broad	24	lbw b Panesar	20
*5	B. B. McCullum	(Otago)	b Panesar	19	c Ambrose b Anderson	24
6	D. R. Flynn	(Northern Districts)	b Anderson	97	not out	29
7	J. D. P. Oram	(Central Districts)	c Strauss b Sidebottom	9	b Sidebottom	101
†8	D. L. Vettori	(Northern Districts)	b Sidebottom	28	not out	0
9	K. D. Mills	(Auckland)	b Sidebottom	48		
10	T. G. Southee	(Northern Districts)	b Sidebottom	10		
11	C. S. Martin	(Auckland)	not out	1		
				0		
			b16, l-b14, w 1, n-b 3, p ,	34	b 4, l-b 5, w , n-b 1, p ,	10
			Total ....(86.2 overs)	277	Total (6 wkts, 86.2 overs)	269

FALL OF THE WICKETS

1—2	2—18	3—41	4—76	5—104	6—203	7—222	8—258	9—260	10—277
1—47	2—52	3—99	4—115	5—252	6—269	7—	8—	9—	10—

ANALYSIS OF BOWLING

Name	1st Innings						2nd Innings					
	O.	M.	R.	W.	Wd.	N-b	O.	M.	R.	W.	Wd.	N-b
Sidebottom	28.2	12	55	4	...	...	21.2	4	65	2	...	...
Anderson	20	5	66	3	1	1	19	5	64	2	...	...
Broad	24	4	85	2	...	2	17	4	54	1	...	1
Collingwood	3	1	11	0	...	...	...	...	...	...	...	...
Panesar	11	2	30	1	...	...	24	8	56	1	...	...
Pietersen	...	...	...	...	...	...	5	0	21	0	...	...

ENGLAND

			First Innings		Second Innings	
1	A. J. Strauss	(Middlesex)	lbw b Oram	63		
2	A. N. Cook	(Essex)	c McCullum b Martin	61		
†3	M. P. Vaughan	(Yorkshire)	c Marshall b Vettori	106		
4	K. P. Pietersen	(Hampshire)	lbw b Vettori	3		
5	I. R. Bell	(Warwickshire)	c McCullum b Martin	16		
6	P. D. Collingwood	(Durham)	c Taylor b Vettori	6		
*7	T. R. Ambrose	(Warwickshire)	lbw b Vettori	0		
8	S. C. J. Broad	(Nottinghamshire)	b Oram	25		
9	R. J. Sidebottom	(Nottinghamshire)	c Taylor b Mills	16		
10	M. S. Panesar	(Northamptonshire)	c Flynn b Vettori	0		
11	J. M. Anderson	(Lancashire)	not out	0		
			b 3, l-b 7, w 1, n-b 12, p ,	23	b , l-b , w , n-b , p ,	
			Total ....(111.3 overs)	319	Total	

FALL OF THE WICKETS

1—121	2—148	3—152	4—180	5—208	6—208	7—269	8—317	9—318	10—319
1—	2—	3—	4—	5—	6—	7—	8—	9—	10—

ANALYSIS OF BOWLING

Name	1st Innings						2nd Innings					
	O.	M.	R.	W.	Wd.	N-b	O.	M.	R.	W.	Wd.	N-b
Martin	32	8	76	2	...	6	...	...	...	...	...	...
Mills	22	3	60	1	...	6	...	...	...	...	...	...
Southee	16	2	59	0	...	...	...	...	...	...	...	...
Oram	19	5	45	2	1	...	...	...	...	...	...	...
Vettori	22.3	4	69	5	...	...	...	...	...	...	...	...

Umpires—S. J. A. Taufel & S. A. Bucknor (3rd Umpire—N. J. Llong; 4th Umpire—J.W. Lloyds)
Match Referee—R. S. Madugalle   Scorers—D. Kendix & J. M. Brown

†Captain   *Wicket-keeper
Play begins at 11.00 each day
Tea Interval 3.40—4.00 (may be varied according to state of game)   Luncheon Interval 1.00—1.40
Stumps drawn at 6.00 on the 1st, 2nd, 3rd and 4th days, or after 90 overs have been bowled save that play cannot continue after 6.30 except for the purpose of making up time lost due to bad weather. The Umpires may agree to play a further 30 minutes of extra time at the end of any of the first four days if a definite result can be obtained.
Any alteration to the hours of play will be announced over the public address system.
Stumps drawn on the fifth day at 6.00 or after 90 overs have been bowled, save that at 5.00, or after 75 overs have been bowled on that day, the last hour – during which a minimum of 15 overs shall be bowled, but otherwise Laws of Cricket 16.6, 16.7 and 16.8 shall apply – will commence. If there is no prospect of a definite result, play may cease when a minimum of 15 overs remain to be bowled.

England won the toss and elected to field
Match drawn

---

patient 68, New Zealand were wobbling at 115 for four, a lead of just 73 runs. Five runs later, McCullum, the first innings hero, though not necessarily a man in the Trevor Bailey mould which they now required, had to retire hurt after being hit on the elbow by Broad, and had Oram or Flynn then failed, England's chances would have risen from a glimmer to a flicker.

But they stayed together. Oram in particular played a muscular hand, scoring 101 out of the 132 the pair added together, hitting fifteen fours and two sixes, and bringing New Zealand safely out of danger. When he was out, bowled by Sidebottom for 101, it only remained for Vettori to walk out to bat, and very quickly agree to shake hands with Vaughan on the draw.

2008: England v South Africa

(1st Test) July 10, 11, 12, 13, 14
Match Drawn

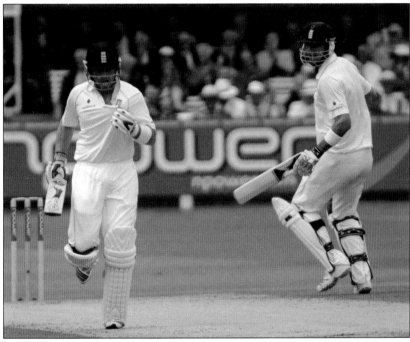

Ian Bell and Kevin Pietersen in their record fourth wicket partnership for England.

The sixth consecutive drawn Lord's Test was not a rain-affected bore draw. It contained 1,233 runs, six centuries and only 21 wickets on a track that was as helpful to batsmen as Mick Hunt, the groundsman, can ever have served up. Not that Graeme Smith noticed that when it came to the toss. He won it, and promptly put England in to bat. By the time the hosts had piled up 593 for eight declared, Smith was unlikely to have been consoled by the knowledge that Vaughan would have asked South Africa to bat if he had won the toss.

For this match, England fielded the same eleven for the sixth match in a row, a feat of selectorial consistency unequalled in the annals of English Test cricket. England's innings revolved around

three stands: 114 for the first wicket between Strauss and Cook, 152 for the seventh wicket between Bell and Broad, and 286 for the fourth wicket between Pietersen and Bell. This partnership was the sixth highest of all time in Lord's Tests, and the highest ever for the fourth wicket. The first wicket partnership was only broken by an appalling lbw decision against Strauss, but as England had declined to use the infant and still mistrusted referral system, they had only themselves to blame. The other five partnerships produced only 41 runs between them.

Bell's innings of 199 was his highest in Tests to date, and he became the first Englishman ever to be dismissed on that score in a Test. Until his final

LORD'S GROUND

ENGLAND v. SOUTH AFRICA

THURSDAY, FRIDAY, SATURDAY, SUNDAY & MONDAY, JULY 10, 11, 12, 13 & 14, 2008
(5-day Match)

ENGLAND

			First Innings		Second Innings
1	A. J. Strauss	(Middlesex)	lbw b Morkel	44	
2	A. N. Cook	(Essex)	c de Villiers b Morkel	60	
†3	M. P. Vaughan	(Yorkshire)	b Steyn	2	
4	K. P. Pietersen	(Hampshire)	c Boucher b Morkel	152	
5	I. R. Bell	(Warwickshire)	c and b Harris	199	
6	P. D. Collingwood	(Durham)	c Amla b Harris	7	
*7	T. R. Ambrose	(Warwickshire)	c Smith b Morkel	4	
8	S. C. J. Broad	(Nottinghamshire)	b Harris	76	
9	R. J. Sidebottom	(Nottinghamshire)	not out	1	
10	M. S. Panesar	(Northamptonshire)			
11	J. M. Anderson	(Lancashire)			
			b14, l-b12, w 7, n-b15, p	48	b , l-b , w , n-b , p
			Total (8 wkts, dec)	593	Total

FALL OF THE WICKETS

1—114 2—117 3—117 4—403 5—413 6—422 7—574 8—593 9— 10—
1— 2— 3— 4— 5— 6— 7— 8— 9— 10—

ANALYSIS OF BOWLING

Name	1st Innings						2nd Innings					
	O.	M.	R.	W.	Wd.	N-b	O.	M.	R.	W.	Wd.	N-b
Steyn	35	8	117	1	2	2	...	...	...	...	...	...
Ntini	29	2	130	0			...	...	...	...	...	...
Morkel	34	3	121	4		5	...	...	...	...	...	...
Kallis	20	3	70	0	1		...	...	...	...	...	...
Harris	38.2	8	129	3		4	...	...	...	...	...	...
	...											

SOUTH AFRICA

			First Innings		Second Innings	
†1	G. C. Smith	(Western Province)	c Bell b Anderson	8	c Pietersen b Anderson	107
2	N. D. McKenzie	(Gauteng)	b Panesar	40	c Ambrose b Anderson	138
3	H. M. Amla	(Natal)	c Ambrose b Broad	6	not out	104
4	J. H. Kallis	(Western Province)	c Strauss b Sidebottom	7	b Sidebottom	13
5	A. G. Prince	(Western Province)	c Ambrose b Sidebottom	101	not out	9
6	A. B. de Villiers	(Northerns)	c Anderson b Panesar	42		
*7	M. V. Boucher	(Border)	b Broad	4		
8	M. Morkel	(Northerns)	b Panesar	6		
9	P. L. Harris	(Northerns)	c Anderson b Panesar	6		
10	D. W. Steyn	(Northerns)	c Sidebottom b Pietersen	19		
11	M. Ntini	(Border)	not out	0		
			b 1, l-b 4, w 3, n-b , p	8	b 8, l-b 8, w 5, n-b 1, p	22
			Total (93.3 overs)	247	Total (3 wkts, dec)	393

FALL OF THE WICKETS

1—13 2—28 3—47 4—83 5—161 6—166 7—191 8—203 9—245 10—247
1—204 2—329 3—357 4— 5— 6— 7— 8— 9— 10—

ANALYSIS OF BOWLING

Name	1st Innings						2nd Innings					
	O.	M.	R.	W.	Wd.	N-b	O.	M.	R.	W.	Wd.	N-b
Sidebottom	19	3	41	2	...	...	30	9	46	1	...	1
Anderson	21	7	36	1	1	...	32	7	78	2	3	...
Broad	23	3	88	2	2	...	26	7	78	0	2	...
Panesar	26	4	74	4	...	...	60	15	116	0	...	...
Collingwood	4	1	3	0	...	...	11	4	37	0	...	...
Pietersen	0.3	0	0	1	...	...	7	1	21	0	...	...
Cook					...	...	1	0	1	0		

Umpires—D. J. Harper & B. F. Bowden (3rd Umpire—N. J. Llong; 4th Umpire—R. T. Robinson)
Match Referee—J. J. Crowe   Scorers—D. Kendix & B. L. Rodwell

†Captain   *Wicket-keeper
Play begins at 11.00 each day   Luncheon Interval 1.00—1.40
Tea Interval 3.40—4.00 (may be varied according to state of game)
Stumps drawn at 6.00 on the 1st, 2nd, 3rd and 4th days, or after 90 overs have been bowled save that play cannot continue after 6.30 except for the purpose of making up time lost due to bad weather. The Umpires may agree to play a further 30 minutes of extra time at the end of any of the first four days if a definite result can be obtained.
Any alteration to the hours of play will be announced over the public address system.
Stumps drawn on the fifth day at 6.00 or after 90 overs have been bowled, save that at 5.00, or after 75 overs have been bowled on that day, the last hour – during which a minimum of 15 overs shall be bowled, but otherwise Laws of Cricket 16.6, 16.7 and 16.8 shall apply – will commence. If there is no prospect of a definite result, play may cease when a minimum of 15 overs remain to be bowled.

South Africa won the toss and elected to field

Match drawn

---

stroke which gave Harris a very smart caught and bowled, Bell had played superbly, showing the talent that everybody knew he had but which he displayed all too rarely in the early part of his Test career. When Bell was out, Vaughan declared and gave South Africa three overs to negotiate before the end of the rain affected day. On the next day, England ran through the South African batsmen, with the honourable exception of Ashwell Prince, and secured a first innings lead of 346. With two days' play to go and the follow-on enforced, it looked as though an England victory was in the bag, but we had not reckoned with the South Africans' fighting spirit, and the flatness of this Lord's wicket.

England began their task in bad light at the end of the third day, which meant that Vaughan gave the new ball to Panesar and Pietersen – a ploy that did not work. The next day, even with Sidebottom, Anderson and Broad in harness. South Africa knuckled down and Smith and McKenzie put on 204 for the first wicket. This broke yet another record – the highest opening stand in Test history by a team following on. When Anderson finally prised out Smith, all that did was to let in Amla who carried on the good work. He and McKenzie added a further 125, with Amla becoming the sixth centurion of the match. McKenzie's innings lasted for 447 balls, while Panesar bowled 360 balls in the innings, for no wickets but an economy rate of under two per over. It was attritional stuff, and not the sort of cricket to bring in the crowds. However, it was South Africa who came away from Lord's in the happier frame of mind.

2009: England v West Indies

(1st Test) May 6, 7, 8
England won by ten wickets

For the first time – apart from the 1970 Rest of the World 'Test' – a Test match at Lord's started on a Wednesday. The hope that this would set up an exciting weekend for the final two days' play was dashed when England strolled to victory within three days and Lord's was left empty at the weekend. Mind you, it had hardly been more than half full on any of the first three days: a far cry from the days when the West Indies playing at Lord's meant queues round the block. There was a suspicion that some of the visiting team had their minds elsewhere – their captain Chris Gayle had only arrived from the money-spinning IPL in South Africa two days before the start of the match – but

Ravi Bopara's innings of 143 paved the way for England's victory.

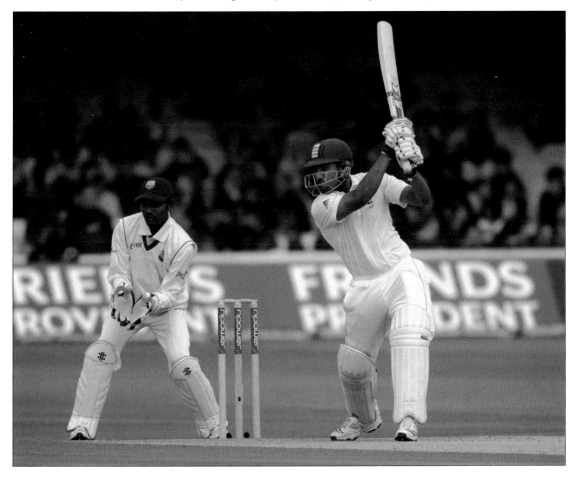

LORD'S GROUND

£1   £1

ENGLAND v. WEST INDIES

WEDNESDAY, THURSDAY, FRIDAY, SATURDAY & SUNDAY, MAY 6, 7, 8, 9, 10, 2009
(5-day Match)

ENGLAND

No	Batsman	County	First Innings	Runs	Second Innings	Runs
†1	A. J. Strauss	(Middlesex)	c Ramdin b Taylor	16	not out	14
2	A. N. Cook	(Essex)	b Edwards	35	not out	14
3	R. Bopara	(Essex)	c Nash b Taylor	143		
4	K. P. Pietersen	(Hampshire)	c Ramdin b Edwards	0		
5	P. D. Collingwood	(Durham)	c Smith b Edwards	8		
*6	M. J. Prior	(Sussex)	c Simmons b Edwards	42		
7	S. C. J. Broad	(Nottinghamshire)	c Taylor b Benn	38		
8	T. T. Bresnan	(Yorkshire)	lbw b Benn	9		
9	G. P. Swann	(Nottinghamshire)	not out	63		
10	J. M. Anderson	(Lancashire)	c Ramdin b Edwards	1		
11	G. Onions	(Durham)	b Edwards	0		
			b 1, l-b 5, w 7, n-b 9, p ,	22	b , l-b , w , n-b 4, p ,	4
			Total (111.3 overs)	377	Total (6.1 overs)	32

FALL OF THE WICKETS

1—28 2—92 3—92 4—109 5—193 6—262 7—275 8—368 9—377 10—377
1— 2— 3— 4— 5— 6— 7— 8— 9— 10—

ANALYSIS OF BOWLING

Name	1st Innings O.	M.	R.	W.	Wd.	N-b	2nd Innings O.	M.	R.	W.	Wd.	N-b
Taylor	24	2	83	2	1	2	3	0	20	0	...	1
Edwards	26.3	4	92	6	1	7	3.1	0	12	0	...	3
Baker	24	5	75	0	2	...						
Benn	27	4	84	2	...	...						
Nash	2	1	2	0	...	...						
Simmons	5	1	24	0	3	...						
Gayle	3	0	11	0	...	...						

WEST INDIES

No	Batsman	Origin	First Innings	Runs	Second Innings	Runs
†1	C. H. Gayle	(Jamaica)	b Broad	28	c Swann b Anderson	0
2	D. S. Smith	(Grenada)	b Swann	46	b Onions	41
3	R. R. Sarwan	(Guyana)	c Prior b Broad	13	b Anderson	1
4	L. M. P. Simmons	(Trinidad)	c Strauss b Onions	16	c Cook b Onions	21
5	S. Chanderpaul	(Guyana)	c Collingwood b Swann	0	c Bopara b Swann	4
6	B. P. Nash	(Jamaica)	c Collingwood b Swann	4	c Cook b Broad	81
*7	D. Ramdin	(Trinidad)	lbw b Onions	0	b Broad	61
8	J. E. Taylor	(Jamaica)	c Prior b Onions	2	lbw b Swann	15
9	S. J. Benn	(Barbados)	c Swann b Onions	10	b Swann	0
10	F. H. Edwards	(Barbados)	not out	17	c Bresnan b Broad	2
11	L. S. Baker	(Leeward Islands)	lbw b Onions	11	not out	2
			b , l-b 10, w 1, n-b , p ,	11	b 8, l-b 18, w 2, n-b , p ,	28
			Total (32.3 overs)	152	Total (72.2 overs)	256

FALL OF THE WICKETS

1—46 2—70 3—99 4—99 5—117 6—117 7—117 8—119 9—128 10—152
1—14 2—22 3—70 4—75 5—79 6—222 7—243 8—246 9—249 10—256

ANALYSIS OF BOWLING

Name	1st Innings O.	M.	R.	W.	Wd.	N-b	2nd Innings O.	M.	R.	W.	Wd.	N-b
Broad	11	0	56	2	...	...	19.2	2	64	3	1	...
Swann	5	2	16	3	...	...	15	4	39	3	...	...
Anderson	7	0	32	0	1	...	15	6	38	2	...	...
Onions	9.3	1	38	5	...	...	12	2	64	2	1	...
Bresnan	...	...	...	...	...	...	7	3	17	0	...	...
Bopara	...	...	...	...	...	...	2	0	8	0	...	...

Umpires—E. A. R. De Silva & S. J. Davis (3rd Umpire—I. J. Gould; 4th Umpire—N. A. Mallender)
Match Referee—A. J. Pycroft   Scorers—D. Kendix & A. E. Choat

†Captain   *Wicket-keeper

West Indies won the toss and elected to field

England won by 10 wickets

England, under the new management of Andy Flower and captain Andrew Strauss, were in no mood to let their opponents get used to the conditions. The cold wind that blew over Lord's for much of the time did not help the visitors one bit.

England's victory was due largely to the batting of Ravi Bopara, who scored his second successive century against West Indies, and would go on to score a third in the next (even colder) Test match at Chester-le-Street. The two Grahams, Swann and Onions (which sounds like the menu for a medieval banquet) were the bowling heroes for England, Onions getting himself on the honours board with five for 38 in the first innings. Man of the Match Swann, who opened the bowling with Broad in the first innings, took six wickets for only 55 runs in the match, and also scored 63 not out, his highest Test score thus far, as he flayed the ball around at the end of England's first innings.

The West Indian first innings collapsed from 99 for two to 152 all out in 32.3 overs, and they only reached the 150 thanks to a last wicket stand of 24 between Edwards and Baker. Batting at almost five an over, but still not totalling much more than 150 smacks of a side made up of one-day specialists, and not very good ones at that, and it certainly appeared that none of the West Indians were in Test match mood. Their second innings was better, thanks mainly to a stand of 143 for the sixth wicket between West Indies' Australian born all-rounder Brendan Nash (81) and Dinesh Ramdin (61), but the batting above and below them in the order was fairly feeble.

This Test marked the debut of Tim Bresnan, who did very little in the game, but went on to become

Graham Onions wrecked the visitors' first innings taking five wickets for 38 runs.

something of a talisman for England, being on the winning side in every one of his first thirteen Tests. Only Australia's Adam Gilchrist, who was on the winning side in each of his first fifteen Tests, enjoyed a more successful start to his Test career than Bresnan.

2009: England v Australia

(2nd Test) July 16, 17, 18, 19, 20
England won by 115 runs

Seventy five years after England last won a Test match against Australia at Lord's, Andrew Strauss and his team finally broke the headquarters hoodoo to win a very one-sided match and put themselves one up in the series.

The England team were unrecognizable from the eleven who had so nearly been crushed at Cardiff. Only one change in the side, maybe, but a change in attitude so complete that after the first session of the first day, England looked on top, and they stayed there. Flintoff, who before the match announced his retirement from Test cricket at the end of the summer, bowled like a man possessed to pocket the Man of the Match award for his five wickets in the Australian second innings, a performance which put him among the select few to appear on both the batting and bowling honours boards, but in many ways the match turned on the opening partnership between Andrew Strauss and Alastair Cook, who put on 196 together. Although the next highest partnership of the innings was the 47 added by Anderson and Onions for the last wicket, England's total of 425 set an imposing target, made all the more difficult by the quality of England's attack, led by James Anderson (four for 55). The light was poor, too, which did not help batting, and on the second morning the new floodlights were used for the first time in a Test. Australia could only manage 215, again thanks to a late order flurry as Hauritz, Siddle and Hilfenhaus added 63 for the last two wickets.

The use of electronic aids by the third umpire did not eliminate controversy: Ponting, a man who should by now have been used to unlucky dismissals in England, was apparently caught at slip off Anderson, but the on field umpires asked third umpire Nigel Llong for confirmation that the catch was good. It was, so Ponting had to go. The

Andrew Flintoff took five wickets in Australia's second innings to secure England's win.

ENGLAND

			First Innings		Second Innings	
†1	A. J. Strauss	(Middlesex)	b Hilfenhaus	161	c Clarke b Hauritz	32
2	A. N. Cook	(Essex)	lbw b Johnson	95	lbw b Hauritz	32
3	R. S. Bopara	(Essex)	lbw b Hilfenhaus	18	c Katich b Hauritz	27
4	K. P. Pietersen	(Hampshire)	c Haddin b Siddle	32	c Haddin b Siddle	44
5	P. D. Collingwood	(Durham)	c Siddle b Clarke	16	c Haddin b Siddle	54
*6	M. J. Prior	(Sussex)	b Johnson	8	run out	61
7	A. Flintoff	(Lancashire)	c Ponting b Hilfenhaus	4	not out	30
8	S. C. J. Broad	(Nottinghamshire)	b Hilfenhaus	16	not out	0
9	G. P. Swann	(Nottinghamshire)	c Ponting b Siddle	4		
10	J. M. Anderson	(Lancashire)	c Hussey b Johnson	29		
11	G. Onions	(Durham)	not out	17		
			b15, l-b 2, w , n-b 8, p ,	25	b16, l-b 9, w 1, n-b 5, p ,	31
			Total ....(101.4 overs)	425	Total ....(6 wkts, dec)	311

FALL OF THE WICKETS

1—196 2—222 3—267 4—302 5—317 6—333 7—364 8—370 9—378 10—425
1—61   2—74   3—147 4—174 5—260 6—311 7—   8—   9—   10—

ANALYSIS OF BOWLING

Name		1st Innings								2nd Innings				
	O.	M.	R.	W.	Wd.	N-b			O.	M.	R.	W.	Wd.	N-b
Hilfenhaus	31	12	103	4	...				19	5	59	0	...	3
Johnson	21.4	2	132	3	...	4			17	2	68	0	1	1
Siddle	20	1	76	2	...	4			15.2	4	64	2	...	
Hauritz	8.3	1	26	0	...				16	1	80	3	...	1
North	16.3	2	59	0	...				...	...	...	...	...	...
Clarke	4	1	12	1	...				4	0	15	0	...	

AUSTRALIA

			First Innings		Second Innings	
1	P. J. Hughes	(New South Wales)	c Prior b Anderson	4	c Strauss b Flintoff	17
2	S. M. Katich	(New South Wales)	c Broad b Onions	48	c Pietersen b Flintoff	6
†3	R. T. Ponting	(Tasmania)	c Strauss b Anderson	2	b Broad	38
4	M. E. K. Hussey	(Western Australia)	b Flintoff	51	c Collingwood b Swann	27
5	M. J. Clarke	(New South Wales)	c Cook b Anderson	1	b Swann	136
6	M. J. North	(Western Australia)	b Anderson	0	b Swann	6
*7	B. J. Haddin	(New South Wales)	c Cook b Broad	28	c Collingwood b Flintoff	80
8	M. G. Johnson	(Queensland)	c Cook b Broad	24	b Swann	63
9	N. M. Hauritz	(New South Wales)	c Collingwood b Onions	35	b Flintoff	1
10	P. M. Siddle	(Victoria)	c Strauss b Onions	6	b Flintoff	7
11	B. W. Hilfenhaus	(Tasmania)	not out	12	not out	4
			b 4, l-b 6, w , n-b 2, p ,		b 5, l-b 8, w , n-b 8, p ,	21
			Total ....(63 overs)	215	Total ....(107 overs)	406

FALL OF THE WICKETS

1—4   2—10   3—103 4—111 5—111 6—139 7—148 8—152 9—196 10—215
1—17 2—34   3—78   4—120 5—128 6—313 7—356 8—363 9—388 10—406

ANALYSIS OF BOWLING

Name		1st Innings								2nd Innings				
	O.	M.	R.	W.	Wd.	N-b			O.	M.	R.	W.	Wd.	N-b
Anderson	21	5	55	4	...				21	4	86	0	...	
Flintoff	12	4	27	1	...	2			27	4	92	5	...	8
Broad	18	1	78	2	...				16	3	49	1	...	
Onions	11	1	41	3	...				9	0	50	0	...	
Swann	1	0	4	0	...				28	3	87	4	...	
Collingwood	...	...	...	...	...				6	1	29	0	...	

Umpires—R. E. Koertzen & B. R. Doctrove (3rd Umpire—N. J. Llong; 4th Umpire—R. J. Bailey)

Match Referee—J. J. Crowe   Scorers—D. Kendix & M. A. Fowler

†Captain   *Wicket-keeper

Play begins at 11.00 each day   Luncheon Interval 1.00—1.40
Tea Interval 3.40—4.00 (may be varied according to state of game)
Stumps drawn at 6.00 on the 1st, 2nd, 3rd and 4th days, or after 90 overs have been bowled save that play cannot continue after 6.30 except for the purpose of making up time lost due to bad weather. The Umpires may agree to play a further 30 minutes of extra time at the end of any of the first four days if a definite result can be obtained. Any alteration to the hours of play will be announced over the public address system.
Stumps drawn on the fifth day at 6.00 or after 90 overs have been bowled, save that at 5.00, or after 75 overs have been bowled on that day, the last hour – during which a minimum of 15 overs shall be bowled, but otherwise Laws of Cricket 16.6, 16.7 and 16.8 shall apply – will commence. If there is no prospect of a definite result, play may cease when a minimum of 15 overs remain to be bowled.

England won the toss

England won by 115 runs

question that should have been asked – did he hit it? – would have elicited the answer "No", so he could not have been caught. But if he did not hit it, then Ponting was clearly lbw, so justice was largely served.

England did not enforce the follow-on, but their efforts to build an unbeatable lead were hesitant until Collingwood arrived at the crease. He, with Prior batting more like Gilchrist than an English keeper, put on 86 and when Collingwood fell, Flintoff and Prior carried on the mayhem to such an extent that between tea and close on the third day, England added 181 in 31 overs – virtually a run a ball. England's declaration left Australia with 522 to win and two days to make the runs.

England made an excellent start, reducing Australia to 128 for five, but a remarkable partnership between Clarke and Haddin brought Australia to 313 for five at the close of the fourth day, needing 209 more to win, with five wickets in hand. But Flintoff, bowling at over 90 mph, trapped Haddin before Australia had added to their overnight score, and the game was up. Flintoff bowled unchanged from the Pavilion End until just before lunch, when Swann bowled Johnson with a quicker arm ball, and the celebrations began.

2010: England v Bangladesh

(1st Test) May 27, 28, 29, 30, 31
England won by eight wickets

England would expect to beat Bangladesh at Lord's. This is not just arrogance, but a statement of simple logic: England have been playing Tests at Lord's for a century and a quarter, while Bangladesh were making only their second visit to the ground. For many of the side, it was their first experience of English conditions. England should have coasted home. But it was less than two weeks after England's World Twenty20 victory in the West Indies, and several of the players on both sides seemed to have difficulty in adapting to the different demands of Test cricket. They either played far too slowly and defensively, or with reckless ebullience, as if they had forgotten the range of gears that need to be used in Test cricket.

England did win – eight wickets is a comfortable margin – but when they had piled up a score of 505, built around Jonathan Trott's massive 226, most of their supporters might have anticipated an overwhelming innings victory. They did not expect still to be waiting for the win at tea on the final day.

Bangladesh did not have a bowling attack that was really of Test class, even though Shahadat Hossain got his name onto the honours board with five for 98 in the first innings, so England's batsmen had the chance to make hay. Only Andrew Strauss (83) and Trott (226) really tucked into the attack, although Eoin Morgan, on his debut, made 44 with style and confidence. After a somewhat docile performance in the field from the visitors,

Spectators taking a keen interest in the wicket at Lord's.

nobody expected much better from their batting. However, the Bangladesh team exceeded all expectations, especially the top four in the batting order, led by the dashing Tamim Iqbal. In the first innings, Bangladesh made only 282 (Iqbal 55), and were asked to follow on 223 behind. Even with the uncertain weather which took roughly two sessions off the Test, an innings victory should have been a formality for the home side.

England's attack was theoretically weakened by the absence of the injured Stuart Broad, which gave Steven Finn a chance to show his worth on his home ground. He made the most of the opportunity and took nine wickets and the Man of the Match Award, but he conceded 187 runs in 49 overs in the process. Indeed, England's four-man attack (plus Trott for six overs) was severely stretched by the end. Tamim Iqbal's second innings century, which allowed Bangladesh to avoid the innings defeat with plenty to spare, took him only 94 balls, and his opening partnership with Imrul Kayes of 185 was a new Bangladesh Test record. It was an astonishing display, and when he left, the good work was carried on by Junaid Siddique and Jahurul Islam. At the end of the fourth day, Bangladesh were on 328 for five, over 100 ahead with five wickets in hand and a draw was a distinct possibility. But it was all too good to last. Finn and Bresnan cleaned up the next morning, and England's batsmen chased down the target at a rate of more than four an over.

MARYLEBONE CRICKET CLUB
LORD'S GROUND
ENGLAND v. BANGLADESH
THURSDAY, FRIDAY, SATURDAY, SUNDAY & MONDAY MAY 27, 28, 29, 30 & 31, 2010
(5-day Match)

£1   £1

ENGLAND		First Innings		Second Innings	
†1 A. J. Strauss	(Middlesex)	b Mahmudullah	83	c Mushfiqur b Shakib	82
2 A. N. Cook	(Essex)	lbw b Shahadat	7	lbw b Mahmudullah	23
3 I. J. L. Trott	(Warwickshire)	c Kayes b Shahadat	226	not out	36
4 K. P. Pietersen	(Hampshire)	b Shakib	18	not out	10
5 I. R. Bell	(Warwickshire)	b Rubel	17		
6 E. J. G. Morgan	(Middlesex)	c Mushfiqur b Shahadat	44		
*7 M. J. Prior	(Sussex)	run out	16		
8 T. T. Bresnan	(Yorkshire)	c Siddique b Shahadat	25		
9 G. P. Swann	(Nottinghamshire)	c Rubel b Shakib	22		
10 J. M. Anderson	(Lancashire)	b Shahadat	13		
11 S. T. Finn	(Middlesex)	not out	3		
		b , l-b10, w 8, n-b13, p ,	31	b , l-b 5, w 1, n-b 6, p ,	12
		Total ....(125 overs)	505	Total ....(35.1 overs)	163

FALL OF THE WICKETS

1—7　2—188　3—227　4—258　5—370　6—400　7—463　8—478　9—498　10—505
1—67　2—147　3—　4—　5—　6—　7—　8—　9—　10—

ANALYSIS OF BOWLING		1st Innings					2nd Innings				
Name	O.	M.	R.	W.	Wd.	N-b	O.	M.	R.	W.	Wd.	N-b
Shahadat	28	3	98	5	1	2	2	0	19	0	1	4
Robiul	22	2	107	0	...	4	1	0	12	0	...	1
Shakib	27	3	109	2	...	...	16	1	48	1	...	...
Rubel	23	0	109	1	7	3	1	0	8	0	...	1
Mahmudullah	23	3	59	1	...	...	15.1	1	71	1	...	...
Ashraful	2	0	13	0	...	...	...	...	...	...	...	...

BANGLADESH		First Innings		Second Innings	
1 Tamim Iqbal	(Chittagong Div.)	run out	55	c Trott b Finn	103
2 Imrul Kayes	(Khulna Div.)	c Strauss b Finn	43	c Bell b Finn	75
3 Junaid Siddique	(Rajshahi Div.)	c Prior b Finn	58	c Bresnan b Finn	74
4 Jahurul Islam	(Rajshahi Div.)	c Prior b Anderson	20	c and b Trott	46
5 Mohammad Ashraful	(Dhaka Div.)	lbw b Finn	4	c Prior b Anderson	21
†6 Shakib Al Hasan	(Khulna Div.)	c Strauss b Anderson	25	c Morgan b Finn	16
*7 Mushfiqur Rahim	(Rajshahi Div.)	b Finn	16	c Prior b Finn	19
8 Mahmudullah	(Dhaka Div.)	b Anderson	17	c Prior b Bresnan	0
9 Shahadat Hossain	(Dhaka Div.)	b Anderson	20	b Bresnan	4
10 Rubel Hossain	(Chittagong Div.)	c Cook b Bresnan	9	c Strauss b Bresnan	0
11 Robiul Islam	(Khulna Div.)	not out	9	not out	0
		b , l-b 2, w 3, n-b 1, p ,	6	b 7, l-b14, w 2, n-b , p ,	24
		Total ....(93 overs)	282	Total ....(110.2 overs)	382

FALL OF THE WICKETS

1—88　2—134　3—179　4—185　5—191　6—221　7—234　8—255　9—266　10—282
1—185　2—189　3—289　4—321　5—322　6—347　7—354　8—361　9—381　10—382

ANALYSIS OF BOWLING		1st Innings					2nd Innings				
Name	O.	M.	R.	W.	Wd.	N-b	O.	M.	R.	W.	Wd.	N-b
Anderson	31	6	78	4	1	...	29	8	84	1	1	...
Bresnan	24	5	76	1	2	...	26.2	9	93	3	1	...
Finn	25	5	100	4	...	1	24	6	87	5	...	...
Swann	11	6	19	0	...	...	27	5	81	0	...	...
Trott	2	0	7	0	...	...	4	0	16	1	...	...
	...	...	...	...	...	...	...	...	...	...	...	...

Umpires—B. F. Bowden & E. A. R. De Silva　(3rd Umpire—R. K. Illingworth 4th Umpire—J. W. Lloyds)
Match Referee—A. G. Hurst　Scorers—D. Kendix & N. T. Harris
†Captain　*Wicket-keeper
Play begins at 11.00 each day　Luncheon Interval 1.00—1.40
Tea Interval 3.40—4.00 (may be varied according to state of game)
Stumps drawn at 6.00 on the 1st, 2nd, 3rd and 4th days, or after 90 overs have been bowled save that play cannot continue after 6.30 except for the purpose of making up time lost due to bad weather. The Umpires may agree to play a further 30 minutes of extra time at the end of any of the first four days if a definite result can be obtained.
Any alteration to the hours of play will be announced over the public address system.
Stumps drawn on the fifth day at 6.00 or after 90 overs have been bowled, save that at 5.00, or after 75 overs have been bowled on that day, the last hour – during which a minimum of 15 overs shall be bowled, but otherwise Laws of Cricket 16.6, 16.7 and 16.8 shall apply – will commence. If there is no prospect of a definite result, play may cease when a minimum of 15 overs remain to be bowled.

Bangladesh won the toss and elected to field
England won by 8 wickets

2010: Pakistan v Australia

(1st Test) July 13, 14, 15, 16
Australia won by 150 runs

For the first time for 98 years, three Tests were played at Lord's in one season, and for the first time in 98 years, two overseas teams met for a Test on neutral ground in England. The security situation in Pakistan after the attack on the Sri Lankans in Lahore in March 2009 meant that no team's safety could be guaranteed, and Pakistan were obliged to play their Tests elsewhere. The ECB offered to let them play in England, and a series of two Tests against Australia was arranged to take place before Pakistan toured England officially in the second half of the summer. It cannot be denied that Pakistan betrayed the goodwill showed to them by the ECB, and by the end of the summer were the pariahs of Test cricket, and not just

because of the political situation back at home. The sponsorship of the series by MCC, under their 'Spirit of Cricket' banner, soon became the hollowest joke of the season.

Both teams were experimental to a degree. Australia, with the prospect of facing England at home six months later, were looking for the men who could fill the enormous gaps left by the retirements of Warne, McGrath, Hayden and Gilchrist, while Pakistan were going through one of their regular sack-and-rehire processes which meant that some top class players were left behind, while others – the captain Shahid Afridi for example – were back in the Test side after time in the wilderness.

The "Baggy Greens" celebrate the fall of another Pakistani wicket.

MARYLEBONE CRICKET CLUB

LORD'S GROUND

£1 £1

PAKISTAN v. AUSTRALIA

TUESDAY, WEDNESDAY, THURSDAY, FRIDAY & SATURDAY, JULY 13, 14, 15, 16 & 17, 2010

(5-day Match)

AUSTRALIA

			First Innings		Second Innings	
1	S. R. Watson	(New South Wales)	b Amir	4	c Farhat b Asif	31
2	S. M. Katich	(New South Wales)	c Akmal b Asif	80	c Akmal b Gul	83
†3	R. T. Ponting	(Tasmania)	c Amin b Amir	26	lbw b Asif	0
4	M. J. Clarke	(New South Wales)	lbw b Asif	47	b Gul	12
5	M. E. K. Hussey	(Western Australia)	not out	56	c Farhat b Gul	0
6	M. J. North	(Western Australia)	b Asif	0	c Akmal b Asif	20
*7	T. D. Paine	(Tasmania)	c Akmal b Gul	7	b Afridi	47
8	S. P. D. Smith	(New South Wales)	lbw b Kaneria	1	lbw b Kaneria	12
9	M. G. Johnson	(Western Australia)	b Kaneria	3	b Gul	30
10	B. W. Hilfenhaus	(Tasmania)	b Amir	1	not out	56
11	D. E. Bollinger	(New South Wales)	b Amir	4	b Kaneria	21
			b 10, l-b 2, w 2, n-b 10, p	24	b 6, l-b 5, w 2, n-b 9, p	22
			Total ....(76.5 overs)	253	Total ....(91 overs)	334

FALL OF THE WICKETS

1—8   2—51   3—171   4—174   5—174   6—206   7—208   8—213   9—222   10—253

1—61   2—73   3—97   4—97   5—149   6—188   7—188   8—208   9—282   10—334

ANALYSIS OF BOWLING

Name		1st Innings						2nd Innings				
	O.	M.	R.	W.	Wd.	N-b	O.	M.	R.	W.	Wd.	N-b
Amir	19.5	2	72	4	2		18	3	67	0		
Asif	19	5	63	3			21	3	77	3		2
Gul	17	3	32	1		9	21	5	61	4	2	3
Afridi	3	0	25	0			14	0	44	1		1
Kaneria	18	7	49	2		1	17	2	74	2		3

PAKISTAN

			First Innings		Second Innings	
1	Imran Farhat	(Lahore)	c Paine b Hilfenhaus	4	c Watson b Smith	24
2	Salman Butt	(Lahore)	b Watson	63	st Paine b North	92
3	Azhar Ali	(Lahore)	c Paine b Hilfenhaus	16	c Paine b Hilfenhaus	42
4	Umar Amin	(Rawalpindi)	c Paine b Johnson	1	c Katich b North	33
5	Umar Akmal	(Lahore)	lbw b Watson	5	c Clarke b North	22
*6	Kamran Akmal	(Lahore)	lbw b Watson	0	b Smith	46
†7	Shahid Afridi	(Karachi)	c Johnson b Watson	31	c Hussey b North	2
8	Muhammad Amir	(Rawalpindi)	c Paine b Bollinger	0	c Hussey b North	19
9	Umar Gul	(Peshawar)	c Watson b Bollinger	7	c Ponting b Smith	1
10	Danish Kaneria	(Karachi)	c Smith b Watson	14	c Ponting b North	1
11	Mohammad Asif	(Lahore)	not out	4	not out	1
			b , l-b 2, w , n-b 1, p	3	b 2, l-b 1, w , n-b 2, p	5
			Total ....(40.5 overs)	148	Total ....(91.1 overs)	289

FALL OF THE WICKETS

1—11   2—45   3—54   4—75   5—83   6—117   7—117   8—129   9—133   10—148

1—50   2—152   3—186   4—216   5—227   6—229   7—283   8—285   9—287   10—289

ANALYSIS OF BOWLING

Name		1st Innings					2nd Innings				
	O.	M.	R.	W.	Wd.	N-b	O.	M.	R.	W.	Wd.	N-b
Bollinger	11	3	38	2			12	4	43			2
Hilfenhaus	12	2	37	2		1	16	8	37	1		
Johnson	10	2	31	1			18	5	74			
Watson	7.5	1	40	5			6	0	26			
Smith							21	5	51	3		
North							18.1	1	55	6		

Umpires—I. J. Gould & R. E. Koertzen (3rd Umpire—Ahsan Raza; 4th Umpire—Nadeem Ghouri)

Scorers—D. Kendix & N. D. Smith

Match Referee—B. C. Broad   *Wicket-keeper

†Captain   Luncheon Interval 12.30—1.10

Play begins at 10.30 each day

Tea Interval 3.10—3.30 (may be varied according to state of game)

Stumps drawn at 5.30 on the 1st, 2nd, 3rd and 4th days, or after 90 overs have been bowled save that play cannot continue after 6.00 except for the purpose of making up time lost due to bad weather. The Umpires may agree to play a further 30 minutes of extra time at the end of any of the first four days if a definite result can be obtained.

Any alteration to the hours of play will be announced over the public address system.

Stumps drawn on the fifth day at 5.30 or after 90 overs have been bowled, save that at 4.30, or after 75 overs have been bowled on that day, the last hour – during which a minimum of 15 overs shall be bowled, but otherwise Laws of Cricket 16.6, 16.7 and 16.8 shall apply – will commence. If there is no prospect of a definite result, play may cease when a minimum of 15 overs remain to be bowled.

Pakistan won the toss and elected to field

Australia won by 150 runs

Pakistan won the toss and put Australia in. Pakistan's opening bowlers, Muhammad Amir and Mohammad Asif made life difficult for their opponents, and showed what great skills they both have and what a loss to fast bowling they will be. But Australia's old guard gradually gained the upper hand on an overcast day, clawing their way to 206 for five, before Danish Kaneria and Umar Gul reduced Australia to 229 for 9 overnight and 253 all out next morning, enough to give Australia a first innings lead of 105. For Pakistan, apart from Salman Butt, with a solid 63, and Shahid Afridi, who hit 31 in 15 balls, nobody looked like troubling the Australian bowlers for long, and the decidedly average attack of Bollinger, Hilfenhaus, Johnson and Watson sliced through the Pakistan batting order in 40.5 overs.

Australia's second innings was in trouble at 97 for four, but Katich and the lower order brought them up to 334, setting Pakistan 440 to win. That they came anywhere near was thanks to Salman Butt (92) and lesser contributions from Azhar Ali and Kamran Akmal. That they failed to reach their target was mainly due to Marcus North's part-time off-breaks. North took a career-best six for 55, to earn a place on the new 'neutral' honours board, along with Shane Watson, who took five for 40 in the first innings.

As a result of this defeat, Shahid Afridi not only resigned the captaincy but also retired with immediate effect from Test cricket. His place as captain was taken by Salman Butt, joint Man of the Match with Simon Katich. It was an appointment that would have far-reaching consequences.

2010: England v Pakistan

(4th Test) August 26, 27, 28, 29
England won by an innings and 225 runs

This was the latest ever start date for a Lord's Test, apart from the Centenary Test of 1980 which began on 28 August that year. It was also the fourth and last in the series against Pakistan, an order decided upon because of the Pakistan v Australia match at Lord's in mid-July. If Lord's had staged the first or second Tests, as is the custom, then Pakistan would have been back at the ground barely two weeks after the Australia game, and tickets might have been harder to sell.

The weather did play its part, curtailing the first day to just 75 balls, but there was still plenty of time for England to win before lunch on the fourth day. And the weather was not what was being talked about in the press box and all around the ground – indeed, all around the cricket world.

Having come into the match only five days after beating England at the Oval, the visitors should have been looking to draw the series by winning the final game. Instead, captain Salman Butt, hailed a few weeks earlier as the potential saviour of Pakistan cricket, organized a betting scam involving his two opening bowlers, Mohammad Amir and Mohammad Asif, which ultimately ended in all three serving jail sentences. England's victory was thus easily gained but even more easily tarnished.

Which was a great pity, because the partnership of 332 for England's eighth wicket between Jonathan Trott and Stuart Broad, which transformed England's innings from 102 for seven to 434 all out, was not only the highest eighth wicket

A Test match triumph for Stuart Broad was marred by the betting scandal as ECB chairman Giles Clarke's demeanour at the Man of the Series presentation clearly shows.

partnership in Test history but also owed nothing to the scheming mind of Salman Butt and his henchmen, and everything to the superb batting of Broad and Trott, by now England's most reliable number three since the days of David Gower or before him Ken Barrington. Stuart Broad's 169 was his maiden first-class hundred, and the highest score ever by an England number nine. Only Ian Smith of New Zealand had ever made more, 173 against India in Auckland in 1989-90. It was also seven runs more than his father's highest Test score for England: they were the first father and son to make Test hundreds for England.

Mohammad Asif and Mohammad Amir each bowled no-balls to order, to satisfy a bookmaker somewhere on the sub-continent, but have always claimed that Pakistan were nevertheless always trying to win the match. Their pitiful batting, especially in the first innings, casts doubt on that, but perhaps it was just that they came up against a bowling attack of superb quality. Graeme Swann, with nine for 74 in the match, led the line, but Anderson, Broad and Finn were not far behind in quality and effectiveness. For Pakistan, the shame of crashing to their heaviest ever Test defeat was almost hidden beneath the shame of the betting scandal.

Bizarrely, despite all of the above, Mohammad Amir was voted Pakistan's Man of the Series. ECB chairman Giles Clarke refused to shake his hand or look him in the eye as he handed over the cheque for £4,000.

MARYLEBONE CRICKET CLUB

LORD'S GROUND

£1   £1

ENGLAND v. PAKISTAN

THURSDAY, FRIDAY, SATURDAY, SUNDAY & MONDAY, AUGUST 26, 27, 28, 29 & 30, 2010
(5-day Match)

ENGLAND

			First Innings		Second Innings
†1	A. J. Strauss	(Middlesex)	b Asif	13	
2	A. N. Cook	(Essex)	c K. Akmal b Amir	10	
3	I. J. L. Trott	(Warwickshire)	c K. Akmal b Riaz	184	
4	K. P. Pietersen	(Hampshire)	c K. Akmal b Amir	0	
5	P. D. Collingwood	(Durham)	lbw b Amir	0	
6	E. J. G. Morgan	(Middlesex)	c Hameed b Amir	0	
*7	M. J. Prior	(Sussex)	c K. Akmal b Amir	22	
8	G. P. Swann	(Nottinghamshire)	c Ali b Amir	0	
9	S. C. J. Broad	(Nottinghamshire)	lbw b Ajmal	169	
10	J. M. Anderson	(Lancashire)	c Hameed b Ajmal	6	
11	S. T. Finn	(Middlesex)	not out	0	
			b 4, l-b 17, w 7, n-b 14, p ,	42	b , l-b , w , n-b , p ,
			Total ......(139.2 overs)	446	Total ....

FALL OF THE WICKETS

1—31   2—39   3—39   4—39   5—47   6—102   7—102   8—434   9—446   10—446
1—   2—   3—   4—   5—   6—   7—   8—   9—   10—

ANALYSIS OF BOWLING

Name	1st Innings						2nd Innings					
	O.	M.	R.	W.	Wd.	N-b	O.	M.	R.	W.	Wd.	N-b
Amir	28	6	84	6	1	4	...	...	...	...	...	...
Asif	29	6	97	1	...	2	...	...	...	...	...	...
Riaz	27.2	6	92	1	2	8	...	...	...	...	...	...
Ajmal	44	5	126	2	...	...	...	...	...	...	...	...
Hameed	1	1	0	0	...	...	...	...	...	...	...	...
Farhat	10	1	26	0	...	...	...	...	...	...	...	...

PAKISTAN

			First Innings		Second Innings	
1	Imran Farhat	(Habib Bank)	c Prior b Anderson	6	c Cook b Broad	5
2	Yasir Hameed	(P.I.A.)	c Swann b Broad	2	lbw b Anderson	3
†3	Salman Butt	(National Bank)	b Swann	26	lbw b Swann	21
4	Mohammad Yousuf	(W.A.P.D.A.)	b Broad	0	c Trott b Finn	10
5	Azhar Ali	(K.R.L.)	c Cook b Swann	10	b Swann	12
6	Umar Akmal	(Sui Northern)	b Finn	6	not out	79
*7	Kamran Akmal	(National Bank)	c Prior b Finn	13	c Prior b Anderson	1
8	Mohammad Amir	(National Bank)	lbw b Finn	0	b Swann	0
9	Wahab Riaz	(National Bank)	lbw b Swann	2	c Pietersen b Swann	0
10	Saeed Ajmal	(K.R.L.)	not out	4	run out	8
11	Mohammad Asif	(National Bank)	c and b Swann	0	c Collingwood b Swann	1
			b , l-b 4, w , n-b 1, p ,	5	b 1, l-b 2, w 3, n-b 1, p ,	7
			Total ....(33 overs)	74	Total ....(36.5 overs)	147

FALL OF THE WICKETS

1—9   2—9   3—10   4—46   5—53   6—57   7—57   8—70   9—74   10—74
1—7   2—9   3—41   4—41   5—63   6—64   7—65   8—73   9—97   10—147

ANALYSIS OF BOWLING

Name	1st Innings						2nd Innings					
	O.	M.	R.	W.	Wd.	N-b	O.	M.	R.	W.	Wd.	N-b
Anderson	10	6	10	1	...	1	13	4	35	2	1	...
Broad	6	4	10	2	...	...	6	1	24	1	2	...
Finn	9	4	38	3	...	...	4	0	23	1	...	1
Swann	8	3	12	4	...	...	13.5	1	62	5	...	...

Umpires—B. F. Bowden & A. L. Hill (3rd Umpire—S. J. Davis 4th Umpire—R. T. Robinson)
Match Referee—R. S. Madugalle
Scorers—D. Kendix & Lt. Cdr. P. J. W. Danks R.N.
†Captain   *Wicket-keeper
Play begins at 11.00 each day   Luncheon Interval 1.00—1.40
Tea Interval 3.40—4.00 (may be varied according to state of game)
Stumps drawn at 6.00 on the 1st, 2nd, 3rd and 4th days, or after 90 overs have been bowled save that play cannot continue after 6.30 except for the purpose of making up time lost due to bad weather. The Umpires may agree to play a further 30 minutes of extra time at the end of any of the first four days if a definite result can be obtained. Any alteration to the hours of play will be announced over the public address system. Stumps drawn on the fifth day at 6.00 or after 90 overs have been bowled, save that at 5.00, or after 75 overs have been bowled on that day, the last hour – during which a minimum of 15 overs shall be bowled, but otherwise Laws of Cricket 16.6, 16.7 and 16.8 shall apply – will commence. If there is no prospect of a definite result, play may cease when a minimum of 15 overs remain to be bowled.

Pakistan won the toss and elected to field

England won by an innings and 225 runs

2011: England v Sri Lanka

(2nd Test) June 3, 4, 5, 6, 7
Match drawn

This was Sri Lanka's 200th Test match, and coming so soon after the debacle at Cardiff, where England had dismissed them for 82 in fewer than 25 overs to win the first Test by an innings and 14 runs, the visitors showed a great deal more fighting spirit and skill than they had a week earlier. The first drawn Test at Lord's since the South African match in July 2008 had moments when the game might have swung to either side, but in the end a draw was the fair result. The wicket was too good a batting strip and the bowling attacks were not quite up to the job of taking the twenty wickets required.

England were without the injured Jimmy Anderson and for the first time in a long time, three England bowlers conceded over 100 runs in an innings as Sri Lanka notched up 479, just seven runs short of England's impressive first innings total.

England's innings was built around a relentlessly patient 96 from Alastair Cook at the top of the order, and some solid middle order batting from Bell (52), Morgan (79), Prior (126) and Broad (54). Prior and Broad hardly deserved the adjective 'solid' for their run-a-ball partnership, but once again the strength of England's lower

The visitor's captain Dishan made 193 to set the highest score by a Sri Lankan at Lord's.

£1

LORD'S GROUND

£1

ENGLAND v. SRI LANKA

FRIDAY, SATURDAY, SUNDAY, MONDAY & TUESDAY, JUNE 3, 4, 5, 6 & 7, 2011
(5-day Match)

ENGLAND

			First Innings		Second Innings	
†1	A. J. Strauss	(Middlesex)	lbw b Welegedara	4	lbw b Welegedara	0
2	A. N. Cook	(Essex)	c Maharoof b Fernando	96	st H. Jaya'dene b Herath	106
3	I. J. L. Trott	(Warwickshire)	lbw b Lakmal	2	b Herath	58
4	K. P. Pietersen	(Surrey)	c Dilshan b Lakmal	2	b Herath	72
5	I. R. Bell	(Warwickshire)	c Pa'vitana b Welegedara	52	not out	57
6	E. J. G. Morgan	(Middlesex)	lbw b Lakmal	79	c Lakmal b Fernando	4
*7	M. J. Prior	(Sussex)	b Herath	126	run out	4
8	S. C. J. Broad	(Nottinghamshire)	lbw b Welegedara	54	c H. Jaya'dene b Fernando	3
9	G. P. Swann	(Nottinghamshire)	c Pa'vitana b Welegedara	4		
10	C. T. Tremlett	(Surrey)	not out	24		
11	S. T. Finn	(Middlesex)	b Herath	19		
			b 3, l-b 7, w 4, n-b 10, p	24	b , l-b 12, w 1, n-b 18, p	31
			Total .... (112.5 overs)	486	Total .... (6 wkts, dec.)	335

FALL OF THE WICKETS

1—5 2—18 3—22 4—130 5—201 6—302 7—410 8—414 9—452 10—486
1—0 2—117 3—244 4—305 5—312 6—319 7—335 8— 9— 10—

ANALYSIS OF BOWLING

Name	1st Innings						2nd Innings					
	O.	M.	R.	W.	Wd.	N-b	O.	M.	R.	W.	Wd.	N-b
Welegedara	28	4	122	4	2	5	10	1	50	1		3
Lakmal	25	2	126	3	1		17	0	70	0	1	7
Maharoof	17	5	57	0	1	5	7	0	24	0		2
Fernando	17	2	77	1			20.1	2	92	2		6
Herath	18.5	1	64	2			24	2	87	3		
Dilshan	7	1	30	0								

SRI LANKA

			First Innings		Second Innings	
1	N. T. Paranavitana	(Sinhalese)	c Strauss b Finn	65	lbw b Trott	44
†2	T. M. Dilshan	(Tamil Union)	b Finn	193		
3	K. C. Sangakkara	(Nondescripts)	c Prior b Tremlett	26	c Morgan b Tremlett	12
4	D. P. M. D. Jayawardene	(Sinhalese)	c Cook b Finn	49	c Pietersen b Broad	23
5	T. T. Samaraweera	(Sinhalese)	c Prior b Tremlett	9	not out	17
*6	H. A. P. W. Jayawardene	(Bloomfield)	c Swann b Finn	40	not out	12
7	M. F. Maharoof	(Nondescripts)	lbw b Broad	2		
8	H. M. R. K. B. Herath	(Tamil Union)	st Prior b Swann	26		
9	C. R. D. Fernando	(Sinhalese)	c Strauss b Swann	5		
10	R. A. S. Lakmal	(Tamil Union)	not out	0		
11	C. Welegedara	(Tamil Union)	c Broad b Swann	6		
			b 25, l-b 23, w 8, n-b 2, p	58	b 7, l-b 3, w 6, n-b 1, p	17
			Total .... (131.4 overs)	479	Total ... (3 wkts, 43 overs)	127

FALL OF THE WICKETS

1—207 2—288 3—370 4—394 5—394 6—409 7—466 8—472 9—472 10—479
1—13 2—64 3—96 4— 5— 6— 7— 8— 9— 10—

ANALYSIS OF BOWLING

Name	1st Innings						2nd Innings					
	O.	M.	R.	W.	Wd.	N-b	O.	M.	R.	W.	Wd.	N-b
Broad	32	5	125	1			9	2	29	1	1	
Tremlett	30	8	85	2		1	9	1	31	1		1
Finn	33	8	108	4	3	1	8	2	31	0	1	
Swann	32.4	5	101	3			12	2	19	0		
Pietersen	4	0	12	0			1	0	2	0		
Trott							4	1	5	1		

Umpires—R. J. Tucker & B. R. Doctrove (3rd Umpire—A. S. Dar; 4th Umpire—R. K. Illingworth)
Match Referee—J. Srinath   Scorers—M. J. Charman & D. Kendix
†Captain   *Wicket-keeper
Play begins at 11.00 each day   Luncheon Interval 1.00—1.40
Tea Interval 3.40—4.00 (may be varied according to state of game)
Stumps drawn at 6.00 on the 1st, 2nd, 3rd and 4th days, or after 90 overs have been bowled save that play cannot continue after 6.30 except for the purpose of making up time lost due to bad weather. The Umpires may agree to play a further 30 minutes of extra time at the end of any of the first four days if a definite result can be obtained.
Any alteration to the hours of play will be announced over the public address system.
Stumps drawn on the fifth day at 6.00 or after 90 overs have been bowled, save that at 5.00, or after 75 overs have been bowled on that day, the last hour – during which a minimum of 15 overs shall be bowled, but otherwise Laws of Cricket 16.6, 16.7 and 16.8 shall apply – will commence. If there is no prospect of a definite result, play may cease when a minimum of 15 overs remain to be bowled.

Sri Lanka won the toss and elected to field

Match drawn

---

middle order took them from a potentially shaky 201 for 5 to 486 all out scored at more than four an over.

Anything England could do Sri Lanka could do almost as well. Tillekeratne Dilshan played a true captain's innings, beating the highest score made by a Sri Lankan at Lord's by three runs. The previous record holder, Sidath Wettimuny, was at the ground to watch his record being beaten. It was batting at its best. His runs came in only 253 balls with 20 fours and two sixes, and despite being hit on the thumb by Finn, he played aggressively as much as he could, but defended with patience when the ball warranted it. The blow to his thumb proved to be a hairline fracture, so Dilshan was unable to bat in the second innings, but by then the game had been made safe.

Dilshan and his opening partner Paranavitana put on 207 for the first wicket, a record for England v Sri Lanka Tests, but thereafter the biggest contributor to the Sri Lanka total was Extras, with 58 including 25 byes and 23 leg byes. Only twice had a wicket-keeper conceded that many byes in a Test at Lord's, but Prior made up for it partially by stumping Herath – his first Test stumping victim.

England's second innings provided the opportunity for Cook to hit yet another hundred (rather slowly), and for Trott, Pietersen and Bell to make fifties. In this match seven of the eight England batsmen who batted twice made at least one fifty. The only exception was the captain, Strauss. The critics were beginning to sharpen their knives.

2011: England v India

(1st Test) July 21, 22, 23, 24, 25
England won by 196 runs

According to the ICC counting system, this was the 2,000th Test of all time. More certainly, it was the one hundredth Test encounter between England and India (even though the first few were between England and All-India, before Pakistan and Bangladesh became separate countries). It may not have had one of the closest finishes of all those Tests, but it will certainly remain one of the most memorable.

The Man of the Match was Kevin Pietersen, who hit a brilliant if – by his standards – cautious double century to provide the backbone of England's 474 for eight. Praveen Kumar, in only his fourth Test, took five of those eight wickets, swinging the ball effectively after Zaheer Khan, who took the first two wickets to fall, had limped out of the attack with hamstring trouble.

In 1996, on his debut, Rahul Dravid had made 95 at Lord's while his fellow debutant Saurav Ganguly made a hundred. Now, aged 38 and in what was his fourth and almost certainly final Test appearance at Lord's, Dravid finally scored the century that had eluded him for fifteen years. As always with Dravid, the runs were made elegantly but with a defence that remained one of the most stubborn in world cricket. His 103 took exactly one hundred balls more than Matt Prior took to make the same score in England's second innings, but it was still 14 balls quicker than Pietersen's first hundred. With Broad and Anderson both bowling at their best, and with Chris Tremlett in support, batting was never easy for the Indians and their much vaunted if ageing batsmen allowed the total to slip from 158 for two to 286 all out. In contrast, when England were in a spot of difficulty at 107 for six in their second innings, Prior and Broad added an unbeaten 162 for the seventh wicket, a new record for that wicket against India, to set up

England's declaration and ultimate victory. This was, incidentally, Prior's third Test century at Lord's, making him the first wicket-keeper to achieve that landmark. Anderson (5 for 65 in India's second innings) and Kumar (5 for 106 in England's first innings) also qualified for the honours board.

By the end of this match, which came on the last evening when Broad trapped Ishant Sharma

Kevin Pietersen in aggressive form on the way to a double century.

leg before, England could claim five batsmen and five bowlers (one of whom, Steven Finn, was not even picked for this match) in the top 20 of the Test rankings. Only Andrew Strauss, probably the best Test captain in the world at this time, and Test newcomer Eoin Morgan were not ranked among the twenty best in the world, and England seemed to be on an unstoppable march towards the world number one ranking, a feat they duly achieved by the end of the series against India, and which they would be defending on their next visit to headquarters.

MARYLEBONE CRICKET CLUB
LORD'S GROUND
ENGLAND v. INDIA
100TH TEST MATCH

£1 **£1**

THURSDAY, FRIDAY, SATURDAY, SUNDAY & MONDAY, JULY 21, 22, 23, 24 & 25, 2011

ENGLAND		First Innings		Second Innings	
†1 A. J. Strauss	(Middlesex)	c Sharma b Khan	22	lbw b Singh	32
2 A. N. Cook	(Essex)	lbw b Khan	12	c Dhoni b Kumar	1
3 I. J. L. Trott	(Warwickshire)	lbw b Kumar	70	b Sharma	22
4 K. P. Pietersen	(Surrey)	not out	202	c Dhoni b Sharma	1
5 I. R. Bell	(Warwickshire)	c Dhoni b Kumar	45	c Dhoni b Sharma	0
6 E. J. G. Morgan	(Middlesex)	c Dhoni b Kumar	0	c Gambhir b Sharma	19
*7 M. J. Prior	(Sussex)	c Dhoni b Kumar	71	not out	103
8 S. C. J. Broad	(Nottinghamshire)	lbw b Kumar	0	not out	74
9 G. P. Swann	(Nottinghamshire)	b Raina	24		
10 C. T. Tremlett	(Surrey)	not out	4		
11 J. M. Anderson	(Lancashire)				
		b14, l-b 8, w 1, n-b 1, p ,	24	b 8, l-b 7, w 2, n-b , p ,	17
		Total (8 wkts, dec.)	474	Total (6 wkts, dec.)	269

FALL OF THE WICKETS

1—19	2—62	3—160	4—270	5—270	6—390	7—390	8—451	9—	10—
1—23	2—54	3—55	4—55	5—62	6—107	7—	8—	9—	10—

ANALYSIS OF BOWLING

Name	1st Innings						2nd Innings					
	O.	M.	R.	W.	Wd.	N-b	O.	M.	R.	W.	Wd.	N-b
Khan	13.3	8	18	2	…	…	20	2	70	1	1	…
Kumar	40.3	10	106	5	…	…	22	6	59	4	1	…
Sharma	32	5	128	0	1	…	21	1	66	1	…	…
Singh	35	3	152	0	…	1	2	0	16	0	…	…
Dhoni	8	1	23	0	…	…	6	1	43	0	…	…
Raina	2.4	1	25	1	…	…						
	…	…	…	…	…	…						

INDIA		First Innings		Second Innings	
1 A. Mukund	(Tamil Nadu)	b Broad	49	b Broad	12
2 G. Gambhir	(Delhi)	b Broad	15	lbw b Swann	22
3 R. S. Dravid	(Karnataka)	not out	103	c Prior b Anderson	36
4 S. R. Tendulkar	(Mumbai)	c Swann b Broad	34	lbw b Anderson	12
5 V. V. S. Laxman	(Hyderabad)	c Trott b Tremlett	10	c Bell b Anderson	56
6 S. K. Raina	(Uttar Pradesh)	lbw b Swann	28	c Prior b Anderson	78
†*7 M. S. Dhoni	(Jharkand)	c Swann b Tremlett	0	c Prior b Tremlett	16
8 Harbhajan Singh	(Punjab)	c Prior b Tremlett	17	c Tremlett b Anderson	12
9 P. Kumar	(Uttar Pradesh)	c Strauss b Broad	0	b Broad	2
10 Z. Khan	(Mumbai)	b Anderson	0	not out	0
11 I. Sharma	(Delhi)	c Prior b Anderson	0	lbw b Broad	1
		b 5, l-b12, w 1, n-b12, p ,	30	b 2, l-b 6, w , n-b 6, p ,	14
		Total (95.5 overs)	286	Total (96.3 overs)	261

FALL OF THE WICKETS

1—63	2—77	3—158	4—182	5—183	6—240	7—241	8—276	9—284	10—286
1—19	2—94	3—131	4—135	5—165	6—225	7—243	8—256	9—260	10—261

ANALYSIS OF BOWLING

Name	1st Innings						2nd Innings					
	O.	M.	R.	W.	Wd.	N-b	O.	M.	R.	W.	Wd.	N-b
Anderson	23.5	6	87	2	…	…	28	7	65	5	…	…
Tremlett	24	6	80	3	…	10	21	4	44	1	…	6
Broad	22	8	37	4	1	2	20.3	4	57	3	…	…
Trott	6	1	12	0	…	…	2	0	11	0	…	…
Swann	19	3	50	1	…	…	22	3	64	1	…	…
Pietersen	1	0	3	0	…	…	3	0	12	0	…	…
	…	…	…	…	…	…	…	…	…	…	…	…

Umpires—B. F. Bowden & A. Rauf (3rd Umpire—M. Erasmus; 4th Umpire—R. J. Bailey)
Match Referee—R. S. Madugalle   Scorers—A. P. Scarlett & D. Kendix
†Captain   *Wicket-keeper

Play begins at 11.00 each day   Luncheon Interval 1.00—1.40
Tea Interval 3.40—4.00 (may be varied according to state of game)
Stumps drawn at 6.00 on the 1st, 2nd, 3rd and 4th days, or after 90 overs have been bowled save that play cannot continue after 6.30 except for the purpose of making up time lost due to bad weather. The Umpires may agree to play a further 30 minutes of extra time at the end of any of the first four days if a definite result can be obtained.
Any alteration to the hours of play will be announced over the public address system.
Stumps drawn on the fifth day at 6.00 or after 90 overs have been bowled, save that at 5.00, or after 75 overs have been bowled on that day, the last hour – during which a minimum of 15 overs shall be bowled, but otherwise Laws of Cricket 16.6, 16.7 and 16.8 shall apply – will commence. If there is no prospect of a definite result, play may cease when a minimum of 15 overs remain to be bowled.

India won the toss and elected to field

England won by 196 runs

2012: England v West Indies

(1st Test) May 17, 18, 19, 20, 21
England won by five wickets

Stuart Broad with eleven wickets was England's match winner.

Originally this Test match was not scheduled to be played at Lord's. When the ECB awarded the 2012 Tests to the grounds involved in the bidding process, this match was awarded to the Swalec Stadium in Cardiff, which meant that for the first time since 1882, a touring team would come to England and not play a Test at Lord's. However, Glamorgan CCC had lost so much money on their hosting of the 2011 Test against Sri Lanka (despite the very exciting finish) that they decided to allow ECB to put the match out to re-tender, and Lord's won the right to the game.

The West Indies touring party was, for one reason or another, severely weakened by unavailability. Whether the players or the administrators were at fault was very difficult to assess, but with Chris Gayle making plenty of runs with the IPL rather than the national side, and

MARYLEBONE CRICKET CLUB

LORD'S GROUND

£1 £1

ENGLAND v. WEST INDIES

Investec Test Match

Thursday 17th May – Monday 21st May 2012

WEST INDIES	First Innings		Second Innings	
1 A.B. Barath.............(Trinidad & Tobago)	c Anderson b Broad	42	c Prior b Bresnan	24
2 K.O.A. Powell........(Leeward Islands)	b Anderson	5	c Bell b Broad	8
3 K.A. Edwards...................(Barbados)	lbw b Anderson	1	run out	0
4 D.M. Bravo ....(Trinidad & Tobago)	run out	29	b Swann	21
5 S. Chanderpaul.............(Guyana)	not out	87	lbw b Swann	91
6 M.N. Samuels.................(Jamaica)	c Bairstow b Broad	31	c Swann b Broad	86
*7 D. Ramdin.........(Trinidad & Tobago)	c Strauss b Broad	6	b Anderson	43
†8 D.J.G. Sammy......(Windward Islands)	c Bresnan b Broad	17	c Prior b Broad	37
9 K.A.J. Roach.................(Barbados)	c and b Broad	6	c Bell b Broad	4
10 F.H. Edwards................(Barbados)	c Prior b Broad	2	not out	10
11 S.T. Gabriel ....(Trinidad & Tobago)	c Swann b Broad	0	b Swann	13
	b 6, l-b 8, w , n-b 3, p ,	17	b , l-b 7, w , n-b 1, p ,	8
	Total ....(89.5 overs)	243	Total ....(130.5 overs)	345

FALL OF THE WICKETS

1—13   2—32   3—86   4—100   5—181   6—187   7—219   8—231   9—243   10—243
1—36   2—36   3—36   4—65   5—222   6—261   7—307   8—313   9—325   10—345

ANALYSIS OF BOWLING	First Innings					Second Innings				
Name	O.	M.	R.	W.	W. N-b.	O.	M.	R.	W.	W. N-b.
Anderson	25	8	59	2	...	36	11	67	1	... 1
Broad	24.5	6	72	7	... 3	34	6	93	4	...
Bresnan	20	7	39	0	...	36	11	105	1	...
Swann	18	6	52	0	...	18.5	4	59	3	...
Trott	2	0	7	0	...	6	0	14	0	...

ENGLAND	First Innings		Second Innings	
†1 A.J. Strauss.....................(Middlesex)	c Ramdin b Roach	122	c Powell b Roach	1
2 A.N. Cook.........................(Essex)	b Roach	26	c K. Edwards b Sammy	79
3 I.J.L. Trott ....(Warwickshire)	c Ramdin b Sammy	58	c Sammy b Roach	13
4 K.P. Pietersen ....(Surrey)	c Ramdin b Samuels	32	c Ramdin b Gabriel	13
5 I.R. Bell ....(Warwickshire)	c Powell b Gabriel	61	not out	63
6 J.M. Bairstow ....(Yorkshire)	lbw b Roach	16	not out	0
*7 M.J. Prior ....(Sussex)	b Gabriel	19		
8 T.T. Bresnan ....(Yorkshire)	c Ramdin b Sammy	0		
9 S.C.J. Broad ....(Nottinghamshire)	b F. Edwards	10		
10 G.P. Swann ....(Nottinghamshire)	b Gabriel	30		
11 J.M. Anderson ....(Lancashire)	not out	0	c Ramdin b Roach	6
	b 9, l-b 3, w , n-b 12, p ,	24	b 4, l-b 3, w , n-b 11, p ,	18
	Total ....(113.3 overs)	398	Total ....(5 wkts, 46.1 overs)	193

FALL OF THE WICKETS

1—47   2—194   3—244   4—266   5—292   6—320   7—323   8—342   9—397   10—398
1—1   2—10   3—29   4—57   5—189   6—   7—   8—   9—   10—

ANALYSIS OF BOWLING	First Innings					Second Innings				
Name	O.	M.	R.	W.	W. N-b.	O.	M.	R.	W.	W. N-b.
F. Edwards	25	1	88	1	... 3	8	0	24	0	... 1
Roach	25	3	108	3	... 8	13	2	60	3	... 10
Gabriel	21.3	2	60	3	...	5	1	26	1	...
Sammy	28	1	92	2	... 1	10	1	25	1	...
Samuels	14	3	38	1	...	10.1	0	51	0	...

Umpires—A.S. Dar & M. Erasmus (3rd Umpire—A. Rauf; 4th Umpire—R.T. Robinson)
Match Referee—R.S. Mahanama   Scorers—D.K. Shelley & D. Kendix
†Captain   *Wicket-keeper

Play begins at 11.00 each day   Luncheon Interval 1.00—1.40   Tea Interval 3.40—4.00
(The intervals may be varied according to the state of the match.)
Stumps drawn at 6.00 on the 1st, 2nd, 3rd and 4th days, or after 90 overs have been bowled save that play cannot continue after 6.30
except for the purpose of making up time lost due to bad weather. The Umpires may agree that a further 30 minutes
of extra time may be played at the end of any of the first four days if there is the prospect of a definite result.
Any alteration to the hours of play will be announced over the public address system.
Stumps drawn on the fifth day at 6.00 or after 90 overs have been bowled, save that if after 75 overs have been bowled on
that day, the last hour – during which a minimum of 15 overs shall be bowled, but otherwise Laws of Cricket 16.6, 16.7 and 16.8 shall
apply – will commence. If there is no prospect of a definite result, play may cease when a minimum of 15 overs remain to be bowled.

England won the toss and elected to field

England won by 5 wickets

Ramnaresh Sarwan and Brendan Nash, to name but two, scoring hundreds for county sides rather than for the touring party, it was no surprise that the West Indies team were written off as also-rans before the series started. However, although England won the game, it was not as one-sided as the pundits had been predicting.

England's match-winner was Stuart Broad, who took eleven wickets in the game, to become only the fourth man to get his name on all three honours boards – for a century, for five wickets in an innings, and for ten wickets in a match. Only Gubby Allen, Ian Botham and Keith Miller had achieved this before Broad.

One man whom Broad did not dismiss was Shivnarine Chanderpaul, the only experienced Test batsman in the West Indies side. He ranked as world number one at the time of this Test, and proved his status by scoring 178 runs for once out in the match – nearly a third of his side's runs – and alongside Marlon Samuels, dismissed twice by Broad for a total of 117 runs, took the match into the fifth day. When Andrew Strauss was caught off a vicious lifter from Kemar Roach on the fourth evening, and night-watchman Jimmy Anderson followed shortly thereafter, there was a real possibility that West Indies might conjure a victory out of nothing. The next morning, they got rid of Trott and Pietersen quickly enough, but Cook and Bell added 132 to bring England to the very edge of victory before Cook slashed to gully with just two runs needed. Debutant Jonny Bairstow, having to come in with two to win, must have cursed Cook under his breath as he strode out to bat. He survived a close lbw appeal and faced only three balls before Bell finished off the match.

2012: England v South Africa

(3rd Test) August 16, 17, 18, 19, 20
South Africa won by 51 runs

This match was a great occasion for Andrew Strauss. It was his 100th Test match and he was the first man to celebrate his 100th cap at headquarters since Geoff Boycott did so in 1981. It was also his 50th Test as captain and it was a match that England had to win if they were to retain their position as the top Test nation. South Africa went into the match 1-0 up in the three match series and victory would elevate them to the number one spot. It was also the first match at Lord's after the ground had hosted the Olympic Games archery competition and the outfield had been relaid, so there was plenty to talk about.

However, the only talking point for spectators as they arrived at the ground on the first morning was the dropping of Kevin Pietersen for reasons of team morale. Despite his truly brilliant innings of 149 in the previous Test at Headingley, he had sent texts to members of the South African team, apparently critical of Strauss and his captaincy, and this proved to be the final straw for the England management team in dealing with their mercurial superstar batsman.

Once the Test got under way, though, Pietersen was quickly forgotten. The game – eventually won by South Africa who thus superseded England as the top Test nation – was a gripping contest throughout, full of great individual and team performances, which went all the way to the final session of the fifth day. The margin of victory was in the end reasonably comfortable, but it was nevertheless the closest victory margin in terms of runs of any of the 127 Tests at Lord's.

Pietersen's replacement Jonny Bairstow shook off the disappointment of his performances earlier in the summer against West Indies with two

England's captain Andrew Strauss leads his team through the Long Room in his final Test match.

excellent innings which promised to establish him as a key player for the future, and the South African run machine Hashim Amla responded with a century of his own. Vernon Philander showed for the first time in the series why he is such a successful bowler at Test level, and Jacques Kallis, in what was almost certainly his final Test at Lord's, took a catch to remove Trott which will be remembered for many years. We should not forget, either, a superb spell of fast bowling by Steve Finn on the fourth day: he joined a list that includes such famous names as Bobby Peel, Ted McDonald and Fred Trueman in taking four wickets in each innings of a Lord's Test.

Andrew Strauss – in what proved to be his finale – did manage to break the Test record for catches by an England outfielder when he caught de Villiers in the second innings, but England's short-comings in the top order batting and in the field, where they dropped several crucial chances, proved to be the differences between the two sides. The final day began with England on 16 for 2, needing another 330 to win, and the media were talking of miracles being needed. They very nearly got one. Despite the early loss of Bell and Taylor (run out going for a fourth run), the rest of the batsmen played superbly as they chased their target down. But it was too much to ask: despite the best efforts of Prior, Broad and Swann, all of whom hit their highest scores of the series in England's second innings, the hosts fell 51 runs short. They have not beaten South Africa at Lord's since 1960.

LORD'S GROUND

ENGLAND v. SOUTH AFRICA
Investec Test Match
Thursday 16th August – Monday 20th August 2012

SOUTH AFRICA

Batsman		First Innings		Second Innings	
†1 G.C. Smith	(Cape Cobras)	c Prior b Anderson	14	lbw b Swann	23
2 A.N. Petersen	(Titans)	c Prior b Finn	22	lbw b Broad	24
3 H.M. Amla	(Dolphins)	b Finn	13	b Finn	121
4 J.H. Kallis	(Cape Cobras)	c Prior b Finn	3	lbw b Finn	31
*5 A.B. de Villiers	(Titans)	c Cook b Anderson	27	c Strauss b Finn	43
6 J.A. Rudolph	(Titans)	b Swann	42	c Prior b Finn	11
7 J.P. Duminy	(Cape Cobras)	c Prior b Anderson	61	not out	26
8 V.D. Philander	(Cape Cobras)	st Prior b Swann	61	c Bairstow b Anderson	35
9 D.W. Steyn	(Cape Cobras)	c Swann b Broad	26	c Taylor b Broad	9
10 M. Morkel	(Titans)	c Prior b Finn	25	st Prior b Swann	9
11 Imran Tahir	(Dolphins)	not out	2	b Anderson	1
		b 7, l-b 5, w 1, n-b , p	13	b 6, l-b 8, w 2, n-b 2, p	18
		Total (101.2 overs)	309	Total (124.2 overs)	351

FALL OF THE WICKETS

1—22	2—49	3—50	4—54	5—105	6—164	7—235	8—270	9—307	10—309
1—46	2—50	3—131	4—164	5—259	6—268	7—282	8—336	9—348	10—351

ANALYSIS OF BOWLING

Name	First Innings					Second Innings				
	O.	M.	R.	W.	W. N-b.	O.	M.	R.	W.	W. N-b.
Anderson	29	5	76	3	... ...	25.2	4	73	2	1 1
Broad	24	4	69	1	... ...	21	2	85	2	... 1
Finn	18	2	75	4	1 ...	27	5	74	4	1 ...
Swann	24.2	6	63	2	... ...	47	14	94	2	... ...
Trott	6	1	14	0	... ...	4	0	11	0	... ...

ENGLAND

Batsman		First Innings		Second Innings	
†1 A.J. Strauss	(Middlesex)	b Morkel	20	lbw b Philander	1
2 A.N. Cook	(Essex)	c Kallis b Steyn	7	lbw b Philander	3
3 I.J.L. Trott	(Warwickshire)	lbw b Steyn	8	c Kallis b Steyn	63
4 I.R. Bell	(Warwickshire)	c Petersen b Philander	58	c Smith b Philander	4
5 J.W.A. Taylor	(Nottinghamshire)	c Smith b Morkel	10	run out	4
6 J.M. Bairstow	(Yorkshire)	b Morkel	95	b Tahir	54
*7 M.J. Prior	(Sussex)	c Kallis b Philander	27	c Smith b Philander	73
8 S.C.J. Broad	(Nottinghamshire)	c Amla b Steyn	16	c Amla b Kallis	37
9 G.P. Swann	(Nottinghamshire)	not out	37	run out	41
10 J.M. Anderson	(Lancashire)	c Rudolph b Steyn	12	not out	4
11 S.T. Finn	(Middlesex)	c Duminy b Morkel	10	c Kallis b Philander	0
		b , l-b 10, w 1, n-b 4, p	15	b 7, l-b , w 2, n-b 1, p	10
		Total (107.3 overs)	315	Total (82.5 overs)	294

FALL OF THE WICKETS

1—29	2—38	3—39	4—54	5—178	6—221	7—252	8—264	9—283	10—315
1—1	2—6	3—34	4—45	5—134	6—146	7—208	8—282	9—294	10—294

ANALYSIS OF BOWLING

Name	First Innings					Second Innings				
	O.	M.	R.	W.	W. N-b.	O.	M.	R.	W.	W. N-b.
Morkel	28.3	6	80	4	... 4	17	3	58	0	2 1
Philander	24	9	48	2	... ...	14.5	4	30	5	... ...
Steyn	29	4	94	4	... ...	16	4	61	1	... ...
Kallis	12	3	29	0	1 ...	11	2	50	1	... ...
Tahir	14	3	54	0	... ...	24	3	88	1	... ...

Umpires—S.J.A. Taufel & H.D.P.K. Dharmasena (3rd Umpire—R.J. Tucker; 4th Umpire—P.J. Hartley)
Match Referee—J.J. Crowe   Scorers—D. Kendix & M.G. Archer
†Captain   *Wicket-keeper

Play begins at 11.00 each day   Luncheon Interval 1.00—1.40   Tea Interval 3.40—4.00
(The intervals may be varied according to the state of the match.)
Stumps drawn at 6.00 on the 1st, 2nd, 3rd and 4th days, or after 90 overs have been bowled save that play cannot continue after 6.30 except for the purpose of making up time lost due to bad weather. The Umpires may agree that a further 30 minutes of extra time may be played at the end of any of the first four days if there is the prospect of a definite result.
Any alteration to the hours of play will be announced over the public address system.
Stumps drawn on the fifth day at 6.00 or after 90 overs have been bowled, save that at 5.00, or after 75 overs have been bowled on that day, the last hour – during which a minimum of 15 overs shall be bowled, but otherwise Laws of Cricket 16.6, 16.7 and 16.8 shall apply – will commence. If there is no prospect of a definite result, play may cease when a minimum of 15 overs remain to be bowled.

South Africa won the toss
South Africa won by 51 runs

2013: England v New Zealand

(1st Test) May 16, 17, 18, 19
England won by 170 runs

Test cricket is said to be losing its appeal in many parts of the world, but even during a cold and damp late spring, Lord's was still packed to the rafters for four days. Perhaps the closely fought Test series in New Zealand a couple of months earlier, which had ended 0-0 with England bravely holding on for a draw in the third and final Test, had added to the gate, or perhaps the English no longer believe the weather forecasters, but for whatever reason they came, they got their money's worth with a fascinating game of cricket. The final margin of 170 runs, which looks like an overwhelming victory for England, was still in doubt until towards the end of the fourth morning, after nine and a half sessions of gripping cricket.

The difference between the two teams turned out to be Stuart Broad. His explosively brilliant spell of 7 for 44 decided the match as New Zealand, trying to press for victory, were dismissed for 68 in just 22.3 overs. Broad and Anderson bowled unchanged through the complete innings, the first time since 1912 that two England bowlers had done so at Lord's.

Before that, the match had been as well balanced as the weather was cold. Cook, captaining England at home for the first time, won the toss and batted. But nobody could score big runs: the highest score was Jonny Bairstow's 41, and England crumbled to 232 all out at barely two runs an over. The outfield, relaid after the Olympic archery of the previous summer, took much of the blame and certainly it was as lush as many had ever seen it. The number of threes which did not turn into fours was remarkable. England's 232 turned out to be the highest score of the match. New Zealand replied with 207, built mainly around Taylor's aggressive 66 in 72 balls, and Williamson's rather more sedate 59, but the highlight of the

innings was the wicket of Fulton, caught low down at slip by Swann, which gave Jimmy Anderson his 300th wicket in Tests, only the fourth England bowler to reach that target, and the first to do so at Lord's.

England's second innings featured a stand of 123 between Trott and Root, but the other nine

Jonny Bairstow top scored in England's first innings.

MARYLEBONE CRICKET CLUB
LORD'S GROUND
£1   £1
ENGLAND v. NEW ZEALAND
Investec Test Match
Thursday 16th May – Monday 20th May 2013

wickets contributed just 90 runs between them. Tim Southee took 6 for 50, the best figures for a New Zealand bowler at Lord's, to go with his four in the first innings, and New Zealand set about making a mere 239 to win. That they made only 68 meant that Southee joined Courtney Walsh as one of only two overseas bowlers to have taken ten wickets in a Test at Lord's and still ended on the losing side.

Wicketkeepers added to the list of curiosities: Prior, fresh from being voted England's Player of the Year, became the first man to score a century on debut at Lord's and then subsequently make a pair, while McCullum, who took over behind the stumps from the injured Watling, kept without pads for quite some time. It had been three years since he kept in a Test for New Zealand: he had obviously sold his pads in the meantime.

ENGLAND

			First Innings		Second Innings	
†1	A.N. Cook	(Essex)	c Watling b Boult	32	c Brownlie b Boult	21
2	N.R.D. Compton	(Somerset)	c Southee b Martin	16	b Wagner	15
3	I.J.L. Trott	(Warwickshire)	c Brownlie b Boult	39	b Williamson	56
4	I.R. Bell	(Warwickshire)	c Watling b Wagner	31	c Brownlie b Southee	6
5	J.E. Root	(Yorkshire)	c Watling b Southee	40	b Southee	71
6	J.M. Bairstow	(Yorkshire)	c and b Southee	41	b Southee	5
*7	M.J. Prior	(Sussex)	lbw b Southee	0	c sub b Southee	0
8	S.C.J. Broad	(Nottinghamshire)	lbw b Wagner	0	not out	26
9	G.P. Swann	(Nottinghamshire)	c Watling b Wagner	5	c McCullum b Southee	1
10	S.T. Finn	(Middlesex)	lbw b Southee	4	c sub b Southee	6
11	J.M. Anderson	(Lancashire)	not out	7	c Southee b Williamson	0
			b 1, l-b 9, w 2, n-b 5, p ,	17	b 3, l-b , w 1, n-b 2, p ,	6
			Total (112.2 overs)	232	Total (68.3 overs)	213

FALL OF THE WICKETS

1—43 2—67 3—112 4—157 5—192 6—192 7—195 8—201 9—221 10—232
1—36 2—36 3—159 4—167 5—171 6—171 7—183 8—200 9—210 10—213

ANALYSIS OF BOWLING

Name	First Innings						Second Innings					
	O.	M.	R.	W.	W.	N-b.	O.	M.	R.	W.	W.	N-b.
Boult	27	10	48	2	...	2	15	3	56	1	...	...
Southee	28.2	8	58	4	...		19	4	50	6	...	1
Wagner	28	8	70	3	2	2	14	2	44	1	1	1
Martin	26	12	38	1	...	1	13	2	40	0	...	1
Williamson	3	1	7	0	...		8.3	2	20	2	...	

NEW ZEALAND

			First Innings		Second Innings	
1	P.G. Fulton	(Canterbury)	c Swann b Anderson	2	c Prior b Broad	1
2	H.D. Rutherford	(Otago)	c Cook b Anderson	4	b Broad	9
3	K.S. Williamson	(Northern Districts)	c Prior b Anderson	60	c Finn b Broad	6
4	L.R.P.L. Taylor	(Central Districts)	lbw b Anderson	66	c Cook b Broad	0
5	D.G. Brownlie	(Canterbury)	lbw b Finn	23	c Cook b Anderson	5
†6	B.B. McCullum	(Otago)	c Prior b Broad	2	lbw b Broad	8
*7	B.J. Watling	(Northern Districts)	c Prior b Finn	17	c Trott b Anderson	13
8	T.G. Southee	(Northern Districts)	c Root b Finn	12	c Root b Broad	7
9	B.P. Martin	(Auckland)	b Anderson	0	b Broad	1
10	N. Wagner	(Otago)	not out	6	run out	17
11	T.A. Boult	(Northern Districts)	c Anderson b Finn	0	not out	0
			b 4, l-b 8, w , n-b 3, p ,	15	b , l-b , w 1, n-b , p ,	1
			Total (69 overs)	207	Total (22.3 overs)	68

FALL OF THE WICKETS

1—5 2—7 3—100 4—147 5—155 6—177 7—194 8—195 9—207 10—207
1—1 2—16 3—16 4—21 5—25 6—29 7—41 8—54 9—67 10—68

ANALYSIS OF BOWLING

Name	First Innings						Second Innings					
	O.	M.	R.	W.	W.	N-b.	O.	M.	R.	W.	W.	N-b.
Anderson	24	11	47	5	...	...	11.3	5	23	2	...	...
Broad	21	4	64	1	...	2	11	0	44	7	...	...
Finn	15	3	63	4	...	1						
Swann	8	0	19	0	...							
Trott	1	0	2	0	...							

Umpires—A.S. Dar and S.J. Davis (3rd Umpire—M. Erasmus, 4th Umpire—P.J. Hartley)
Match Referee—D.C. Boon   Scorers—C. Mulholland and D. Kendix
†Captain   *Wicket-keeper

Play begins at 11.00 each day   Luncheon Interval 1.00—1.40   Tea Interval 3.40—4.00
(The intervals may be varied according to the state of the match.)
Stumps drawn at 6.00 on the 1st, 2nd, 3rd and 4th days, or after 90 overs have been bowled save that play cannot continue after 6.30 except for the purpose of making up time lost due to bad weather. The Umpires may agree that a further 30 minutes of extra time may be played at the end of any of the first four days if there is the prospect of a definite result.
Any alteration to the hours of play will be announced over the public address system.
Stumps drawn on the fifth day at 6.00 or after 90 overs have been bowled, save that at 5.00, or after 75 overs have been bowled on that day, the last hour – during which a minimum of 15 overs shall be bowled, but otherwise Laws of Cricket 16.6, 16.7 and 16.8 shall apply – will commence. If there is no prospect of a definite result, play may cease when a minimum of 15 overs remain to be bowled.

England won the toss
England won by 170 runs

2013: England v Australia

(2nd Test) July 18, 19, 20, 21
England won by 347 runs

England's fiftieth Test victory at Lord's was the biggest victory in terms of runs they had ever had, but it was not so much the records as the hapless performance of the once mighty Australians that took the headlines.

The weather was most unEnglish: after a cold spring and early summer, the weather changed almost as soon as the Australians arrived in England, and by mid-July the forecasters were using phrases like 'heat health watch amber level three' rather than the more commonly heard 'cloudy with blustery showers.' It was more Kalgoorlie than St. John's Wood, but that did not help the visitors. The first Test at Trent Bridge, which finished only five days earlier, had resulted in a narrow English victory by 14 runs, so hopes were high for a close series. When England won the toss and quickly slipped to 28 for three, there were those who wanted to blame the Queen, to whom the teams had been presented at 11 a.m. before the match began and whose grandfather, George V, was known as 'the best change bowler in England', so regularly did wickets fall after he had met the teams. Perhaps the Queen of Britain and Australia was hoping for an even contest between her two teams, a hope that was dashed from the moment that Ian Bell came to the crease and settled in for his third century in consecutive Ashes Tests, and certainly his most valuable. With help from Trott and Bairstow, and a last wicket flourish from Swann and Broad, England battled to 361.

The Decision Review System (DRS) came in for more criticism following the errors made in its name at Trent Bridge. At Lord's, the machinery decided that Hughes and Agar were both out caught behind, despite there being very little evidence of any contact between bat and ball, and

Bairstow and Root both batted well against Australia.

it allowed Ian Bell to continue his second innings when to most eyes he had been cleanly caught by Smith when he had made just 3. But the Australians were largely the architects of their own downfall. From the moment Watson decided to review his lbw decision in the first innings (he was as plumb as could be), they got it wrong. Rogers failed to review his lbw decision, to a truly dreadful waist high full toss from Swann which was missing the stumps by some distance, and from then on their confidence in using the DRS was gone. Good decisions were questioned, bad decisions un-challenged. On top of that, their batting was lamentable, and all out for 128 in good batting conditions showed how poor the Australians' morale and their cricket had become.

In among the technological dramas were some excellent individual performances. Joe Root became the youngest Ashes centurion at Lord's, and won the Man of the Match award for his 180 and a couple of top order wickets. Both Harris and Swann took five wickets in an innings. When he took the final wicket with the third ball of the final over of Day Four, there must have been mixed feelings at Lord's: two-nil up with three to play against the once mighty Australians is all very well, but what about the fifth day income? There were 20,000 tickets or more to be refunded, and no bar sales on a hot and humid Monday.

MARYLEBONE CRICKET CLUB
LORD'S GROUND
ENGLAND v. AUSTRALIA
Investec Test Match
Thursday 18th July – Monday 22nd July 2013

£1   £1

ENGLAND

		First Innings		Second Innings	
†1 A.N. Cook	(Essex)	lbw b Watson	12	b Siddle	8
2 J.E. Root	(Yorkshire)	lbw b Harris	6	c Smith b Harris	180
3 I.J.L. Trott	(Warwickshire)	c Khawaja b Harris	58	b Siddle	0
4 K.P. Pietersen	(Surrey)	c Haddin b Harris	2	c Rogers b Siddle	5
5 I.R. Bell	(Warwickshire)	c Clarke b Smith	109	c Rogers b Smith	74
6 J.M. Bairstow	(Yorkshire)	c and b Smith	67	c Haddin b Harris	20
*7 M.J. Prior	(Sussex)	c Haddin b Smith	6	not out	1
8 T.T. Bresnan	(Yorkshire)	c Haddin b Harris	7	c Rogers b Pattinson	38
9 J.M. Anderson	(Lancashire)	c Haddin b Harris	12		
10 S.C.J. Broad	(Nottinghamshire)	c Haddin b Pattinson	33		
11 G.P. Swann	(Nottinghamshire)	not out	28		
		b , l-b 11, w 4, n-b 6, p ,	21	b 15, l-b 8, w , n-b , p ,	23
		Total .... (100.1 overs)	361	Total .... (7 wkts, dec.)	349

FALL OF THE WICKETS

1—18	2—26	3—28	4—127	5—271	6—274	7—283	8—289	9—313	10—361
1—22	2—22	3—30	4—129	5—282	6—344	7—349	8—	9—	10—

ANALYSIS OF BOWLING

Name	First Innings						Second Innings					
	O.	M.	R.	W.	W.	N-b.	O.	M.	R.	W.	W.	N-b.
Pattinson	20.1	3	95	1	4	3	20	8	42	1		
Harris	26	6	72	5			18.1	4	31	2		
Watson	13	4	45	1			12	5	25	0		
Siddle	22	6	76	0		1	21	6	65	3		
Agar	13	2	44	0		2	29	5	98	0		
Smith	6	1	18	3			14	6	65	1		

AUSTRALIA

		First Innings		Second Innings	
1 S.R. Watson	(New South Wales)	lbw b Bresnan	30	lbw b Anderson	20
2 C.J.L. Rogers	(Victoria)	lbw b Swann	15	b Swann	6
3 U.T. Khawaja	(Queensland)	c Pietersen b Swann	14	c Anderson b Root	54
4 P.J. Hughes	(South Australia)	c Prior b Bresnan	1	lbw b Swann	1
†5 M.J. Clarke	(New South Wales)	lbw b Broad	28	c Cook b Root	51
6 S.P.D. Smith	(New South Wales)	c Bell b Swann	2	c Prior b Bresnan	1
*7 B.J. Haddin	(New South Wales)	c Trott b Swann	7	lbw b Swann	7
8 A.C. Agar	(Western Australia)	run out	2	c Prior b Bresnan	16
9 P.M. Siddle	(Victoria)	c Swann b Anderson	2	b Anderson	18
10 J.L. Pattinson	(Victoria)	not out	10	lbw b Swann	35
11 R.J. Harris	(Queensland)	c Pietersen b Swann	10	not out	16
		b 4, l-b 1, w 2, n-b , p ,	7	b 4, l-b 5, w 1, n-b , p ,	10
		Total .... (53.3 overs)	128	Total .... (90.3 overs)	235

FALL OF THE WICKETS

1—42	2—50	3—53	4—69	5—86	6—91	7—96	8—104	9—104	10—128
1—24	2—32	3—36	4—134	5—135	6—136	7—154	8—162	9—192	10—235

ANALYSIS OF BOWLING

Name	First Innings						Second Innings					
	O.	M.	R.	W.	W.	N-b.	O.	M.	R.	W.	W.	N-b.
Anderson	14	8	25	1	1		18	2	55	2		
Broad	11	3	26	1		1	21	4	54	0		
Bresnan	7	1	28	2			14	8	30	2	1	
Swann	21.3	5	44	5			30.3	5	78	4		
Root							7	3	9	2		

Umpires—M. Erasmus & H.D.P.K. Dharmasena (3rd Umpire—A.L. Hill, 4th Umpire—R.T. Robinson)
Match Referee—R.S. Madugalle   Scorers—D. Kendix & Mrs. D.E. Pugh
†Captain   *Wicket-keeper

First Day—play begins at 11.15 Luncheon 1.15—1.55 Tea 3.55—4.15
Other Days—play begins at 11.00 Luncheon 1.00—1.40 Tea 3.40—4.00
(The intervals may be varied according to the state of the match.)
Stumps drawn at 6.15 on the first day, and at 6.00 on the second, third and fourth days, or after 90 overs have been bowled save that play cannot continue for more than 30 minutes except for the purpose of making up time lost due to bad weather. The Umpires may agree that a further 30 minutes of extra time may be played at the end of any of the first four days if there is the prospect of a definite result. Any alteration to the hours of play will be announced over the public address system.
Stumps drawn on the fifth day at 6.00 or after 90 overs have been bowled, save that at 5.00, or after 75 overs have been bowled on that day, the last hour – during which a minimum of 15 overs shall be bowled, but otherwise Laws of Cricket 16.6, 16.7 and 16.8 shall apply – will commence. If there is no prospect of a definite result, play may cease when a minimum of 15 overs remain to be bowled.

England won the toss
England won by 347 runs

1970: England v Rest of the World

(1st Test) June 17, 19, 20, 22
Rest of the World won by an innings and 80 runs

THE TEST MATCH THAT WASN'T

The proposed tour by South Africa in 1970 was cancelled on government advice after protests against the tour had created unacceptable strains on police resources, so the T.C.C.B. announced that in place of the South Africans, a Rest of the World side would play a series of five Tests against England. This team was to be led by Gary Sobers, and was truly representative of the strength of world cricket at the time – as England duly found to their cost.

From the beginning there was confusion over the status of these matches. The T.C.C.B. stated that England caps would be awarded for the games, and that, in the words of *Wisden*, 'the matches would be accorded the dignity of unofficial Test status.' They even found a sponsor for the series, Guinness, who put £20,000 into the pot, something they probably would not have done if they had thought that these were not real Test matches.

The editor of *Wisden*, Norman Preston, had no doubt. 'I have never regarded them as anything other than proper Test matches,' he wrote, and pointed out that in football, matches between England and representative 'Rest of the World' sides have always counted as full internationals. He also pointed out that although these matches were not played between two members of the International Cricket Conference, thus giving them official status, South Africa had left the Commonwealth – and therefore the I.C.C. – in 1961 and that therefore all Tests played against South Africa since then should also be counted as unofficial, 'which to my mind is a ridiculous situation.'

Wisden's records included these matches within the Test records, but over the years it became clear that they were fighting a losing battle. And even though the I.C.C. sanctioned the frankly far less competitive I.C.C. XI v Australia Test in 2005-06 as an official Test, there is no prospect of the 1970 matches being readmitted into the ranks of Tests. This is a pity. At the very least there should be consistency: either matches against World XIs are Tests or they are not, and to classify one match as a Test and five others as non-Tests smacks of expediency and inconsistent politicking.

The match itself was a one-sided triumph for the Rest of the World, which included four South Africans, four West Indians, an Indian, a Pakistani and an Australian. Their captain, Sobers, produced one of the great all-round performances by scoring 183 out of his side's 546, after having first taken six wickets for 21 runs as England crumbled to 44 for 7 at lunch on the first day, and thence to 127 all out. In England's second innings Sobers only took two more wickets, but at least d'Oliveira, the unwitting cause of the cancellation of the South African tour, hit a fine 78 and Illingworth 94 as England fell woefully short.

The Lord's honours boards, which record the achievements of century-making batsmen and bowlers who take five wickets in an innings, still include the names of Sobers (twice), Eddie Barlow (119) and Intikhab Alam (6 for 113). For the M.C.C. dressing room attendants, at least, this match will always be a Test.

The most unfortunate man on either side was undoubtedly debutant Alan Jones, the Glamorgan opening batsman, who was presented with his England cap before striding out with Brian Luckhurst to bat on the first morning. He only scored

ENGLAND

BW Luckhurst	c Richards b Sobers	1
A Jones	c Engineer b Proctor	5
MH Denness	c Barlow b McKenzie	13
BL D'Oliveira	c Engineer b Sobers	0
PJ Sharpe	c Barlow b Sobers	4
† R Illingworth	c Engineer b Sobers	63
* APE Knott	c Kanhai b Sobers	2
JA Snow	c Engineer b Sobers	2
DL Underwood	c Lloyd b Barlow	19
A Ward	c Sobers b McKenzie	11
K Suttleworth	not out	1
	(LB 5, NB 1)	6
Total		127

c Engineer b Intikhab Alam	67
c Engineer b Proctor	0
c Sobers b Intikhab Alam	24
c Lloyd b Intikhab Alam	78
b Sobers	2
c Barlow b Sobers	94
lbw b Gibbs	39
b Intikhab Alam	10
c Kanhai b Intikhab Alam	7
st Engineer b Intikhab Alam	0
not out	0
(B4, LB 8, NB 6))	18
	339

REST OF THE WORLD

BA Richards	c Sharpe b Ward	35
EJ Barlow	c Underwood b Illingworth	119
RB Kanhai	c Knott b D'Oliveira	21
RG Pollock	b Underwood	55
CH Lloyd	b Ward	20
† GS Sobers	c Underwood b Snow	183
* FM Engineer	b Ward	2
Intikhab Alam	b Ward	61
MJ Proctor	b Snow	26
GD McKenzie	c Snow b Underwood	0
LR Gibbs	not out	2
	(B 10, LB 5, NB 7)	22
Total		546

REST OF THE WORLD	O.	M.	R.	W.		O.	M.	R.	W.
McKenzie	16.1	3	43	2		15	8	25	0
Proctor	13	6	20	1		15	4	36	1
Sobers	20	11	21	6		31	13	43	2
Barlow	4	0	26	1		7	2	10	0
Intikhab Alam	2	0	11	0		54	24	113	6
Lloyd						1	0	3	0
Gibbs						51	17	91	1

ENGLAND	O.	M.	R.	W.
Snow	27	7	109	2
Ward	33	4	121	4
Shuttleworth	21	2	85	0
D'Oliveira	18	5	45	1
Underwood	25.5	8	81	2
Illingworth	30	8	83	1

FALL OF WICKETS

	Eng.	RoW.	Eng.
Wkt	1st	1st	2nd
1st	5	69	0
2nd	17	106	39
3rd	23	237	140
4th	23	237	148
5th	29	293	196
6th	31	298	313
7th	44	496	323
8th	94	537	334
9th	125	544	338
10th	127	546	339

† Captain   * Wicketkeeper

five runs in the match, was dropped and never selected for England again – but cannot even call himself a one-cap wonder because his is the cap that was not a cap. He was only playing because Geoffrey Boycott and Colin Cowdrey had both asked not to be considered for the match, citing lack of form, and John Edrich was injured. The out of form Cowdrey, incidentally, made 126 for Kent against Sussex while the 'Test' was being played.

Over 35,000 people turned up to see this non-Test, which began on a Wednesday because the Thursday was the date of the General Election and was made a rest day. England's defeat in four days was thus spread over six days.

Appendix: The Records

The records do not include the 1970 match v Rest of the World.

Team records:

Team	Played	Won	Drawn	Lost
England	125	50	47	28
Australia	37	16	14	7
West Indies	20	4	7	9
South Africa	16	5	4	7
India	16	1	4	11
New Zealand	16	1	8	7
Pakistan	14	3	6	5
Sri Lanka	6	0	4	2
Zimbabwe	2	0	0	2
Bangladesh	2	0	0	2

Highest totals:

729 for 6 dec.	Australia v England	1930
682 for 6 dec.	South Africa v England	2003
653 for 4 dec.	England v India	1990
652 for 8 dec.	West Indies v England	1973
632 for 4 dec.	Australia v England	1993
629	England v India	1974

Highest scores by other teams:

555 for 8 dec.	Sri Lanka v England	2002
551 for 9 dec.	New Zealand v England	1973
454	India v England	1990
445	Pakistan v England	2006
382	Bangladesh v England	2010
233	Zimbabwe v England	2003

Lowest totals:

42	India v England	1974
47	New Zealand v England	1958
53	England v Australia	1888
53	Australia v England	1896
54	West Indies v England	2000
58	South Africa v England	1912

Lowest scores by other teams:

74	Pakistan v England	2010
83	Zimbabwe v England	2000
108	Bangladesh v England	2005
192	Sri Lanka v England	2006

Largest victories:

Largest innings victories:

Innings and 285 runs	England v India	1974
Innings and 261 runs	England v Bangladesh	2005
Innings and 226 runs	West Indies v England	1973
Innings and 225 runs	England v Pakistan	2010
Innings and 209 runs	England v Zimbabwe	2000
Innings and 148 runs	England v New Zealand	1958
Innings and 124 runs	England v India	1967
Innings and 120 runs	England v Pakistan	1978
Innings and 106 runs	England v Australia	1886

Largest victories by a runs margin:

409 runs	Australia v England	1948
356 runs	South Africa v England	1994
347 runs	England v Australia	2013
326 runs	West Indies v England	1950
247 runs	England v India	1990
239 runs	Australia v England	2005
230 runs	England v New Zealand	1969
210 runs	England v West Indies	2004

Smallest victory margins:

By a runs margin:

51 runs	South Africa v England	2012
61 runs	Australia v England	1888
71 runs	England v South Africa	1955
72 runs	England v West Indies	1995

By a wickets margin:

2 wickets	Pakistan v England	1992
2 wickets	England v West Indies	2000

Most appearances in a Lord's Test:

For England

21	G.A. Gooch
20	A.J. Stewart
18	A.J. Strauss
17	D.I. Gower
16	G. Boycott
16	A.N. Cook
15	M.A. Atherton
15	I.T. Botham
15	K.P. Pietersen

Most from other countries:

9	S.E. Gregory	(Australia)
5	W. Bardsley	(Australia)
5	J.M. Blackham	(Australia)
5	A.R. Border	(Australia)
5	C.G. Macartney	(Australia)
5	R.W. Marsh	(Australia)
5	S. Chanderpaul	(West Indies)
5	C.H. Lloyd	(West Indies)
5	G.S. Sobers	(West Indies)
5	S.M. Gavaskar	(India)
5	S.R. Tendulkar	(India)
5	Wasim Bari	(Pakistan)
4	G.A. Faulkner	(South Africa)
4	A.W. Nourse	(South Africa)
4	B.F. Congdon	(New Zealand)
4	M.D. Crowe	(New Zealand)
4	R.J. Hadlee	(New Zealand)
4	J.G. Wright	(New Zealand)
4	P.A. de Silva	(Sri Lanka)
2	Mohammad Ashraful	(Bangladesh)
2	Mushfiqur Rahim	(Bangladesh)
2	Shahadat Hossain	(Bangladesh)
2	G.W. Flower	(Zimbabwe)
2	H.H. Streak	(Zimbabwe)

1,202 cricketers have played Tests at Lord's; 607 of them played here only once.

Batting records:

Highest partnerships:

370 for 3rd wkt	W.J. Edrich and D.C.S. Compton, E v SA	1947
332 for 8th wkt	I.J.L. Trott and S.C.J. Broad, E v P	2010
308 for 3rd wkt	G.A. Gooch and A.J. Lamb, E v I	1990
291 for 2nd wkt	A.J. Strauss and R.W.T. Key, E v WI	2004
287* for 2nd wkt	C.G. Greenidge and H.A. Gomes, WI v E	1984
286 for 4th wkt	K.P. Pietersen and I.R. Bell, E v SA	2008
274* for 5th wkt	G.S. Sobers and D.A.J. Holford, WI v E	1966
268 for 1st wkt	J.B. Hobbs and H. Sutcliffe, E v SA	1924
260 for 1st wkt	M.A. Taylor and M.J. Slater, A v E	1993
257 for 2nd wkt	G.C. Smith and G. Kirsten, SA v E	2003

Highest partnerships for other nations:

211 for 3rd wkt	V. Mankad and V.S. Hazare, I v E	1952
210 for 3rd wkt	M.D. Crowe and B.A. Edgar, NZ v E	1986
207 for 1st wkt	N.T. Paranavitana and T.M. Dilshan, SL v E	2011
197 for 5th wkt	J. Burki and Nasim-ul-Ghani, P v E	1962
185 for 1st wkt	Tamim Iqbal and Imrul Kayes, B v E	2010
80 for 2nd wkt	M.A. Vermeulen and S.V. Carlisle, Z v E	2003

Highest partnerships for each wicket:

268 for 1st wkt	J.B. Hobbs and H. Sutcliffe, E v SA	1924
291 for 2nd wkt	A.J. Strauss and R.W.T. Key, E v WI	2004
370 for 3rd wkt	W.J. Edrich and D.C.S. Compton, E v SA	1947
286 for 4th wkt	K.P. Pietersen and I.R. Bell, E v SA	2008
216 for 5th wkt	A.R. Border and G.M. Ritchie, A v E	1985
274* for 6th wkt	G.S. Sobers and D.A.J. Holford, WI v E	1966
174 for 7th wkt	M.C. Cowdrey and T.G. Evans, E v WI	1957
332 for 8th wkt	I.J.L. Trott and S.C.J. Broad, E v P	2010
130 for 9th wkt	S.R. Waugh and G.F. Lawson, A v E	1989
83 for 10th wkt	R. Illingworth and J.A. Snow, E v WI	1969

Highest individual scores:

333	G.A. Gooch	England v India	1990
259	G.C. Smith	South Africa v England	2003
254	D.G. Bradman	Australia v England	1930
240	W.R. Hammond	England v Australia	1938
226	I.J.L. Trott	England v Bangladesh	2010
221	R.W.T. Key	England v West Indies	2004
214*	C.G. Greenidge	West Indies v England	1984
211	J.B. Hobbs	England v South Africa	1924
208	D.C.S. Compton	England v South Africa	1947
206*	W.A. Brown	Australia v England	1938
206	M.P. Donnelly	New Zealand v England	1949
205*	J. Hardstaff jr.	England v India	1946
202*	K.P. Pietersen	England v India	2011
202	Mohammad Yousuf	Pakistan v England	2006
200	Mohsin Khan	Pakistan v England	1982

Batting records (continued)

The highest scores for other countries are:

193	T.M. Dilshan	Sri Lanka v England	2011
184	V. Mankad	India v England	1952
103	Tamim Iqbal	Bangladesh v England	2010
68	D.D. Ebrahim	Zimbabwe v England	2003

A total of 222 centuries have been scored in Tests at Lord's.
The lowest score on which nobody has yet finished an innings in a Lord's Test is 125.

Most Runs at Lord's

2015	G.A. Gooch	(England)	21 matches	Ave: 53.02
1562	A.J. Strauss	(England)	18 matches	Ave: 52.06
1476	A.J. Stewart	(England)	20 matches	Ave: 44.72
1241	D.I. Gower	(England)	17 matches	Ave: 44.32
1235	K.P. Pietersen	(England)	15 matches	Ave: 56.13
1189	G. Boycott	(England)	16 matches	Ave: 45.73
1161	A.N. Cook	(England)	15 matches	Ave: 43.00
1140	I.R. Bell	(England)	14 matches	Ave: 60.00

Highest from other countries:

575	W. Bardsley	(Australia)	5 matches	Ave: 115.00
571	G.S. Sobers	(West Indies)	5 matches	Ave: 95.16
508	D.B. Vengsarkar	(India)	4 matches	Ave: 72.57
411	G.C.Smith	(South Africa)	3 matches	Ave: 82.20
384	Inzamam-ul-Haq	(Pakistan)	4 matches	Ave: 54.85
375	D.P.M.D. Jayawardene	(Sri Lanka)	3 matches	Ave: 75.00
327	M.D. Crowe	(New Zealand)	4 matches	Ave: 54.50
158	Tamim Iqbal	(Bangladesh)	1 match	Ave: 79.00
74	D.D. Ebrahim	(Zimbabwe)	1 match	Ave: 37.00

Warren Bardsley and Allan Border (Australia - 503 runs at 100.60) are the only two players to have scored more than 500 runs at Lord's with an average above 100.

Two centuries in a match:

G.A. Headley	106 and 107	West Indies v England	1939
G.A. Gooch	333 and 123	England v India	1990
M.P. Vaughan	103 and 101*	England v West Indies	2004

Bowling records

Most wickets:

69	I.T. Botham (England)	15 matches	Ave: 24.53
63	F.S. Trueman (England)	12 matches	Ave: 22.12
61	J.M. Anderson (England)	14 matches	Ave: 26.09
48	S.C.J. Broad (England)	11 matches	Ave: 27.93
47	R.G.D. Willis (England)	9 matches	Ave: 18.76
45	J.B. Statham (England)	9 matches	Ave: 17.46
42	H. Verity (England)	7 matches	Ave: 14.59
40	G.P. Swann (England)	10 matches	Ave: 24.07

Most wickets for other countries:

26	R.J. Hadlee (New Zealand)	4 matches	Ave: 21.26
26	G.D. McGrath (Australia)	3 matches	Ave: 11.50
20	M.D. Marshall (West Indies)	3 matches	Ave: 17.00
20	C.A. Walsh (West Indies)	4 matches	Ave: 22.95
17	B.S. Bedi (India)	4 matches	Ave: 28.94
17	Kapil Dev (India)	4 matches	Ave: 32.52
17	Waqar Younis (Pakistan)	3 matches	Ave: 21.29
12	A.A. Donald (South Africa)	2 matches	Ave: 18.08
9	H.H. Streak (Zimbabwe)	2 matches	Ave: 20.66
5	S.D. Anurasiri (Sri Lanka)	1 match	Ave: 36.00
5	H.M.R.K.B. Herath (Sri Lanka)	1 match	Ave: 30.20
5	P.D.R.L. Perera (Sri Lanka)	1 match	Ave: 27.60
5	R.J. Ratnayake (Sri Lanka)	1 match	Ave: 32.00
5	U.W.M.B.C.A. Welegedara (Sri Lanka)	1 match	Ave: 34.40
5	Shahadat Hossain (Bangladesh)	2 matches	Ave: 43.60

Best bowling analyses:

8 for 34	I.T. Botham	England v Pakistan	1978
8 for 38	G.D. McGrath	Australia v England	1997
8 for 43	H. Verity	England v Australia	1934
8 for 51	D.L. Underwood	England v Pakistan	1974
8 for 53	R.A.L. Massie	Australia v England	1972
8 for 84	R.A.L. Massie	Australia v England	1972
8 for 103	I.T. Botham	England v West Indies	1984

Best for other teams:

7 for 65	S.J. Pegler	South Africa v England	1912
6 for 32	Mudassar Nazar	Pakistan v England	1982
6 for 32	M.D. Marshall	West Indies v England	1988
6 for 35	L. Amar Singh	India v England	1936
6 for 76	D.J. Nash	New Zealand v England	1994
6 for 87	H.H. Streak	Zimbabwe v England	2000
5 for 69	R.J. Ratnayake	Sri Lanka v England	1991
5 for 98	Shahadat Hossain	Bangladesh v England	2010

Bowling records (continued)

Five wickets in an innings has been achieved 172 times in Tests at Lord's, 90 times by England bowlers and 82 times by others. Ian Botham has taken five wickets in an innings eight times.

Twelve wickets in a match:

16 for 137	R.A.L. Massie	Australia v England	1972
15 for 104	H. Verity	England v Australia	1934
13 for 71	D.L. Underwood	England v Pakistan	1974
12 for 101	R. Tattersall	England v South Africa	1951

Ten wickets in a match has been achieved 26 times, 15 times by English bowlers and 11 times by other nationalities. Derek Underwood is the only man to achieve this feat twice (in 1969 and 1974).

All-round records

Five wickets in an innings and a century in the same match:

I.T. Botham	108 and 8 for 34	England v Pakistan	1978
V. Mankad	184 and 5 for 196	India v England	1952

Five wickets in an innings and a century – not in the same match:

K.R. Miller	109	Australia v England	1953
	5-72 and 5-80	Australia v England	1956
R. Illingworth	113	England v West Indies	1969
	6-29	England v India	1967
G.O.B. Allen	122	England v New Zealand	1931
	5-35 and 5-43	England v India	1936
A. Flintoff	142	England v South Africa	2003
	5-92	England v Australia	2009
S.C.J. Broad	169	England v Pakistan	2010
	7-72	England v West Indies	2012
	7-44	England v New Zealand	2013

Botham, Allen, Miller and Broad are the only four players to have scored a century in a Lord's Test, and also to have taken ten wickets in a match.

Fielding records:

Most catches:

A.J. Strauss	(England)	22
M.C. Cowdrey	(England)	20
W.R. Hammond	(England)	20
A.N. Cook	(England)	18
G.A. Gooch	(England)	18

Most from other countries:

A.R. Border	(Australia)	9
G.S. Sobers	(West Indies)	8
B.E. Congdon	(New Zealand)	6
M.D. Crowe	(New Zealand)	6
Javed Miandad	(Pakistan)	6
J.H. Kallis	(South Africa)	6
P.A. de Silva	(Sri Lanka)	5
R. Dravid	(India)	5
D.D. Ebrahim	(Zimbabwe)	2
N.C. Johnson	(Zimbabwe)	2
Imrul Kayes	(Bangladesh)	1
Junaid Siddique	(Bangladesh)	1
Rubel Hossain	(Bangladesh)	1

Most catches in an innings:

G.S. Sobers	4	West Indies v England	1973
A.J. Lamb	4	England v New Zealand	1983
M.E. Trescothick	4	England v Sri Lanka	2002
M.E. Trescothick	4	England v Zimbabwe	2003

Wicket-keeping records:

Most dismissals:

M.J. Prior	(England)	40	(c37, st3)
A.J. Stewart	(England)	37	(c36, st1)
T.G. Evans	(England)	37	(c25, st12)
A.P.E. Knott	(England)	33	(c32, st1)
G.O. Jones	(England)	32	(c30, st2)

Stewart also made 4 catches as an outfielder.

Most from other countries:

D.L. Murray	(West Indies)	15	(c15)
R.W. Marsh	(Australia)	14	(c14)
Kamran Akmal	(Pakistan)	13	(c11, st2)
M.V. Boucher	(South Africa)	11	(c10, st1)
M.S. Dhoni	(India)	9	(c9)
A.C. Parore	(New Zealand)	8	(c8)
K.C. Sangakkara	(Sri Lanka)	7	(c7)
Khaled Mashud	(Bangladesh)	2	(c2)
Mushfiqur Rahim	(Bangladesh)	2	(c2)
T. Taibu	(Zimbabwe)	2	(c2)

Most dismissals in a Test:

9 (8ct, 1 st)	G.R.A. Langley	Australia v England	1956

Most dismissals in an innings:

6 (6c)	J.T. Murray	England v India	1967
6 (5c 1st)	M.J. Prior	England v South Africa	2012

Index

AUSTRALIA
versus England 2–19, 22–3,
26–7, 30–1, 34–5, 40–2, 50–1,
58–9, 66–7, 76–7, 82–3, 92–3,
98–9, 110–1, 120–1, 130–1,
134–5, 144–7 (centenary Test),
148–9, 160–1, 174–6, 188–9,
200–1, 213–5, 230–1, 248–9,
266–7
versus Pakistan 252–3
versus South Africa 28–9

BANGLADESH
versus England 228–9, 250–1

ENGLAND
versus Australia 2–19, 22–3,
26–7, 30–31, 34–5, 40–42,
50–51, 58–9, 66–7, 76–7, 82–3,
92–3, 98–9, 110–11, 120–21,
130–31, 134–5, 144–7
(centenary Test), 148–9,
160–61, 174–6, 188–9, 200–1,
213–5, 230–1, 248–9, 266–7
versus Bangladesh 228–9, 250–1
versus India 46–7, 54–5, 62–3,
74–5, 88–9, 106–7, 118–19,
126–7, 140–41, 150–51, 162–4,
179–81, 195–7, 218–9, 239–40,
258–9
versus New Zealand 43–5, 56–7,
68–9, 86–7, 100–101, 114–15,

122–3, 138–9, 154–5, 165–6,
177–8, 190–91, 204–6, 224–5,
241–2, 264–5
versus Pakistan 78–9, 94–5,
108–9, 116–17, 128–9, 136–7,
152–3, 167–8, 186–7, 197–199,
210–12, 235–6, 254–5
versus Rest of World 268–9
versus South Africa 20–21, 24–5,
32–3, 38–9, 52–3, 64–5, 72–3,
80–81, 90–91, 102–3, 191–3,
202–4, 222–3, 243–4, 262–3
versus Sri Lanka 158–9, 172–3,
184–5, 216–7, 232–4, 256–7
versus West Indies 36–7, 48–9,
60–61, 70–71, 84–5, 96–7,
104–5, 112–13, 124–5, 132–3,
142–3, 156–7, 169–71, 182–3,
193–5, 208–9, 226–7, 237–8,
245–7, 260–1
versus Zimbabwe 206–7, 220–1

INDIA
versus England 46–7, 54–5,
62–3, 74–5, 88–9, 106–7,
118–9, 126–7, 140–1, 150–1,
162–4, 179–81, 195–7, 218–9,
239–40, 258–9

NEW ZEALAND
versus England 43–5, 56–7,
68–9, 86–7, 100–1, 114–5,

122–3, 138–9, 154–5, 165–6,
177–8, 190–1, 204–6, 224–5,
241–2, 264–5

PAKISTAN
versus Australia 252–3
versus England 78–9, 94–5,
108–9, 116–7, 128–9, 136–7,
152–3, 167–8, 186–7, 197–9,
210–12, 235–6, 254–5

SOUTH AFRICA
versus Australia 28–9
versus England 20–1, 24–5,
32–3, 38–9, 52–3, 64–5, 72–3,
80–1, 90–1, 102–3, 191–3,
202–4, 222–3, 243–4, 262–3

SRI LANKA
versus England 158–9, 172–3,
184–5, 216–7, 232–4, 256–7

WEST INDIES
versus England 36–7, 48–9,
60–1, 70–1, 84–5, 96–7, 104–5,
112–3, 124–5, 132–3, 142–3,
156–7, 169–71, 182–3, 193–5,
208–9, 226–7, 237–8, 245–7,
260–1

ZIMBABWE
versus England 206–7, 220–1